"This collection demonstrates effectively the remarkable scope, contribution, and soul of planning scholarship. Unconstrained by traditional disciplinary perspectives, planning scholars engage and contribute to other fields in crosscutting ways. Sustaining the common soul of this unique configuration of scholars depends importantly on the link to practice."

Lewis D. Hopkins, FAICP, University of Illinois at Urbana-Champaign, USA

"Thomas Sanchez and his co-authors' book is truly a unique synthesis. Bringing together thinkers from almost all realms of planning, it illuminates how planners now think about planning theory and research. From Ernest Alexander on theory to Michael Batty on planning science, teachers, researchers, and students will find valuable insight into what they do."

Michael B. Teitz, University of California, Berkeley, USA

PLANNING KNOWLEDGE AND RESEARCH

The field of urban planning is far-reaching in breadth and depth. This is due to the complex nature of cities, regions, and development processes. The knowledge domain of planning includes social, economic, technological, environmental, and political systems that continue to evolve and expand rapidly. Understanding these systems is an inter-disciplinary endeavor at the scale of several academic fields. The wide range of topics considered by planning educators and practitioners are often based on varying definitions of "planning" and modes of planning practice. This unique book discusses various elements and contributions to urban planning research to show that seemingly disparate topics do in fact intersect and together, contribute to ways of understanding urban planning. The objective is not to discuss how to "do" research, but rather, to explore the context of urban planning scholarship with implications for the planning academy and planning practice.

This edited volume includes chapters contributed by a diverse range of planning scholars who consider the corpus of planning scholarship both historically and critically in their area of expertise. It is essential reading for students of planning research and planning theory from around the world.

Thomas W. Sanchez earned his PhD in City Planning from Georgia Tech in 1996 and has since taught at Iowa State University, Portland State University, and the University of Utah. He is currently chair and professor of Urban Affairs and Planning at Virginia Tech. Sanchez conducts research in the areas of transport equity, environmental justice, technology, and scholarly impact. He currently serves as the editor-in-chief of *Housing Policy Debate*, a leading journal on housing and community development policy. In 2012 he co-authored, *Planning as if People Matter: Governing for Social Equity* with Marc Brenman. In 2007 they co-authored *The Right to Transportation: Moving to Equity*. Also in 2007 he co-authored *The Social Impacts of Urban Containment* with Arthur C. Nelson and Casey Dawkins.

PLANNING KNOWLEDGE AND RESEARCH

Edited by Thomas W. Sanchez

NEW YORK AND LONDON

First published 2018
by Routledge
711 Third Avenue, New York, NY 10017

and by Routledge
2 Park Square, Milton Park, Abingdon, Oxon, OX14 4RN

Routledge is an imprint of the Taylor & Francis Group, an informa business

© 2018 Taylor & Francis

The right of Thomas W. Sanchez to be identified as the author
of the editorial material, and of the authors for their individual chapters,
has been asserted in accordance with sections 77 and 78 of the
Copyright, Designs and Patents Act 1988.

All rights reserved. No part of this book may be reprinted or
reproduced or utilised in any form or by any electronic, mechanical,
or other means, now known or hereafter invented, including photocopying
and recording, or in any information storage or retrieval system,
without permission in writing from the publishers.

Trademark notice: Product or corporate names may be trademarks
or registered trademarks, and are used only for identification
and explanation without intent to infringe.

Library of Congress Cataloging-in-Publication Data
Names: Sanchez, Thomas W., author.
Title: Planning knowledge and research / edited by Thomas W. Sanchez.
Description: New York, NY : Routledge, 2018.
Identifiers: LCCN 2017029116| ISBN 9781138233751 (hardback) |
ISBN 9781138233768 (pbk.)
Subjects: LCSH: City planning. | City planning—Research.
Classification: LCC HT166 .P534 2018 | DDC 307.1/216—dc23
LC record available at https://lccn.loc.gov/2017029116

ISBN: 978-1-138-23375-1 (hbk)
ISBN: 978-1-138-23376-8 (pbk)
ISBN: 978-1-315-30871-5 (ebk)

Typeset in Bembo and Stone Sans
by Florence Production Ltd, Stoodleigh, Devon, UK

CONTENTS

List of illustrations   *x*
Dedication   *xii*
Acknowledgement   *xiii*
Contributors   *xiv*

    Introduction: Planning Knowledge and Research   1
    Thomas W. Sanchez

PART I
The Context of Planning Research   **5**

1 How Theory Links Research and Practice. 70 Years' Planning Theory: A Critical Review   7
    Ernest R. Alexander

2 Learning from Practice, Learning for Practice in Local Land Use Planning Research   24
    Carolyn G. Loh

3 Planning Culture: Research Heuristics and Explanatory Value   35
    Karsten Zimmermann, Robin Chang, and Andreas Putlitz

4 Striving for Impact Beyond the Academy? Planning Research in Australia   51
    Paul Burton

PART II
Types and Topics of Planning Research   67

5 Mapping the Knowledge Domain of Urban Planning   69
    Thomas W. Sanchez and Nader Afzalan

6 The Relationship between Green Places and Urban Society: Understanding the Evolution and Integration of City Planning and the Ecological Sciences   85
    Charles Hostovsky

7 Evolution in Land Use and Transportation Research   110
    Dea van Lierop, Geneviève Boisjoly, Emily Grisé, and Ahmed El-Geneidy

8 Monitoring Sustainability Culture: An Overview of a Multi-Year Program of Evaluation Research at the University of Michigan   132
    Robert W. Marans and John Callewaert

PART III
Planning Research on Objects and Design   151

9 Towards an Object-Oriented Case Methodology for Planners   153
    Robert Beauregard and Laura Lieto

10 Urban Morphology as a Research Method   167
    Brenda Case Scheer

11 The Unwarranted Boundaries between Urban Planning and Design in Theory, Practice and Research   182
    Davide Ponzini

PART IV
Planning Methods, Science, and Technology   197

12 Use of *Planning* Magazine to Bridge the Gap Between Researchers and Practitioners   199
    Kathryn R. Terzano and Reid Ewing

13 Planning Our Future Cities: The Role Computer
   Technologies Can Play   210
   Robert Goodspeed, Peter Pelzer, and Christopher Pettit

14 Citizen Science as a Research Approach   226
   Michelle M. Thompson

15 Science in Planning: Theory, Methods and Models   241
   Michael Batty

   Postscript   255
   Thomas W. Sanchez

Index   *256*

ILLUSTRATIONS

FIGURES

5.1	Reduced network of 11 mode faculty research topics	76
6.1	Olmsted's design of Central Park	89
6.2	Rachel Carson	90
6.3	McHarg's overlay mapping technique	91
6.4	City of Ottawa, concept of greenway connectivity	93
7.1	Evolution of land use and transportation research	113
8.1	University of Michigan campuses and regions	142
8.2	Bursley composting evaluation	145
10.1	Morphological data is usually comparative	169
10.2	Categories of morphological data	170
10.3	An overlay of two maps of lower Manhattan	172
10.4	A few examples of common patterns of urban form	173
10.5	Brownstone rowhouses in Bedford-Stuyvesant	174
13.1	CityViz Housing Indicator	215
13.2	CityViz City movement indicator	216
13.3	Dutch stakeholders	220
14.1	Property condition survey	234
14.2	The Thompson Technology Tree	235
15.1	The classical scientific method	244
15.2	Models in scientific method	248

TABLES

1.1	Planning theories, practices and research	14
3.1	Four types of planning systems in Europe	39

4.1	*Australian Planner* – paper topics, 2006–2016	56
4.2	Ranking of main planning challenges	58
5.1	Graph components in planning and design field	74
6.1	Refereed Place-Based Journal Articles on Greenway Planning	102
8.1	CSIA themes, guiding principles, and 2025 goals	135
8.2	SCIP survey questions by module and question type	137
8.3	Items used for creating sustainability indicators	139
8.4	Index scores for students, staff and faculty	140

DEDICATION

To Linn for her love, generosity, and inspiration.

ACKNOWLEDGEMENT

I would like to acknowledge all of the authors for their thoughtful contributions.

CONTRIBUTORS

Nader Afzalan is visiting Assistant Professor of Urban Planning and Geodesign at the University of Redlands and Chair of the American Planning Association, Technology Division. His research focuses on the potentials and challenges of using communication technologies and data sources in collaborative land use and environmental planning.

Ernest R. Alexander is Professor of Urban Planning emeritus at the University of Wisconsin-Milwaukee, USA, and now lives in Israel. His research focuses on planning systems and processes, organizations, institutions and institutional design, and design and evaluation in the planning process. The author of *Approaches to Planning* (1992) and *How Organizations Act Together: Interorganizational Coordination in Theory and Practice* (1995), Alexander also edited *Evaluation in Planning* (2006) and co-edited *Place–Based Evaluation in Integrated Land Use Management* (2016). He is Editor of *Planning: Journal of the Israel Association of Planners*.

Michael Batty is Bartlett Professor of Planning at University College London where he is also Chairman of the Centre for Advanced Spatial Analysis (CASA), which he set up in 1995. Previously he was Chair and Dean of City and Regional Planning at the University of Cardiff (1979–1990) and Director of the National Center for Geographic Information and Analysis at the State University of New York at Buffalo (1990–1995). He has worked on computer models of cities and their visualization since the 1970s and has published several books, such as *Cities and Complexity* (2005) and, most recently, *The New Science of Cities* (2013). He is Editor of the journal *Environment and Planning B*. His research group is working on simulating long-term structural change and dynamics in cities, as well as urban analytics for smart cities.

Robert Beauregard is Professor of Urban Planning in the Graduate School of Architecture, Planning, and Preservation at Columbia University. He writes on both planning theory and urbanism. His most recent books are *Planning Matter: Acting with Things* (2015) and *Cities in the Urban Age: A Dissent* (forthcoming in 2018). With Laura Lieto, he edited *Planning for a Material World* (2016).

Geneviève Boisjoly is currently a PhD student in Urban Planning at McGill University. After acquiring a Bachelor of Engineering at École Polytechnique de Montréal, Geneviève received a Master in Environmental Studies and Sustainability Science from Lund University, Sweden, with a focus on urban sustainable transportation. Concerned with the impacts of car-oriented transport systems on disadvantaged populations, Geneviève is interested in land use and transportation planning from a social equity perspective. She is currently working on measurements of accessibility in North American cities.

Paul Burton is Professor of Urban Management and Planning and Director of the Cities Research Institute at Griffith University, Queensland, Australia. He is a founding member of Regional Development Australia Gold Coast and an elected member of the National Education Committee of the Planning Institute of Australia. Having trained and worked as a planner in London in the late 1970s, Paul joined the School for Advanced Urban Studies at the University of Bristol and, before moving to Australia, served as Head of the university's School for Policy Studies.

John Callewaert, PhD, is Emerging Opportunities Program Director at the Graham Sustainability Institute and Lecturer in the College of Literature, Science, and the Arts at the University of Michigan. At the Graham Institute, John is responsible for designing, implementing, and overseeing a wide range of activities that support translational knowledge efforts involving subject matter experts, decision-makers, and key stakeholders. Dr. Callewaert serves as an Associate Editor for the *Journal of Environmental Studies and Sciences* and as an advisory board member for The Integrated Assessment Society and the Association for the Advancement of Sustainability in Higher Education.

Robin Chang (Canada) is a researcher and lecturer in the Department of European Planning Cultures at the Technical University of Dortmund, Germany. She received her MSc in Spatial Planning from the Technical University of Dortmund and a BPl in Environmental Planning from the University of Northern British Columbia. Robin has assisted with research investigating climate change impacts and developing climate change strategies, and she has worked as a land use planner at the municipal level in Canada. She also extended her urban policy and research experience in the European context through work with the European Urban Research Association (EURA) Secretariat. Currently, Robin is researching temporary land use in German and Dutch planning.

xvi Contributors

Ahmed El-Geneidy is Associate Professor at School of Urban Planning, McGill University. His research interests include land use and transportation planning, transit operations and planning, travel behavior analysis concentrating on the use of motorized and non-motorized modes of transportation, and measurements of accessibility and mobility in urban contexts. Ahmed has a special interest in measuring and understanding the transportation needs of disadvantaged populations. He is currently serving on the board of the new planning authority of Montreal, Autorité régionale de transport métropolitain (ARTM). He is currently serving as an Editor for the *Journal of Transport and Land Use*. He has also served as a board member at the World Society on Transport and Land Use Research (WSTLUR) (2011–2013). He is a member of the Transportation Research Board (TRB) Committee on Public Transportation Planning and Development, AP025 (2011–2014; 2014–2017), and he was on the Committee on Public Transportation Marketing and Fare Policy, AP030 (2012–2015).

Reid Ewing is Chair of the Department of City and Metropolitan Planning at the University of Utah, Associate Editor of the *Journal of the American Planning Association*, and columnist for *Planning* magazine, writing the bimonthly column "Research You Can Use." He holds master's degrees in Engineering and City Planning from Harvard University, and he received a PhD in Urban Planning and Transportation Systems from the Massachusetts Institute of Technology. Ewing's work is aimed at planning practitioners. His eight books include *Pedestrian and Transit-Oriented Design* (2013); and *Best Development Practices* (1996), listed by the American Planning Association (APA) as one of the 100 "essential" books in planning over the past 100 years. Ewing authored two of the ten most highly cited articles in the 80-year history of the *Journal of the American Planning Association*.

Robert Goodspeed, PhD, AICP, is Assistant Professor of Urban Planning at the University of Michigan's Taubman College of Architecture and Urban Planning. His research investigates how new information technologies can be used to improve the planning process and planning outcomes, and involves mixed-method studies of innovative urban planning practice, the use of GIS to develop novel methods, and theoretical analysis of sociotechnical practices like crowdfunding and smart cities. He teaches in the areas of geographic information systems (GIS), collaborative planning, and scenario planning theory and methods. He holds a PhD in Urban and Regional Planning from the Massachusetts Institute of Technology, an MCP from the University of Maryland, and a BA in History from the University of Michigan.

Emily Grisé is a PhD student at McGill University in the School of Urban Planning. After completing an undergraduate degree from the University of Waterloo in Geography and Environmental Management, she graduated from the University of Toronto with a Master in Geography. Her master's thesis was on pedestrian injury in the City of Toronto with a particular focus on pedestrian planning and policy implications for children and the elderly. Her main research interests are on public transit satisfaction and loyalty, urban public transit planning and operations, and land use and transportation planning. More specifically, her doctoral research is focused on examining customer satisfaction and service quality using a spatial analysis approach.

Charles Hostovsky is a Canadian Registered Professional Planner and has been a practitioner-educator in urban environmental planning for 30 years. He is presently a Lecturer at Brock University's Department of Geography and Tourism Studies and an adjunct faculty member at McMaster University's School of Geography and Earth Sciences. Previously he was a faculty member at the University of Toronto for 12 years. Professionally he has been a planner with a medium-sized Canadian city, the Ontario Ministry of the Environment and Climate Change, and a major consulting engineering firm. For the past 12 years he has been the Consulting Environmental Planner to the Six Nations of the Grand River, Canada's largest by population and most biodiverse First Nation territory. Chuck holds the 2011 Government of Canada CMHC Award for Teaching Sustainability as well as awards from the Canadian Association of Geographers and the Canadian Institute of Planners.

Laura Lieto is Professor of Urban Planning at "Federico II" University, Napoli (Italy). She is a planning theorist and writes extensively on urban informality and transnational urbanism. She is Managing Editor of the planning journal *CRIOS*. Her most recent publications are *Planning for a Material World*, co-edited with R. Beauregard (2016) and "Does Actor Network Theory Help Planners Think about Change?" co-authored with R. Beauregard (in Y. Rydin and L. Tate, eds., *Actor Networks of Planning*, 2016).

Carolyn G. Loh is Associate Professor in the Department of Urban Studies and Planning at Wayne State University. A former planning consultant, her research interests include land use, the local government planning process, planning practice, implementation, regional planning, and spatial analysis.

Robert W. Marans, PhD, is a research professor at the Institute for Social Research and Professor Emeritus of Architecture and Urban Planning in the Taubman College of Architecture and Urban Planning at the University of Michigan. He is the recipient of the 2012 Career Award of the Environmental Design Research Association (EDRA), and he was elected to the College of Fellows of the American Institute of Certified Planners (FAICP) in 2014. He is the co-editor of *Investigating Quality of Urban Life: Theory, Methods, and Empirical Research* (2011) and has lectured extensively throughout the United States and in Europe, Asia, South Africa, South America, Australia, and the Middle East. His current work deals with cultural issues of sustainability and energy conservation in institutional settings including universities and the impact of the built and natural environments on quality of life.

Peter Pelzer is Researcher and Lecturer at the Urban Futures Studio, Utrecht University. His research interests include futuring, Planning Support Systems, the sharing economy, and urban mobility. His work has been published in several journals including *Transportation Research Part A*, *Computers Environment and Urban Systems*, and *Planning Theory and Practice*. He is currently working on the Post-Fossil City Contest, an initiative to unchain the imagination about the future of our cities.

Christopher Pettit is the inaugural Chair of Urban Science at the University of New South Wales, Director of the newly launched City Analytics Postgraduate Program (https://www.be.unsw.edu.au/postgraduate-degrees/city-analytics/how-apply) and Associate Director of the City Futures Research Centre (https://cityfutures.be.unsw.edu.au/research/city-analytics/). His expertise is in the convergence of the fields of urban planning and Geographical Information Sciences (GIS). For the last 20 years, he has been undertaking research and development in the use of spatial information and mapping technologies for envisioning what if? scenarios across both urban and regional landscapes. His recent interests also span applications, development and the critique of geographical visualization tools including advanced spatial decision support systems and city dashboards.

Davide Ponzini is currently Associate Professor of Urban Planning at Politecnico di Milano and Visiting Professor at TU Munich. His research activity focuses on planning theory, urban and cultural policy, transnational issues in contemporary architecture and the urban environment. His research has been published extensively in international scientific journals and edited volumes. He is the co-author, with Pier Carlo Palermo, of *Place–Making and Urban Development: New Challenges for Planning and Design* (2015) and, with the photographer Michele Nastasi, of *Starchitecture: Scenes, Actors and Spectacles in Contemporary Cities* (2016, second edition).

Andreas Putlitz studied Urban Planning at the Technical Universities of Vienna and Madrid. After obtaining his master's degree he worked for the Karlsruhe Institute of Technology and the University of Heidelberg before beginning his doctoral studies at the Technical University of Dortmund. His current research is centered around planning culture in the smart cities of Amsterdam and Vienna, with particular focus on complexity and practice-theoretical approaches.

Thomas W. Sanchez is Professor and Chair of Urban Affairs and Planning at Virginia Tech. He conducts research in the areas of transportation, environmental justice, technology, and scholarly impact. His research over the past 20 years has resulted in over 100 articles, reports, and conference presentations on these topics. He is Editor-in-Chief of *Housing Policy Debate*, a leading journal on the topics of housing and community development policy. In 2012 he co-authored *Planning as if People Matter: Governing for Social Equity* with Marc Brenman. In 2007 they authored *The*

Right to Transportation: Moving to Equity. Also in 2007, he co-authored *The Social Impacts of Urban Containment* with Arthur C. Nelson and Casey J. Dawkins.

Brenda Case Scheer, FAIA, FAICP, is an urban designer and architect. Following a successful architecture practice and academic career, she was Dean of Architecture and Planning at the University of Utah from 2002 to 2013. Scheer has published more than 32 papers and book chapters as well as 3 books, and she has held 32 research grants. Recent publications include "Performance the Urban Form-Based Codes as a Method of Architectural Critique" in *Architecture Beyond Criticism: Expert Judgment and Performance Evaluation* (2015) and "Strip Development and How to Read It" in *Fixing Sprawl* (2015). Her most recent book is *The Evolution of Urban Form: Typology for Planners and Architects* (2010). She is currently Co-Director of the University of Utah's Master of Real Estate Development and a jointly appointed Professor of Architecture and Urban Planning.

Kathryn R. Terzano serves as Associate Director of the Metropolitan Research Center and Book Review Editor for the *Journal of Planning Literature*. Her research focuses on the intersection of human behavior and the built and natural environments. Under this research umbrella, Dr. Terzano has studied branding and urban design in ethnic enclaves, neighborhood satisfaction in the face of commercial and residential real estate changes, and non-motorized travel behavior, preferences, and attitudes. Dr. Terzano earned a PhD in City and Regional Planning and a Master of City and Regional Planning (MCRP), both from The Ohio State University, as well as a Bachelor of Arts in Sociology from Ohio University.

Michelle M. Thompson, PhD, GISP, is Associate Professor at the University of New Orleans in the Department of Planning and Urban Studies. Thompson combines her passion for applied research and service learning with public participation geographic information systems (PPGIS) to evaluate quality of life changes in urban environments. In 2009 Thompson created a community data information system, WhoData.org, which has been used primarily in New Orleans, LA, to model citizen science policies and practice. Thompson volunteers for Cross World Africa, Inc. to increase economic and educational opportunities in Kenya through micro-finance grants to youth and their families.

Dea van Lierop recently graduated from McGill University with a PhD in Urban Planning. Rapidly growing urban populations and environmental concerns have motivated her to question how cities can become more environmentally and socially sustainable. She is inspired by collaborations between academic researchers, planners, policymakers, and other stakeholders that question how initiatives in clean technology can become normative rather than alternative in urban centers around the world. Dea's current interests include public transit satisfaction and loyalty, land use and transportation planning, pedestrian and cyclist safety, and innovations in Transit Oriented Development.

Since 2012 **Karsten Zimmermann** has been Professor in the Faculty of Spatial Planning at the Technical University of Dortmund, where he holds the Chair for European Planning Cultures. He is educated as a political scientist and dedicated most of his academic work to the study of cities and regions. Currently he is President of the European Urban Research Association (EURA) and Dean of the Faculty. His list of publications includes numerous articles and books on metropolitan governance, European urban policy, knowledge and planning, and local climate policies.

INTRODUCTION

Planning Knowledge and Research

Thomas W. Sanchez

As an academic field, urban planning straddles traditional social sciences and professional training. The role and nature of research is quite different in these two cases, as are the professional expectations. The expectation for planning academics is to produce scholarship (i.e., published works) adding to the body of knowledge about planning thought and processes. Practice-oriented research focuses on the elements of plan-making. Contributions to academic literature are very different products and activities compared to planning reports or plans, although both draw upon and contribute to planning knowledge. The objective of this book is to reflect on the purposes of planning research, especially among planning academics.

Planning research and scholarship attempts to improve our understanding of place and society. Urban planning is a very broad field, and the variety of topics can appear fractured or disjointed to non-planners. This book discusses elements of urban planning research to illustrate the knowledge domain, showing how seemingly disparate topics are interconnected through an urban planning lens. An objective is to highlight perspectives on planning scholarship in relation to the planning academy and profession. Underlying each chapter is the question, "How do we better understand place and society through planning research?" This involves a variety of viewpoints from planning scholars who consider planning scholarship historically, critically, and speculatively from their area of expertise.

Readers of this book are encouraged to reflect on the themes that connect each chapter. These chapters are not meant to be about planning research methods, but instead are about the intention and meaning of the research. While much of the discussion focuses on the United States, there are significant contributions about international planning scholarship and experience. Despite differences in institutional landscapes, patterns of international planning scholarship are strikingly similar to those of the United States. Taken together, these chapters provide a rich discussion on urban planning research and knowledge. The book may also appeal to professional planners who work with research or have research interests.

The discussion is broken into four parts.

Part I: The Context of Planning Research

These chapters set the context for the purpose of planning research. There are differing opinions about the level of emphasis that should be placed upon research that is purely academic and research that directly serves the planning profession. This varies according to the type of academic institutions where planning faculty reside and the mission of their institutions. These chapters discuss how the two foci complement each other as well as create tension within academic and professional communities. Ernest Alexander connects planning theory, research, and practice in a historical context. This has direct implications for the purposes and approaches to planning problems. The inherent "gap" between research and practice is reviewed by Carolyn Loh, who notes that many planning academics lack professional planning experience. She sees the gap narrowing with greater attention being paid to practice-oriented research. From a European perspective, Karsten Zimmermann, Robin Chang, and Andreas Putlitz identify "planning cultures" that influence the directions of planning research. In addition, they refer to research traditions which pervade academia. Paul Burton provides more depth on these traditions as he relates his experiences in Australia.

Part II: Types and Topics of Planning Research

The knowledge domain of planning is comprised of many interwoven elements. Given that the urbanization process is at the confluence of natural, human, and built environment systems, we would expect that planning scholarship would be a reflection of this. While some integration occurs, particular research areas develop their own cultures and communities of scholarship. This section begins with a chapter by Thomas Sanchez and Nader Afzalan that examines the research interests of approximately 900 US planning faculty. Their results describe the footprint of planning research topics. The next two chapters examine particular streams of planning research. Charles Hostovsky presents the case of greenway planning; and Dea van Lierop, Geneviève Boisjoly, Emily Grisé, and Ahmed El-Geneidy present the case of land use and transportation research. Both show the evolution of research and explicit connections in an interdisciplinary context. The chapter by Robert Marans and John Callewaert profiles a case of evaluation research. The multilayered approach is a rich case study that illustrates a project-level process, with direct applications to a range of planning problems.

Part III: Planning Research on Objects and Design

Planning scholarship traditionally employs a variety of methods that are both quantitative and qualitative, with studies also ranging in scale. The three chapters in this section discuss the "boundary" between planning research and design. Robert Beauregard and Laura Lieto argue that large-N, quantitative analyses often lead us to overgeneralize, while real planning problems are specific and case-based. In discussing urban morphology, Brenda Case Scheer refers to several ways in which "form" cannot currently be easily quantified. She points out that change detection and pattern recognition to understand built environments and settlement activities have fascinating pedagogies with deep connections to theory. In his chapter, Davide Ponzini questions the boundary between planning and design, arguing for strengthening this critical connection. These discussions challenge scholars and students in terms of research design and methods selection, especially those with non-design backgrounds.

Part IV: Planning Methods, Science, and Technology

The last section focuses on methods, science, and technology in urban planning research. There has been increasing interest in analytical methods and modeling at the urban scale. These applications have broadened to include information and communications technologies (ICTs) and distributed analytic capabilities. The first chapter, by Kathryn Terzano and Reid Ewing, recaps the "Research You Can Use" columns that have appeared for the past few years in *Planning* magazine. The column's author, Reid Ewing, is an academic but places particular emphasis on research for practitioners. These are valuable insights that connect to "research to practice" themes in prior chapters. The chapter by Robert Goodspeed, Peter Pelzer, and Christopher Pettit elaborates on the advances in ICTs and their potential for planning research opportunities. Previously referred to as "planning support systems," these technologies can be used to collect, analyse, and communicate a vast array of data types. At the same time, these tools can be made available to "citizen scientists," who are extending the traditional model of citizen participation. In her chapter, Michelle Thompson demonstrates how this happened in the case of New Orleans after Katrina. Citizen science is a collaborative model well-suited to urban planning research activities that can build grassroots capacity. Finally, Michael Batty's chapter on planning theory, methods, and models articulates how the scientific method underlies urban planning research traditions. He brings us back to where we started, with planning theory being a platform from which to understand planning research and knowledge.

PART I
The Context of Planning Research

1
HOW THEORY LINKS RESEARCH AND PRACTICE

70 Years' Planning Theory: A Critical Review

Ernest R. Alexander

Introduction: Planning, Planning Theories and Practices

For any sensible discussion of how planning theory relates planning research to planning practice, we need to understand what "planning" we are talking about. That's not as obvious as it may seem: planning, it turns out, has defied simple definition. Jean Hillier, a leading planning theorist, could only offer a variety of definitions with different "referents in specialist theories and approaches" (2010: 4; see pp. 3–5). Tim Chapin's "[p]lanning is a funny field" (2015: 315) seems as good an answer as any.

The futility of trying to define planning led me to a contrarian conclusion: there is no "planning". But, even if no definable planning exists, we can still recognize a variety of diverse planning practices. Among these are the professional planning practices we know: spatial, urban, environmental or transportation planning. This is what people usually mean when they talk about planning, and this is what is captured by the American Planning Association (APA) in its definition: "Planning, also called urban planning or city and regional planning, is . . ." (APA, 2016).

Not planning, then, but this set of diverse planning practices, is the true subject of planning theories and research. I will go on to discuss what this implies for planning theories, and how they link planning-related research to different kinds of planning practice. First, if there is no "planning", it follows that there is no planning theory either: accordingly, I did not refer above to planning theory, but to planning *theories*. Recognizing diversity in planning theories suggests that there are different kinds of planning theories, related to various types of planning practices.

This relation offers the missing link between planning theory and practice, which planning academics and practitioners have been seeking for years. Complaints about the planning theory-practice gap[1] prompted a search for explanations, but none is really satisfactory.

The conceptual framework developed here shows how and why different kinds of planning theories are associated with particular forms of planning practices, making some theories more useful than others for those types of practices we think of as "planning". Research in planning and related areas has an important role here: it generates the knowledge behind some planning theories — not all — that links them to their respective knowledge-based planning practices. My exposition of this argument concludes with a classification of the different kinds of planning theories, which shows their links to the diverse types of identifiable planning practices.

In the section that follows, I review the body of thought that is generally called planning theory, identifying three diverging "streams" that planning theorists have followed over the last 70 years or so. Finally, combining these classifications provides the framework to explain how different kinds of planning study and planning-related research contribute to various planning theories and how these, in turn, relate to the diverse planning practices that make up "planning".

From Planning Theory to Planning Theories[2]

There is No Planning – Only Planning Practices

For decades, planning theorists have tried to answer the question: what is planning? Today's popular answer is Friedmann's (1987: 38–44) definition of planning as the link between knowledge and action. Other answers range from planning as rational choice (Davidoff and Reiner, 1962) through planning as storytelling (Throgmorton, 1992) to planning as expectation management (Hartmann, 2012) or as a "language game" (Lord, 2014: 37–39). The problem with all these definitions is not that they are not true; it is that they are too abstract for closure.[3]

Vickers' (1968) definition – planning is what planners do – looks like a tautology, but it offers a pragmatic answer. Expanding this definition in the light of its validation principle, the social construction of knowledge, we can say that "planners" are the people who a particular community acknowledges are involved in a process it recognizes as "planning".

This leads to an interesting discovery: only one set of people talks about "planning" without any qualification – planning theorists. Everyone else refers to "planning" with a substantive descriptor (explicit or implied[4]): spatial planning; urban, regional or town and country planning; transportation, environmental or social planning; strategic, advocacy or e-planning. The qualifier is practically universal. It applies in academe, in practice and anywhere one can think of: politics, legislation, the media and common conversation. Nobody else talks about "planning", or really means *generic* planning if they do.

What does this imply for planning? If planning theorists are the only ones who refer to "planning" and talk of "planners", perhaps there is no planning at all – if "planning" is understood as a recognizable practice. But that begs the question:

what *is* a practice? In one sense, practices are descriptions of what some people do, a set of activities linked by common understandings and abilities – the practice of cooking, banking, tennis, etc. (Schatzki, 2001).

In another, more normative, sense, practices are what people learn as the best ways to fulfill their purposes. These are knowledge-centered practices: "socially recognized forms of activity, done on the basis of what members learn . . . capable of being done well or badly, correctly or incorrectly" and endowing their "membership with the power to perform" (Barnes, 2001: 19–20). Knorr-Cetina (2001) calls this "epistemic practice", demanding specialized knowledge and expertise and operating in various fields, each with its distinct epistemic culture, its specific "epistemic objects"[5] and its relevant expert-object relationship.

Now we can revisit the original question to ask: is planning a knowledge-centered practice? The conclusive answer is: no. Planning may be a practice in the broader, descriptive sense: such generic planning is what people do – just as cooking is a practice – when they are planning. Generic planning is not an epistemic practice, because it is not related to any identifiable epistemic object.[6] Specific knowledge-centered planning practices do exist. Common-sense recognition of these planning practices identifies them by their epistemic objects: spatial, regional, environmental, transportation, social, strategic or e-planning.

At the concrete level, diverse identifiable practices (per Schatzki's definition) also exist: planning practices that are definable, observable and researchable. These are planning practices enacted in their real-world settings. For simplification, we can give them three descriptors: the planning sector (indicating purpose), planning level (associated with scale and scope) and country (summarizing socioeconomic, political and cultural traits).

Such contextuated planning practices range from advocacy planning for a Colombian *barrio* and municipal planning for a Swedish city at the local level, through environmental planning in the greater Los Angeles area and transportation planning for the Mexican Distrito Federál at the metropolitan-regional level, to national statutory planning in the Netherlands, European Union TEN[7] transportation planning and World Bank development planning at the national, transnational and international levels. These real-life planning practices are the subject of study and research that form the building blocks of constructive theories, norms and methods, which are relevant and useful to practitioners of knowledge-based planning – theories of spatial, environmental, social, strategic or advocacy planning.

Planning Practices and Theories

This review confirms my previous intuitive conclusion. There is no planning, in the sense of *a* definable and identifiable "planning" practice, but "planning" exists as a set of different and diverse planning practices. These can be grouped in a rough hierarchy that is linked to different types of theories and research.

At the highest level of abstraction and generality, there is a "planning" practice that can be described and theorized. This is planning as "organized nexuses of activity" generating actions that intervene in the world (Schatzki, 2001: 48). As planning theory is supposed to be a theory of practice (Harrison, 2014: 68; De Neufville, 1983), generic "planning" theories will be at the same level of abstraction as the subject practice.[8]

At the next level, "planning" is a diverse set of specific knowledge-centered practices, each identifiable by its domain or subject of concern – its "epistemic object" (Knorr-Cetina, 2001). In contrast to generic "planning" practice, these knowledge-based planning practices are normative, not just positive-descriptive. These "epistemic" planning practices must be the subjects of ("something") planning theories, prescriptions and methodologies.

At the concrete level of real-life planning we again find diverse planning practices: descriptions and explanations of what these planners do. These contextuated planning practices are the subject of study, research and generalizations that form the building blocks of constructive theory. This will be at a mid level of (something) planning theories that relate to a specific "epistemic" planning practice.

The conventional qualifiers of "planning" can serve as a tentative list of such planning practices. These include substantive fields (e.g. spatial-territorial planning, transportation planning, environmental planning); planning domains (e.g. state planning, metro-regional planning); and forms of practice (e.g. advocacy planning, strategic planning, e-planning). Any of those is a potential field for such (something) planning theories.

70 Years' Planning Theory – Three Streams[9]

The above review divided planning theory and research by its links to different planning practices. Next, I review the last 70 years of planning theory in a different way, linking theories by their common orientation and roots. This account of developments from the 1950s to the present was inspired by John Friedmann's (1987) magisterial review of 200 years of planning thought. Just as he reduced the complex interactions and influences that produced modern planning theory to four "traditions", I see the diversity of recent planning thought coalescing – not converging – into three streams: the radical-communicative, the post-structuralist and the institutionalist streams.

The Radical–Communicative Stream

Among the critics of the rational planning model that prevailed up to the 1950s, whose ideas invaded planning thought, we can recognize divergent directions. From the conservative-reformist side, revisionists like Simon and Lindblom proposed various forms of bounded rationality, while political economists and philosophers like Popper, Mannheim and Hayek explored alternative models of thought and action. Proto-planning theorists (e.g. systems theorist Churchman) and conscious planning theorists (e.g. Perloff, Webber, Schön) reflected Friedmann's "policy analysis", "social learning" and "social reform" traditions.

The ancestor of the radical-communicative stream is Friedmann's "social mobilization" tradition. The radical part reflects neo-Marxist thought (e.g. Gramsci), later represented by proto-planning theorists such as the political philosopher Herbert Marcuse, the sociologist Castells and geographers Harvey and Soja. Its leading member today is John Friedmann. Another, younger, group of the radical branch learned from Foucault's critique of modern rationality and society.

The communicative part descends from another branch of the same tradition: the critical school of philosophy. This body of planning thought was rounded out by John Forester's translation of Habermas' (1981) communicative rationality into the would-be planning paradigm (Beauregard, 1996) of communicative practice. Most of today's planning theory community belongs in this stream. After Friedmann, Forester, Healey, Hoch and Innes are among prominent anglophone members of this stream, with Sager (from Norway) representing the others. The radical branch includes Fainstein, Peter Marcuse, Moulaert, Watson and Yiftachel, with fewer anglophones and more "southerners".[10]

The radical-communicative stream is quite diverse, but all its members share some beliefs in varying degrees. Their main common concept is communicative practice, seeing planning as discourse deploying good communication to reach a common consensus through reasoned argument. Another guiding idea is the social construction of knowledge (Berger and Luckmann, 1967), rejecting objective empiricism and the primacy of scientific expertise to privilege "lay" knowledge instead. Finally, they share a progressive agenda (e.g. see Friedmann) rooted in experiential knowledge, focused not on governments and states but on people and households. Planning is to promote system change toward the "Good Society"; radical-communicative planning means "transformative development . . . bring(ing) knowledge to bear on the flow of action" (Healey, 2011: xii–xiii).

The Post–Structuralist Stream

This stream in planning theory emerged later than the mainstream (in the 1970s to 1980s) and contains a much smaller and younger cohort of scholars. Its ancestry resembles that of the Foucaultian radicals, but its members draw on other postmodern theorists. A leading member of this stream described post-structuralist planning theory as

> represent(ing) theoretical inquiry which includes not only relationality, multiplicity and fragmentation, but also performativity and immanence . . . not allowing definitions . . . of planning or politics to be detailed in advance . . . less seeking some underlying structure but rather about searching for how and why transformation takes place.
>
> (Hillier, 2005: 276)

The post-structuralists' common denominator is their role as translators of continental-European theorists, following Forester's lead as the exponent of

Habermas. Many postmodern European thinkers' theories and concepts have been imported into planning theory in this way. Most of these thinkers are post-structuralists: Deleuze, Derrida, Guattari, Lacan and Mouffe; some, such as Bourdieu and Lefebvre,[11] are not. All these are the subjects of planning-related expositions by Gunder, Hillier, and others.

This stream is striking in its variety and lack of convergence, making it difficult to characterize or stereotype. Its diversity shows in the range of concepts that are proposed to enhance planning theory and improve – even revolutionize – practice, from Bourdieu's habitus through Mouffe's agonism, Deleuze's *bricolage* and Lacan's Real to Lefebvre's "right to the city". Critical reflection asks: what do these ideas from other fields (e.g. semiotics, sociology and psychoanalysis) contribute to planning theory or practice? While we must be open to our intellectual environment, this is a legitimate question. Such transfers can be judged by their relevance to some real-world context (Alexander, 2010: 104). By this criterion, some imports fare quite well but others seem to fail.[12]

The Institutionalist Stream

Like its predecessors, this stream is an arbitrary label for a subset of the planning theory discourse community, linked by what they share: their common interest in institutions. Institutions are important: "the rules of the game in society . . . that shape human interaction" (North, 1990: 3). They range from major institutions (e.g. the U.S. Constitution) through important sectoral ones (e.g. the Swedish planning system) to small informal ones (like the weekly card game at Brady's Bar – still important to its players). For members of this stream, institutions are the focus of their study and research.

The institutionalist stream reflects the "new institutionalism" that emerged in economics, political science and sociology, modifying classical theory in these disciplines. Institutional economics questioned classic assumptions to account for corporations in markets. In political science, institutions explain political stability. In international relations, regime theory accounts for treaties restraining nations' power. In planning, too, institutionalists are making contributions; for example, Healey (1999) situates institutions in the context of transformative planning, and Alexander (1992) refutes the conflict between planning and the market (Verma, 2007: 4–7).

Institutionalists' intellectual ancestries and ideological orientations range from progressive to libertarian. At one extreme Healey reads institutionalism into communicative practice; at the other, Hayekian liberalism inspires Lai, Moroni and Webster. Between these poles, pragmatism and the "social reform" tradition in planning theory inspire others in this set; for example, Albrechts, Alexander, Faludi, Mazza, Sanyal, Teitz and Verma. Simplifying this continuum, we can distinguish two branches in the institutionalist stream: a liberal branch and a progressive one.

Their work involves institutions in various ways, from the general-abstract to the specific and concrete particular. Healey's (2006) collaborative planning is one example of the first approach, shifting scale from communicative planning to governance and focusing on institutional dynamics and transformations; her work fits into the progressive branch of the institutionalists. Alexander (1992, 1995) introduces institutional economics into planning theory to see planning as coordination (Verma, 2007: 6–7). Moroni (2010) adopts this approach from the liberal side, proposing radical change in conventional planning and development control. Also in the liberal branch, Webster and Lai (2003) offer a well-developed institutional model of urban governance.

At the concrete level, planning scholars in this stream adopt an institutional approach in their specific research. Examples of this work are Aarts evaluating Port Authorities' planning and implementation, Buitelaar on the famous non-zoning in Houston, Texas, Ganapatti analyzing Indian housing cooperatives, Matthews on planning for climate adaptation, Moroni on contractual communities and Verma on U.S. fiscal impact analysis.[13] Here Verma (2007) also places institutional design (e.g. Bolan, 1996). Later contributions and applications (Alexander, 2001, 2006; Gualini, 2001; Faludi and Waterhout, 2002; Woltjer, 2000) show its diffusion in the field.

Relating Planning Theories, Practices and Research

Now we can identify different kinds of planning theories, link them to the diverse planning practices we have found, and explore how these relations could explain how planning and planning-related research informs planning theory and practices. First, there is the link between "levels" of planning theory and research, and the three types of planning practices: generic "planning" practice, knowledge-centered planning practices with their epistemic objects (such as spatial, environmental, or e-planning) and the diverse real-life planning practices enacted in their specific contexts (from community planning in a Cali barrio to transportation planning of the European TEN). Then we can situate various planning theories that fit into the streams suggested above – the radical-communicative, post-structuralist and institutionalist approaches – into the appropriate cells formed by the theory-practice intersections, shown in Table 1.1, to see how they relate to the different types of planning practices.

Planning Theories and Research

Decades ago, Andreas Faludi (1973) divided planning theory into "theory *of* planning" and "theory *in* planning". "Theory *in* planning" is substantive theory, related to "planners' specific concern about their particular core subject" (e.g. land use planning) (Faludi, in Mukhopadhyay, 2015: 12). This is the planning theory Batty (2018, this volume) is talking about in his explanation of how theory is constructed from scientific research.

But, as Faludi suggested, procedural "theory *of* planning" is more commonly the stuff of planning theory, and much of that consists of (in terms of this

TABLE 1.1 Planning theories, practices and research

		KNOWLEDGE Planning theories/research			ACTION Planning practices		
		Level	Type	Content	*"Planning"* Generic	*(Something) planning* Knowledge centered on epistemic object	*Contextuated planning* Enacted in defined real-life context
					P.1	**P.2**	**P.3**
Theory	**T.1**	Abstract/general	Generic "planning" theories	Procedural: Descriptive-explanatory	Rational planning: Bounded rationality Communicative practice Strategic planning "Fluid" planning Adaptive planning		
	T.2	Abstract/practice-specific	(Something) planning theories	1. Procedural: Descriptive-explanatory/normative 2. Substantive: Descriptive-explanatory		[*Spatial planning*] Comprehensive planning Collaborative planning New Urbanism	
Research	**R.1**	General/abstract [Quantitative]				1. <u>Procedural:</u> 2. <u>Substantive:</u>	1. <u>Procedural:</u> 2. <u>Substantive:</u>
	R.2	Concrete/case-specific [Qualitative]					1. <u>Procedural:</u> 2. <u>Substantive:</u>

discussion) generic "planning" theories that relate to (generic) planning practice. These "planning" theories (row T.1 in Table 1.1) make up most of what planning academics, students and practitioners understand as planning theory.

Like the generic planning practice to which they relate, such "planning" theories are necessarily general and abstract. And because their subject – generic "planning" practice (column P.1 in Table 1.1) – is defined as descriptive (planning is what planners do), they must be descriptive or explanatory too. So the normative value of "planning" theories is limited: they cannot prescribe (something) planners' roles or actions in their real-life planning practices.[14]

"Theory *in* planning" is planning theory related to planners' "particular core subject"; that is, a specific knowledge-centered planning practice's epistemic object. For the cited example of land use planning, that would be: land and making the best use of land for human activities. Accordingly, we can identify several sets of planning theories, each related to a recognized knowledge-centered planning practice: theories of spatial planning, of social planning, of regional, transportation or community development planning, etc. (column P.2 in Table 1.1). These (something) planning theories (row T.2) are procedural and substantive, and since they relate to knowledge-centered practices that are defined as normative,[15] they include normative theories too.

Since theories are generalized abstractions of reality, there cannot be planning theories relating directly to enacted planning practices in specified real-life settings. That is why cells P.3/T.1 and P.3/T.2 in Table 1.1 are empty. But it is these contextuated planning practices (column P.3) that are the subjects of most planning and planning-related research. Such research includes general/abstract studies and analyses, which are usually quantitative and may be mainly *procedural* (cell P.3/R.1.1) – for example, vulnerability assessment in environmental planning (Hall, 2009) – or *substantive* (P.3/R.1.2) – such as "big data" analysis of urban structures and trends (Batty, 2013).

Planning and planning-related research in real situations also draws on contextuated planning practices (cell P.3/R.2 in Table 1.1): particular case studies (usually more qualitative) in specified contexts. Procedural case studies (P.3/R.2.1) are the bases for more general spatial planning models,[16] and substantive case analyses (P.3/R.2.2) make up most planning-related empirical research. This covers a wide range of fields from neighborhood segregation in social geography through housing markets in urban economics to local government models in public administration.

Spatial Planning Theories and Research[17]

An exhaustive survey of planning theories for (something) planning practices (i.e. knowledge-centered practices in specified fields)[18] is impossible. It is hard to imagine such a review, considering their multiplicity, diversity and indeterminacy.[19] Here, I discuss spatial planning as an illustrative case of a (something) planning practice. This is for two reasons: first, spatial planning is a recognized specialized planning practice; and second, this is a field I know something about.[20]

Davoudi (2015) has identified three kinds of knowledge that enable good practice: knowing what (theories, concepts), knowing how (crafts, skills) and knowing to what end (moral choices). Under "knowing what", there are two basic aspects of theories of spatial planning: the material object of spatial planning and spatial planning processes (Needham, 2013). We can combine these dimensions as follows to frame the field of spatial planning theories.

1. **What?** *The object* of spatial planning is human activities in space and their environment; for practical purposes, the land-property market can serve as a surrogate. The land-property market, which is not a "normal" market and needs spatial planning to work, can be seen as the object of spatial planners' practice (Alexander, 2014a) and is one of the subjects of empirical spatial planning theories.

   Other subjects of empirical spatial planning theories are drawn from planning-related disciplines (e.g. geography, economics, sociology, environmental sciences)[21] and fields that address specific aspects of social activities and human behavior (e.g. demography, housing, transportation). Research in these disciplines and fields is not necessarily planning research. But as planning-related research, the subjects of these studies are the settings and environments of real-life spatial planning practices in identified contexts; that is how such research contributes to empirical theories and models for spatial planning.[22]

2. **Where?** *The context* for spatial planning is the social-institutional environment of spatial planners' practice. Spatial planning institutions, spanning the public, private and "third" sectors in various combinations (Alexander, 2001), are the workplaces of most planners. This suggests analysis of the relevant institutional environment and demands institutional design of spatial planning institutions and processes. This is being done through case studies and institutional analyses by scholars and researchers in the institutionalist stream of planning theory.

3. **How?** Spatial planning *tools* are the concepts, methods, skills and competencies needed for effective practice. These are the expert spatial planner's contribution to the social co-construction of knowledge involved in all planning. Spatial planning concepts and methodologies are a central theme of spatial planning theories, though many of them are transferred from related disciplines, such as social and urban geography, urban economics, and sociology.

   Integrating concepts and models in spatial planning theory is perhaps the most important aspect of "How?" These take different forms: some are mainly procedural, others more substantive; many combine these with being normative to imply that this is what makes a good plan.

   The first type, procedural models, are adaptations for spatial planning of generic "planning" paradigms, e.g. comprehensive planning (Kent, 1964; Hollander et al., 1988, 71–91; Herman et al., 2016) applying the rational planning model, collaborative planning (Innes and Booher, 2010) as communicative practice, or adaptive planning (De Roo, 2003) as planning in complexity. The second type includes influential substantive concepts reflecting normative elements of urban morphology, which have come and gone over time. A notable historical example is the grid (Mazza, 2016: 6–17); a more recent one is the neighborhood unit (Mumford, 1954; Gillette, 1983); a contemporary one is concentrated decentralization (Zonneveld, 1989). The last kind is better called movements in spatial planning; these range from the New Towns movement, which began in the 1930s but is still alive (Hall, 2002: 88–100), to the New Urbanism (Talen, 2005) today.

How these draw on planning research and planning-related research is a question almost impossible to answer: it would demand an exhaustive intellectual history. Speculation suggests that these concepts and models are the product of innovative ideas responding to reflected experience: the result of intuitive reflection and systematic evaluation in case studies and phronetic research (Flyvberg, 2001) involving active participation.

A good example of this research approach is Flyvbjerg's (1998) Foucaultian strategic planning. Here, the author's successful participation as an actor in the Aalborg Project supported his advocacy of spatial planners engaging strategically in the local political arena. His case was a decades-long urban revitalization project for central Aalborg, which involved local planners, politicians and interests in conflict over proposed plans and development.

A more problematic example is Hillier's post-structuralist proposal for "fluid" spatial planning – "planning (of) space in which representations are unsettled and destabilized" (2005: 299), illustrated with the redevelopment of Melbourne Docklands in Australia. But here the research contradicts her conclusions: "fluid" planning in the cited case did not work. The Redevelopment Agency's first "fluid" plan was too uncertain for potential investors; it had to be supplemented by an urban design "Vision" and a conventional public plan.

4   **What for?** *The purpose* of planning is the topic of much "planning" theory, but prescribing roles for "planners" has not been very useful. For spatial planning, I have suggested planners' role as expert professionals intervening in the public interest in the land-property markets that are in their remit (Alexander, 2016: 100). This implies two areas for the normative side of spatial planning theories. One is the public interest, which explores the objectives of planning decisions and spatial plans (Alexander, 2002); the other is ethics, concerned with planners' subjective values and professional behavior (Hendler, 1995).

Discussion: Planning Theories, Research and Practices

Now we have a matrix linking types of planning theories with planning practices and planning research. For one cell, a more detailed frame for spatial planning theories relates these to planning and planning-related research. How does "planning" theory, in the streams reviewed above, fit into this framework? The answers to this question may tell us something about the relation between planning theory and planning practices, and go towards explaining the planning theory-practice gap.

Another question is: how does planning theory relate to planning research? For this, too, we can look at the different planning theory streams. But what do I mean by planning research? Here I adopt the conventional understanding of research: positivist[23] empirical investigation applying the scientific method,[24] as done in the physical and natural sciences. Most research in social science disciplines (including planning) takes this approach, but some theorizing in these fields uses a different approach. Hermeneutic[25] analysis, rather than positivist research, is behind most critical and postmodernist theory in the social sciences; as we will see, this applies to planning theory as well.

The *radical–communicative stream* is true "planning" theory for generic planning practice. Its paradigms and models are general and abstract and have limited applicability to other planning practices. Without appropriate development, they offer little for specific knowledge-centered practices or planning practices in real-life contexts. This stream's central paradigm, communicative practice, is a good example. Defining planning as communication, it proposes "listening" and mediating roles for planners (Forester, 1999). Another model, radical-insurgent planning, prescribes abstract normative roles for "planners"; for example, the planner as a moral agent in the public domain (Friedmann, 1978).

But some models adapt generic planning theories to specific planning practices. Abstract radical-transformative planning becomes "transactive planning" for real planning practice in small-scale interactive contexts (Friedmann, 1973).[26] Communicative practice (in its institutional settings) is enacted in more concrete models that contribute to the body of spatial planning theories relevant for spatial planning practice, such as Healey's and Innes' collaborative planning (Healey, 1997; Innes and Booher, 2010) and Albrechts' (2004) strategic spatial planning. Foucaultian approaches are applied to specific planning practices, such as infrastructure planning (Flyvberg, 2005) and ethnocratic spatial planning (Yiftachel, 2006). Finally, prescribed roles for generic planners are developed and transformed into supplementary fields and useful methods for spatial planners, such as mediation and conflict resolution (Susskind and Ozawa, 1984).

Critiques of traditional rationality are at the intellectual root of this stream (Alexander, 2000). So, most of its members invoke hermeneutic thinking rather than positivistic research. Empirical planning research supporting the applied planning models offered here (e.g. collaborative planning or strategic planning for spatial planners) is often phronetic research, combining analysis with active participation, or evaluative case study learning from experience.

More than its predecessor, the *post–structuralist stream* is only for generic planning practice: most of the exposition is very abstract and general. There have been few attempts to adapt imported concepts for real-world application, and these have had limited success.[27] Post-structuralist planning theories, like their European sources, are the consistent products of hermeneutic analysis; facts revealed through empirical research are disregarded or ignored.[28]

I have called my approach to planning theory "post-postmodernist", a perspective my colleagues in the *institutionalist stream* consciously or unconsciously share. This implies a different way of theorizing than the other streams, where hermeneutic argument is preferred, and a different attitude to planning research. Contrary to the postmodern dismissal of scientific knowledge, empirical research is the basis of institutionalist analysis. Unlike radical-communicative and post-structuralist planning theories for generic planning practice, institutionalists' work relates to specific planning practices.[29] Our general models are for knowledge-centered practices, such as spatial, environmental or strategic planning; our research focuses on enacted planning practices in specific real-world contexts.

This summary review suggests a simple explanation of the planning theory-practice gap: "planning" theory is not for planning practices. Most of what the planning community – scholars, teachers, and students of planning, and practicing planners – commonly thinks of as planning theory is what I have reviewed here as theories and models in the radical-communicative and post-structural streams of "planning" theory. These streams are about generic "planning" practice; they are not planning theories for the diverse recognized planning practices or for (something) planners. Their links with planning practices enacted in real-life contexts are also weak, ignoring these as sources of research-based knowledge and hardly communicating with their practitioners. Given this kind of theory, it is not surprising to find a gap between "planning" theory and real planning practices.

But there is room for hope: communicative practice has provided some insights,[30] useful models and methods for spatial planning,[31] and it may contribute more. This also reflects the influence of the institutionalist approach as it infiltrates other streams. As trends in planning theory discourse suggest a retreat from postmodernism, if planning theorists recognize the nature and diversity of planning practices, we may at least "mind the gap".

Notes

1 See Burton (2018, this volume) for an Australian case confirming this gap by showing the limited impact of planning theories and research on local planning practice.
2 The following sections are based on Alexander (2016).
3 We can see this by simply substituting another term for "planning"; for example, "plumbing links knowledge with action" or "politics as a language game".
4 For example, the APA definition of "planning" above.
5 These may be real-objective natural things, or cognitive-cultural artifacts. The epistemic object of neurosurgery, for example, is the brain, while for economists, it is the economy.
6 This is obvious if we review the "objects" that definitions associate with (generic) planning; for example, knowledge and action, decisions, the future, rational choice.
7 Trans-European Network.
8 For example, the "planning" addressed in such planning theories may be any practice in the public domain that links knowledge with action. Undoubtedly, some "planning" theories and paradigms at this level of abstraction have enhanced our understanding. But since this "planning" is not a normative or "epistemic" practice, their normative validity or utility for practitioners is questionable.
9 The following sections are based on Alexander (2015).

10 These lists are the arbitrary response of my selective memory to the constraints of time and space; they should not be read with any connotation of rating or importance – many equally valid references may be missing. Error is inevitable, given the (over)simplification of my taxonomy and the complexity of planning theorists' real work and roles.
11 Nevertheless, I have lumped them into this stream for simplicity and convenience. This stream might have been more aptly called "postmodernist" to include them, but then it should properly include the Foucaultians as well.
12 Forester's translation of Habermas' communicative rationality is the successful prototype; ideas/concepts from this stream that pass this test include habitus (analytically useful) and the "right to the city" (normatively stimulating), while agonism and bricolage have yet to prove their value.
13 See Brunetta and Moroni (2012), Buitelaar (2009), Ganapatti (2007), Hijdra et al. (2014), Matthews (2013) and Raja and Verma (2010).
14 Also because their possible epistemic objects are vague or absent; see note 6.
15 See Schatzi's and Knorr-Cetina's definitions of practices, p. 9.
16 For examples, see the next section: Spatial Planning Theories and Research.
17 Much of this section is based on Alexander (2016: 97–98).
18 Filling cell P.2/T.2 in Table 1.1.
19 What is a knowledge-centered planning practice, and what is not, is unresolved (Alexander, 2016: 94–95).
20 But see Alexander (2014b) for a discussion of e-planning, a planning practice of which I know nothing.
21 I am not qualified for a systematic review, but examples that come to mind include: central place theory and gravity models (geography); land-rent functions and growth poles (urban and development economics); neighborhood succession and segregation (urban sociology); and ecosystem concepts and climate change adaptation (environmental sciences).
22 Batty (2018, this volume) explains how empirical research, theories and models (such as urban density–land rent) enable the construction of models (e.g. land use–transportation models) for practical planning application.
23 Positivism assumes that there is a discoverable reality out there, and "truth" is in findings that correspond best to that reality.
24 This involves testing falsifiable hypotheses to arrive at agreement on verifiable facts or "truths" – see Batty (2018, this volume).
25 Hermenuetics is a way of extracting meaning through systematic interpretation of data – usually applying selected theoretical models or ideological frames – and "true" findings reflect collective understanding.
26 For example, neighborhood planning, community development, or local urban revitalization.
27 See note 12; other examples include Hillier's (2005) "fluid" planning and Gunder and Hillier's (2009) Lacanian application to planning (see Alexander, 2011).
28 See, for example, Hillier's case study (p. 17). This is consistent with postmodernist epistemology, which does not recognize the objective reality of "facts".
29 Exceptions to this generalization are rare; one of the few is my own "transaction cost theory of planning" (Alexander, 1992), which associates (generic) planning with organization – public and market alike.
30 For example, the importance of public and stakeholder involvement in participative planning; this produced the field of public participation in planning and related methods and applications.
31 See point 4, p. 17.

References

Albrechts, L. (2004) Strategic spatial planning reexamined. *Environment and Planning B: Planning & Design* 31 (5): 743–758.

Alexander, E.R. (1992) A transaction cost theory of planning. *Journal of the American Planning Association* 58 (2): 190–200.

Alexander, E.R. (1995) *How Organizations Act Together: Interorganizational Coordination in Theory and Practice*. Amsterdam: Gordon & Breach.

Alexander, E.R. (2000) Rationality revisited: planning paradigms in a post-modernist perspective. *Journal of Planning Education and Research* 19 (3): 242–256.

Alexander, E.R. (2001) A transaction-cost theory of land use planning and development control. *Town Planning Review* 72 (1): 45–76.

Alexander, E.R. (2002) The public interest in planning: from legitimation to substantive plan evaluation. *Planning Theory* 1 (3): 226–249.

Alexander, E.R. (2005) What do planners need to know? Identifying needed competencies, methods and skills. *Journal of Architectural and Planning Research* 22 (2): 91–106.

Alexander, E.R. (2006) Institutional design for sustainable development. *Town Planning Review* 77 (1): 1–28.

Alexander, E.R. (2010) Introduction: does planning theory affect practice, and if so, how? *Planning Theory* 9 (2): 99–107.

Alexander, E.R. (2011) Book review: Gunder and Hillier (2009) Planning in ten words or less. *Planning Theory* 10 (4): 379–382.

Alexander, E.R. (2014a) Land-property markets and planning: a special case. *Land Use Policy* 41: 533–540.

Alexander, E.R. (2014b) "Planning" or e-planning? Implications for theory, education and practice. *International Journal of E–Planning & Research* 3 (1): 1–15.

Alexander, E.R. (2015) 70 years' planning theory: a post-postmodernist perspective. *Scienze Regionali – Italian Journal of Regional Science* 14 (1): 5–18.

Alexander, E.R. (2016) There is no planning – only planning practices. *Planning Theory* 15 (1): 91–103.

APA (2016) About planning. https://www.planning.org/about planning/whatisplanning/htm (accessed 21 January, 2016).

Barnes, B. (2001) Practice as collective action, in T.R. Schatzki, K. Knorr-Cetina and E. von Savigny (eds.) *The Practice Turn in Contemporary Theory*, pp. 17–28. New York: Routledge.

Batty, M. (2013) *The New Science of Cities*. Cambridge, MA: MIT Press.

Batty, M. (2017) Science in planning: theory, methods and models, in T.W. Sanchez (ed.) *Planning Research and Knowledge*, pp. 241–254. Abingdon, U.K.: Routledge.

Beauregard, R.A. (1996) Commentary – Advocating preeminence: anthologies as politics, in S.J. Mandelbaum, L. Mazza and R.W. Burchell (eds.) *Explorations in Planning Theory*, pp. 105–110. New Brunswick, NJ: CUPR, Rutgers The State University of New Jersey.

Berger, P.L. and T. Luckmann (1967) *The Social Construction of Reality: A Treatise in the Sociology of Knowledge*. New York: Doubleday.

Bolan, R.S. (1996) Planning and institutional design, in S.J. Mandelbaum, L. Mazza and R.W. Burchell (eds.) *Explorations in Planning Theory*, pp. 497–513. New Brunswick, NJ: CUPR – Rutgers The State University of New Jersey.

Brunetta, G. and S. Moroni (2012) *Contractual Communities in the Self–Organizing City: Freedom, Creativity, Subsidiarity*. Dordrecht: Springer.

Buitelaar, E. (2009). Zoning, more than just a tool: explaining Houston's regulatory practice. *European Planning Studies* 17 (7): 1049–1065.

Burton, P. (2018) Striving for impact beyond the academy? Planning research in Australia, in T.W. Sanchez (ed.) *Planning Research and Knowledge*, pp. 51–65. Abingdon, U.K.: Routledge.

Chapin, T. (2015) Notes from the review editor. *Journal of the American Planning Association* 81 (4): 315.

Davidoff, P. and T.A. Reiner (1962) A choice theory of planning. *Journal of the American Institute of Planners* 28 (3): 103–115.

Davoudi, S. (2015) Planning as practice of knowing. *Planning Theory* 14 (3): 316–331.

De Neufville, J.I. (1983) Planning theory and practice: bridging the gap. *Journal of Planning Education & Research* 3 (1): 35–45.

De Roo, G. (2003) *Environmental Planning in the Netherlands: Too Good to be True – from Command–and–Control Planning to Shared Governance*. Aldershot, U.K.: Ashgate.

Faludi, A. (1973) *Planning Theory*. Oxford: Pergamon.

Faludi, A. and B. Waterhout (2002) *The Making of the European Spatial Development Perspective: No Masterplan*. London: Routledge.

Flyvbjerg, B. (1998) *Rationality and Power: Democracy in Practice*. Chicago, IL: University of Chicago Press.

Flyvbjerg, B. (2001) *Making Social Science Matter*. Cambridge, U.K.: Cambridge University Press.

Flyvbjerg, B. (2005) *Policy and Planning for Large Infrastructure Projects: Problems, Causes, Cures*. World Bank Policy Research WP 3781, Dec. 2005. Washington, DC: The World Bank.

Forester, J. (1999) *The Deliberative Practitioner: Encouraging Participative Planning Processes*. Cambridge, MA: MIT Press.

Friedmann, J. (1973) *Retracking America: A Theory of Transactive Planning*. Garden City, NY: Anchor Press.

Friedmann, J. (1978). The epistomology of social practice: a critique of objective knowledge. *Theory & Society* 6 (1): 75–92.

Friedmann, J. (1987) *Planning in the Public Domain*. Princeton, NJ: Princeton University Press.

Ganapatti, S. (2007) An institutional analysis of the evolution of housing cooperatives in India, in N. Verma (ed.) *Institutions and Planning*, pp. 155–174. Amsterdam: Elsevier.

Gillette, H. (1983) The evolution of neighborhood planning: from the progressive era to the 1949 Housing Act. *Journal of Urban History* 9 (4): 421–436.

Gualini, E. (2001) *Planning and the Intelligence of Institutions*. Farnham, U.K.: Ashgate.

Gunder, M. and J. Hillier (2009) *Planning in Ten Words or Less: A Lacanian Entanglement with Spatial Planning*. Farnham, U.K.: Ashgate.

Habermas, J. (1981) *Theorie des Kommunikativen Handelns. Band I Handlungsrationalität und Gesellschaftliche Rationalisierung*. Frankfurt am Main: Suhrkamp.

Hall, J. (2009) Integrated assessment to support regional and local decision making, in S. Davoudi, J. Crawford and A. Mehmood (eds.) *Planning for Climate Change: Strategies for Mitigation and Adaptation for Spatial Planners*, pp. 236–248. London: Earthscan.

Hall, P. (2002) *Cities of Tomorrow: An Intellectual History of Urban Planning and Design in the Twentieth Century*. Oxford, U.K.: Blackwell.

Harrison, P. (2014) Making planning theory real. *Planning Theory* 13 (1): 65–81.

Hartmann, T. (2012) Wicked problems and clumsy solutions: planning as expectation management. *Planning Theory* 11 (3): 242–256.

Healey, P. (1997) *Collaborative Planning: Shaping Places in Fragmented Societies*. Vancouver, BC: UBC Press.

Healey, P. (1999) Institutional analysis, communicative planning and shaping places. *Journal of Planning Education & Research* 19 (2): 111–121.

Healey, P. (2005) On the project of "institutional transformation" in the planning field: commenting on the contributors. *Planning Theory* 4 (3): 301–310.

Healey, P. (2006) The new institutionalism and the transformative goals of planning, in N. Verma (ed.) *Institutions and Planning*, pp. 61–87. Amsterdam: Elsevier.

Healey, P. (2011) Foreword, in J. Friedmann (ed.), *Insurgencies: Essays in Planning Theory*, pp. xi–xiv. London/New York: Routledge.

Hendler, S. (1995) *Planning Ethics: A Reader in Planning Theory, Practice and Education*. New Brunswick, NJ: Center for Urban Policy, Rutgers State University of New Jersey.

Herman, B., D. White, S. Vargas, N. O'Neill, D. Rouse and R. Holywell (2016) The 21st century comprehensive plan. *Planning* 82 (3): 15–31.

Hijdra, A., J. Woltjer and J. Arts (2014) Value creation in capital waterway projects: application of a transaction cost and transaction benefit framework for the Miami River and the New Orleans Inner Harbor Navigation Canal. *Land Use Policy* 38 (1): 91–103.

Hillier, J. (2005) Straddling the post-structuralist abyss: between transcendence and immanence. *Planning Theory* 4 (3): 271–299.
Hillier, J. (2010) Introduction, in J. Hillier and P. Healey (eds.) *The Ashgate Research Companion to Planning Theory: Conceptual Challenges for Spatial Planning*, pp. 1–34. Farnham, U.K.: Ashgate.
Hollander, E.L., L.S. Pollock, J.D. Rockinger and F. Beal (1988) General development plans, in F.S. So and J. Getzels (eds.) *The Practice of Local Government Planning*, pp. 60–91. Washington, DC: ICMA.
Innes, J.E. and D.E. Booher (2010) *Planning with Complexity: An Introduction to Collaborative Rationality for Public Policy*. New York/London: Routledge.
Kent, T.J. (1964) *Urban General Plan*. San Francisco, CA: Chandler.
Knorr-Cetina, K. (2001) Objectual practice, in T.R. Schatzki, K. Knorr-Cetina and E. von Savigny (eds.) *The Practice Turn in Contemporary Theory*, pp. 175–188. New York: Routledge.
Lord, A. (2014) Towards a non-theoretical understanding of planning. *Planning Theory* 13 (1): 26–43.
Matthews, T. (2013) Institutional perspectives on operationalising climate adaptation through planning. *Planning Theory & Practice* 14 (2): 198–210.
Mazza, L. (2016) *Planning and Citizenship*. New York/London: Routledge.
Moroni, S. (2010) Rethinking the theory and practice of land use regulation: towards nomocracy. *Planning Theory* 9 (2): 137–155.
Mukhopadhyay, C. (2015) *Faludi: Introducing a Theory of Planning*. AESOP Young Academics Booklet Series B: Exploring the Abstractions in the Planning Debate, Booklet 2. Groningen, NL: I-plan. http//:reader.inplanning.eu/web/viewer.htm/?/file=/pubs/AESOP-YA_booklet_B_ Faludi.pdf (retrieved 20 June, 2016).
Mumford, L. (1954) The neighborhood and the neighborhood unit. *Town Planning Review* 24 (4): 256–270.
Needham, B. (2013) *A Significant Contribution to Knowledge*. Nijmegen, The Netherlands: Radboud University.
North, D.C. (1990) *Institutions, Institutional Change and Economic Performance*. Cambridge, U.K.: Cambridge University Press.
Raja, S. and N. Verma (2010) Got perspective? A theoretical view of fiscal-impact analysis. *Planning Theory* 9 (2): 126–136.
Schatzki, T.R. (2001) Practice-mind-ed orders, in T.R. Schatzki, K. Knorr-Cetina and E. von Savigny (eds.) *The Practice Turn in Contemporary Theory*, pp. 42–55. New York: Routledge.
Susskind, L. and C. Ozawa (1984) Mediated negotiation in the public sector: the planner as mediator. *Journal of Planning Education & Research* 4 (1): 5–15.
Talen, E. (2005) *New Urbanism and American Planning: The Conflict of Cultures*. New York/London: Routledge.
Throgmorton, J.A. (1992) Planning as persuasive storytelling about the future: negotiating an electric power rate settlement in Illinois. *Journal of Planning Education & Research* 12 (1): 17–31.
Verma, N. (2007). Institutions and planning: an analogical enquiry, in N. Verma (ed.) *Institutions and Planning*, pp. 1–14. Amsterdam: Elsevier.
Vickers, Sir G. (1968) *Value Systems and Social Process*. New York: Basic Books.
Webster, C. and L.W.-C Lai (2003). *Property Rights, Planning and Markets: Managing Spontaneous Cities*. Cheltenham, U.K.: Edward Elgar.
Woltjer, J. (2000) *Consensus Planning: The Relevance of Communicative Planning Theory in Dutch Infrastructure Development*. Aldershot, U.K.: Ashgate.
Yiftachel, O. (2006) *Ethnocracy: Land and Identity Politics in Israel/Palestine*. Philadelphia, PA: University of Pennsylvania Press.
Zonneveld, W. (1989) Conceptual complexes and shifts in post-war urban planning in the Netherlands. *Built Environment* 15 (1): 40–48.

2
LEARNING FROM PRACTICE, LEARNING FOR PRACTICE IN LOCAL LAND USE PLANNING RESEARCH

Carolyn G. Loh

Introduction

Planning is a professional field that depends on strong relationships between practitioners and academics. In planning education, academics train students who go on to take professional planning jobs; thus, the planning education curriculum must speak to what practitioners actually do. Planning academics devote considerable effort to understanding the state of the field and what skills practitioners need and expect from new graduates (Ozawa and Seltzer 1999; Guzzetta and Bollens 2003; Dalton 2007; Edwards and Bates 2011; Greenlee et al. 2015; Dawkins 2016). Planning research depends on a similar link with the "real world" of planning practice, both for legitimacy and for practical value (Klosterman 2011). For the vast majority of planning research, there should be a direct relationship between what researchers do and what practitioners do (Birch 2001). This relationship goes both ways. Researchers have a responsibility to take the space and time they are afforded by the academy and help evaluate practice—the impact of planners, plans, and processes. Although there is certainly a place for higher-level theoretical discussions about planners and planning, here I refer to the creation of practical knowledge about the impacts of what planners are doing and insights into how they might improve on their practice. Researchers then need to make this research accessible to practitioners. Practitioners have a responsibility to keep up with current research so that they are using current best practice. They also have a responsibility to share their experiences and collaborate with researchers to inform the scholarly agenda. Despite a well-established "practice movement" in planning research, some argue that there has not been enough pragmatic research to inspire students and help them do their jobs (Klosterman 2011, 326). This review explores how those who study local land use planning practice have responded.

This review explores two key avenues for local land use planning research that can particularly help practitioners do their jobs. The first deals with what the planner does and why and how s/he matters. Studies in this vein can include case studies of planning processes that examine the role of the planner (Hibbard and Lurie 2000; Hanna 2005; Grant 2009), survey or qualitative research that investigates how planners do their jobs (Loh and Norton 2013), and research that investigates the impact of planners' involvement (Lyles et al. 2014; Loh and Norton 2015). The second avenue for research examines what the plan does and how and why the plan matters (Talen 1996a; Knaap et al. 1998; Brody and Highfield 2005; Koontz 2005; Berke et al. 2006). Given that planners spend a great deal of their time and effort to make and implement plans, researchers need to provide planners with good information about what impact plans have and how plans can be more effective. The review concludes with recommendations about how to make this scholarship more effective in the real world.

The Practice Movement in Planning Scholarship

For many years, scholars involved in the "practice movement" have advocated studying and learning from planning practice (Liggett 1996). Planning is very much an action-oriented field, and so planning scholars have argued that research that is too theoretical and not closely focused on what planners actually do is of limited relevance to the profession. Others have concerns that planning research lacks enough specificity and materiality to allow practitioners to adapt findings to their own situations (Lieto and Beauregard, 2018, this volume). Both practitioners and planning students need inspirational research that speaks directly to what they do (Klosterman 2011) and gives them enough detail and grounding so that they can assess differences and similarities with situations in their own localities (Lieto and Beauregard, 2018, this volume). Innes (1995) argues that pragmatic research grounded in planning practice can eliminate the bemoaned gap between theory and practice, making research relevant again. The purpose of such research is to "document what planners do [and] to reflect critically on that practice" rather than to generate "bottom-line prescriptions or simple models for how to proceed" (183). Watson points out that the results of such an approach might not look much like theory, yet its proponents argue that they "are able to give better insight into the nature and possibilities of planning practice than previous theories were able to do" (2002, 179). Forester suggests that in this way "practice can lead theory" rather than the other way around (1997, 1). The detailed case studies described by Innes are a valuable resource for academics and practitioners alike as they allow readers to understand what happened through storytelling, an effective way of learning (Sandercock 2003). Some researchers interested in planning practice have also taken a more positivist approach in studying what planners do, specifically with the aim of providing guidance for future practice. These planners are not theorists per se, but the body of work they produce may itself one day lead to the production of grounded theory explaining; for example, how and why comprehensive plan implementation does and does not happen (Hoch 2011).

Learning from/Learning for Planners

The most logical place to begin for researchers interested in learning from and learning for planners is with the planners themselves. These researchers try to answer questions like: What was the role of the planner in the process? What was the result of the planner's actions? How did the planner interact with other stakeholders? What might the planner have done differently? Researchers have investigated these questions through both detailed case studies and larger-scale quantitative research.

A planner can take on many different roles in a planning process (Berke and Kaiser 2006). These roles can change between different processes, and public expectations of what role is appropriate can change over time. A planner as technocrat makes decisions based on "facts." The planner as "scientific prophet" is an independent analyst who calls attention to the facts about current conditions, trends, and likely future conditions (295). The planner as facilitator engages in a communicative process, using participatory issue identification, scenario-building, and direction-setting to focus the technical analysis (Innes 1995; Ozawa and Seltzer 1999). As Kevin Hanna writes in his study of two Canadian coastal community planning processes, the planner must find a balance between these roles:

> They must facilitate inclusive participation without unduly shaping a community's identification of what is to be sustained, but planners must also be sources of information and ideas. This dual role can create tension, as planners are expected to generate proposals, but not be seen as overly invested in them.
>
> (2005, 29)

In Jill Grant's in-depth case study of Vancouver planner Larry Beasley's long career, Beasley explains that he helped steer local planning in Vancouver through a combination of listening to what people wanted from the city and educating them about what would need to happen for that outcome to be achieved. For example, Beasley asked whether the residents' grown children would want to live in the city someday, and whether they would be able to. He asked what kinds of services and community programs people might want. Residents began to see how there needed to be a certain critical mass of people, and a certain range of housing types, in order for them to have the kind of things they wanted. Beasley calls this experiential planning, where the planner ties the information and scenario-building directly to how people want to experience their city (Grant 2009). Over the decades of Beasley's career, Vancouver became a dense, thriving, livable city. The planner's role here was clear: showing people how their own interests might lead to an environmentally, economically, and socially sustainable city.

Both Hanna and Hibbard and Lurie, in their case study of a Teton County/Jackson Hole comprehensive planning process, emphasize that part of the work of planning is defining what planning is capable of so that stakeholders develop realistic expectations about what the process can accomplish. In the Jackson Hole process, some of the largest problems in the community (extreme income inequality and loss of community cohesion) were ones land use planning could not directly solve, but no one made this clear at the beginning of the process, leaving stakeholders disappointed (Hibbard and Lurie 2000). In the Canadian communities, community members relied on the planners to show them the boundaries of the process. In Vancouver, although Grant says that "staff saw their role as facilitating engagement and documenting its outcomes, allowing city council to identify the consensus and set policy," it is clear from the interviews that the planners helped shape policy and claimed a major role for planning and the CityPlan process (Grant 2009, 363). In a larger-scale study of planners' involvement in land use planning for natural hazard mitigation, Lyles et al. (2014) found that communities were more likely to pursue land use policies (which the authors argue are among the most effective) when their own planners were involved to help shape the discussion.

Larry Beasley had the luxury of a long career in the same city. Planners in the private sector may have much less time to effect change, and the planner may not have full control over balancing his or her role. As Hibbard and Lurie found in Teton County/Jackson Hole, the planning consultant's role was made problematic when local officials, at one extreme, chose the consultant and managed the process without any meaningful public involvement and, at the other extreme, fired the consultant and failed to show leadership during a more participatory process, letting the process get off track (Hibbard and Lurie 2000). In our own larger-scale survey work on planning consultants, Richard Norton and I found that while public and private sector planners believe they have different values, in fact their values are very similar (Loh and Norton 2013); yet the involvement of consultants does have an effect on the policy orientation of plans, making them more likely to reflect smart growth principles (Loh and Norton 2015). So, under the right circumstances, planners can be influential on future land use planning even if their relationship with the community is short term, but the wrong expectations and/or problematic local leadership can doom the process even with the involvement of an experienced planner.

What Does the Plan Do?

Case studies of planners always include the plan as a major supporting character in the narrative, but often it is unclear what the plan actually did or how effective it was. Planning scholars were aware at least as far back as the 1970s of the tendency of plans to remain on the shelf after adoption (Calkins 1979). Planners and other stakeholders were often eager to begin new planning processes, but that enthusiasm seemed to wane through the protracted time period involved and multiple actors needed to actually implement the plan. Calkins calls this "new plan syndrome," where it is easier to get people excited about a new planning process than to follow through on (or even remember) the last one. If plan implementation routinely remained unfulfilled, there was a real danger of plans, and the planning field, eventually becoming irrelevant (Burby 2003). Why spend the time and resources to go through a planning process if the plan never affected the actual development that occurred? Academics also found it difficult to pin down what implementation meant. How could one measure plan implementation? What constituted planning success (Talen 1997)? These concerns about plan outcomes led to two separate but related areas of local land use planning research. Motivating both was an interest in helping practitioners make better, more effective plans.

Making Better Plans

Some researchers interested in planning outcomes focused on the plans themselves —perhaps if local government officials and staff were not seeing good land use and regulatory outcomes, the problem was with poorly written or conceived plans (Burby 2003). Conversely, these researchers found that higher-quality plans were more likely to be implemented (Dalton and Burby 1994; Knaap et al. 1998; Norton 2005; Berke and Godschalk 2009). These researchers, initially mainly focused on coastal and hazard management (Berke and Godschalk 2009) and based at the University of North Carolina, were tremendously influential in defining the characteristics of a good plan and determining how to evaluate them (Lyles and Stevens 2014). These researchers developed plan evaluation protocols and coded hundreds, if not thousands, of plans (Norton 2008), to answer their main research questions: What elements should a "good plan" include? What levers could be employed to increase plan quality? This line of inquiry ultimately often focused on actions state governments might take to proscribe local plan goals and other content (Dalton and Burby 1994; Burby and May 1997; Norton 2005). These studies often found that state governments could mandate higher-quality plans by requiring them to plan and dictating certain elements that the plan must include; although Pendall (2001) found in Maine that a voluntary program resulted in plans that were more consistent with state goals.

A consensus gradually emerged around the characteristics of a good plan as well as how these characteristics could be measured (Baer 1997; Berke and Godschalk 2009; Lyles and Stevens 2014). Berke and Godschalk divide those components of plan quality into internal and external factors:

> (1) *internal plan quality* that includes the content and format of key components of the plan (e.g., issues and vision statement, fact base, goal and policy framework, implementation, monitoring) needed to guide land use in the future and (2) *external plan quality* that accounts for the relevance of the scope and coverage to reflect stakeholder values and the local situation to maximize use and influence of the plan.
>
> (2009, 229)

So it is not enough for the plan to be researched, written, and organized well. A good plan needs to reflect reality and rest on a broad base of stakeholder support so that it can be effective in the world. This component of plan quality helps explain its direct relevance to implementation.

According to the details of Berke and Godschalk's meta-analysis, a good plan is externally consistent: it takes into account conditions in neighboring communities as well as county-, regional-, and state-level policies. A good plan is also internally well organized and well written and relies on a strong fact base. A good plan includes a realistic overall vision, well-articulated goals, specific, actionable, and measurable objectives, and implementation timelines and assignments. A good plan should also be the result of a good planning process, one that relies on an open and inclusive public visioning process, with goals arrived at through consensus of mutually respectful stakeholders (Innes 1995; Berke and Godschalk 2009). The influence of this view of the good plan is embodied in the most widely assigned general land use planning textbook, Berke and Kaiser's *Urban Land Use Planning* (2006). This textbook explains in detail the components of the "good plan" and how to produce one. The authors even include a plan evaluation protocol like the ones they use in their research to allow student planners to determine for themselves how well a plan meets generally accepted plan quality standards. In other words, the plan quality researchers studied what practitioners were doing to figure out what made a good plan, and they now teach that to future practitioners. The motivation for the plan quality research, then, is to improve the quality of real plans that practitioners write.

After the Plans

Another group of researchers, responding to concerns raised by Calkins and others, looked at plans as part of a larger process including implementation. The plan quality research made clear that higher-quality plans were associated with higher levels of implementation, but it wasn't clear exactly why. The plan quality research still did not explain what happened after the adoption of the plan, and it gave few insights as to how to ensure the plan's effectiveness at guiding land use outcomes. This was ultimately the type of guidance planners would need to ensure the relevance and impact of planning. Initially there was a debate in the literature about how to think about a plan's effectiveness. Some thought that a plan should be considered effective if it was conceived through a robust process and succeeded in generating discussion (performance) (Alexander and Faludi 1989). Others argued that performance was too loose a standard and that the plan should only be considered effective if it could be demonstrated to have influenced subsequent land use decision-making (conformance) (Wildavsky 1973; Talen 1996b; Laurian et al. 2004). While almost every study of plan implementation references this debate, the vast majority of later work on plan implementation has fallen squarely into the conformance camp (so far) (Laurian et al. 2004; Brody and Highfield 2005; Chapin et al. 2008; Oliveira and Pinho 2009; Loh 2011; Padeiro 2016). One major reason for this is, as Brody and Highfield (2005) point out, we should hold planners, planning processes, and plans responsible for outcomes; otherwise, we risk the continuing legitimacy of the profession. Another reason is probably that conformance is more concrete and, as technology has improved, has become easier to measure, as I will discuss below.

Talen's work in the mid-1990s called attention to the lack of implementation studies focusing on actual land use outcomes: she pointed out that most planning studies were not of actual practice, but of *proposed* practice (1996b). As the practice movement scholars point out, such studies often tell planners what they should do, but do not base that guidance on evidence about what they are actually doing. Evaluating plan implementation is difficult. As Laurian et al. write, "Plans address complex issues using multiple methods, outcomes are sometimes seen years after implementation, and change processes in the natural and built environment are complex in and of themselves" (2010, 747). These complexities persist, and researchers have tried to address them in various ways, discussed below. Initially, however, measuring conformance was difficult and time-consuming, partly because of technological limitations: mapping land use decisions and matching them with policy was tedious when done by hand.

Probably for this reason, for many years studies evaluating implementation by measuring land use outcomes against plan goals or subsequent policies were very rare: Alterman and Hill's (1978) study was one of the few to directly compare land use outcomes to planned uses. Comparing plans and issued building permits, they found that plans with built-in flexibility were able to be adhered to more closely, yet areas with high growth pressure experienced more deviation from the plans. Alterman and Hill's study suggests a more flexible idea of conformance that allows the plan to set parameters without necessarily having to dictate specifics.

With the development of GIS, such studies became much more feasible. Brody and Highfield (2005) looked at plans and permits in Florida and determined that areas under extreme development pressure are more likely to have wetlands development permits granted that do not conform to the legally binding comprehensive plan. Laurian et al. (2004) found in their own study of building permits that there was more implementation breadth than depth: many policies had been implemented, but not many had been implemented fully, as measured through the permitting process. Chapin et al. (2008) used parcel-level land use data to determine that there had been significant development inside areas that were most susceptible to hurricane damage, contrary to state policy. These studies showed that plan implementation is complex and often incompletely realized. My own work on plan implementation was conducted directly in response to Talen's work and sought to help explain why implementation tended to break down. I found that, as Pressman and Wildavsky (1973) had suggested years earlier, every time additional complexity was introduced into the process, either in the form of a handoff between documents or between agents/agencies, the chances of a breakdown increased (Loh 2012). Echoing findings by Alterman and Hill as well as Brody and Highfield, I found that planning agencies that were short-staffed or under high development pressure were more likely to experience problems with implementation. Laurian et al. (2010) performed some of the same evaluative work I did as part of their POE (plan outcome evaluation) approach—first examining the plan writing to see if the plan was logically capable of producing the desired outcome if followed—and found that many are not.

There were still methodological questions to be answered, however, since time passes between the adoption of a plan and its implementation—standards of success may even change over time (Berke and Godschalk 2009). I tried to tackle the question of how to interpret instances of nonconformance between plans and outcomes; in other words, how one could tell if a plan was on the path to implementation or was running into trouble even while it remained only partially implemented. I argued that some nonconformance was benign, simply due to a time lag between a plan and its eventual implementation (such as agricultural land not yet developed according to its planned use). Other, more concerning instances of nonconformance indicated an accidental or deliberate disregard of the plan's recommendations, putting the plan's legitimacy at risk (Loh 2011). Others have taken this characterization a step further, arguing that even seemingly benign instances of nonconformance, such as my time lag example, may lead to entrenched differences between the plan and land use outcomes, such as leapfrog development (Padeiro 2016).

How does all of this work on implementation help practicing planners? First, identifying lack of implementation as a problem that needs attention is important to remind all planners that work doesn't end with the plan. Pointing out specific harms that lack of implementation can cause can help planners advocate for processes and resources (such as a staff member at least partly dedicated to supervising implementation) needed to ensure that the plan gets translated into land use outcomes. Highlighting the conditions under which implementation breaks down allows planners to be vigilant about moving the process past likely obstacles. All of this research is specifically intended to increase plans' efficacy and to help planners better do their jobs.

Conclusion

Almost 30 years ago, Michael Brooks (1988) wrote that most planning scholars did not have practitioner experience and that their research was conducted primarily for an audience of other academics. He and others called for a body of research that tries to make planning more effective. Today, in the field of land use planning, many researchers have experience as practitioners, and that experience strongly informs their choice of research topics.

In this review I have explored how land use planning scholars are addressing the need for practice-oriented research through an incrementally building body of work that seeks to understand: what planners do and how they influence plans and development: and what plans do and how to make them work better. Most of this research is directly informed by practice, through surveying and interviewing planners, examining planning documents, and assessing planning outcomes. Some planning scholars even produce work jointly with practitioners, ensuring the research's relevance for real-world planning.

Methodologically, some academics have responded to calls by Innes and others for in-depth case studies with in-depth qualitative research that provides rich narratives of planning experience for others to draw from. Other researchers have taken a more bird's eye quantitative approach that seeks to evaluate many plans or processes at once to see if there are generalizable conclusions to be made about how those plans can be best written and carried out.

From this review, it should be clear that land use planning researchers take seriously the responsibility to conduct practice-relevant and practice-oriented research. Academics could still do a better job of both translating and disseminating that research to the practitioners who might actually want to use it. Siemiatycki (2012) calls upon planning researchers to move outside their comfortable roles as dispassionate observers and into direct engagement with practice through public scholarship, consulting, activism, or community-based planning. For land use planning scholars, this could mean writing about their research for practitioner-oriented publications, giving talks to their local APA chapter, serving on a planning commission, or advocating for land use decision-making that balances the planner's triangle (Campbell 1996).

References

Alexander, E. R. and A. Faludi (1989). Planning and plan implementation: Notes on evaluation criteria. *Environment and Planning B: Planning and Design* 16(2): 127–140.

Alterman, R. and M. Hill (1978). Implementation of urban land use plans. *Journal of the American Institute of Planners* 44(3): 274–285.

Baer, W. C. (1997). General plan evaluation criteria: An approach to making better plans. *Journal of the American Planning Association* 63(3): 329–344.

Berke, P., M. Backhurst, M. Day, N. Ericksen, L. Laurian, J. Crawford and J. Dixon (2006). What makes plan implementation successful? An evaluation of local plans and implementation practices in New Zealand. *Environment and Planning B: Planning and Design* 33(4): 581–600.

Berke, P. and D. Godschalk (2009). Searching for the good plan: A meta-analysis of plan quality studies. *Journal of Planning Literature* 23(3): 227–240.

Berke, P. and E. J. Kaiser (2006). *Urban Land Use Planning*. Urbana-Champaign, IL: University of Illinois Press.

Birch, E. L. (2001). Practitioners and the art of planning. *Journal of Planning Education and Research* 20(4): 407–422.

Brody, S. D. and W. E. Highfield (2005). Does planning work? Testing the implementation of local environmental planning in Florida. *Journal of the American Planning Association* 71(2): 159–175.

Brooks, M. P. (1988). Four critical junctures in the history of the urban planning profession: An exercise in hindsight. *Journal of the American Planning Association* 54(2): 241–248.

Burby, R. J. (2003). Making plans that matter: Citizen involvement and government action. *Journal of the American Planning Association* 69(1): 33–49.

Burby, R. J. and P. J. May (1997). *Making Governments Plan: State Experiments in Managing Land Use*. Baltimore, MD: Johns Hopkins University Press.

Calkins, H. W. (1979). The planning monitor: An accountability theory of plan evaluation. *Environment and Planning A* 11(7): 745–758.

Campbell, S. (1996). Green cities, growing cities, just cities? Urban planning and the contradictions of sustainable development. *Journal of the American Planning Association* 62(3): 296–312.

Chapin, T. S., R. E. Deyle and E. J. Baker (2008). A parcel-based GIS method for evaluating conformance of local land-use planning with a state mandate to reduce exposure to hurricane flooding. *Environment and Planning B: Planning and Design* 35(2): 261–279.

Dalton, L. C. (2007). Preparing planners for the breadth of practice: What we need to know depends on whom we ask. *Journal of the American Planning Association* 73(1): 35–48.

Dalton, L. C. and R. J. Burby (1994). Mandates, plans, and planners: Building local commitment to development management. *Journal of the American Planning Association* 60(4): 444–461.

Dawkins, C. J. (2016). Preparing planners: The role of graduate planning education. *Journal of Planning Education and Research*: 36(4): 414–426.

Edwards, M. M. and L. K. Bates (2011). Planning's core curriculum: Knowledge, practice, and implementation. *Journal of Planning Education and Research* 31(2): 172–183.

Forester, J. (1997). *Learning from Practice: Democratic Deliberations and the Promise of Planning Practice*. College Park, MD: Urban Studies and Planning Program, University of Maryland.

Grant, J. (2009). Experiential planning: A practitioner's account of Vancouver's success. *Journal of the American Planning Association* 75(3): 358–370.

Greenlee, A. J., M. Edwards and J. Anthony (2015). Planning skills: An examination of supply and local government demand. *Journal of Planning Education and Research* 35(2): 161–173.

Guzzetta, J. D. and S. A. Bollens (2003). Urban planners' skills and competencies: Are we different from other professions? Does context matter? Do we evolve? *Journal of Planning Education and Research* 23(1): 96–106.

Hanna, K. S. (2005). Planning for sustainability: Experiences in two contrasting communities. *Journal of the American Planning Association* 71(1): 27–40.

Hibbard, M. and S. Lurie (2000). Saving land but losing ground challenges to community planning in the era of participation. *Journal of Planning Education and Research* 20(2): 187–195.

Hoch, C. (2011). Viewpoint: The planning research agenda: Planning theory for practice. *Town Planning Review* 82(2): vii–xvi.

Innes, J. E. (1995). Planning theory's emerging paradigm: Communicative action and interactive practice. *Journal of Planning Education and Research* 14(3): 183–189.

Klosterman, R. E. (2011). Planning theory education: A thirty-year review. *Journal of Planning Education and Research* 31(3): 319–331.

Knaap, G., L. D. Hopkins and K. P. Donaghy (1998). Do plans matter? A game-theoretic model for examining the logic and effects of land use planning. *Journal of Planning Education and Research* 18(1): 25–34.

Koontz, T. M. (2005). We finished the plan, so now what? Impacts of collaborative stakeholder participation on land use policy. *Policy Studies Journal* 33(3): 459–481.

Laurian, L., M. Day, P. Berke, N. Ericksen, M. Backhurst, J. Crawford and J. Dixon (2004). Evaluating plan implementation: A conformance-based methodology. *Journal of the American Planning Association* 70(4): 471–480.

Laurian, L., J. Crawford, M. Day, P. Kouwenhoven, G. Mason, N. Ericksen and L. Beattie (2010). Evaluating the outcomes of plans: Theory, practice, and methodology. *Environment and Planning B: Planning and Design* 37(4): 740–757.

Liggett, H. (1996). Examining the planning practice conscious(ness), in S. J. Mandelbaum, L. Mazza and R. W. Burchell (eds.) *Explorations in Planning Theory*, pp. 299–306. New Brunswick, NJ: Center for Urban Policy Research, Rutgers.

Loh, C. G. (2011). Assessing and interpreting non-conformance in land-use planning implementation. *Planning Practice & Research* 26(3): 271–287.

Loh, C. G. (2012). Four potential disconnects in the local planning process. *Journal of Planning Education and Research* 32(1): 33–47.

Loh, C. G. and R. K. Norton (2013). Planning consultants and local planning: Roles and values. *Journal of the American Planning Association* 79(2): 138–147.

Loh, C. G. and R. K. Norton (2015). Planning consultants' influence on local comprehensive plans. *Journal of Planning Education and Research* 35(2): 199–208.

Lyles, W. and M. Stevens (2014). Plan quality evaluation 1994–2012: Growth and contributions, limitations, and new directions. *Journal of Planning Education and Research* 34(4): 433–450.

Lyles, L. W., P. Berke and G. Smith (2014). Do planners matter? Examining factors driving incorporation of land use approaches into hazard mitigation plans. *Journal of Environmental Planning and Management* 57(5): 792–811.

Norton, R. K. (2005). More and better local planning: State-mandated local planning in coastal North Carolina. *Journal of the American Planning Association* 71(1): 55–71.

Norton, R. K. (2008). Using content analysis to evaluate local master plans and zoning codes. *Land Use Policy* 25(3): 432–454.

Oliveira, V. and P. Pinho (2009). Evaluating plans, processes and results. *Planning Theory and Practice* 10(1): 35–63.

Ozawa, C. P. and E. P. Seltzer (1999). Taking our bearings: Mapping a relationship among planning practice, theory, and education. *Journal of Planning Education and Research* 18(3): 257–266.

Padeiro, M. (2016). Conformance in land-use planning: The determinants of decision, conversion and transgression. *Land Use Policy* 55: 285–299.

Pendall, R. (2001). Municipal plans, state mandates, and property rights lessons from Maine. *Journal of Planning Education and Research* 21(2): 154–165.

Pressman, J. L. and A. Wildavsky (1973). *Implementation*. Berkeley, CA: University of California Press.

Sandercock, L. (2003). Out of the closet: The importance of stories and storytelling in planning practice. *Planning Theory & Practice* 4(1): 11–28.

Siemiatycki, M. (2012). The role of the planning scholar research, conflict, and social change. *Journal of Planning Education and Research* 32(2): 147–159.

Talen, E. (1996a). After the plans: Methods to evaluate the implementation success of plans. *Journal of Planning Education and Research* 16(2): 79–91.

Talen, E. (1996b). Do plans get implemented? A review of evaluation in planning. *Journal of Planning Literature* 10(3): 248–259.

Talen, E. (1997). Success, failure, and conformance: An alternative approach to planning evaluation. *Environment and Planning B: Planning and Design* 24(4): 573–587.

Watson, V. (2002). Do we learn from planning practice? The contribution of the practice movement to planning theory. *Journal of Planning Education and Research* 22(2): 178–187.

Wildavsky, A. (1973). If planning is everything, maybe it's nothing. *Policy Sciences* 4(2): 127–153.

3
PLANNING CULTURE

Research Heuristics and Explanatory Value

Karsten Zimmermann, Robin Chang, and Andreas Putlitz

The Relevance of Planning Culture and the Need to Deepen Contemporary Research

The recent discussion on planning culture in Europe results from the debate on the diversity of European planning systems that emerged during the 1990s. While the debate around planning culture is still evolving, it is nevertheless, in our view, a substantial contribution to current planning debate and the understanding of the differences and the directions of change as well as the performance of planning systems. This is valid not only in the European context but also for North America.

In our chapter, we argue that the notion of planning culture has considerable value as a research heuristic and explanatory variable in comparative research, particularly concerning how planning culture is performed in relation to what some consider the main purpose of the debate: to explain change and persistence leading to specific outcomes. Like Sanyal, we claim that comparative research in planning cultures has its highest potential for analysis of change or, to put it in a more pragmatic way, when a practice that has been long accepted as appropriate and self-evident erodes and loses legitimacy (Sanyal 2016).

In contrast to institutionalist and actor-based approaches, the planning cultures approach discerns frames (in the sense of Rein and Schön 1993; see Ernste 2012) and, in parallel, perceives professional ethics (in the sense of Max Weber) and symbolic representations as a source for inertia as well as change in planning systems (Reimer and Blotevogel 2012).

For instance, the persistence of planning culture may explain the opposition to and consequent abolishment of English regional spatial strategies in 2011 (Sykes and O'Brien 2016). Although regional policy as a form of territorial development policy is not completely unknown in England, the implementation of the idea of strategic regional policymaking or regional planning was resisted in communities. Even though the narrative in England – from 'traditional land use planning' to 'strategic spatial planning' in the 1990s and then to localism and neighborhood planning since 2011 – was not stringent, the planning culture approach has additional potential to explain why reforms fail or are only half-implemented (this also applies to political ideological backgrounds such as neo-liberalism).

However, the scholarly debate needs to evolve beyond duplicating existing stereotypes that represent national planning traditions. In a recent paper, Sanyal (2016) argues that planning culture – understood in an earlier volume as "the collective ethos and dominant attitudes of professional planners in different nations towards the appropriate role of the state, market, and civil society in urban, regional, and national development" (Sanyal 2005b, p. 3) – is "a result of both exogenous and endogenous factors" (Sanyal 2016, p. 658). Acknowledging such influences means that any essentialist notion of planning culture or 'national planning tradition' is unable to grasp the diversity and hybridity of contemporary planning practice. Thus, it is questionable whether a characterization of a planning culture as 'German' or 'Italian' (see Othengrafen and Reimer 2013, p. 1280) is appropriate as this disregards the complexity of norms and values in contemporary planning practice. Moreover, this debate has to accept that even within national planning systems, a diversity of hybrid planning practices are discernible and transcend the stereotypic understanding of national and subnational planning traditions.

Having said this, we suggest following cultural theories based on 'practice' – or 'habitus' – (as introduced by Schatzki, Bourdieu, and Giddens; see also Luukkonen 2017) that allow for a more nuanced understanding of planning culture. Understood in this way, planning culture is of heuristical and explanatory value not just in the European debate, but may introduce some points of discussion to American planning discourse as well.

Planning Culture: Two Strands of Discussion

To elaborate, we begin by distinguishing two strands of the debate. The initial strand follows planning culture as practice that is specific to nations undergoing their own processes of change in a globalized world (Sanyal 2005a). The second strand follows the debate resulting from the Europeanization of planning discussions (not necessarily spatial planning) since the 1990s and will be the focus of this chapter (Knieling and Othengrafen 2015; De Vries 2015). Before we go into detail about the latter, let us contextualize the discussion with a more expansive sense of planning cultures and the need for a more comparative and dynamic understanding of how changes occur in globalized planning practice (Sanyal 2005a).

The American Debate: Globalized Planning Culture and National Planning Practice

As a continuation of discussions from a symposium about the effects of planning cultures on planning practices, Sanyal released a collection of case studies in 2005 demonstrating a "continuous process of social, political, and technological change, which affects the way planners in different settings conceptualize problems and structure institutional responses to them" (Sanyal 2005b, p. 22). In other words, Sanyal's intent is not to demarcate the unchanging social attributes that distinguish different cultures and practices, but to go beyond the "exclusionary, parochial, and . . . inaccurate representation of history" that constitutes the "cultural essentialism" typical of work on planning cultures (Sanyal 2005b, p. 22). The case studies examine planning in European, North American, Asian, and Oceanic settings with individual and comparative perspectives, sorting through the multilayered discourse. A notable aim is the reiteration of institutional and practical differences both between nations and within nations at local and regional levels (Sanyal 2005b; Friedmann 2005b). Moreover, the collection of studies provides an initially comprehensive exploration of "temporally fluid" (Leaf 2005, p. 91) planning culture that presents "unconscious" qualities that are developed and inherited, thus resistive to quick change (Tajbakhsh 2005, p. 69) and tension – change advocated by planners against the persistence of broader societal norms (Leaf 2005).

Expanding on Sanyal's call for a refined understanding of globalized planning cultures, Friedmann reviews the roles for which planners are responsible: "coach, player, manager, and even . . . [sometimes] simply . . . spectator" and emerging roles in the transition from pedestalized planning to complex chaos that proves what was once "state of the art" is no longer enough (Friedmann 2005b). The only clear option to assuage the strains of this brisk change is communication of imperfect, but real, cultural and practical differences grounded in the local and the regional that color narrated matters ranging from claims of new rights to newly active local citizenship in areas of need (Friedmann 2005b, p. 43). Compared to more qualitative definitions of planning cultures previously circulated, Friedmann presents practice- and process-oriented meaning through 'formal' and 'informal' measures that give birth to, legitimize, and implement a spatial type of planning that is also more strategic (facilitating long-term priorities) and entrepreneurial (facilitating economic development) in nature (Friedmann 2005a).

In a more recent review of globalized planning cultures, Sanyal cites the outcome of current global migration as an opportunity to rethink how planning culture as change and reaction needs to be more rigorously researched (Sanyal 2016, p. 659). For example, the processes of change embodied through culture could be investigated through outcomes of industrialization and democracy or using national territories as units for analysis in the wake of the current global flow and local settlement of refugees (Sanyal 2016, p. 660). What this recent review suggests is that subnational and national planning actions and practices in particular instances define and differentiate planning cultures – not only because of the specific global circumstances, but also because they are in themselves a change in behavior and change future norms for planning cultures.

The European Debate: Comparison of European Planning Systems

One of the first comparative empirical studies on planning cultures in Europe was attempted by Keller, Koch and Selle (1993, 1996). Based on the premise that domestic planning practices change, the authors of this study completed surveys in Italy, Switzerland, France and Germany. The work focused on urban planning and directly addresses planning practitioners. The authors wanted to find out whether convergence in planning practices could be observed (in relation to communicative or cooperative turns in planning). Although an interesting and early contribution to the debate, the study is limited in terms of theoretical grounding and representativeness.

A further contribution has been made by Philip Booth (1993). He highlights the "cultural dimension in comparative research" in his seminal paper on development control in France and shows that "it is a culture of decision-making, and the ways in which that culture is expressed in the institutions of the state and the legal system, that shapes the way in which planning is understood and put into effect" (Booth 2011, p. 16).

The Three Phases of the European Debate

The main thrust of the European debate is kindled by the European integration process. While borders blurred, cross-border cooperation increased, and pan-European planning concepts (such as the European Spatial Development Perspective) emerged, two contradictory phenomena became apparent: first, an increasing convergence of the different styles and systems of spatial planning in Europe was both expected and partially reported; and second, a tenacious persistence of differences in planning practices across borders remained. Moreover, the latter was not elegantly ascribable to national regulatory frameworks or neatly demarcated geographical spaces. The progress of the European debate up until now can thus be viewed as an unsuccessful attempt to pinpoint a European convergence of planning systems in the course of a continuous European integration process in the 1990s, as well as a quest to identify the underlying driving forces for the persistent differences between planning systems, styles and practices between European regions and states.

Static Models of Comparison of National Containers

During the late 1990s a broader discussion on planning system typologies in Europe emerged (Healey and Williams 1993; Newman and Thornley 1996). Comparative work characteristic of this phase was motivated by the question of convergence or divergence of planning systems in Europe. A strong influence was the preparation of the European Spatial Development Perspective (ESDP), which was published in 1999 as a non-binding intergovernmental document. Besides the question of whether the European Commission should strengthen or profile competencies for spatial planning or spatial development policies, an issue arising out of these developments was whether a common European approach to spatial planning existed. The planning systems in member states resulted from the different paths of development of welfare states in Europe (Nadin and Stead 2013). As a result, the notion of 'European spatial planning' was born out of this debate, though it has since remained vague. A common European approach in spatial planning needed to take into consideration the highly differing planning systems and practices in Europe. The first studies in the field of European spatial planning arranged European planning systems into four families of planning systems (Newman and Thornley 1996; Williams 1996; Healey and Williams 1993; see also Balchin, Sykora and Bull 1999). (A description of the specific typology is given in the next paragraph.) Following a comprehensive study resulting in a compendium of spatial planning systems in Europe, published in 1997 – two years prior to the ratification of the ESDP – this approach was later adopted by the European Commission (Commission of the European Communities 1997).

The four types or families of planning systems in Europe use four ideal types (in the sense of Max Weber) to abstractly describe planning systems in Europe. Each of the four types represents European planning systems as an archetype in order to describe more general features of planning. The economic development type is certainly based on the French *aménagement du territoire*, while the 'land use management' type strongly reveals features of the British planning system. The Southern European *urbanismo* reflects planning practice in Italy, Spain and Greece, while the 'integrated comprehensive planning' type (in Austria, Switzerland, also formerly Denmark) reflects the German planning system.

The weakness of this way of thinking about planning systems is the institutional and structural perspective that hinders meaningful consideration of planning practice and performance. Also, these studies view the nation state as a major point of reference (territorial container). Building on this perspective, the ESPON study 2.3.2, "Governance of territorial and urban policies from EU to local level", elaborates with dimensions and indicative development trends relevant for the new

TABLE 3.1 Four types of planning systems in Europe

Economic development	*Comprehensive integrated*
Positive planning (implementation oriented)	Broad scope of planning
Socioeconomic development	Plan-led systems (regulatory, binding)
State responsibility (central–local relationship) France	Multi-level governance (state planning, regional planning, local planning) Germany, Austria, Switzerland
Land use management	*Urbanismo*
Development control	Architecture and urban design
Plans less relevant	Regulation on building permission
Role for regional planning unstable UK, Ireland, partly Belgium	Weak or no regional tier Italy, Spain, Greece
Source: based on Commission of the European Communities (1997)	

Central and Eastern European members of the European Union (Farinos Dasi 2007). However, as observed by Karel Maier, most of the comparative studies that focus on legal and formal aspects of planning systems fail to fully grasp the specific path dependencies in post-communist countries (Maier 2012, p. 139, p. 147).

The approach – to taxonomize European planning systems into families of planning traditions based on legal and formal characteristics – though often cited, has rarely been used to conduct a dense comparative study of the performance of planning practices or systems in Europe. One reason for this, amongst others, is that a formalized perspective on planning systems probably does not tell much about what happens in actuality (see Loh, 2018, this volume, on the value of practice-based studies). To a certain extent, Booth's comment from 1993 on the matter of comparing planning systems still holds true:

> the source of this conceptual weakness stems from an attitude towards planning, that holds it to be essentially a technical exercise, normative in intent. The attitude invites us to believe that the relationship between policy, its articulation in planning documents and its applications through a control mechanism is essentially constant and understood by anyone, regardless of nationality, involved in land use planning.
>
> (1993, p. 218)

Despite its limitations, this approach is useful as it better describes the changes in the transformation states in Eastern and Central Europe (Farinos Dasi 2007). These post-socialist states reinvented their planning systems and combined existing planning traditions with imported principles, instruments and institutional orders from other European states. However, the dynamic changes and reforms of planning systems in the Netherlands, Belgium, the Czech Republic, England, Italy, and Denmark show that the typology of four planning systems is no longer appropriate for empirical research (Reimer, Getimis and Blotevogel 2014). What we observe now is a process of hybridization and the emergence of new institutional orders instead of harmonization or convergence of spatial planning in Europe.

More recent publications attempt to broaden the field and integrate other approaches, such as Esping-Anderson's typologies of welfare states (Nadin and Stead 2013). This discussion is motivated by the question of whether planning practice in Europe is based on broader societal norms, ideas and values (Knieling and Othengrafen 2015, p. 2134). Nevertheless, the plurality of styles of doing planning and the question of what differentiates and integrates European spatial planning is resulting in an epistemological shift in comparative planning research.

An Epistemological Shift to Planning Culture

The recent turn to planning culture in Europe started with the contributions from Knieling and Othengrafen's edited volume (Knieling and Othengrafen 2009; see Fürst 2009), followed since by many other publications (Othengrafen and Reimer

2013; Othengrafen 2010; Taylor 2013; Ernste 2012; Stead, de Vries and Tasan-Kok 2015). This debate on planning cultures is still diverse and in its infancy. In general, we can distinguish a political cultures approach and a cultural studies approach. The latter is dominant, but some authors amalgamate both approaches.

The political culture approach is elaborated less; nevertheless, it is referenced by many authors (Othengrafen and Reimer 2013; Stead, de Vries and Tasan-Kok 2015). From the political culture perspective, societal acceptance of planning as a state activity and the embeddedness of the planning idea in society or a local milieu is of interest (a view of planning culture also held by Neuman 2007, p. 157). This understanding goes back to the seminal book by Almond and Verba entitled *The civic culture: Political attitudes and democracy in five nations* (1963). It focuses on acceptance and support of the idea of planning by societal groups (de Olde 2016). It also stresses that the relationship between market, state and civil society is of relevance for the political culture of planning.

The second and more widespread approach sees planning as a culturalized activity that considers traditions, beliefs, symbols, frames and values but also artefacts such as maps or plans as the objects of study. The motivation of this approach is to better understand (a) planning processes and results and (b) change of planning practice (Fürst 2009; Othengrafen 2010; Reimer and Blotevogel 2012). This implies that scientific approaches used so far (such as institutional or organizational theories, rational choice approaches, actor-based theories) have considerable weaknesses in explaining performance and change in planning practice (see Loh's chapter in this volume). The explanatory potential of the cultural studies approach is highlighted with regards to the comparison of planning systems. Planning systems may show similarities in formal structure or instruments in use (such as regulatory land use plans) but differ with regard to execution or results. Although finding increased recognition, we see the following weaknesses of this approach:

1 The outcome of this debate in terms of sound comparative studies so far is rather weak and runs the risk of reproducing existing stereotypes of national planning traditions. Knieling and Othengrafen (2015, p. 2142), for example, refer – without strong empirical evidence – to traditional Prussian values to characterize the German planning system, while they see a Mediterranean tradition of familism and clientelism prevailing in Southern Europe. This demonstrates weaknesses as it is unclear if the planning culture approach used is normative.
2 The definition of culture refers to a specific way of life of a social group bound to a territory – the 'nation' – which risks essentialism or territorial traps.

Concerning the first weakness mentioned, we can ask: what is a good planning culture? If studies in planning culture merely describe a typical way of doing planning in a given socio-institutional context, or if they point to 'good practice' without giving clear criteria for the evaluation of this practice, the studies are somehow positivistic. This also relates to the question of causality. Is planning culture a driver for change ('new planning culture') or, in contrast, is planning culture the reason for stability or inertia in times when change is wanted (crisis or reform)? In fact, quite a few European planning systems (England, Netherlands, Denmark) were recently extensively reformed, and the outcome is still hard to judge. The existing observations point out that a change in legal and procedural frameworks is a test for implicit assumptions of the purpose and form of planning in the given context (Sykes and O'Brien 2016; Damsgaard 2014; Zonneveld and Evers 2014). The same applies for planning systems in post-socialist countries in Central and Eastern Europe (Maier 2012).

Concerning the second weakness mentioned, it is not clear if a 'planning culture' is seen as a system of practice (including institutions and norms). Following more recent discussions in cultural studies and cultural sociology, we believe that a definition of 'culture' anchored in a social collective (community or *Gemeinschaft*), a shared territory or a period of time (tradition) needs revision (Reckwitz 2005). We argue that studies in planning culture have to accept that a diversity of hybrid planning practices can be observed – even within national planning systems (see Loh 2018, this volume). Hence, we suggest following Reckwitz (2005), who states that comparison of culture is not a comparison of cultural cleavages or differences between collectives or territories; rather, it is about building relationships between hybrid combinations of planning practice elements from different periods in time and different places in Europe and probably worldwide.

This theory avoids essentialist and traditionalist notions of culture and sees practices as the unit for scrutiny and comparison. Such a perspective on planning cultures also considers the objections of the cultural studies approach to the then dominant discourse in cultural sociology (Williams 1958; During 2007). The cultural studies approach considers culture as a practice embedded in ordinary life and, therefore, sensitive to hegemonic cultures. The question of hegemony and power in relation to change, reform and crisis has so far not been addressed in the discussion on planning cultures. This opens up our methodological repertoire to the use of ethnological methods for the study of the everyday practice of planning (Healey 1992; Loh 2018, this volume). Lastly, an advantage of such an approach is also that culture is not bound to territorial containers by definition because practice is the unit for empirical observation (which does not imply that a city or region may, or may not, reveal a stable configuration of routines and patterned practices that can be called planning culture).

The 'Turn to Practice'

Practice-based sociological theories have been introduced into the planning culture debate recently, offering a promising approach for the comparative study of planning culture (Luukkonen 2017). Theories of practice see planning as knowledge-based social routine actions, not as a structure, a tradition, or a configuration of symbols, text or artefacts. There is a broad range of theories on practice, including from authors such as Giddens, Bourdieu and Schatzki (see Reckwitz 2002).

Schatzki (2001) defines practices as sets of actions or patterned activities that reveal a degree of regularity. These activities are considered meaningful behavior in a particular social context. Other notions in use in this discussion are practical knowledge, know-how or routines. This approach clearly focuses on action and interaction at the micro level (Wagenaar and Cook 2003). Luukkonen (2017) demonstrates the potential of this strand of practice theory in a study on the Europeanization of planning.

The work of Bourdieu goes beyond this micro-level perspective and represents a voluminous theory and methodology about how practices are classified in a given society. Using the notion of 'sense of practice' or 'logic of practice' and focusing on discrete empirical actions and interactions in spatial and material settings, he gives a broader framework for understanding power relations and distinction of social milieus (Bourdieu 1984). Practices show a degree of regularity but are fuzzy in the sense that they don't predict actual behavior. On the other hand, the sense of practice generates spontaneous and pre-reflexive activities that are considered accepted practice in the field (of planning). Actors continuously apply premises that they often don't confirm explicitly (Bourdieu 1990).

The social classification schemes and evaluation of practices highlight the difference between Bourdieu and more recent contributions to practice theory, with Bourdieu's concept of practices embedded in a wider theory of societal stratification and distinction (Bourdieu 1984). The sense of orientation or 'getting the idea' for the game played in the field of planning refers to generative rules that produce practices (theory of practice). In contrast to other theories of practice, Bourdieu focuses more on these generative rules and less on the practical accomplishments. Using Bourdieu's approach, we can ask: What makes a professional planner a professional planner in a given context? What is the impact of the education of planners in this regard (socialization)? We have a rough idea of what is considered accepted practice, but we don't know from where the underlying classification schemes come.

Practice theory also refers to the work of sociologist Anthony Giddens (1984). In his theory of structuration, Giddens aims at overcoming the widespread dichotomy between structure and agency by replacing it with a duality of structure and agency (Gregory 1984). This he calls "structured systems of recursively reproducing practices" (in Gregory 1984). Giddens argues that action is not necessarily intentional. It is, rather, to be seen as the practical capacity to effect changes in the world. In Giddens' view, social structure has to be continuously enacted, while the enacting of structure preconditions its own reproduction. The enacting of social structure hereby draws upon the collective knowledge of everyday conduct practices. This individual as well as collective practical knowledge of the everyday conduct of practices is what Giddens calls the 'practical consciousness'. In detail, this refers to a quality of practical know-how oftentimes routinized, automatic and even unconscious, as opposed to the so-called 'discursive consciousness', which comprises knowledge that we can articulate and which we are aware of.

Gidden's notion of the practical consciousness displays a certain overlap with the idea of a practice-based notion of planning culture. He describes it as "tacitly assumed and unexpressed knowledge about how to proceed in the various instances of everyday life" (in Gregory 1984, p. 129), which in the case of planning can be suitably applied to the various instances of everyday professional planning practice.

Discussion

Shortcomings of the Debate

Besides the already mentioned lack of sound empirical comparative studies of planning cultures, we see the following shortcomings:

- Lack of a definitive theory distinguishing planning culture from other approaches (institutional thought, governance, policy analysis).
- Lack of historically sensitive study on the evolution of planning systems and cultures (see, for example, Sykes and O'Brien 2016, for the English planning culture; Sutcliffe 1981). A historical perspective also teaches us to see, methodologically, critical junctures or path-breaking interventions, such as the Thatcher government in the UK in the 1980s, as situations where planning culture can be studied best because old ideas of planning are challenged with the crystallization of new ideologies.
- In their study on the attitudes of American, Spanish and Dutch planners, Kaufman and Escuin expected a lot of variation but conclude that "the dominant planning ideology shared by the planners we sampled in these three countries is more similar than would be expected" (2000, p. 37). This explorative study is not comprehensively empirical, but it indicates that all planners might share an idea of planning or a common set of norms. Compared with the European discussion on planning culture that also emphasizes diversity and hybridization, this result is contra-intuitive. At a very minimum, comparative studies in planning cultures need a more nuanced understanding of what the planning cultures under scrutiny have in common and how they differ.
- Lack of a clear unit of empirical investigation to allow for rigid international comparisons, in contrast to anecdotic compilations of perceived stereotypes.

Where Can a Practice-Based Notion of Planning Culture Be Useful?

Considering the aforementioned aspects and shortcomings of a practice-based approach to planning culture, how could this be applied in empirical studies? The number of well-designed comparative studies in planning culture is still limited (de Vries 2015). In order to illustrate a possible framework, we would like to outline an exemplar of a European comparative study of planning culture. For this purpose, we will present two cases: the European Capital of Culture Essen/Ruhr 2010 and the European Capital of Culture Marseille-Provence 2013. The following narratives will help illustrate the potentials and methodological challenges of empirical work on planning cultures. In his contribution to the special issue of the *Town Planning Review* on European Capitals of Culture (ECoC), Philip Booth convincingly describes the potential of comparative studies of planning cultures within the ECoC context:

> With the ECoC Programme, comparison might appear to be more hopeful. Here, after all, is a single programme that applies throughout the EU whose impact might reasonably be explored in the places to which it is applied. The places and cultures are nothing like as different from each other as the entirely separate cultural domains that Porter (2007)[1] explores. Yet there are differences nevertheless, and the question of how we may account for the differences between the way in which different cities have responded to the opportunities of the programme remains unanswered.
>
> (2011, p. 18)

The ECoC is a festivalized programme for city marketing and development, established by the European Union in 1983. Each year, the title is conferred for one entire calendar year during which the city organizes social and cultural events and initiates projects with a symbolic or thematic character, often creating positive spin-offs for urban development and urban regeneration (Andres 2011). The programme usually raises the visibility and attractiveness of the city, gathers local stakeholders and streamlines decision-making processes. Long-term sustainability and profitability of the programme, however, are disputed.

Traditionally, the ECoC is awarded to a single municipality, which in the case of our narrative, are the cities of Marseille and Essen. This decision was influenced by their relative size, regional role and international visibility. Nevertheless, the events were explicitly branded in reference to their regional character: "Marseille-Provence 2013" and "Ruhr.2010 'Essen for the Ruhr'" (Provence and Ruhr being the regions' names).

The cities of Essen and Marseille are both part of integrated metropolitan regions in which they are well connected and closely interlaced through strong work and leisure commuting patterns as well as relatively compact settlement structures. The governance frameworks in both cases, however, do not necessarily reflect this interdependency. While in the case of the Ruhr, the similarity of the four major cities – Essen, Dortmund, Duisburg and Bochum – leads to competition, the Marseille-Provence area suffers from the dichotomic difference between the two leaders of the region, Marseille and Aix, Marseille being larger, with strong former industrial activity, and currently struggling with structural change (Andres 2011).

In both cases, the ECoC was bundled with ongoing processes for stronger regional-metropolitan integration through the implementation of an overarching regional institution, expected to come into being shortly after the ending of the event. In Marseille, this was the implementation of the new regional territorial authority, or the Métropole: a new spatial layer in the French 'territorial puff pastry' created by the latest decentralization law in 2014. In the Ruhr region, this process was the re-implementation of a binding regional plan, which would cover the entire functional region for the first time since 1966.

In each of these cases, the programs are consistently viewed as having been successful due to intensified regional cooperation, increased external self-marketing and internal identity creation, effective project implementation, and the function of the program as a regionally unifying initiative. Additionally, local stakeholders claim the events raised awareness of the benefits of regional cooperation, although concerns about a 'falling back into old patterns' were also expressed. However, in the aftermath of the programs, the follow-up varied greatly. While the preparation of the regional plan in the Ruhr advanced successfully and a new law came into effect in 2015 giving more powers to the inter-municipal planning body, the Marseille-Provence region suffered from fierce resistance to stronger regional integration in the course of implementing the Métropole (Andres 2011).

These differences in outcome could also be attributed to elements of the local governance framework, as it seems that the framing parameters described do not fully explain such a strong divergence in outcomes. We suggest that an analysis of local planning cultural practices and evaluation frames could provide a deeper understanding of the reasons for this discrepancy.

In both cases, we look at situations with established evaluation guidelines and patterns of practice, which up until the initiatives, were led by fragmented municipalities in the areas, which then moved incrementally towards stronger regional integration. It can be assumed that these value frames and practice patterns surface in everyday professional practice in the form of skepticism towards the usefulness of more cooperation as well as in the lack of established sets of rules of good practices and habits to successfully initiate and carry out more integrated cooperation. In consequence, even though external perturbation of well-established patterns of action – like the designation of European Capital of Culture – is tolerated temporarily, patterns of action are very likely to 'fall back into old habits' due to the routinization and professionalization of previously entrenched know-how.

Conclusion and Outlook

A practice-based study of spatial planning is useful as it tells us a lot about hidden assumptions of planning practice that are not manifested in formal regulations. Based on a comparative approach, we are able to differentiate outcomes and performances in different cases and can identify the specific relevant variables that relate to more desirable performance of spatial planning in different cases (Booth 2011). This includes the potential to learn from best practice examples. With regards to policy and knowledge transfer, planning culture may explain what works in a particular local or regional context and why reforms fail, but exact transfer from a different context cannot be guaranteed.

In the introduction, we referred to Sanyal (2016) and claimed that comparative research in planning cultures has its highest potential when change is being analyzed. The analysis of the impact of crisis and reforms on planning systems, that can be observed in many European states in the last 15 years (Ponzini 2016; and the discussion above), may illustrate the relevance of planning culture, as we are able to give a more concise picture of what has changed and what has not. One of the hypotheses would be: Culture is a brake for change, because – compared to formal regulations – cultures change very slowly and are inherently resistant to change. Long-term change manifests in planning culture. Planning culture as understood by protagonists of the cultural studies approach may illuminate hegemony, mechanisms of distinction and power in the planning field. This also allows for an improved understanding of the planning profession and the ethics of planning (and planners).

Note

1 Booth refers to: L. Porter (2007) Producing forests: A colonial genealogy of environmental planning in Victoria, Australia, *Journal of Planning Education and Research*, 26 (4), 466–477.

References

Almond, G., Verba, S. (1963) *The Civic Culture. Political Attitudes and Democracy in Five Nations*. Princeton, NJ: Princeton University Press.

Andres, L. (2011) Marseille 2013 or the final round of a long and complex regeneration strategy? *Town Planning Review* 82 (1): 61–75.

Balchin, P., Sykora, L., Bull, G. (1999) *Regional Policy and Planning in Europe*. London: Routledge.

Booth, P. (1993) The cultural dimension in comparative research: Making sense of development control in France. *European Planning Studies* 1 (2): 217–229.

Booth, P. (2011) Culture, planning and path dependence: Some reflections on the problems of comparison. *Town Planning Review* 82 (1): 14–28.

Bourdieu, P. (1984) *Distinction: A Social Critique of the Judgement of Taste*. London: Routledge.

Bourdieu, P. (1990) *The Logic of Practice*. Cambridge: Polity Press.

Commission of the European Communities (1997) *The EU Compendium of Spatial Planning Systems and Policies*. Luxembourg: European Commission.

Damsgaard, O. (2014) The Danish planning system 1990–2010: Continuity and decay. In: Reimer, M., Getimis, P., Blotevogel, H. H. (eds.) *Spatial Planning Systems and Practices in Europe: A Comparative Perspective on Continuity and Changes*. New York: Routledge, pp. 21–40.

de Olde, C. (2016) Capturing planning cultures in Flanders and The Netherlands. Paper presented at the *AESOP 10th Young Academics Conference*, Ghent, March 21–24.

de Vries, J. (2015) Planning and culture unfolded: The cases of Flanders and the Netherlands. *European Planning Studies* 23 (11): 2148–2164.

During, S. (2007) *The Cultural Studies Reader*, 3rd Edition. London: Routledge.

Ernste, H. (2012) Framing cultures of spatial planning. *Planning Practice & Research* 27 (1): 87–101.

Farinos Dasi, J. (2007) *ESPON Project 2.3.2. Governance of Territorial and Urban Policies from EU to Local Level: Final Report*. Esch-sur-Alzette, Luxembourg: ESPON Coordination Unit.

Friedmann, J. (2005a) Globalization and the emerging culture of planning. *Progress in Planning* 64 (3): 183–234.

Friedmann, J. (2005b) Planning cultures in transition. In: Sanyal, B. (ed.) *Comparative Planning Cultures*. New York: Routledge, pp. 29–44.

Fürst, D. (2009) Planning cultures en route to a better comprehension of "planning processes"? In: Knieling, J., Othengrafen, F. (eds.) *Planning Cultures in Europe: Decoding Cultural Phenomena in Urban and Regional Planning*. Farnham, UK: Ashgate, pp. 23–38.

Giddens, A. (1984) *The Constitution of Society: Outline of the Theory of Structuration*. Berkeley, CA: University of California Press.

Gregory, D. (1984) Space, time, and politics in social theory: An interview with Anthony Giddens. *Environment and Planning D. Society and Space* 1984 (2): 123–132.

Healey, P. (1992). Planning through debate: The communicative turn in planning theory. *Town Planning Review* 63 (2): 143–162.

Healey, P., Williams, R. (1993) European urban planning systems: Diversity and convergence. *Urban Studies* 30 (4/5): 701–720.

Kaufman, J., Escuin, M. (2000) Thinking alike: Similarities in attitudes of Dutch, Spanish, and American planners. *Journal of the American Planning Association* 66 (1): 34–45.

Keller, D. A., Koch, M., Selle, K. (eds.) (1993) *Planungskulturen in Europa. Erkundungen in Deutschland, Frankreich, Italien und in der Schweiz*. Darmstadt: Verlag für Wissenschaftliche Publikationen.

Keller, D. A., Koch, M., Selle, K. (1996) "Either/or" and "and": First impressions of a journey into the planning cultures of four countries. *Planning Perspectives* 11 (1): 41–54.

Knieling, J., Othengrafen, F. (2009) Planning cultures in Europe between convergence and divergence: Findings, explanations and perspectives. In: Knieling, J., Othengrafen, F. (eds.) *Planning Cultures in Europe: Decoding Cultural Phenomena in Urban and Regional Planning*. London: Ashgate, pp. 301–321.

Knieling, J., Othengrafen, F. (2015) Planning culture: A concept to explain the evolution of planning policies and processes in Europe? *European Planning Studies* 23 (11): 2133–2147.

Leaf, Michael (2005) Modernity confronts tradition: The professional planner and local corporatism in the rebuilding of China's cities. In: Sanyal, B. (ed.) *Comparative Planning Cultures*. New York: Routledge, pp. 91–111.

Loh, C. G. (2018) Learning from practice, learning for practice in local land use planning research. In: Sanchez, T. W. (ed.) *Planning Research and Knowledge*. Abingdon, UK: Routledge, pp. 24–34.

Luukkonen, J. (2017) A practice theoretical perspective on the Europeanization of spatial planning. *European Planning Studies* 25 (2): 259–277.

Maier, K. (2012) Europeanization and changing planning in East-Central Europe: An Easterner's view. *Planning Practice & Research* 27 (1): 137–154.

Nadin, V., Stead, D. (2013) Opening up the compendium: An evaluation of international comparative planning research methodologies. *European Planning Studies* 21 (10): 1542–1561.

Neuman, M. (2007) How we use planning: Planning cultures and images of future. In: Hopkins, L. D., Zapata, M. (eds.) *Engaging the Future: Forecasts, Scenarios, Plans, and Projects*. Cambridge, MA: Lincoln Institute of Land Policy, pp. 155–174.

Newman, P., Thornley, A. (1996) *Urban Planning in Europe: International Competition, National Systems, and Planning Projects*. London: Routledge.

Othengrafen, F. (2010) Spatial planning as expression of culturised planning practices: The examples of Athens and Helsinki. *Town Planning Review* 81 (1): 83–110.

Othengrafen, F., Reimer, M. (2013) The embeddedness of planning in cultural contexts: Theoretical foundations for the analysis of dynamic planning cultures. *Environment and Planning A* 45 (6): 1269–1284.

Ponzini, D. (2016) Introduction: Crisis and renewal of contemporary urban planning. *European Planning Studies* 24 (7): 1237–1245.

Reckwitz, A. (2002) Toward a theory of social practices. *European Journal of Social Theory* 5 (2): 243–263.

Reckwitz, A. (2005) Kulturelle Differenzen aus praxeologischer Perspektive: Kulturelle Globalisierung jenseits von Modernisierungstheorie und Kulturessentialismus. In: Srubar, I., Renn, J., Wenzel, U. (eds.) *Kulturen Vergleichen. Sozial– und kulturwissenschaftliche Grundlagen und Kontroversen.* Wiesbaden: VS Verlag für Sozialwissenschaften, pp. 92–111.

Reimer, M., Blotevogel, H. H. (2012) Comparing spatial planning practice in Europe: A plea for cultural sensitization. *Planning Practice & Research* 27 (1): 7–24.

Reimer, M., Getimis, P., Blotevogel, H. H. (2014) *Spatial Planning Systems and Practices in Europe: A Comparative Perspective on Continuity and Changes.* New York: Routledge.

Rein, M., Schön, D. (1993) Reframing policy discourse. In: Fischer, F., Forester, J. (eds.) *The Argumentative Turn in Policy Analysis and Planning.* Durham, NC: Duke University Press, pp. 145–166.

Sanyal, B. (ed.) (2005a) *Comparative Planning Cultures.* New York: Routledge.

Sanyal, B. (2005b) Hybrid planning cultures: The search for the global cultural commons. In: Sanyal, B. (ed.) *Comparative Planning Cultures.* New York: Routledge, pp. 3–25.

Sanyal, B. (2016) Revisiting comparative planning cultures. Is culture a reactionary rhetoric? *Planning Theory & Practice* 17 (4): 658–662.

Schatzki, T. R. (2001) Introduction: Practice theory. In: Schatzki, T. R., Knorr, C. K., von Savigny, E. (eds.) *The Practice Turn in Contemporary Theory.* London: Routledge, pp. 1–15.

Stead, D., de Vries, J., Tasan-Kok, T. (2015) Planning cultures and histories: Influences on the evolution of planning systems and spatial development patterns. *European Planning Studies* 23 (11): 2127–2132.

Sutcliffe, A. (1981) *Towards the Planned City: Germany, Britain, the United States and France, 1780–1914.* Oxford: Blackwell.

Sykes, O., O'Brien, P. (2016) "So you say you want a (permanent) revolution?" – Planning under the shadow of constant reform, the case of the United Kingdom. In: Farinós, D. J. (ed.) *Achieving Territory becomes Matter of State Importance. Essentials for Coordination of Spatial Planning Policies* (in print).

Tajbakhsh, K. (2005) Planning culture in Iran: Centralization and decentralization and local governance in the twentieth century. In: Bishwapriya, S. (ed.) *Comparative Planning Cultures.* New York: Routledge, pp. 67–89.

Taylor, Z. (2013) Rethinking planning culture: A new institutionalist approach. *Town Planning Review* 84 (6): 683–702.

Wagenaar, H., Cook, S. D. N. (2003) Understanding policy practices: Action, dialectic and deliberation in policy analysis. In: Hajer, M. A., Wagenaar, H. (eds) *Deliberative policy analysis: Understanding governance in the network society.* Cambridge: Cambridge University Press, 139–171.

Williams, R. (1989) Culture is ordinary. In: *Resources of Hope.* London/New York: Verso, pp. 3–18 (originally published 1958).

Williams, R. H. (1996) *European Union Spatial Policy and Planning.* London: Paul Chapman Publishing.

Zonneveld, W., Evers, D. (2014) Dutch national spatial planning at the end of an era. In: Reimer, M., Getimis, P., Blotevogel, H. H. (eds.) *Spatial Planning Systems and Practices in Europe: A Comparative Perspective on Continuity and Changes*. New York: Routledge, pp. 61–82.

4

STRIVING FOR IMPACT BEYOND THE ACADEMY?

Planning Research in Australia

Paul Burton

Introduction

The distinction between theory and practice in planning, while itself subject to considerable debate, is often manifest in the distinctive practices and world views of planning academics and planning practitioners. A significant aspect of this distinction lies in the tendency for planning academics to do research and write *about* planning, while practitioners devote more time to *doing* planning, albeit often in reflexive ways (Schön, 1983). The question sometimes arises of how the research done by planning academics is connected to the planning done by practitioners? Is academic planning research designed specifically to meet the needs of practitioners, and if so, how are these needs determined and does the research in fact meet the needs of planning practitioners? Or is academic research less directly connected with day-to-day practices of planning and more concerned with broader and perhaps more abstract questions of the relationship between place and society, and with the nature of planning and its social, political and economic role in contemporary and indeed historical settings? If the second of these positions seems attractive, does this research nevertheless prove useful, perhaps in the longer term, to practitioners who want to reflect on their broader role and impact as well as dealing with the important but more prosaic challenges of land use regulation and growth management? Of course, each of these positions is plausible, and for years they have coexisted. Nevertheless, there is an enduring sense that academic planning research should be more sensitive to the imperative to be of practical relevance and to aspire to a degree of usefulness, and a prevailing view among many practitioners and some academics that it could do better in this regard. Finally, there is a widespread although not unanimous view that the nature of the contemporary university is changing and that the expectations held of academics and their labors are increasingly driven by a broad set of neoliberal imperatives.

This chapter takes as its starting point the assumption that planning research could and should be of greater practical value, but subjects this assumption to critical scrutiny. It does so in the context of planning research and practice in Australia, a place that has been dominated by British planning traditions but is now subject to a more global set of values and expectations about the theory and practice of planning. The chapter also explores what we mean by 'planning research': who conducts this research, in what settings and for what purposes? While most of what might be claimed as and regarded as planning research is conducted by academics working within university settings, a smaller but significant amount is conducted elsewhere – by local, national and international planning consultancies, by think tanks and by practising planners as part of their practice – and this cannot be ignored.

The argument developed here reflects my position as a planning academic based in an Australian university. I am currently Professor of Urban Management and Planning and Director of the Cities Research Centre at Griffith University in Queensland. The Cities Research Centre supports research on all aspects of cities and processes of urban development and strives to ensure our research is both academically rigorous and practically useful, and this aspiration reflects my belief that such an accommodation between scholarly and practitioner imperatives is desirable and possible. Before moving to Australia I was a member of the School for Advanced Urban Studies and then the School for Policy Studies at the University of Bristol in the UK, where I conducted a wide range of research on urban policy issues, often with the financial support of central or local governments, and on the relationship between evidence and policy. But before re-entering the academy to carry out research for my PhD (on the ways in which planning theory might help us understand the redevelopment of London's Docklands), I trained as a town planner at what was then the Polytechnic of the South Bank in London and worked, subsequently, as a development control planner with the London Borough of Richmond upon Thames and as a planning researcher with the London Borough of Southwark. So, over a career spanning 40 years, I have worked mainly as a research-active planning academic and also as a planning practitioner.

Engaged Planning Scholarship

The relationship between scholarly and more applied research has been a subject of debate within universities for centuries. In her history of European universities, Zonta (2002) notes that there has always been great variety in both the founding principles and the emphasis given to different scholarly traditions. This variety is illustrated by the importance of monastic traditions in France and Spain compared with the primacy of service to local rulers embodied in the establishment of the central European universities of Prague, Krakow and Vilnius. But the principles espoused by two of Europe's oldest universities, Paris and Bologna, typify two essential and different roles for universities both ancient and modern: presenting and criticizing the theoretical foundations of knowledge imparted to students and providing training 'in the practical solution of problems of importance to society'

(Zonta, 2002: 29). In other words, there has always been a clear European tradition both in extending knowledge *and* in putting this to the service of contemporary problem-solvers. This tradition lives on in many contemporary universities in their commitment to service as well as to 'pure research' and to teaching.

In the USA during the second half of the 19th century, the higher education system expanded in scale but also, more importantly, in its scope with President Lincoln's signing of the Morrill Act in 1862. Later known as the Land Grant College Act, this saw the federal government provide land to the states to use as collateral in creating public universities and colleges 'for the liberal and practical education of the industrial classes in the several pursuits and professions of life' (Morrill Act, quoted in Hambleton, 2015: 293). This practical and ideological commitment to local service remains, although some like Rhodes, a former president of Cornell University, have lamented a loss of local engagement and the conviction that 'the pursuit of knowledge is best undertaken by scholars, living and working, not in isolation, but in the yeasty and challenging atmosphere of community' (2001: 47).

Despite the significance of these historical roots for European and North American universities and their relevance to contemporary Australian universities, for many academics a spectre is now haunting the contemporary university. Against a background of nostalgia for levels of public funding for universities in Australia not seen since the 1970s, the form and function of contemporary universities is a source of profound disquiet to many. While the expanding opportunity to attend university is not often criticized openly, it is possible to detect mutterings in senior common rooms or their contemporary equivalent about the proliferation of 'degrees in basket-weaving and golf course management' as an unwelcome symptom of this expansion. Current concern about the state of the modern university in Australia and elsewhere tends to focus on a number of very different developments from the consequences of the outright expansion of the sector, through 'intolerable' work pressures, to a growing publish or perish culture (Davis, 2012; Thornton, 2014; McCamish, 2016). Much of this critique is inextricably linked to a broader critique of neoliberalism and its apparent application within the contemporary academy (see, for example, Readings, 1996; Whelan, 2015; Carlin, 2016).

But there is also, among some academics, a powerful strand of criticism aimed at the growing emphasis on relevance and application in research and an apparent retreat from disengaged scholarship (McLennan, 2008; Gaita, 2012; West, 2016). This is less evident among academic planners who have traditionally acknowledged the importance of basing planning theory on planning practice and, in turn, on providing both a theoretical explanation and a justification for planning in practice. However, theorists of planning have not been immune to the linguistic complexities and conceptual contortions associated with postmodern, post-structuralist and post-normal dispositions (for example, Gunder and Hillier, 2009).

It is one thing to be more or less comfortable with the relationship between planning theory and planning practice, but what of the slightly different relationship between planning research and planning practice? To be sure, planning research might seek to test with empirical evidence existing planning theory and to develop new theories on the basis of this testing; however, much published planning research does not involve the explicit testing or development of theory, but something rather more vague and diffuse. In her insightful and substantial critique of Hillier and Healey's *Research Companion to Planning Theory*, Sandercock (2011) refers somewhat scathingly to a contemporary tendency towards 'theoretical musings' at the expense of what Healey suggests should be the principle task of planning theorists: 'to learn from practices, through methodologically careful and thick accounts'. In other words, much of what passes for planning theory involves abstract musings on the institutions of government (federal, state or local) or the repressive consequences of political ideologies, such as neoliberalism, that are held to frame and constrain planning practice. The empirical testing of clearly stated hypotheses that seek to uncover causal connections is less often seen and more often condemned as a remnant attachment to discredited forms of positivism. Of course planning theory is not alone in this, but struggles alongside other social science disciplines to reconcile the sometimes conflicting imperatives of academic freedom and social relevance.

Planning Research in Australia: Who Does it and What Does it Focus Upon?

The main domestic outlets for Australian planning research are two journals: *Urban Policy and Research* (of which I am a member of the Editorial Board) and *Australian Planner*, which is associated with the Planning Institute of Australia (PIA). Of course, planning research by Australian-based researchers is also published in a variety of other, international academic journals, and research about Australian planning issues is conducted by researchers based in other countries. Nevertheless, we look below at the profile of research published in *Australian Planner* and at debates about the state of planning or urban research conducted in *Urban Policy and Research*.

Planning research is also presented at conferences. The main conferences for practising planners are the annual state conferences and annual national congress of the PIA, which provide opportunities for planners (academic and practice-based) to present their research. The main conferences for planning academics in Australasia are the annual Australia and New Zealand Association of Planning Schools (ANZAPS) conferences and the biennial State of Australian Cities (SOAC) conferences. Other conferences attended by planners include those organised by the Urban Development Institute of Australia (UDIA), the Property Council of Australia (PCA), the Housing Institute of Australia (HIA) and the Green Building Council of Australia (GBCA). We should note that few planning practitioners attend the SOAC conferences and few planning academics attend the PIA conferences and congress. While there may be good reasons for this, it does little to foster productive and constructive debate across the theory/practice or academic/practitioner divide.

So, not all research about planning or research designed to be of benefit to practising planners is produced by academics working within Australian universities.

Professional bodies such as the PIA, the UDIA, the PCA and the HIA produce and commission research and publish reports with a research base; and numerous think tanks, both global and local, publish work intended to be of benefit to planners. In Australia, for example, the Grattan Institute was formed in 2008 to contribute to public policy debates in ways that are (in their own words) rigorous, practical and independent. They do this through a number of policy-focused programs of work, including one on transport and cities, and they have published reports on cities as the engines of prosperity (Kelly, Donegan, Chisholm, and Oberklaid, 2014), on the need for new approaches to housing policy (Kelly, Hunter, Harrison, and Donegan, 2013) and on suburbs of the future (Kelly, Breadon, Mares, Ginnivan, Jackson, Gregson, and Viney, 2012). At the global scale, work is carried out by bodies such as: the JLL Cities Research Centre, who recently published a study of benchmarking techniques for current and emerging world cities (see Hu, Blakely, and Zhou, 2013); Global Cities, Inc. of Bloomberg Philanthropies, which looks to build communication among global city leaders to promote innovation; and the 100 Resilient Cities initiative of the Rockefeller Foundation, which focuses on building the capacity of member cities to cope with global shocks and disruptions. While front-line planning practitioners may not be the target audience of these initiatives, their research does appear to have some traction among some senior planners and city leaders, insofar as cities elect to join these networks and bring leading members to local conferences.

To provide a snapshot of one element of the state of planning research in Australia, data is presented on the profile of papers published in *Australian Planner*. Formerly published as the *Royal Australian Planning Institute Journal* (1958–1981), the journal now claims to be 'Australia's leading peer-reviewed journal for the planning profession, and is the most read and influential planning journal in Australia and the Pacific Region' (*Australian Planner* website) and is published in association with the Planning Institute of Australia. Over the last decade (2006–2016), this quarterly journal has published 350 peer-reviewed papers, excluding letters to the editor and book reviews, on a variety of topics and by different types of planner. For the purpose of this short analysis, we have classified the authorship of papers as academic only, practitioner only or a mix of academic and practitioner. We also subjectively classified the subject area of each paper into one of 28 categories, although we acknowledge that papers might in fact cover more than one topic (history and transport, or climate change and healthy cities, for example). Thirteen categories have more than ten papers in each, and to simplify the data, we have limited the subsequent analysis to this narrower range of categories, which are listed in Table 4.1.

Papers classified as being about planning practice have been the most popular (31 papers), followed by papers on planning history (27), climate change (25), transport (23) and urban form (21); other topics include healthy cities (17), smart cities (11), community engagement (10) and international issues (10). We also classified the type of paper, distinguishing discussion/review papers; modelling and analysis; case studies; policy analysis papers; research results; histories; and critiques.

TABLE 4.1 *Australian Planner* – paper topics, 2006–2016

Topic	Number of papers
Planning practice	31
History	27
Climate change	25
Transport	23
Urban form	21
Housing	18
Healthy cities	17
Planning education	17
Architecture and design	14
Smart cities & Internet	11
Community consultation	10
Development	10
International	10

Again, we recognize that these categories are not entirely mutually exclusive, but they serve to indicate something of the range of types of paper.

By cross-tabulating the type of author with the topic and type of paper, we begin to see areas that are often dominated by particular types of author. For example, papers on planning history, planning education, oil depletion and social issues were almost the exclusive preserve of academic authors, while papers on planning practice, climate change, housing, development, economics and water quality had the highest proportion of practitioner authors.

What can we conclude from this? In some instances the correlation between author type and topic is unsurprising. It is understandable that planning academics write about planning education more than practitioners; although in the next section, a recent survey shows that practitioners have strong views about the nature of planning education and the work-readiness of recent graduates. It is also not surprising that practitioners are willing to write about economic issues and about development, though it is likely that the practitioners in these cases are consultant researchers rather than employees of statutory planning agencies.

But we should remember that research about and for planning is produced by a wide range of people and that while academic researchers constitute a major source, practitioners themselves produce a lot of research, as do consultants and researchers working for industry bodies, think tanks and lobby organizations. While the latter have a vested interest in making their work available, even if on a commercial basis, the research of practitioners does not always enter the public domain.

Researchers in the commercial sector face an imperative to carry out research that someone is prepared to pay for – whether or not it is subsequently made more widely available. This is not to say that the results of their research will be tailored to the beliefs or predilections of their clients although, in some cases, this is manifestly the case. Market research commissioned by developers will in the long run stand or fall by the rigor and reliability of the analysis, and research commissioned to support the policy preferences of industry groups such as the UDIA, the PCA or the HIA may be more susceptible to accusations of partisanship.

Academic research is not immune from similar accusations, and there is a clear and long-standing tradition among some academic planning researchers of producing research that is explicitly and unapologetically supportive of particular groups or political positions. Sandercock, for example, has for many years articulated an approach to planning that is unashamedly radical and progressive, and she has shown ongoing support for the Planners Network, a body whose constant objective has been 'to advocate that planning be used to eliminate inequalities and promote peace and racial, economic and environmental justice.'[1]

What does the Profession Think about the Focus of Contemporary Planning Research?

There is little by way of systematic or robust evidence of the views of Australian planners about the focus, the quality or the usefulness of contemporary planning research. However, a recent survey of Australian planners captured their views on a range of issues, including the relationship between theory and practice and the matters of greatest concern. This survey replicated many of the questions posed to European planners by Klaus Kunzmann and Martina Koll-Schretzenmayr (2015), but was conducted among a larger sample of planners in Australia and New Zealand. The online survey was directed at planners through a number of channels, including the listserv RePlan (350 planners mostly in Australasia) and notices on the PIA website. Over 250 responses were received from a mix of practitioners (69% of the achieved sample) and academics (31%), although not all respondents completed the full range of questions. The gender distribution was more even, with male respondents making up 53% of the sample and female respondents making up 45%. In terms of length of service in the profession, the largest group of respondents had worked as planners for over 20 years (30%), while recent entrants (0–5 years) accounted for 23% of respondents.

Table 4.2 summarizes the main planning challenges identified by respondents as well as their popularity for different groups of planners (women, men, practitioners, academics). It is notable that academics tended to rank highly some of the 'big issue' topics such as climate change, governance, social justice and sustainability, while the practitioners included more substantive topics such as housing and transport alongside these big issues. Of perhaps even greater significance is that planning education and indigenous issues are at the bottom of these lists for all

TABLE 4.2 Ranking of main planning challenges

Ranking	Practitioners	Academics	Women	Men
1	Housing	Climate change	Climate change	Transport
2	Climate change	Governance	Housing	Climate change
3	Transport	Social justice[a]	Governance	Governance
4	Governance	Sustainability[a]	Sustainability	Sustainability[a]
5	Sustainability	Housing	Social justice[a]	Housing[a]
6	Social justice	Transport	Transport[a]	Social justice
7	Planning education	Planning education[a]	Planning education[b]	Planning education
8	Indigenous	Indigenous[a]	Indigenous[b]	Indigenous

Note: a, b = equal rankings.
Source: Freestone, Goodman, and Burton (2016)

types of planner, though it should be noted that a much longer list of issues exists for all respondents.

In terms of the links between theory and practice, the survey asked respondents about the relative importance of three specific relationships: academic research and planning practice; planning theory and planning practice; and working relationships between academics and practitioners. Overall, all respondents agreed that the relationship of academic research to planning practice was important or extremely important, and the same was found for the relationship between planning theory and planning practice. They also felt that the relationship between academics and practitioners was important. The strength of these relationships were seen somewhat differently by academics and practitioners, with the former believing they have good connections with the latter to a greater extent than in the opposite direction. Around half of all practitioners said they used academic research, while slightly fewer (46%) said that research was relevant and useful to them.

When asked about their views on what could be done to make academic research more relevant to them, the practitioners offered a number of suggestions, including:

- creating more opportunities for collaboration;
- providing better access to research findings;
- allowing academics more opportunities to work directly with practitioners; and
- carrying out more applied research, including research commissioned by practitioners.

From the academics' perspective, most felt they had good connections with the planning profession and that these connections were important in maintaining the relevance and the quality of their research. Far fewer believed that it was similarly important to maintain good relations with members of the development industry; indeed some suggested that close relations of this nature might compromise the integrity of academic planning researchers. The complex nature of these relationships was summed up well by one respondent, who said,

> At present we know a bit, but probably not enough to properly understand the different pressures and priorities of working in each sector and as a consequence sometimes slip into making glib statements about what others should do: why don't practitioners take the time to read my work; why don't academics write for me rather than for themselves; why don't commercial researchers stop just writing what their clients pay for . . . and so on.

While discussions of the practical relevance of academic planning scholarship have waxed and waned over the decades in Australia, some recent contributions have reignited the debate. Randolph's (2013) editorial in the journal *Urban Policy and Research* highlighted the failure of planning research to receive support from successive rounds of funding from the Australian Research Council (the principal funder of scholarly research in Australia) and concluded:

> The research funding drought is a corrosive situation. Without new research funding at scale, we will fail to train the next generation of urban researchers. Without the new researchers, our discipline area will simply wither away. Moreover, without an active research community, the forces creating our cities will continue to roll forward without a thoroughgoing understanding of the drivers of urban change and the options for planning and other interventions.
>
> (p. 133)

In the same issue, Troy (2013) offers a typically trenchant review of the history of urban research in Australia, pointing to a colonial legacy of physical determinism that eschewed critical research of the type that was becoming commonplace in many leading North American universities. While sharing Randolph's pessimistic analysis, Troy concludes rather more optimistically by advocating the establishment of a Town Planning Bureau to provide rigorous, independent advice to government on the development and management of Australian cities. While I see considerable merit in Troy's proposal for a Bureau, the approach to urban policy taken by the relatively new Assistant Minister for Cities and Digital Transformation, Angus Taylor, suggests that global consultancy firms are at present a more favored source of urban research than Australian universities.

Hurley and Taylor (2016) recently published an important and provocative paper that explores the use of urban research in planning practice, presenting evidence of why time-poor practitioners find it difficult to access and utilize most of the published academic research. A telling phrase uttered by one of their respondents,

'Not a lot of people read this stuff', captured the painful reality for those committed to engaged scholarship. But Hurley and Taylor do not just describe; they suggest a number of ways in which academic research might become more accessible and useful to planning practitioners. These include translating often long and complex research reports into more digestible summaries and bringing academic work out from behind the paywalls of journals and more into the public domain. But they also suggest that it might require reducing research to 'only one page, with a click-bait title, a nifty graphic and, even more difficult, a simple unambiguous answer' (2016, p. 129). These may well help, but there is a danger in believing that uptake and application is necessarily part of a rational process of policymaking (Burton, 2006).

Finally, Bunker (2015) addresses the paradox of why Australian urban research, which is judged to be of high quality, is used so little in local planning practice. His critique raises important questions about how the quality of research is judged and how traditional academic and scholarly criteria might need to be supplemented by factors of value to practitioners. But they also remind us that for some academics, obligations and expectations of greater engagement with policy and practice are to be resisted or treated with suspicion.

Conclusion: Is There a Case for a Renewed Focus on Greater 'Engagement' in Planning Research by Academics?

An Australian tabloid newspaper recently carried one of its regular items condemning the expenditure of public funds on 'absurd' research (Brooks, 2016). While such attacks are easy to dismiss and ignore, slightly more worrying was the response of the Australian Federal Treasurer, the Honorable Scott Morrison, who agreed with the suggestion that research supported by the Australian Research Council (ARC) should be able to withstand the 'pub test'. While the Treasurer no doubt meant that decisions about public expenditure should in general be tested against notions of the public interest, in this particular case it represented a thinly veiled attack on the alleged disconnection between academic research agendas and the apparent interests of the public at large. This itself is part of a wider and long-running debate about the extent to which publicly funded research in universities should make a contribution to meeting public needs, addressing government priorities and solving social problems (Gardner, 2016). While these are entirely laudable aims, the question remains as to whether each and every piece of publically funded research should be able to demonstrate in advance how it will contribute to the public good or solve contemporary social problems and policy challenges.

When presented in this way, further questions are raised about the relationship between research and policy or practice. First, it can be difficult to establish with any degree of precision trajectories of policy development and the role of research in these trajectories, for as Rein famously observed, 'Social science does contribute to policy and practice but the link is neither consensual, graceful nor self-evident'

(1976, 12). Second, the temporal connection between the publication of research and its possible impact on policy and practice is unpredictable and variable. The policy streams conception of policymaking (Kingdon, 1995) suggests that a number of factors must come together in order for a 'policy window' to open and allow relatively rapid policy development, and the availability of relevant research is only one of these factors. Third, the application of research to policy and practice can be unpredictable. There are many cases where excellent research on topics of great significance is ignored in policy processes, and there are also cases (admittedly far fewer) where seemingly obscure research on arcane topics become tremendously influential. Few would have imagined that Robert Putnam's (1994) economic history of the performance of Italian local governments and their relationship with local democracy would serve as the intellectual foundation for governments around the world to develop policies for the building of social capital.

We are left with the questions: Is the relationship between planning research, policy and practice in Australia in need of renewal? And if so, what should be the basis of that renewal? First, we should recognize that the relationship will never be one in which every piece of conducted and published research about planning will be of immediate value to practitioners. Some research is designed to address wider issues of the social, political and economic context of planning. Some will be critical of contemporary planning practice, perhaps even wantonly so, but we academics might strive to ensure that our critiques are more sophisticated in the benchmarks upon which we build them and the political assumptions that underpin them. For example, the critique of planning that claims it no longer sets out to redress deep-seated social and political inequalities might itself be critiqued for advancing a naïve and unsophisticated conception of planning both now and in the past. Similarly, academic papers that decry the neoliberalization of contemporary planning thought and practice often fail to define the structural and material conditions of neoliberalism despite persistent calls for research on 'actually existing' neoliberal forms and practices (Peck, Theodore, and Brenner, 2009).

There are various steps that can be taken by academic and practitioner planners to work more closely together in defining shared research agendas, collaborating in the conduct of research and drawing out the possible practical implications flowing from research. But we should also recognize that the imperatives and obligations facing academic planners working in universities are not the same as those of planners working for statutory planning agencies or in the commercial sector. Practising planners have to develop and implement planning policies as they regulate development, while academic planners have to educate students, conduct research and publish their findings. To be sure, part of the education of planning students involves preparing them for the world of planning as it is actually practised in different settings, and there are trends in the assessment (and reward) of academic research quality to give greater credence to impact beyond the academy. At the same time, practising planners should continue to recognize that devoting some time to reading more abstract and reflective work on planning may well help them in becoming more reflective practitioners and hence better planners.

To some extent the take-up or readership of planning research by practitioners might be helped if published research was described and catalogued more clearly. The growing field of systematic reviews, often carried out as part of the broader evidence-based policy movement, has revealed how published research in some fields – and planning would almost certainly be one of them – is very poorly described. Titles often seem to reflect the practices of popular magazines with little attempt to accurately describe the work in question, and some abstracts fail to describe the research methods used or the scope of the work. In contrast to journals in the sciences or medical sciences, the metadata associated with papers in planning is very limited. One consequence of this is that papers must be read in full in order to determine their relevance or to discover their irrelevance, which is not conducive to broadening readership among fellow academics, let alone pressed-for-time practitioners. But even here, there can be profound differences in the expectations of academics and practitioners. At a recent round table of academics and practitioners held at the national congress of the Planning Institute of Australia, it emerged that while *Australian Planner* was seen by some academics as a low-ranking journal in terms of academic prestige, it was viewed by some practitioners as an overly academic journal with few papers of great practical relevance.

Research on planning in Australia, as elsewhere, is produced by a range of different people, working in different settings and to different sets of imperatives. Academics are rewarded for securing certain types of research grants – nationally competitive grants provided by the Australian Research Council, for example – for publishing in prestigious 'high-impact' journals and for procuring as many possible citations of their work. While there are moves to give greater weight to 'engaged scholarship' and to the demonstrable social impact of one's research, planning academics still tend to measure their success according to internal rather than external factors. Consultant planning researchers must do work that someone else is willing to pay for, on the basis of their reputation, track record and technical skills; and while some of this work will enter the public domain, publication and promulgation is not typically a key performance indicator. Researchers working for planning think tanks and advocacy organizations have similar obligations to conduct high-quality research, but their principal imperative is to produce work that is influential because of its focus, timeliness, quality and clarity of presentation. Researchers working within planning organizations (typically state or territory governments and local governments) are more likely to carry out research on very closely specified topics that address particular needs in their organization. They are less likely to be called upon to do board-scale or highly conceptual work, and their work may not be available beyond their organization. Despite these different research imperatives, there is scope for each domain to learn from the others. Rigorous systematic reviewing skills learnt within the academy may be useful to consultants, advocacy researchers and internal researchers; clarity of expression is valuable in all domains; and the ability to synthesize quantitative data from a number of sources and present it cogently also has wide appeal.

In conclusion, planning research will continue to be marked by its diversity – of topic, method, focus, outlet and intent. Perhaps the most we can hope for is that this diverse product range is more clearly labelled. As with any other product, customer satisfaction is often undermined when what you get is not what appears on the label. From the perspective of the practitioner, it may be the case that some planning research sells itself as being based on practice and appears to offer readily adoptable solutions to practical problems, but falls short on both counts. Sometimes the practice base of research is so thin it cannot support the weighty recommendations for policy and practice that follow. Sometimes the recommendations and proposed solutions betray an alarming degree of political naiveté and ignorance of actually existing political systems and institutions. However, practitioners searching in academic journals devoted to planning theory should not be surprised if there is a paucity of 'how to fix it' papers; and they might even find that more scholarly and conceptual pieces help them reflect more widely and critically on their own role as practitioners.

Acknowledgements

I would like thank Dr Heather Shearer, Research Fellow in the Cities Research Centre, for her analysis of publications appearing in *Australian Planner* from 2006 to 2016.

The survey of planners in Australasia was conducted by Professor Robin Goodman, RMIT University; Professor Robert Freestone, UNSW; and Professor Paul Burton, Griffith University. Support in the design and administration of the survey and the initial data analysis was provided by Dr Elizabeth Taylor and Raven Cretney, RMIT University, and Dr Heather Shearer, Griffith University, whose contributions are gratefully acknowledged.

Note

1   See Planners Network website: www.plannersnetwork.org/about/history

References

Brooks, R. (2016) If you're going to ridicule research, do your homework, *The Conversation*, August 22. Available at: https://theconversation.com/if-youre-going-to-ridicule-research-do-your-homework-64238.

Bunker, R. (2015) Linking urban research with planning practice. *Urban Policy and Research* 33 (3): 362–369.

Burton, P. (2006) Modernising the policy process: making policy research more significant. *Policy Studies* 27 (3): 173–195.

Carlin, M. (2016) Deleuze and Guattari: Politics and education. In: D. C. Phillips (ed.) *Encyclopedia of Educational Philosophy and Theory*, pp. 1–5. Los Angeles: Sage.

Davis, G. (2012) The Australian idea of a University, *Meanjin*. Available at: https://meanjin.com.au/essays/the-australian-idea-of-a-university/.

Freestone, R., Goodman, R. and Burton, P. (2016) Challenges, complaints and critiques: Australasian planners on the profession, education and research in 2016. Paper for the *ANZAPS 2016 Conference*, Western Sydney University, Parramatta, 28–30 October.

Gaita, R. (2012) To civilise the City? *Meanjin* 71 (1). Available at: https://meanjin.com.au/essays/to-civilise-the-city/.

Gardner, A. (2016) The war between higher education and the right. *Inquisitr*, May 4. Available at: www.inquisitr.com/3060902/the-war-between-higher-education-and-the-right/.

Gunder, M. and Hillier, J. (2009) *Planning in Ten Words or Less: A Lacanian Entanglement with Spatial Planning*. Aldershot, UK: Ashgate.

Hambleton, R. (2015) *Leading the Inclusive City: Place–Based Innovation for a Bounded Planet*. Bristol: Policy Press.

Hu, R., Blakely, E. J. and Zhou, Y. (2013). Benchmarking the competitiveness of Australian global cities: Sydney and Melbourne in the global context. *Urban Policy and Research*, 31 (4), 435–452.

Hurley, J. and Taylor, E. (2016) Not a lot of people read this stuff: Australian urban research in planning practice. *Urban Policy and Research* 34 (2): 116–131.

Kelly, J.-F., Breadon, P., Mares, P., Ginnivan, L., Jackson, P., Gregson, J. and Viney, B. (2012) *Tomorrow's Suburbs*. Melbourne: Grattan Institute.

Kelly, J.-F., Hunter, J., Harrison, C. and Donegan, P. (2013) *Renovating Housing Policy*. Melbourne: Grattan Institute.

Kelly, J.-F., Donegan, P., Chisholm, C. and Oberklaid, M. (2014) *Mapping Australia's Economy: Cities as Engines of Prosperity*. Melbourne: Grattan Institute.

Kingdon, J. (1995) *Agendas, Alternatives and Public Policies*. London: Longman.

Kunzmann, K. and Koll-Schretzenmayr, M. (2015) The state of the art of planning in Europe. *disP – The Planning Review* 51 (4): 42–51.

McCamish, T. (2016) Thinking caps on: Where has demand driven our universities? *The Monthly*, September. Available at: https://www.themonthly.com.au/issue/2016/september/1472652000/thornton-mccamish/thinking-caps.

McLennan, G. (2008) Disinterested, disengaged, useless: Conservative or progressive idea of the university? *Globalisation, Societies and Education* 6 (2): 195–200.

Peck, J., Theodore, N. and Brenner, N. (2009) Neoliberal urbanism: Models, moments and mutations. *SAIS Review* 24 (1): 49–60.

Putnam, R. (1994). *Making Democracy Work: Civic Traditions in Modern Italy*. Princeton, NJ: Princeton University Press.

Randolph, B. (2013) Wither urban research? Yes, you read it right first time! *Urban Policy and Research* 31 (2): 130–133.

Readings, B. (1996) *The University in Ruins*. Cambridge, MA: Harvard University Press.

Rein, M. (1976) *Social Science and Public Policy*. Harmondsworth, UK: Penguin.

Rhodes, F. H. T. (2001) *The Role of the American University*. Ithaca, NY: Cornell University Press.

Sandercock, L. (2011) Book review: J. Hillier and P. Healey, The Ashgate research companion to planning theory: Conceptual challenges to spatial planning, Farnham, England: Ashgate, 2010. *Journal of Planning Education and Research* 31 (4): 461–463.

Schön, D. (1983) *The Reflective Practitioner: How Professionals Think in Action*. London: Temple Smith.

Thornton, M. (2014) *Through the Glass Darkly: The Social Sciences Look at the Neoliberal University*. Canberra: ANU Press.

Troy, P. (2013) Australian urban research and planning. *Urban Policy and Research* 31 (2): 134–149.

West, D. (2016) The managerial university: A failed experiment? *DEMOS*, April 14. Available at: www.demosproject.net/the-managerial-university-a-failed-experiment/.

Whelan, A. (2015) Academic critique of neoliberal academia. *Sites* 12 (1): 1–25.

Zonta, C. (2002) The history of European universities: Overview and background. In: N. Sanz and S. Bergan (eds) *The Heritage of European* Universities, pp. 25–37. Strasbourg: Council of Europe Publishing.

PART II
Types and Topics of Planning Research

5
MAPPING THE KNOWLEDGE DOMAIN OF URBAN PLANNING

Thomas W. Sanchez and Nader Afzalan

Introduction

Wildavsky's "If planning is everything, maybe it's nothing" remark provokes us to think about the breadth of urban planning, recognizing that urban development processes are quite complex, far beyond a singular definition or approach (Alexander, 2018, this volume). These include social, economic, technological, environmental, and political systems that continue to evolve and expand rapidly. Understanding these systems requires extensive interdisciplinary knowledge, while at the same time, the standard practice of higher education is to reward faculty expertise in narrowly defined fields (Shin, 2014). This means that scholars specialize due to institutional norms, leading to fragmented knowledge domains, a challenge to disciplines similar in size to planning. Like general practitioners of medicine, there are practitioners with a general understanding of the planning process, who then defer to professionals with specialized training, like civil engineers, lawyers, landscape architects, etc. (Friedmann, 1996). Friedmann argued for a change in the planning education model from the "generalist-with-a-specialty" to a "mastery of a specialty" (p. 102).

The debate about the wide range of topics considered by planning educators and practitioners is often based on varying definitions of "planning" and modes of planning practice. Definitions differ in how planning considers place and process as well as the objectives and intended outcomes of planning efforts (Edwards and Bates, 2011). Wildavsky acknowledged the challenges of planning in its all-encompassing dimensions when he stated, "Planning requires the resources, knowledge, and power of an entire people" (1973, p. 152). It was in the same issue of *Policy Sciences* that the Wildavsky article appeared (1973, No. 4, Issue 2) that Rittel and Webber described how planning problems are inherently "wicked". Solutions to wicked problems are considered to be elusive due to their complexity and lack of scientific rules. Later insights on these topics shared by Alexander (1981),

Reade (1982), Klosterman (1985), Wadley and Smith (1998), and Alexander (2018, this volume) reiterate that "planning" has several definitions that depend on philosophical and ideological perspectives. Some have seen this as a lack of coherence and expressed concern about the legitimacy of planning (see Levy, 1992; Lucy, 1994). Beauregard drew many of these points together by stating that "rather, planners need to accept the fuzzy boundaries of planning, the endemic incompleteness of professional control, and healthy and relentless internal criticism" (2001, p. 439). In a historical and personal view, Godschalk (2014) drew the distinction between planning practice and education from his experiences over a 50-year span. Like other planning scholars mentioned previously, he alludes to the wickedness of planning as having "complex problems with no perfect solutions" (p. 83).

Related to the broadness of planning, a discussion about planning core curricula and specializations has been ongoing for several years (see Pivo, 1989). The expansiveness and diversity of planning leans toward the need for specializations as students prepare for professional careers. Various scholars have argued how planning education shapes, and is being shaped, by planning practice due to changes in planners' roles and skill requirements (see Perloff, 1956; Birch, 2001). Specific skills have advantages that meet demands for niche roles and expertise that cannot otherwise be met by the planning "generalist". There remains a debate over the content of specified "core" curricula for planners, but it is generally recognized that specializations are important for subdomains of planning. Both the American Planning Association (APA) and the Planning Accreditation Board (PAB) identify specializations as components of planning practice and planning education. Planning academics certainly ascribe to specialization through their scholarly activities, as previously mentioned.

This examination of faculty specializations analyzes the self-reported research and teaching interests of faculty from Association of Collegiate Schools of Planning (ACSP) member schools. These member schools are primarily located in North America, which means that the planning issues identified are likely biased to this region. However, although faculty with degrees from US or Canadian schools represent most of these planning programs, it is also true that many faculty in North American planning schools come from around the world, and several focus on international issues that are directly applicable to non-North American issues. In addition, many planning faculty in the United States and Canada conduct research and teach about issues facing cities and regions around the world. In other words, while the sample is from North American schools, international planning issues are likely well represented.

To explore the constellation of specializations across planning programs, we also considered those identified by the APA. APA identifies 11 specializations on its website, as shown below:[1]

- Community Activism/Empowerment
- Community Development

- Economic Development
- Environmental/Natural Resources Planning
- Historic Preservation
- Housing
- Land Use & Code Enforcement
- Parks & Recreation
- Planning Management/Finance
- Transportation Planning
- Urban Design

While this list is not officially sanctioned by the APA or its members, these specialty areas are commonly associated with the planning profession. These specialties have substantial range in terms of how they address particular planning issues. Some areas, like "planning management/finance", include some technical aspects of organizational process, budgeting process, and program evaluation, but should still be evident from interests reported by faculty.

The *ACSP Guide* reports approximately 400 program specializations (see Appendix B of the *Guide*). There appears to be considerable overlap taking into account many are closely related but use different terminology. We expect that there is a close match between faculty specialties (which reflect program specializations) and the professional specializations mentioned by APA. There may also be topics that do not fit into identified program specializations because they represent emerging (or even lagging) topic areas within the field of planning.

Defining planning through mapping both teaching and research interest produces a web of topics along with derivatives that sometimes result from semantics rather than being actual subdomains. This means that identifying a distinct footprint or delineation of "planning" is challenging; however, mapping the knowledge domain produced by stated teaching and research topics highlights clusters of topics that can be seen as specializations within the overall planning knowledge domain. Specializations are not expected to be discrete but, rather, interconnected foundational themes. Using network analysis, we focus on identifying these specializations and the knowledge domain as reflected by faculty expertise and areas of interest.

The Urban Planning Knowledge Domain

We anticipate that the relationship among the interests of urban planning faculty creates a set of identifiable teaching and research specializations. When viewed as a network and using graph theory, the results will help to identify the knowledge domain or knowledge "footprint" generated by planning academics. As previously mentioned, because the sample is drawn from North American planning academics, the resulting domain structure will likely represent the Northern America context and will not necessarily be generalizable to planning academics around the world. However, in addition to highlighting current faculty specialty areas, delineating research topic areas can provide insights relevant to the definition of planning. This process provides a useful macroscopic view of planning education which can then be used to explore planning research areas, integration of research topics, and the relationship between planning education and practice.

One way to understand the domain of planning is to assess the record of publications by planning scholars (see Goldstein and Carmin, 2006). However, academic scholarship represents a "sample" of planning thought. Some planning academics and practitioners would argue that there is a mismatch between planning education and practice, and despite ongoing cooperation and communications among and between the academic and professional planning organizations (such as the APA, the ACSP, the American Institute of Certified Planners [AICP], and the PAB), the challenge is to link educational objectives and professional needs.

Knowledge Domain Mapping

At the intersection of computer science, information technology, bibliometrics, and library science, knowledge domain mapping is primarily exploratory, but it is useful for describing research activities and visualizing interconnections (Shiffrin and Börner, 2004). The approach often includes mapping to represent a body of knowledge to detect or mine patterns for further analysis. Network analysis and visualization help to illustrate relationships where rankings or lists are not effective (Menaouer, Baghdad, and Matta, 2013; Rafols, Porter, and Leydesdorff, 2010). In map form, it is easier to conceptualize "the *internal* dynamics of a research field or emergent discipline" (Rafols, Porter, and Leydesdorff, 2010, p. 1873). Knowledge domain mapping is often conducted through network analysis of co-citation data, where a relationship between topics, authors, or articles results from one publication citing another. Co-citation implies a type of influence, usually to substantiate or illustrate particular arguments or statements based on similar or related themes. The overall structure of the resulting network (or map), including clusters, represents the knowledge domain.

Besides co-citation, which links publications, the approach can be based on author names, co-author names, and publication keywords. Network relationships are generated as authors collaborate and keywords are shared by publications. Network analysis, whether using citations, authors, or keywords, can help to identify distinctive characteristics such as hubs, turning points, pivot points, and bridges between topics (Chen and Paul, 2001). In the case of interdisciplinarity, this can occur as connections are made between disciplines or specialties. Along with spatial relationships, the temporal dimension can also be associated with the network. Historiographic mapping of knowledge depicts origins and flows of research ideas and influence because sequences can be analyzed (Morris, Yen, Wu, and Asnake, 2003). Challenges involved with historical mapping include having complete sets of publication data to fully capture the corpus of disciplinary knowledge. Garfield (2004) provides an excellent example by mapping the chronological citation activity connected to the Winston-Crick 1953 article identifying the heliacal structure of DNA. Garfield's maps show both the scholarship being cited by the seminal work and those being influenced and published later.

An objective of the analysis presented in this chapter is to identify the knowledge domain of urban planning based on the research and teaching topics reported by planning faculty. Our analysis presents a "snapshot" of current planning topics, and assembles them in relationship to each other and also in terms of the whole. Just as Boyack, Klavans, and Börner (2005) mapped "the backbone" of science, this analysis does the same on a smaller scale, which is the knowledge domain of planning represented by faculty interests. This analysis does not rely on publication citation data, but more directly assesses research interests by using self-reported keywords. The use of keywords for knowledge domain mapping associates primary topics that cluster together, just as co-citation activity does (Ding, Chowdhury, and Foo, 2001), resulting in maps of similar structure and interpretability.

Because faculty self-identify areas of interest,[2] there may be data classification issues. For instance, "transportation" may be reported as an academic's area when in fact their specialty is "public transportation", "freight movement", or "travel modeling". The titles of published works are likely more specific compared to self-reported interest areas. As mentioned earlier, an alternative approach would be to analyze publication topics, keywords, or titles instead of interest areas. Knowledge domains are often analyzed this way with bibliometrics using networks or clusters of authors, papers, or references (Boyack, Klavans, and Börner, 2005, p. 351). However, a challenge is reclassifying or clustering titles so that they can be more easily grouped and analyzed. Another challenge with the method of looking at publication keywords or titles is that publications do not show authors academic interests or expertise, therefore limiting the amount of information available that can be analyzed.

Methodology

Building on graph theory, this study employs network analysis methods to examine how different specialties mentioned by urban planning faculty are connected and clustered. The analysis is performed by using the raw areas of expertise reported by planning faculty in the *ACSP Guide*. Graph theory informs network analysis by exploring parameters that influence network connectivity, including the number of nodes and links between them in the network, the density of sub-networks (clusters), and the distance between the nodes and clusters (Linehan, Gross, and Finn, 1995). In addition, network visualization is increasingly attracting scholarly attention because of its power in identifying network structure and, specifically, sub-networks or communities within networks (Bruns, 2012; Bastian and Heymann, 2009). Table 5.1 describes the graph components as they relate to our study.

Gephi, an open source network analysis and visualization tool, is used to analyze and visualize the faculty research interest data. Using data management methods, we sorted the nodes and edges in the network created based on the data

TABLE 5.1 Graph components in planning and design field

Terms	Definition	Translation in the network created in this study
Node	The main component of a graph	This is a term used by a faculty member as an area of expertise. For example, if a faculty member mentioned "community development" as their area of expertise, the two words "community" and "development" are considered as single nodes in the network.
Edge	Establishes connectivity between nodes	An edge is created between the areas of expertise (nodes) if they are mentioned by one or more faculty member(s).
Degree centrality	The number of edges that are connected to a single node	This shows the number of times that each area of expertise is connected to the other areas. In other words, it shows how many times an area of expertise is mentioned by different faculty members.
Betweenness centrality	A measure of connectivity between nodes, structures, or modules in graphs	This shows bridges or connections among faculty members' areas of expertise. Larger betweenness centrality for a node shows stronger connectivity between the node and other nodes.
Modularity	A measure of network structure; the division of a network into different modules	This shows how a faculty's areas of expertise cluster and create domains of expertise.

Note: See Wilson (1979); Minor and Urban (2007); Zetterberg, Mörtberg, and Balfours (2010).

set. Since different faculty members use different terms for similar topics, we first used single words, instead of terms, as units of analysis for creating the network. For example, if a faculty mentioned "participatory planning" as one of her areas of expertise, we chose the words "participatory" and "planning" as single nodes in the network. We then came up with combined terms through computing modularity and betweenness centrality.

Clusters or subdomains of planning topics were identified by analyzing modularity. Modularity looks for nodes that exhibit stronger connections or greater density compared to the rest of the network. These modes or clusters can be viewed as subdomains or specializations within urban planning research and education. Faculty interests are likely to be associated or complementary to academic training, which encourages specialization to achieve expertise. Network analysis optimizes the placement of nodes based on the number of edges between them. Proximity on the network means that nodes are related, which in this case means that topics near each other are more likely to be mentioned together.

Other conventional multivariate analytical tools such as principal component analysis can also be used for defining clusters in large groups of data sets. However, using network analysis allowed definition of the clusters of the faculties' expertise based on how different types of expertise mentioned by a single faculty is relevant to the other expertise mentioned by the other faculty.

Results

As expected, "Planning" and "Urban" have both the highest degree and betweenness centrality among the 1,150 terms mentioned by planning faculty. High degree centrality indicates that the terms or concepts are core to planning research activities, and betweenness centrality indicates bridges or connections among nodes on the network; but because they are very similar in this case, this suggests a coherent and relatively dense network. We removed these from the top 25 list to more deeply explore the important planning-related domains in the network. If the list with high betweenness centrality were significantly different, then we would expect to see multiple clusters among the core topics being linked by the topics most often lying in between. This is not the case among the top 25 terms. A total of 540 terms act as links, with the remaining 610 being considered non-core or beyond the central cluster of planning topics. These all have a betweenness centrality of zero and were excluded from the list (see the Appendix for the list of topics).

As shown, while single-word terms have been parsed from the *ACSP Guide*, the cluster or modularity analysis allocates terms that are frequently mentioned together like, "community" and "development", in one mode or subdomain. Other examples include terms like "transportation" and "travel", "design" and "sustainable", and "environmental" and "modeling". The clusters of topic titles were consolidated into more summary themes to more easily visualize faculty interests. This process is similar to that of principal component analysis, where statistical attributes are interpreted to create classes or components. The data reduction process (interpretation) is easier in some cases compared to others, especially in cases with many clustered terms.

The results of this analysis suggest that the teaching and research interests of urban planning faculty are represented by a dense and cohesive core. The strength of connections among these 11 core topics is significant and suggests that for a large proportion of urban planning faculty, the focus of teaching and research interests do in fact represent an interconnected knowledge domain. Each group or mode in this domain consists of various interconnected subdomains or topics. Figure 5.1 shows the reduced network that results from the modularity analysis, producing 11 subdomains of planning faculty interests.

The first group, "community, housing and economic development", represents the core of the planning domain. The other topics related to "public policy", "transportation", "land-use management", "sustainable design", "environmental

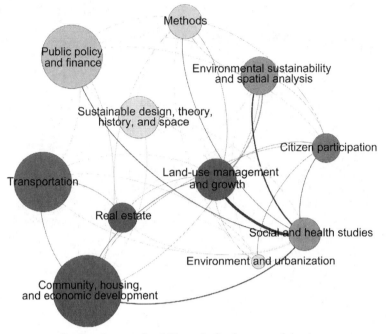

FIGURE 5.1 Reduced network of 11 mode faculty research topics.

sustainability", "methods", "social and health studies", "real estate", and "citizen management" have a major role in shaping the core of the planning domain. However, their effect seems to be lower than that of the first group. Although different areas of planning in these groups are clustered differently from the APA's suggested groups, they cover almost all the APA's suggested groups. The only main difference is that the APA considers "community activism" as one of the main planning areas; however, this does not seem to be a major and important area of research and teaching in the academic environment. It may be that planning academics consider "community activism" as part of "community participation".

The list derived from faculty interests is obviously expansive because research topics tend to be narrow and fall under more general subdomains or specialties. The pattern of topics illustrates the nature of planning and appears to be in general agreement about what is relevant to urban planning research today. The question remains whether urban planning practitioners see these same topics as being central to their professional needs.

Figure 5.1 shows the reduced network based on the 11 identified subdomains or specialties. Each of the specialty areas consists of the topics shown in the Appendix. The result is similar to a semantic analysis that groups terms based on certain relationships related to meaning as well as being co-mentioned faculty interests. Using data from within a single discipline, such as planning, makes this process more reliable than if it were across several disciplines. Adequate sampling, however, will produce more accurate clusters. In this case, the data were drawn from a near complete sample, raising the level of confidence of the results.

Conclusions

The objective of this analysis was to map and identify the knowledge domain of urban planning education in the United States. It has been widely acknowledged that urban planning has many dimensions because cities and regions themselves are dynamic and multifaceted. For this reason, the previous discussion touched on how urban planning has been viewed as dispersed and lacking coherence. An analysis of faculty teaching and research topics was used to identify the specialties that are offered by US planning programs. The data provide a high-resolution analysis because we used the interest areas reported by individual faculty to derive these specialties. The resulting network analysis examined the web of topics that make up the knowledge domain of planning.

The results of the analysis show a relatively compact group of terms to describe planning faculty research and teaching interests. These interest areas have been used as keywords representing the topics important to planning education and, therefore, to planning practice. Overall, 11 subdomains or specialties were identified and were found to cluster tightly as a whole. Had these networks of topics been found to have isolated or disbursed clusters, this would suggest that the domains of urban planning are "too much", drawing in topics or disciplines not well integrated with core planning themes. The results represent a snapshot of current planning research and teaching activities and represent what is happening in the field today. The analysis does not attempt to evaluate whether these are the topics that *should* be emphasized, especially in comparison to those listed by the APA, Dalton (2007), Saghir and Sands (2015), and others. The network shown in Figure 5.1 can be seen as the footprint or knowledge domain of urban planning, which was the primary objective of this analysis. This contributes to previous discussions about the topic by providing an updated analysis as well as applying a different methodology.

Analyses like this are useful for those inside a discipline to get an overall view of current activities. The results also show the interaction between different types of expertise and interests, such as teaching and research efforts being emphasized by planning programs. Planning programs can use this information to identify areas that are *not* being emphasized as well as others. This information can be useful for strategic planning purposes and allocation of resources.

A second way this information can be used is for external purposes. The planning profession suffers from low public visibility and recognition, which has implications for recruitment to planning education as well as the profession. Without more awareness of the profession and degree programs, planning will remain relatively unknown. Many people are not aware of planning's role in shaping places, so efforts to enumerate and highlight the important issues addressed by our discipline can go a long way to raise awareness.

Appendix: Topics for 11-Mode Network

Group #	Topic	Betweenness centrality	Degree	Among the top 20% based on betweenness centrality or degree	Average degree for the group labels*
1	**Community, housing, and economic development****				192.4
	Development	57,889	554	✓	
	Community	26,070	408	✓	
	Economic	14,817	300	✓	
	Housing	11,283	279	✓	
	Regional	7,751	266	✓	
	International	5,876	222	✓	
	Neighborhood	3,433	177	✓	
	Land	2,306	127	✗	
	Markets	1,648	111	✗	
	Poverty	1,400	116	✗	
	Race	1,334	99	✗	
	Labor	967	89	✗	
	Rural	789	112	✗	
	Affordable	784	79	✗	
	Developing	649	73	✗	
	Metropolitan	460	88	✗	
2	**Public policy and finance**				179.7
	Policy	33,290	437	✓	
	Public	25,501	380	✓	
	Finance	4,864	181	✓	
	Local	3,809	156	✗	
	Politics	3,479	160	✗	
	Governance	1,763	144	✗	
	Evaluation	649	95	✗	
	Government	518	83	✗	
	Ethics	439	73	✗	
	Implementation	389	88	✗	

continued ...

Appendix: Continued

Group #	Topic	Betweenness centrality	Degree	Among the top 20% based on betweenness centrality or degree	Average degree for the group labels*
3	**Transportation**				173.0
	Transportation	16,28	302	✓	
	Behavior	2,018	118	✗	
	Travel	1,003	99	✗	
4	**Land-use management and growth**				145.4
	Land use	24,903	380	✓	
	Management	19,160	334	✓	
	Law	4,283	137	✗	
	Disaster	3,480	85	✗	
	Growth	2,123	185	✓	
	Project	1,357	75	✗	
	Property	1,348	87	✗	
	Resource	1,195	108	✗	
	Practice	1,063	132	✗	
	Strategic	1,011	107	✗	
	Mitigation	709	75	✗	
	Natural	604	105	✗	
	Smart	304	81	✗	
5	**Sustainable design, theory, history, and space**				145.3
	Design	28,374	388	✓	
	Theory	12,801	285	✓	
	Sustainable	6,416	258	✓	
	Landscape	6,268	166	✓	
	Geography	5,388	113	✓	
	History	4,541	200	✓	
	Cities	4,482	151	✗	
	Urbanism	3,641	127	✗	
	Physical	3,335	118	✗	
	Preservation	3,149	140	✗	

continued . . .

Appendix: Continued

Group #	Topic	Betweenness centrality	Degree	Among the top 20% based on betweenness centrality or degree	Average degree for the group labels*
	Cultural	2,530	123	✗	
	Environment	2,417	170	✗	
	Space	2,244	134	✗	
	Building	2,123	93	✗	
	Issues	2,047	111	✗	
	Architecture	1,766	85	✗	
	Historic	1,538	121	✗	
	City	1,386	117	✗	
	Built	1,148	120	✗	
	Conservation	1,133	90	✗	
	New	1,021	73	✗	
	Architectural	1,012	77	✗	
	Open	456	83	✗	
6	**Environmental sustainability and spatial analysis**				139.5
	Environmental	23,271	386	✓	
	Analysis	15,730	285	✓	
	GIS	9,371	215	✓	
	Spatial	4,889	171	✓	
	Water	3,903	127	✗	
	Systems	3,179	154	✗	
	Sustainability	2,907	163	✗	
	Change	2,794	174	✗	
	Ecology	2,774	111	✗	
	Technology	2,310	99	✗	
	Process	2,264	136	✗	
	Modeling	2,143	130	✗	
	Science	1,926	92	✗	
	Energy	1,027	99	✗	
	Climate	977	117	✗	

continued ...

Appendix: Continued

Group #	Topic	Betweenness centrality	Degree	Among the top 20% based on betweenness centrality or degree	Average degree for the group labels*
	Resources	904	106	x	
	Participatory	882	94	x	
	Resolution	776	97	x	
	Justice	647	87	x	
	Food	621	78	x	
	Conflict	385	76	x	
	Equity	321	74	x	
7	**Methods**				133.5
	Methods	8,820	235	✓	
	Research	2,965	166	x	
	Quantitative	2,143	116	x	
	Impact	1,522	120	x	
	Qualitative	1,216	83	x	
	Assessment	277	81	x	
8	**Social and health studies**				131.4
	Social	9,900	252	✓	
	Health	5,384	175	✓	
	Studies	3,490	180	✓	
	Human	2,667	114	x	
	Services	2,154	109	x	
	Infrastructure	1,872	147	x	
	Communities	1,214	100	x	
	Gender	393	90	x	
	Demography	289	73	x	
	Redevelopment	231	74	x	
9	**Real estate**				126.0
	Real	2,162	126	x	
	Estate	2,162	126	x	

continued . . .

Appendix: Continued

Group #	Topic	Betweenness centrality	Degree	Among the top 20% based on betweenness centrality or degree	Average degree for the group labels*
10	**Citizen participation**				125.0
	Participation	3,850	176	✓	
	Citizen	301	74	✗	
11	**Environment and Urbanization**				102.8
	Environment	12,643	75	✓	
	Urbanization	2,364	120	✗	
	Political	1,741	124	✗	
	Comparative	895	111	✗	
	Economy	856	112	✗	
	Globalization	608	75	✗	

Notes:

* The average betweenness centrality also correlated with average degree for each group. Ranking the groups based on the average degree is sufficient.

** The group names are mainly based on the labels that are among the top 20% considering their betweenness centrality or degree. For those cases where none or very few of a group's labels are among the top 20%, other group labels are used.

Notes

1. See https://www.planning.org/aboutplanning/whatisplanning.htm.
2. No predefined list of topics is provided in the ACSP survey.

References

Alexander, E. R. (1981). If planning isn't everything, maybe it's something. *Town Planning Review*, 52(2), 131–142.

Alexander, E. R. (2018). How theory links research and practice. 70 years' planning theory: A critical review, in T.W. Sanchez (ed.) *Planning Research and Knowledge*, pp. 7–23. Abingdon, UK: Routledge.

Bastian, M., and Heymann, S. (2009). Gephi: An open source software for exploring and manipulating networks, *International AAAI Conference on Weblogs and Social Media*, pp. 361–362.

Beauregard, R. A. (1990). Bringing the city back in. *Journal of the American Planning Association*, 56(2), 210–215.

Beauregard, R. A. (2001). The multiplicities of planning. *Journal of Planning Education and Research*, 20(4), 437–439.

Birch, E. L. (2001). Practitioners and the art of planning. *Journal of Planning Education and Research*, *20*(4), 407–422.

Boyack, K. W., Klavans, R., and Börner, K. (2005). Mapping the backbone of science. *Scientometrics*, *64*(3), 351–374.

Bruns, A. (2012). How long is a tweet? Mapping dynamic conversation networks on Twitter using Gawk and Gephi. *Information, Communication & Society*, *15*(9), 1323–1351.

Chen, C., and Paul, R. J. (2001). Visualizing a knowledge domain's intellectual structure. *Computer*, *34*(3), 65–71.

Dalton, L. C. (2007). Preparing planners for the breadth of practice: What we need to know depends on whom we ask. *Journal of the American Planning Association*, *73*(1), 35–48.

Ding, Y., Chowdhury, G. G., and Foo, S. (2001). Bibliometric cartography of information retrieval research by using co-word analysis. *Information Processing & Management*, *37*(6), 817–842.

Edwards, M. M., and Bates, L. K. (2011). Planning's core curriculum: Knowledge, practice, and implementation. *Journal of Planning Education and Research*, *31*(2), 172–183.

Friedmann, J. (1996). The core curriculum in planning revisited. *Journal of Planning Education and Research*, *15*(2), 89–104.

Garfield, E. (2004). Historiographic mapping of knowledge domains literature. *Journal of Information Science*, *30*(2), 119–145.

Godschalk, D. R. (2014). A planning life. *Journal of the American Planning Association*, *80*(1), 83–90.

Goldstein, H. A., and Carmin, J. (2006). Compact, diffuse, or would-be discipline? Assessing cohesion in planning scholarship, 1963–2002. *Journal of Planning Education and Research*, *26*(1), 66–79.

Klosterman, R. E. (1985). Arguments for and against planning. *Town Planning Review*, *56*(1), 5–20.

Levy, J. M. (1992). What has happened to planning? *Journal of the American Planning Association*, *58*(1), 81–84.

Linehan, J., Gross, M., and Finn, J. (1995). Greenway planning: Developing a landscape ecological network approach. *Landscape and Urban Planning*, *33*(1–3), 179–193.

Lucy, W. H. (1994). If planning includes too much, maybe it should include more. *Journal of the American Planning Association*, *60*(3), 305–318.

Menaouer, B., Baghdad, A., and Matta, N. (2013). Knowledge mapping evolution guided by data mining. *International Journal of Computer Applications*, *71*(1), 32–39.

Minor, E. S., and Urban, D. L. (2007). Graph theory as a proxy for spatially explicit population models in conservation planning. *Ecological Applications: A Publication of the Ecological Society of America*, *17*(6), 1771–1782.

Morris, S. A., Yen, G., Wu, Z., and Asnake, B. (2003). Time line visualization of research fronts. *Journal of the American Society for Information Science and Technology*, *54*(5), 413–422.

Perloff, H. (1956). Education of city planners: Past, present and future. *Journal of the American Institute of Planners*, *22*(4), 186–217.

Pivo, G. (1989). Specializations, faculty interest, and courses in physical planning subjects at graduate planning schools. *Journal of Planning Education and Research*, *9*(1), 19–27.

Rafols, I., Porter, A. L., and Leydesdorff, L. (2010). Science overlay maps: A new tool for research policy and library management. *Journal of the American Society for Information Science and Technology*, *61*(9), 1871–1887.

Reade, E. (1982). If planning isn't everything . . . A comment. *Town Planning Review*, *53*(1), 65–72.

Rittel, H. W., and Webber, M. M. (1973). Dilemmas in a general theory of planning. *Policy Sciences*, *4*(2), 155–169.

Saghir, C., and Sands, G. (2015). What do city planners need to know? When do they need to know it? *International Journal of Social Science Studies*, *3*(2), 21–29.

Shiffrin, R. M., and Börner, K. (2004). Mapping knowledge domains. *Proceedings of the National Academy of Sciences*, *101*(suppl 1), 5183–5185.

Shin, J. C. (2014). The scholarship of teaching, research, and service, in J. C. Shin and U. Teichler (eds.) *The Future of the Post–Massified University at the Crossroads*, pp. 75–84. Cham, Switzerland: Springer International Publishing.

Stiftel, B. (2009). Planning the paths of planning schools. *Australian Planner*, *46*(1), 38–47.

Wadley, D., and Smith, P. (1998). If planning is about anything, what is it about? *International Journal of Social Economics*, *25*(6/7/8), 1005–1029.

Wildavsky, A. (1973). If planning is everything, maybe it's nothing. *Policy Sciences*, *4*(2), 127–153.

Wilson, R. (1979). *Introduction to Graph Theory* (Longman Gr). Kent, OH: Kent State University Press.

Zetterberg, A., Mörtberg, U. M., and Balfors, B. (2010). Making graph theory operational for landscape ecological assessments, planning, and design. *Landscape and Urban Planning*, *95*(4), 181–191.

6

THE RELATIONSHIP BETWEEN GREEN PLACES AND URBAN SOCIETY

Understanding the Evolution and Integration of City Planning and the Ecological Sciences

Charles Hostovsky

Introduction

Since the birth of the profession in the early 20th century, urban planning has sought to organize and stabilize society through the systematic disposition of land use and rational design. In Canada and the United States planners assumed, until recently, that sufficient greenfield lands have been available to organize and expand urban centers, thus little effort was placed on habitat conservation (FNSGLC 2002). Even though the introduction of environmental impact assessment (EIA) regulations in the 1970s sought to identify and mitigate significant impacts associated with "noxious" urban infrastructure projects (e.g. roads, power plants, waste disposal facilities, sewage treatment, etc.), EIA regulators regarded residential, industrial, commercial, and institutional land development as relatively innocuous, hence exempt from their regulations. EIA tended to examine site- and route-specific impacts while ignoring a more holistic, "big-picture" approach to land use found in municipal comprehensive and official plans (Glasson et al. 1995; Dearden and Mitchell 1998; Hostovsky and Graci 2016). EIA fails to address habitat loss, fragmentation and degradation caused by urbanization and agriculturalization. This history, in part, explains why urban sprawl's consumption of land has been accelerating, with greenfield development doubling in the United States in the period between 1992 and 1997 from the previous ten years (Environmental Protection Agency 2000). By the 1990s less than 10 percent of the landmass in the United States remained in a natural state (Forman 1995), with 85 percent of forest habitat having been permanently destroyed or logged (US Fish & Wildlife

Service 1999). In my region of birth, Southern Ontario, Canada's most populated and fastest-growing region, three-quarters of all natural habitat has been removed and the remaining quarter significantly and negatively altered. Of the 2.2 million hectares in the Lake Erie–Lake Ontario ecoregion in the greater Toronto area – Canada's most biodiverse region and where 25 percent of all Canadians live – only 10 percent contains dense deciduous forest and 2 percent has sparse to mixed forest cover (Riley and Mohr 1994, Crins et al. 2009).

Because of urban sprawl, planning critics have also become concerned with poor urban design, as development that has consumed natural habitat and countryside most commonly took the form of sterilized suburbanization. Underlining how the suburbs can carry a devastating ecological footprint, Kunstler (1993) famously railed against what poorly designed communities they are:

> Cities, towns, and countryside were ravaged equally (by postwar development), as were the lesser orders of things within them—neighborhoods, buildings, streets, farms—and there is scant refuge from the disorders that ensued. . . . [T]his process of destruction, and the realm it spawned, largely became our economy. . . . To me, it is a landscape of scary places, the geography of nowhere, that has simply ceased to be credible human habitat.
> (1993, p. 15)

As a result of these planning concerns, the purpose of this chapter is to better understand the body of literature that interfaces between professional land use planning and ecology, especially in terms of biodiversity. "Place" in this chapter deals specifically with green space, especially natural habitat's interface with anthropogenic development. This paper was originally assembled in 2004 as a tool and resource for my graduate planning students at the University of Toronto (stage 1). John Randolph had just published, in 2003, the first comprehensive planning textbook dedicated to the land use and ecology, *Environmental Land Use Planning and Management*, and I began enthusiastically using this text in class and created an annotated bibliography of the literature that led up to Randolph's text to provide background reading and historical context for my graduate students. Hence, 2003 is used in this writing as a milestone year for environmental planning within our profession. I argue that through the Randolph book, "greenway planning" became fully embraced by planners and accepted as part of our "planners' toolbox", our *modus operandi*.

The emphasis of this chapter is planning at an urban/municipal level, rather than federal/state/provincial parks and wilderness preservation areas. Another objective of this work is to assist with a historical review of ecological research in the planning literature. Beatley (2000) pointed out at the start of this century that only a handful of planning scholars had expertise and training in ecology and conservation. Because I have a baccalaureate degree in Environmental Geography and Biology, I decided to accept this challenge. A literature search was conducted using databases of abstracts in 2004 (stage 2 involved a new literature search from

2004 to 2013). Notwithstanding the emphasis on examining the planning, geography and urban studies literature, as a cross-check I also looked at various environmental and ecological journals to identify the nature of research in the natural sciences that interfaces with municipal land use planning. Although the literature search focused on articles from academic peer-reviewed journals as well as the professional practice journals of the American Planning Association and the Canadian Institute of Planners, I begin this chapter with a background discussion on the seminal ecological research papers and books that influenced environmental planning. An analysis of the themes found within these intersecting bodies of research up until 2004 is presented as stage 1. The chapter concludes with a discussion of the implications of this research and identification of further investigation required in the stage 2 literature search.

To help understand the concepts that are the subject of this discussion, clarification of some terminology commonly used in the field is needed. At the broadest scale, "environmental management" is the means of controlling or guiding human-environmental interactions to protect and enhance human health and welfare and environmental quality; while "environmental planning" applies to the processes of land use planning within the environmental management framework (Randolph 2011 [2003]). In terms of the integration of ecological systems with land use planning, Ahern (2002) points out that there are a wide range of names given to this method of planning, applied inconsistently in the literature. This inconsistent application of terminology is a hindrance to research in the field and part of the rationale for this bibliographic review.

> The net result of this inconsistency in terminology is [that] . . . a tower of Babel is being created . . . [and] this lack of coordination contributes to poor communication and a missed opportunity for new knowledge based on greenway planning and implementation experiments worldwide.
> (Ahern 2002, p. 133)

The roots of these planning methods are based in landscape ecology theory; however, the term "greenway" has become widely accepted in the United States (Ahern 2002; Pollock-Ellwand 2001). Lindsey defined greenways as "linear open spaces or parks along rivers, ridgelines, or historic infrastructure corridors such as canals or railroads that connect people with places and provide opportunities for recreation, conservation, and economic development" (2003, p. 165). Other commonly used terms summarized by Ahern (2002) include: ecological infrastructure/frameworks/networks, open space systems, multiple use modules, habitat networks, wildlife corridors, and ecological restoration. In some jurisdictions government regulations and policies determine the language. For example, Ontario's Planning Act and Provincial Policy Statement identify the term "natural heritage planning", which has become the common vernacular in my home province (OMMAH 2004).

History and Background of Greenway Planning

Early planners were aware of the need for wooded parks and open space in our cities, and every planning student has learned about the City Beautiful Movement at the turn of the 20th century. This paradigm can be traced to Frederick Law Olmsted and Calvert Vaux (Little 1990; Lindsey 2003; Randolph 2011 [2003]). Their 1857 design of New York's Central Park is still considered a masterpiece of the parks movement (see Figure 6.1). Ebenezer Howard's 1898 Garden City design sought to "combine the best of urban and rural – low rents, high wages, beauty of nature, social opportunity; and attract the people to a new, more healthy, more self-fulfilling way of life" (LeGates and Stout 2000, p. 304). However, the parks movement had more to do with aesthetics and the quality of urban life than environmental conservation, especially ecology and biodiversity. Urban design was imposed on built and natural environments rather than being integrated with natural bio-geo-physical systems. In other words natural systems did not provide the framework for the Garden City, although patches of natural systems may have been included.

Aldo Leopold is considered the father of the modern environmental conservation movement, and his 1949 *A Sand County Almanac* did much to make us aware of the need to protect habitat in its natural state. Here he describes his famous "land ethic":

> quit thinking about decent land-use as solely an economic problem. Examine each question in terms of what is ethically and esthetically right, as well as what is economically expedient. A thing is right when it tends to preserve the integrity, stability, and beauty of the biotic community. It is wrong when it tends otherwise.
>
> (1986 [1949], pp. 224–225)

Despite the importance of Leopold's work, species conservation did not receive widespread public appeal until Rachel Carson's book *Silent Spring* was published in 1962. In her fundamental social critique of the religion of science and the dogma of progress, Carson clearly detailed the folly of many human attempts to conquer or sterilize nature:

> The history of life on earth has been a history of interaction between living things and their surroundings. To a large extent, the physical form and the habits of the earth's vegetation and its animal life have been molded by the environment. Considering the whole span of earthly time, the opposite effect, in which life actually modifies its surroundings, has been relatively slight.
>
> (1962, p. 5)

Moreover, Carson popularized Sir Arthur Tansley's term "ecosystem" in the modern vernacular, and she launched the modern environmental movement and

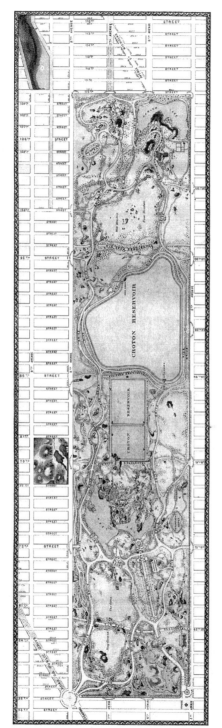

FIGURE 6.1 Olmsted's design of Central Park.[1]

ecofeminism. Carson's efforts led to the creation of the US Environmental Protection Agency and the first credible environmental nongovernmental organization – the Environmental Defense Fund.[2] Carson was one of the first observers to suggest that scientific experts often know little about the environments they are dramatically altering and know especially little about the unseen or long-term effects of their actions.

> The balance of nature is . . . [a] complex, precise, and highly integrated system of relationships between living things which cannot safely be ignored any more than the law of gravity can be defied with impunity by a man perched on the edge of a cliff. The balance of nature is not a *status quo*; it is fluid, ever shifting, in a constant state of adjustment. Man, too, is part of this balance. Sometimes the balance is in his favor; sometimes – and all too often through his own activities – it is shifted to his disadvantage.
>
> (Carson 1962, p. 246)

FIGURE 6.2 Rachel Carson.

No doubt influenced by the ecocentric view of Carson, Ian McHarg became arguably the first well-known "environmental planner" as he spatialized EIA procedures by introducing "constraint" (i.e. overlay) mapping into the planner's toolkit. In municipal comprehensive/official plans, his "design with nature" approach resulted in constraint-based exclusionary planning as a means of avoiding and presumably protecting sensitive habitat. However, McHarg's mapping techniques came to be used in EIA practice for noxious infrastructure facility siting and approvals in and around urban areas, but were not integrated in city comprehensive planning (Hostovsky and Graci 2016). EIA used this reactive and defensive posture to facility-siting based on a simple one-dimensional scale but did little to prevent the problem of fragmentation of the landscape by suburbanization and the resultant biodiversity loss. Further, later research in landscape ecology revealed that isolated patches of habitat are subject to ecological stress that can degrade the size and integrity of that habitat. However, McHarg's simple overlay technique has evolved, especially with the use of remote sensing and GIS, into more sophisticated modeling techniques for ecological conservation, including GAP analysis – identifying "gaps" in the existing protective system that need protection and management (Beatley 2000).

Notwithstanding problems with integrating the tenets of EIA into comprehensive planning, McHarg's important work helped to usher in a paradigm shift – he pointed out that not only are humans not the successful vanquishers of nature, but our fate is determined by the health of the environments in which we live:

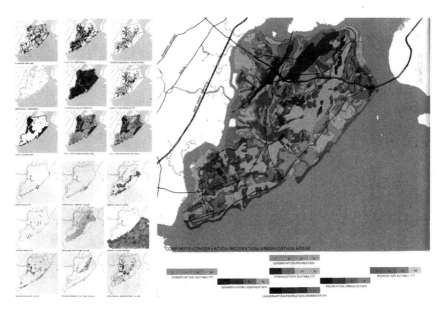

FIGURE 6.3 McHarg's overlay mapping technique, a reactive model of environmental planning.[3]

man's life, in sickness and in health, is bound up with the forces of nature, and that nature, so far from being opposed and conquered, must rather be treated as an ally and a friend, whose ways must be understood, and whose counsel must be respected.

(1969, p. vi)

McHarg saw the main problems associated with the values of anthropomorphic human beings who seek conquest over nature. Yet, all animals and humans are plant parasites completely dependent upon photosynthesis for their survival. Thus, the universe is biocentric not anthropocentric. While Carson was primarily concerned with revealing the madness of our civilization's careless and widespread use of chemicals, Leopold and McHarg linked the need to preserve our natural environment to urban development. Highlighting that humans are a species dependent upon their environment like any other, McHarg affirmed that it is "essential to understand the city as a form, derived in the first instance from geological and biological evolution, existing as a sum of natural processes and adapted by man" (1969, p. 175).

In the 1970s the US Endangered Species Act (1973) was primarily responsible for driving ecological conservation.[4] However, as Beatley (2000) points out, while the Act has been effective in stabilizing and improving listed species, it is a reactive approach leading to "emergency room conservation" in only the most dire of circumstances. In the 1980s the emphasis began to change from a reactive habitat protection posture to the more proactive and holistic concept of biodiversity that emphasizes spatial connectivity of fragmented habitat. Building on the early theories of island biogeography (MacArthur and Wilson 1967), the original work on "landscape ecology" was presented in Forman and Godron's (1986) book, which focused on the distribution patterns of landscape elements, including the flow of flora, fauna, energy, water and mineral cycling, and the changes in landscape ecology over time.

In this author's humble opinion, the most important contribution to progressing the planning discipline from parks planning to ecology-based greenway planning is the research of biologist Reed Noss (1983, 1987; Noss and Harris 1986). Noss and his colleagues explored one of the main problems of urbanization – habitat fragmentation – and they looked at mitigation strategies through their analysis of ecological core areas, corridors, networks, and buffer zones. Ross also highlighted the importance of native flora and fauna and the need to stem the tide of invasive alien species, a consideration largely ignored in urban parks and greenspace planning. Thus Leopold, McHarg, Forman, Godron, Noss, and Harris shifted the emphasis from simplistic notions of green places – from "quantity" (i.e. number of hectares of protected habitat) to the more sophisticated notion of ecological "quality" (i.e. genetic and landscape biodiversity) with an emphasis on the health and resilience of native species.

Biodiversity and the importance of habitat protection became a main focus of sustainability politics and research in the early to mid-1990s. The Convention on Biological Diversity[5] at the 1992 Earth Summit in Rio de Janeiro created momentum, encouraging the protection of habitat at the urban scale. Ecologists and environmentalists in general were concerned about the impact of urbanization and changes in land use on the natural environment. Prior to the 1990s, the planning profession may have been more focused on built form, municipal politics and patterns of urbanization and suburban settlements. As this chapter demonstrates, in the mid-1990s some cities began to more earnestly protect and connect their green areas; for example, the consulting planning work of my colleagues and I in Canada's capital city, Ottawa. The emphasis in the Ottawa official plan was on "connectivity", as this concept is integral to biodiversity resilience (Hostovsky et al. 1995).

As a result of the work of the aforementioned ecology-minded pioneers, planners began to shift their efforts from conserving land in the form of isolated and unconnected parks and corridors to providing larger tracts of open space in the form of "green" connective infrastructure. Planners moved from a reactive EIA model, based on protectionism and mitigation of impacts, to a more proactive approach that, by design, incorporated natural habitat into municipal plans. Environmentalist and historian Charles Little's *Greenways for America* (1990) was the first comprehensive account of the greenways movement. Little overviewed many greenway plans that, up until that time, had improved ecological integrity, stimulated local economies, and protected green space for millions of Americans. Other greenway guidebooks of note include those by Schwarz, Flink and Searns

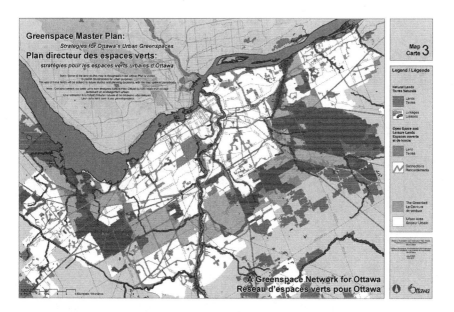

FIGURE 6.4 City of Ottawa, concept of greenway connectivity developed by the author and his associates in 1995 for the Official Plan.[6]

(an environmentalist, a landscape architect and a planner) and Smith and Hellmund (an ecologist and a landscape architect), both published in 1993. Ahern reviewed these early greenway manuals and offered his definition for greenways: "Networks of land containing linear elements that are planned, designed and managed for multiple purposes including ecological, recreational, cultural, aesthetic, or other purposes compatible with the concept of sustainable land use" (2002, p. 42).

A special issue of *Landscape and Urban Planning* in 1995 devoted to greenways (Vol. 33, No. 1–3), later published as a book, further helped city planners better understand places and society in terms of biodiversity (Lindsey 2003). So, by the late 1990s, some state and provincial authorities had begun to create regulations and publish guidelines on how to promote this better understanding of greenways and biodiversity in municipal planning.

Ontario, Canada Greenway Planning Approach

Commencing in 1996, the Ontario Ministry of Municipal Affairs and Housing (OMMAH) issued their Provincial Policy Statement (PPS). The PPS was enabled by the Planning Act, and it set the tone for greenway planning in Ontario. Section 2.3.1 of the PPS directed municipalities to integrate Noss's concepts of ecology into land use planning, as follows:

2.3.1 Natural heritage features and areas will be protected from incompatible development.

  a   Development and site alteration will not be permitted in:

   - significant wetlands south and east of the Canadian Shield; and
   - significant portions of the habitat of endangered and threatened species.

  b   Development and site alteration may be permitted in:

   - fish habitat;
   - significant wetlands in the Canadian Shield2;
   - significant woodlands south and east of the Canadian Shield2;
   - significant valleylands south and east of the Canadian Shield2;
   - significant wildlife habitat; and
   - significant areas of natural and scientific interest
   - if it has been demonstrated that there will be no negative impacts on the natural features or the ecological functions for which the area is identified.

 2.3.2 Development and site alteration may be permitted on adjacent lands to a) and b) if it has been demonstrated that there will be no negative impacts on the natural features or on the ecological functions for which the area is identified.

2.3.3 The diversity of natural features in an area, and the natural connections between them should be maintained, and improved where possible.
(OMMAH 2007)

Therefore, the PPS under clause "a" protected important species. Clauses "b" and "c" introduced the concept of environmental impact assessment (EIA) to land use planning, formerly only associated with large-scale projects such as power plants, highways, etc. under regulations such as the US National Environmental Policy Act (NEPA) and the Canadian and Ontario Environmental Assessment acts (Environmental Protection Agency 2016; Hostovsky and Graci 2016). The emphasis under the PPS moved greenway planning away from the "parks" approach to an ecology-based approach using ecological functions and natural connections. Hence biodiversity became a main theme in land use planning legislation in Ontario in 1996. Municipalities began integrating Noss's ecology-based approach into their Official Plans, and for the first time development projects – from a single new house on a small lot through to large industrial and commercial complexes, adjacent to or containing natural heritage features (e.g. significant wetlands) – required a scoped EIA in support of Official Plan and zoning amendments.

Unfortunately, the PPS on Natural Heritage was still a "piecemeal" approach to planning, examining individual Official Plans and individual development projects without regard to neighboring jurisdictions. But ecology does not respect mapped political boundaries, so the weakness in the PPS statement was that it did not examine "big picture" land use planning and biodiversity on a regional or provincial scale. However, in 2005 Ontario addressed this weakness and introduced the state of the art in greenway planning found in the newly proclaimed Ontario Greenbelt Plan Act and partner Places to Grow Act (OMMAH 2017). The largest municipal greenway plan in the world, the plan covers 1.8 million acres of land, primarily farmland and natural habitat, surrounding the city of Toronto in Southern Ontario (Ali 2008; Macdonald and Keil 2012; Newbold and Scott 2013; Haley 2015). Almost all of this land is protected from future development, except for 338,000 acres between the urban areas.

Greenway Planning in Textbooks

In the late 1990s and early 2000s, published textbooks indicated a synthesis in the disciplines of ecology, landscape architecture and planning. First, Dramstad et al.'s (1996) text describes 55 principles of landscape ecology that involve "patches, edges/boundaries, corridors/connectivity, and mosaics" (p. 69). The work reviews a range of design responses to landscape change. Landscape architect Sheila Peck's (1998) textbook looks at preserving the ecological integrity of open spaces and reserves. She argues that planners need to be guided by seven steps: characterizing biodiversity, developing conservation priorities, incorporating change and disturbance, maintaining connectivity, assessing design priorities, collecting baseline data, and adaptive management.

As previously mentioned, the first land-use-planning-based and planner-written textbook came via John Randolph's (2011 [2003]) *Environmental Land Use Planning and Management*. I consider this work a milestone as the text provides evidence that environmentalism, ecology, conservation, and biodiversity had become fully integrated with the teaching and practice of municipal land use planning. His work presents a comprehensive approach to issues of land use planning and the environment. He synthesizes environmental science, ecology, civil/environmental engineering, and GIS technologies, and the text is a state-of-the-art resource for practicing planners and students. Hence this research identifies 2003 as a milestone year for the planning profession. Again, I argue that the publication of *Environmental Land Use Planning and Management* indicates that greenway planning, including an emphasis on habitat and biodiversity protection, had become fully embraced by planners and accepted as part of our "planners' toolbox" and our *modus operandi*. As a profession, we moved beyond open-space and parks planning for recreation to an ecology-based model for sustainability.

Stage 1 Research Methodology

In order to examine the evolution from parks planning to natural heritage planning, I conducted a literature review focused on journals in abstract databases from the disciplines of planning and the environmental sciences up until 2003; that is, up until the publication of the Randolph textbook. These journals concentrate on planning, landscape, biodiversity, ecology, and the intersection between planning and ecology. Non-refereed trade magazines and government publications were not examined because they are unlikely to publish theoretical research and/or articles addressing the application of theory in practice. However, the search did incorporate planning journals and publications from professional planning institutions, such as *Planning* (American Planning Association) and *Plan Canada* (Canadian Institute of Planners) plus the *Ontario Planning Journal* (Ontario Professional Planners Institute).[7]

Other journals examined in stage 1 included those covering landscape ecology, land use policy and urban design, ecosystems and bioscience, conservation, and restorative and applied ecology as well as planning and environmental management. A wide lens was employed because many professionals had a vital role to play in the development and application of greenway planning until 2003. The scan of computerized databases available in the university library system employed keywords such as: natural heritage (plans), land inventories, environmental inventory, biodiversity, greenbelt, and greenway planning. As the journal articles dated back no further than the 1980s, it is clear that this field is relatively new and very little planning-specific work had been published prior to that decade.

The main intention was to uncover how planners and other practitioners were developing greenway plans and putting those plans to work in the field. As the discussion which follows this section reviews, the vast majority of greenway planning until 2003 took place within the Western world (North America, Europe, plus Australia and New Zealand), but it was conducted by a fairly wide range of professionals. The search was designed to eliminate issues relating primarily to aquatic ecosystems (e.g. watercourses, watersheds) or anything primarily relating to air quality, which were deemed too distinct from the central focus on terrestrial land use planning.

Originally these articles were annotated to create a student resource, but these annotations would be too lengthy for a book chapter. I categorized the articles according to the following subject matter (some articles had two or three areas of focus): (1) biodiversity, (2) rural versus urban, (3) rationale/philosophy, (4) planning tools, and (5) problems or obstacles to successful greenway plan development and implementation. Articles that addressed the first category, biodiversity, tackled its importance to land use planning, how traditional techniques generally excluded it, and how best to utilize new tools to ensure biodiversity in rural and urban land development. Very few articles concentrated on the second issue, the distinction between rural and urban planning environments. The third issue, the rationale behind greenway planning, refers to articles that dealt with the theoretical underpinnings of the movement to include natural heritage in planning as well as the evolution of conservation and ecology theory in general. Zoning, mapping, GIS, and statistical modeling were addressed in the articles on the fourth category, planning tools, while those that tackled the fifth category, obstacles to development and implementation, discussed limitations around data collection and certain forms of technology and, to a much lesser extent, political interference.

Papers were categorized according to the year in which articles were published and the geographical area the research examined in order to identify distinct chronological and geographic trends.

Stage 1 Analysis

A total of 75 journal articles were identified in *stage 1* (listed in the Appendix). Of those 75 articles, excluding non-refereed papers and biology articles from the 1980s, a total of 56 articles appeared in the various refereed journals, with the tally by year as follows:

- 1990 – 1
- 1991 – 0
- 1992 – 1
- 1993 – 1
- 1994 – 1
- 1995 – 12
- 1996 – 7
- 1997 – 1
- 1998 – 6
- 1999 – 6
- 2000 – 7
- 2001 – 5

- 2002 – 1
- 2003 – 7

After just a "trickle" during the early 1990s, clearly 1995 was an important year, having the highest number of papers published of any years covered in stage 1. My speculation is that the World Summit on Sustainable Development held in Rio de Janeiro in 1992 acted as a catalyst for greenway planning. The Summit created, among other agreements, the 1994 Convention on Biological Diversity, an international legally binding treaty. Of the 56 papers, 8 dealt with general methods of greenway planning but did not review geographically based case studies.

The distribution of the 48 case-study-based articles is as follows:

1. United States of America – 21
2. Canada – 13
3. United Kingdom – 7
4. Korea – 2
5. Spain – 2
6. China – 1
7. Holland – 1
8. Japan – 1

Cities and regions in the English-speaking, Western, developed world – predominantly the United States, Canada and the United Kingdom – were the main focus of research for the vast majority of articles. About half of those articles focusing on Western examples discussed Canadian areas, primarily within Ontario. Likely this overrepresenation of Ontario planning can be attributed to the early establishment of the aforementioned provincial biodiversity policies and the early implementation of the capital city of Ottawa's natural heritage plan (Hostovsky et al. 1995) as well as the expansive regional Niagara Escarpment Plan (Louis and Pim 1995).

The majority of articles that focused on regions, counties or cities within the United States examined greenways and open space conservation projects in two main geographic areas, the eastern states (New England, North Carolina, Georgia), and the western states (Washington, Oregon, California, Arizona) with the notable exceptions of Texas, Illinois, Pennsylvania, Michigan and Colorado. The few articles focusing on cases in other countries examined areas within the Netherlands, South Korea, Spain, Japan and China. No case studies were found in any low-income developing countries.

Next the major themes identified in stage 1 while looking for disciplinary differences and similarities are discussed.

Themes in Planning Journals

In planning journals, greenway planning increasingly received attention up until 2003. Interestingly, the main themes that were prevalent in planning journals include biodiversity, greenway planning rationale, planning tools and greenway planning problems. As would be expected, the majority of the articles on greenway planning in planning journals focused on planning tools (24 of the articles identified). The planning tools discussed in the various journals include a wide spectrum of traditional land use planning tools, such as integrating green space and greenways into comprehensive land use plans and zoning, as well as nontraditional tools, such as counterfactual planning (Bae and Jun 2003) and groundwater protection zoning (Tarlock 1993).

The second most frequently discussed topic in planning journal articles in stage 1 was problems or limitations in creating greenways (13 articles). The limitations described in the articles varied widely; however, they could be grouped into three sub-themes: lack of integration of greenway goals with zoning and higher-level government policies; inability or disinterest on the part of the public; and the gap between landscape and ecological knowledge and planning with urban design and zoning.

The third most frequently debated topic was biodiversity. I had expected more discussion in this area because of the 1992 Convention on Biological Diversity, but only 13 articles mentioned or discussed biological diversity. Perhaps many of the articles assumed that the rationale for greenway planning was increasing the level of biodiversity. What is also surprising is that planning journals such as *Plan Canada* and *Landscape and Urban Planning* contained some discussion of biodiversity in the early 1990s – before biodiversity became a Rio Convention "hot topic".

Overall, planning journals discussed that greenways needed to be multifunctional in order to operate successfully. According to Searns (1995), there are three generations of greenways. Generation 1 greenways started out as simple open space areas that acted as public amenities along boulevards. Generation 2 greenways are more complex in that they included trails and access to rivers, lakes or other urban natural areas. Generation 3 greenways are the most complex, attempting to address multiple uses. These evolved multipurpose greenways address various needs such as the need for public green amenities that include trails and contribute to the aesthetics of an urban area, but also go beyond these characteristics to meet the need to create habitat for wildlife (i.e. improve biodiversity). Other articles, such as those by Conine et al. (2004) and Fabos (2004), reinforce Searns' observations of greenways being valued for their environmental benefits in addition to their anthropocentric advantages.

Themes in Environmental Journals

As previously mentioned, the work of Reed Noss (1983, 1987; Noss and Harris 1986) set the tone for biodiversity and planning by introducing land use planners to the problems of habitat fragmentation and mitigation strategies. These strategies include the identification of ecological core areas, corridors/linkages, networks, and buffer zones. I consider this work seminal and pick up the analysis in the 1990s, when other researchers had taken note of their call for action. Thus the following analysis of 28 articles excludes the three papers by Noss in the 1980s.

Practical quantitative tools, including modeling techniques and those used in specific ecologically based projects, was the prevailing topic of the articles (49%)[8] found in the environmental journals. A majority of these papers (12 out of 16) described the development and use of various models by which to calculate, map, and forecast the distribution of certain types of land uses, flora and fauna species, and/or the interaction of these three entities.

The second most frequently discussed topic (24%) up to 2004 were problems facing greenway planners, biologists, engineers, and other practitioners in the field. First among these difficulties were concerns over the nature and restrictions of data collection, followed closely by technological and modeling limitations. The bulk of these articles (5 out of 8) discussed the results of surveys these authors had administered to planning practitioners. Interestingly, despite Ross, biodiversity was only the third most frequently presented issue (15%) from ecologists. Finally, three papers probed the philosophy or rationale behind the greenway movement or specific projects, while only one essay examined the differences and possible tensions between urban and rural environments in terms of greenway planning.

Hence the environmental journals literature reveals some interesting patters in terms of dominant and overlooked themes. For example, despite published research in the 1980s on biodiversity, our planning literature search found no articles on biodiversity until 1998, likely because the 1994 Convention of Biodiversity popularized the term much in the same way Rachel Carson popularized the term "ecology" in the 1960s. Moreover, political and funding concerns were not mentioned in a single environmental journal to 2004. I suspect that the role of natural scientists in greenway planning is not politicized in the manner we as urban planners are traditionally accustomed to.

Literature Search Conclusions

Greenway planning has a 15-year history in the research literature before our planning discipline formalized the field in the 2003 Randolph text. Evidenced by the number of articles recovered in the stage 1 literature search, more attention was given to our topic in the planning literature than the environmental literature. Overall, stage 1 of the evolution of greenway planning documents the benefits of its methods, identifies planning tools to conserve, create, and link current green infrastructure, and highlights barriers to effective greenway design and creation. Greenways evolved from performing a singular recreation (i.e. park) function, and by 2004 greenways were expected to enhance biodiversity, raise property values, perform various natural habitat roles, regulate urban hydrology, and reduce urban heat islands, to name a few. Through this research planners developed a better understanding of greenways as they evolved and took on multiple functions, with a growing emphasis on ecology and biodiversity that was expected to counteract the forces of hard-surface suburbanization and sprawl.

Stage 2 Methodology

The joint AESOP-ACSP 2013 conference acted as an incentive to conduct stage 2 of this research – essentially, updating the literature search to the present. While stage 1 examined publications from various disciplines, including the natural sciences, a literature search using the GEOBASE abstract database was used in stage 2 to identify articles in planning, urban geography, and urban studies journals. The rationale for limiting the scope of the research to planning journals is based on the identification of 2003 as a watershed year for greenway planning in our profession. While stage 1 was exploratory in nature, stage 2 will take the form of a meta-analysis of the greenway planning literature, which I hope to conduct and finalize in the near future. I present only some raw data (Table 6.1) and initial observations in this chapter.

Between 2003 and 2013, a total of 127 published journal articles were found on greenway planning in the planning, geography and urban studies journals – an order of magnitude more than the previous two decades. Science and engineering journal articles were not included unless they specifically identified land use planning as the focus. Table 6.1 provides a chronological and geographic record of the 111 papers found in stage 2 that include studies focusing on a particular area as well as the 48 place-based refereed papers in the stage 1 literature search (pre-2004). Indeed, as the distribution reveals, the geographic coverage of the research and the time period from which the studies were produced are narrow.

It is clear that there has been a significant increase in the number of planning journal articles referring to greenway planning since 2003. It is also clear that in the second decade expanded the geographic scope of greenway planning, moving from exclusively Western countries to include the new economic power of China (n = 12 since 2003) as well as south Asia, southeast Asia, Africa, eastern Europe and South America.

Future research should address the new geography of rapid global urbanization and the role of greenways in terms of changing planning paradigms around the world.

TABLE 6.1 Refereed Place-Based Journal Articles on Greenway Planning by Country and Year

Country	1990	1991	1992	1993	1994	1995	1996	1997	1998	1999	2000	2001	2002	2003	2004	2005	2006	2007	2008	2009	2010	2011	2012	2013	Total
USA	1			1	1	5	2	1	2	2	2	1	1	3	6		4	2	1	4	2	4	2	3	49
Canada			1			5	2			1	1	2						2	1	6		2	1		25
UK							1		2	1	3					1	2	2	1		4		2		19
Argentina																							1		1
Australia															1						1				2
Bangladesh																							1		1
Brazil																	1		1						2
China														1		3	4	2				2			12
Denmark																		1							1
Egypt																					1	1			2
Europe															1						1	2			4
France																					1				1
Germany																1	1								2

Holland	1												1
Italy						2						1	4
Japan		1				1				1			2
Korea	1			1					1		2		5
Latvia								1					1
Portugal					1	1				1			3
Russia							1			1			2
Singapore				1									1
Slovenia										1			1
Spain			1								1		3
Sweden					1			1		1			2
Switzerland									1				1
Taiwan						1							1
Thailand							1						1
Turkey						1				1			2
Vietnam								1		1			2

Appendix: Greenway Bibliography (1990–2003)

Ahern, Jack. 1995. Greenways as a planning strategy. *Landscape and Urban Planning* 33 (1–3): 131–155.

Alario, Margarita. 2000. Urban and ecological planning in Chicago: Science, policy and dissent. *Journal of Environmental Planning and Management* 43 (4): 489–504.

Antrop, M. 2001. The language of landscape ecologists and planners: A comparative content analysis of concepts used in landscape ecology. *Landscape and Urban Planning* 55 (3): 163–173.

Arendt, Randall. 1998. Connecting the dots. *Planning* 64 (8): 20–23.

Bacon, P. J., Cain, J. D., and Howard, D. C. 2002. Belief network models of land manager decisions and land use change. *Journal of Environmental Management* 65 (1): 1–23.

Bae, C.-H. C., and Jun, M.-J. 2003. Counterfactual planning: What if there had been no greenbelt in Seoul? *Journal of Planning Education and Research* 22 (4): 374–383.

Barker, G. M. A., and Box, J. D. 1998. Statutory local nature reserves in the United Kingdom. *Journal of Environmental Planning and Management* 41 (5): 629–642.

Beatley, Timothy. 2000. Preserving biodiversity: Challenges for planners. *Journal of the American Planning Association* 66 (1): 5–20.

Bousfield, John. 2004. One planner's perspective on Bills 26 & 27. *The Ontario Planning Journal* 19 (2): 5–8.

Broberg, Len. 2003. Conserving ecosystems locally: A role for ecologists in land-use planning. *Bioscience* 53 (7): 670–674.

Bruff, Garreth E., and Wood, Adrian P. 2000. Local sustainable development: Land-use planning's contribution to modern local government. *Journal of Environmental Planning and Management* 43 (4): 519–539.

Bryant, Rebecca. 1997. Earth tones. *Planning* 63 (1): 19–21.

Conine, Askley, Xiang, Wei-Ning, Young, Jeff, and Whitley, David. 2004. Planning for multi-purpose greenways in Concord, North Carolina. *Landscape and Urban Planning* 68 (2–3): 271–287.

Cort, Cheryl A. 1996. A survey of the use of natural heritage data in land-use planning. *Conservation Biology* 10 (2): 632–637.

Crist, Patrick. 1996. Helping habitats. *Planning* 62 (7): 16.

Crist, Patrick J., Kohley, Thomas W., and Oakleaf, John. 2000. Assessing land-use impacts on biodiversity using an expert systems tool. *Landscape Ecology* 15 (1): 47–62.

de Pablo, C. L., de Agar, Martin, Barturen, R., Nicholas, J. P., and Pineda, F. D. 1994. Design of an informational system for environmental design and management. *Journal of Environmental Management* 40 (3): 231–243.

Dougan, Jim. 2003. Natural heritage after the Moraine. *The Ontario Planning Journal* 18 (1): 22–24.

Erickson, Donna L. 1995. Rural land use and land cover change. *Land Use Policy* 12 (3): 223–236.

Fabos, J. G. 2004. Greenway planning in the United States: Its origins and recent case studies. *Landscape and Urban Planning* 68 (2–3): 321–342.

Ferguson, Bruce K. 1996. The maintenance of landscape health in the midst of land use change. *Journal of Environmental Management* 48 (4): 387–395.

Gordon, David L. A., and Tamminga, Ken. 2002. Large-scale traditional neighbourhood development and pre-emptive ecosystem planning: The Markham Experience, 1998–2001. *Journal of Urban Design* 7 (3): 321–340.

Hales, Richard. 2000. Land use development planning and the notion of sustainable development. *Journal of Environmental Planning and Management* 43 (1): 99–121.

Hostovsky, Chuck, Miller, David, and Keddy, Cathy. 1995. The Natural Environment Systems Strategy: Protecting Ottawa-Carleton's ecological areas. *Plan Canada* 35 (6): 26–29.

Jim, C. Y., and Chen, Sophia S. 2003. Comprehensive greenspace planning based on landscape ecology principles in compact Nanjing City, China. *Landscape and Urban Planning* 65 (3): 95–116.

Johnson, A. K. L., Cramb, R. A., and McAlpine, J. R. 1994. Integrated land use evaluation as an aid to land use planning in Northern Australia. *Journal of Environmental Management* 40 (2): 139–154.

Jones, Deanne, Cocklin, Chris, and Cutting, Marjorie. 1995. Institutional and landowner perspectives on wetland management in New Zealand. *Journal of Environmental Management* 45 (2): 143–161.

Katz, Geoffrey E. 1995. Natural areas in city, suburb and town and the practical application of landscape ecology. *Plan Canada* 35 (6) 18, 21.

Knack, Ruth Eckdish. 1998. Garden cities. *Planning* 64 (6): 4.

Lee, Chang-Moo. 1999. An intertemporal efficiency test of a greenbelt: Assessing the economic impacts of Seoul's greenbelt. *Journal of Planning Education and Research* 19 (1): 41–52.

Lindsey, Greg. 1999. Use of urban greenways: Insights from Indianapolis. Landscape and Urban Planning 4 (2–3): 145–157. (R, S)

Lindsey, Greg. 2003. Sustainability and urban greenways: Indicators in Indianapolis. Journal of the American Planning Association 69 (2): 165–180. (R, S)

Lindsey, Greg, and Knaap, Gerrit. 1999. Willingness to pay for urban greenway projects. Journal of the American Planning Association 65 (3): 297–313. (R)

Lindsey, G., Maraj, Maltie, and Kuan, SonCheong. 2001. Access, equity, and urban greenways: An exploratory investigation. Professional Geographer 53 (3): 332–346. (R, S, T)

Livey, John. 1995. Urbanizing York Region. *Plan Canada* 35: 25–28.

Louis, Cecil, and Pim, Linda. 1995. The Niagara Escarpment: Planning for environmental protection. *Plan Canada* (Nov.) 39–40.

Marshall, Robert, and Smith, Catherine. 1999. Planning for nature conservation: The role and performance of English district local authorities in the 1990s. *Journal of Environmental Planning and Management* 4 (5): 691–706.

Martin-Duque, Jose, Pedraza, Javier, Sanz, Miguel, Bodoque, Jose, Godfrey, Andrew, Diez, Andres, and Corrasco, Rosa. 2003. Landform classification for land use planning in developed areas: An example in Segovia Province. *Environmental Management* 32 (4): 488–498.

Matusz, Michael, and Campbell, Ashley. 1994. Planners strive for sustainability. *Planning* 60 (4): 32.

Nakamura, Toshihiko, and Short, Kevin. 2001. Land-use planning and distribution of threatened wildlife in a city of Japan. *Landscape and Urban Planning* 53 (1–4): 1–15.

Naveh, Z. 1998. Ecological and cultural landscape restoration and the cultural evolution towards a post-industrial symbiosis between human society and nature. *Restoration Ecology* 6 (2): 135–143.

Newman, Peter. 1996. Greening the city. The ecological and human dimensions of the city can be part of town. *Planning Alternatives Journal* 22 (2): 10–16.

Nicol, Chris, and Blake, Rob. 2000. Classification and use of open space in the context of increasing urban capacity. *Planning Practice and Research* 15 (3): 193–210.

Noss, R. F. 1983. A regional landscape approach to maintain diversity. *BioScience* 33 (11): 700–706.

Noss, R. F., and Harris, L. D. 1986. Nodes, networks, and MUMs: Preserving diversity at all scales. *Environmental Management* 10 (3): 299–309.

Odell, Eric A., Theobald, D. M., and Knight, R. L. 2003. Incorporating ecology into land use planning: the songbird's case for clustered development. *Journal of the American Planning Association* 69 (1): 72–79.

Peccol, Elisabetta, Bird, A. Chris, and Brewer, Tim R. 1996. GIS as a tool for assessing the influence of countryside designations and planning policies on landscape change. *Journal of Environmental Management* 47 (4): 355–367.

Pollock-Ellwand, Nancy. 2001. Landscape policy and planning practice: The gap in understanding, Ontario, Canada. *Landscape Research* 26 (2): 99–118.

Quong, S. P., Larry, R., Martin, G., and Murphy, S. 1999. Ecological rehabilitation: A new challenge for planners. *Plan Canada* 39 (4): 19–21.

Quon, S. P., Larry, R., Martin, G., and Murphy, S. D. 2001. Effective planning and implementation of ecological rehabilitation projects: A case study of the regional municipality of Waterloo (Ontario, Canada). *Environmental Management* 27 (3): 421–433.

Recatal, L., Ive, J. R., Baird, I. A., Hamilton, N., and Sanchez, J. 2000. Land-use planning in the Valencian Mediterranean region: Using LUPIS to generate issue relevant plans. *Journal of Environmental Management* 59 (3): 169–184.

Ricketts, T., and Imhoff, M. 2003. Biodiversity, urban areas, and agriculture: Locating priority ecoregions for conservation. *Conservation Ecology* 8 (2): Article 1. www.consecol.org/vol8/iss2/art1/

Robinson, Paul A. 1995. Protecting the environment in a rapidly urbanizing community. *Plan Canada* (Nov.): 22–25.

Robinson, Robert A., and Sutherland, William J. 2002. Post-war changes in arable farming and biodiversity in Great Britain. *Journal of Applied Ecology* 39 (1): 157–176.

Ryder, Barbara A. 1995. Greenway planning and growth management: Partners in conservation? *Landscape and Urban Planning* 33 (1–3): 417–432.

Rydin, Yvonne. 1998. Land use planning and environmental capacity: Reassessing the use of regulatory policy tools to achieve sustainable development. *Journal of Environmental Planning and Management* 41 (6): 749–765.

Salvesen, David. 1993. Mitigation "banking" proposed to help save wetlands. *Planning* 59 (9): 26.

Salvesen, David. 1995. Banking on wetlands. *Planning* 61 (2): 11–15.

Schneider, R. R., Stelfox, J. B., Boutin, S., and Wasel, S. 2003. Managing the cumulative impacts of land uses in the Western Canadian Sedimentary Basin: A modeling approach. *Conservation Ecology* 7 (1): Article 8. www.consecol.org/vol7/iss1/art8/

Scott, Richard. 1996. Canada's Capital Greenbelt: Reinventing a 1950s plan. *Plan Canada* 36 (5): 19–21.

Searns, Robert M. 1995. The evolution of greenways as an adaptive urban landscape form. *Landscape and Urban Planning* 33 (1–3): 65–80.

Smith, Barry E. and Haid, Susan. 2004. The rural-urban connection: Growing together in Greater Vancouver. *Plan Canada* (Spr.): 36–39.

Sole, Rocard V., Alonso, David, and Saldana, Joan. 2004. Habitat fragmentation and biodiversity collapse in neutral communities. *Ecological Complexity* 1 (1): 65–75.

Tamminga, Ken. 1996. Restoring biodiversity in the urbanizing regions: Toward pre-emptive ecosystem planning. *Plan Canada* 36 (4): 10–15.

Tarlock, A. Dan. 1993. Local government protection of biodiversity: What is its niche? *The University of Chicago Law Review* 60 (2): 555–601.

Taylor, James, Paine, Cecelia, and FitzGibbon, John. 1995. From greenbelt to greenways: Four Canadian case studies. *Landscape and Urban Planning* 33 (1–3): 47–64.

Theobald, D. M. and Hobbs, N. T. 2002. A framework for evaluating land use planning alternatives: Protecting biodiversity on private land. *Conservation Ecology* 6 (1): Article 5. www.consecol.org/vol6/iss1/art5/

Tibbetts, John. 1995. An endangered species of law. *Planning* 61 (9): 16.

Tong, Susanna T. Y., and Chen, Wenli. 2002. Modeling the relationship between land use and surface water quality. *Journal of Environmental Management* 66 (4): 377–393.

Town, Mark A. 1998. Open space conservation in urban environments: Lessons from Thousand Oaks, California. *Urban Ecosystems* 2 (2–3): 85–101.

Tyler, Mary-Ellen. 1999. Ecological planning in an age of myth-information. *Plan Canada* 40 (1): 20–21.

van Lier, Hubert N. 1998. The role of land use planning in sustainable rural systems. *Landscape and Urban Planning* 41 (2): 83–91.

Van Patter, M., and Hilts, S. 1990. Natural heritage protection: Voluntary stewardship or planning control. *Plan Canada* 30 (5): 20–28.

Wilkinson, Chris, and Eagles, Paul. 2003. The OMB's record on natural heritage. *The Ontario Planning Journal* 18 (6): 19–20.

Wilkinson, Chris, and Eagles, Paul. 2003. Natural Heritage Planning in Ontario: The OMB's treatment of PPS. *The Ontario Planning Journal* 18 (5): 31–33.

Notes

1 See: www.fredericklawolmsted.com/central.html
2 See: www.environmentaldefense.org
3 See: http://nvcogct.org/content/maps-0
4 Canada did not pass the federal Species at Risk Act until 2003; previously it was a provincial responsibility (e.g. Ontario Endangered Species Act, 1971).
5 The United States is not a signatory to the convention.
6 See: http://ottawa.ca/en/city-hall/planning-and-development/official-and-master-plans/greenspace-master-plan/2-identifying/24
7 While many other provincial and state planning organizations may publish newsletters or magazines, these do not appear to be included in abstract databases (e.g. GEOBASE). I am familiar with the content of this magazine as I receive it due to my membership in OPPI.
8 Three articles were classified into one or more of the different topic areas, so while a total of 28 articles were collected, the total of topics covered is 33, and the percentages referred to here are based on this total.

References

Ahern, J.F. 2002. *Greenways as Strategic Landscape Planning: Theory and Application*. Doctoral thesis, Wageningen University, The Netherlands.

Ali, Amal K. 2008. Greenbelts to contain urban growth in Ontario Canada: Promises and prospects. *Planning, Practice & Research* 23 (4): 533–548.

Bae, C.H.-C. and M.-J. Jun. 2003. Counterfactual planning: What if there had been no greenbelt in Seoul? *Journal of Planning Education and Research* 22 (4): 374–383.

Beatley, T. 2000. Preserving biodiversity: Challenges for planners. *APA Journal* 66 (1): 5–20.

Carson, Rachel. 1962. *Silent Spring*. Boston: Houghton Mifflin.

Conine, A., W.-N. Xiang, J. Young and D. Whitley. 2004. Planning for multi-purpose greenways in Concord, North Carolina. *Landscape and Urban Planning* 68 (2–3): 271–287.

Crins, William J., Paul A. Grey, Peter W.C. Uhlig and Monique C. Wester. 2009. *The Ecosystems of Ontario, Part 1: Ecozones and Ecoregions.* Sault Ste. Marie, ON: Ontario Ministry of Natural Resources.

Dearden, Philip and Bruce Mitchell. 1998. *Environmental Change and Challenge: A Canadian Perspective.* Toronto: Oxford University Press.

Dramstad, Wenche E., James D. Olson and Richard T.T. Forman. 1996. *Landscape Ecology Principles in Landscape Architecture and Land–Use Planning.* Washington, DC: Island Press.

Fabos, G.J. 2004. Greenway planning in the United States: Its origins and recent case studies. *Landscape and Urban Planning* 68(2–3): 321–342.

Forman, R.T.T. 1995. *Land Mosaics: The Ecology of Landscapes and Regions.* Cambridge: Cambridge University Press.

Forman, Richard T.T. and Michel Godron. 1986. *Landscape Ecology.* New York: Wiley.

Funders' Network for Smart Growth and Livable Communities (FNSGLC). October 2002. *Biodiversity and Smart Growth: Sprawl Threatens Our Natural Heritage.* Translation Paper No. 10. Miami: Collins Center for Public Policy, Inc.

Glasson, John, Riki Therivel and Andrew Chadwick. 1995. *Introduction to Environmental Impact Assessment.* Norwich, UK: UCL Press.

Haley, Emma. 2015. Bigger better greenbelts. *Alternatives Journal* 41 (4): 50–54.

Hostovsky, C. and Sonya Graci. 2016. Environmental assessment in Ontario: Moving from comprehensive planning and decision-making to streamlined approvals, in Kevin S. Hanna (ed.), *Environmental Impact Assessment: Practice and Participation*, third edition. Toronto: Oxford University Press, pp. 373–393.

Hostovsky, C., D. Miller and C. Keddy. 1995. The Natural Environment Systems Strategy: Protecting Ottawa–Carleton's ecological areas. *Plan Canada* 35 (6): 26–29.

Kunstler, James Howard. 1993. *The Geography of Nowhere. The Rise and Decline of America's Man–Made Landscape.* New York: Simon and Schuster.

LeGates, T.R. and F. Stout (eds.). 2000. *The City Reader.* Routledge: New York.

Leopold, Aldo. 1986 [1949]. *A Sand County Almanac, and Sketches Here and There.* New York: Oxford University Press.

Lindsey, Greg. 2003. Sustainability and urban greenways: Indicators in Indianapolis. *Journal of the American Planning Association* 69 (2): 165–180.

Little, C. 1990. *Greenways for America.* Baltimore: Johns Hopkins University Press.

Louis, Cecil and Linda Pim. 1995. The Niagara Escarpment: Planning for environmental protection. *Plan Canada* 35 (1): 39–40.

MacArthur, R.H. and E.O. Wilson. 1967. *The Theory of Island Biogeography.* Princeton, NJ: Princeton University Press.

Macdonald, Sara and Roger Keil. 2012. The Ontario greenbelt: Shifting the scales of the sustainability fix? *The Professional Geographer* 64 (1): 125–145.

McHarg, Ian. 1969. *Design with Nature.* New York: The American Museum of Natural History.

Newbold, K. Bruce and Darren Scott. 2013. Migration, commuting distance, and urban sustainability in Ontario's Greater Golden Horseshoe: Implications of the greenbelt and Places to Grow legislation. *The Canadian Geographer* 57 (4): 474–487.

Noss, R.F. 1983. A regional landscape approach to maintain diversity. *BioScience* 33 (11): 700–706.

Noss, R.F. 1987. Protecting natural areas in fragmented landscapes. *Natural Areas Journal* 7 (1): 2–13.

Noss, R.F. and L.D. Harris. 1986. Nodes, networks, and MUMs: Preserving diversity at all scales. *Environmental Management* 10 (3): 299–309.

Ontario Ministry of Municipal Affairs and Housing (OMMAH). June 2004. *Provincial Policy Statement: Draft Policies Natural Heritage Section 2.1*. Toronto: OMMAH.

Ontario Ministry of Municipal Affairs and Housing (OMMAH). 2007. *Provincial Policy Statement*. www.mah.gov.on.ca, as viewed September 6, 2016.

Ontario Ministry of Municipal Affairs and Housing (OMMAH). 2017. *Greenbelt Plan, 2017*. Toronto: OMMAH. www.mah.gov.on.ca/AssetFactory.aspx?did=18549, as viewed August 31, 2017.

Peck, Sheila. 1998. *Planning for Biodiversity: Issues and Examples*. Washington, DC: Island Press.

Pollock-Ellwand, N. 2001. Landscape policy and planning practice: The gap in understanding, Ontario, Canada. *Landscape Research*, 26 (2), 99–118.

Randolph, John. 2011 [2003]. *Environmental Land Use Planning and Management*. Washington, DC: Island Press.

Riley, John L. and Pat Mohr. 1994. *The Natural Heritage of Southern Ontario's Settled Landscapes*. Aurora: Ontario Ministry of Natural Resources.

Schwarz, Loring, Charles Flink and Robert Searns. 1993. *Greenways: A Guide to Planning, Design, and Development*. Washington DC: Island Press.

Searns, R.M. 1995. The evolution of greenways as an adaptive urban landscape form. *Landscape Urban Planning* 33 (1–3): 65–80.

Smith, Daniel S. and Paul Cawood Hellmund (eds.). 1993. *Ecology of Greenways. Design and Function of Linear Conservation Areas*. Minneapolis, MN: University of Minnesota Press.

Tarlock, A. Dan. 1993. Local government protection of biodiversity: What is its niche? *The University of Chicago Law Review* 60 (2): 555–601.

US Environmental Protection Agency. 2000. *Our Built and Natural Environment: A Technical Review of the Interactions Between Land Use, Transportation, and Environmental Quality*. EPA 231-R-01–0002. Washington, DC: EPA. Available at www.smartgrowth.org.

US Environmental Protection Agency. 2016. National Environmental Policy Act. https://www.epa.gov/nepa, as viewed September 1, 2016.

US Fish & Wildlife Service. 1999. Important Facts About Habitat Loss and Birds. http://digitalmedia.fws.gov/cdm/ref/collection/document/id/272, as viewed May 1, 2013.

7
EVOLUTION IN LAND USE AND TRANSPORTATION RESEARCH

Dea van Lierop, Geneviève Boisjoly, Emily Grisé, and Ahmed El-Geneidy

Introduction

Land use and transportation have a long and complex history of influencing one another, and this relationship has been studied through many dimensions over the past hundred years. The role of land use and transportation researchers has been, and still is, to develop precisely measured, relevant, and reflective research that can help transport and planning professionals design effective policies and plans. While researchers in this domain often conduct studies that lead to changes in planning practice, their areas of research focus are constantly evolving and frequently influenced by the technologies, policies, and implementation of particular approaches to planning within a given context and time. The relationship between land use and transportation research and practice is therefore cyclical: practice is informed by research, and research interests stem from practical issues and trends.

The purpose of this chapter is to highlight and briefly discuss the main themes that land use and transportation researchers have focused on in order to present the evolution of land use and transportation research in a consolidated way. To begin the discussion on the evolution of research in land use and transport, it is useful to discuss the first technological breakthrough that was significant for transportation and urbanization. The invention of James Watt's steam engine circa 1765 enabled the construction of the first steam locomotives and, consequently, the opening of the first railway in 1825 (Vuchic, 2007). Due to the ability to transport agricultural goods from rural regions to the urban core and the increase in manufacturing job opportunities that the Industrial Era presented in urban areas, rural populations began to migrate to cities, causing large-scale urbanization and urban expansion (Davis, 1955). As cities grew in geographic size and walking distances increased, people began to require a system that could transport them throughout urban areas. Accordingly, in the early 19th century, intra-urban public transit systems first arose with the invention of the horse-drawn omnibus, present mainly in European and North American cities (Vuchic, 2007). Soon after, the technology was improved by developing horse-drawn tramways that ran smoothly on rails instead of irregular cobblestone streets. As rails became a common and permanent urban infrastructural component (Neff & Dickens, 2013), land use could now for the first time be planned and developed around existing transportation.

In the late 19th century once electrification was popularized, primarily throughout Europe and the United States, this innovative technology promoted the expansion of rail infrastructure in many cities (Garrison & Levinson, 2006; Vuchic, 2007), and this resulted in substantial changes to land use. For example, based on his analysis of changes in rail network density and population density during the 19th and 20th centuries in London, Levinson (2007) found the presence of a positive feedback loop, which meant that increases in population density motivated the construction of rail stations and vice versa. This suggests that the introduction of electrically run trains had a strong influence on urban land use development as it enabled cities to expand and develop suburbs near commuter rail stations outside of the city centers (Garrison & Levinson, 2006). Consequently, as cities continued to expand and people needed to travel longer distances, the demand for public transit grew stronger as no other modal competition was yet present. Tramway technologies and vehicle design improved, which allowed public transit to service more areas in cities and suburbs, contributing to its popularity (Neff & Dickens, 2013; Vuchic, 2007). Accordingly, by the time WWI started, electric railways had become "the backbone of urban mass transportation" in many North American (Weiner, 1999b, p. 12) and European cities.

As public transit systems, and especially rail, continued to have a more permanent presence in cities (Aman, 1911; Weiner, 1999b), researchers began to study the integration between land use and transportation and the effect it had on where individuals and firms chose to locate (Weber & Pick, 1909). However, this communal way of moving through urban areas changed in the 1920s when the private automobile became increasingly popular and presented a new way of moving around the city. The competition between modes significantly decreased public transit ridership, and the popularity of the automobile led to increased traffic congestion, road accidents, and air pollution in cities (Barrett, 1983; Foster, 1981; Raff, 1991). Due to the new demand for road space resulting from the increase in automobile use, transportation researchers in the 1920s and 1930s focused primarily on traffic studies in order to develop a systematic understanding of traffic flows (Garrison & Levinson, 2006; McClintock, 1926).

No form of urban mobility has affected land use as dramatically as the invention and widespread usage of the automobile, continuing with the creation of an auto-dependent culture that exists in many cities around the world today (Wachs, 1993). The convenience of the personal automobile, availability of inexpensive fuel, and policies such as the 1956 Interstate Highway Act in the United States and the Special Roads Act 1949 in the United Kingdom facilitated the suburban development that reflected urban dwellers' location preferences and, consequently, allowed for outward migration from city centers (Levinson & Krizek, 2008; Special Roads Act

1949). Suburbs could be developed across waterways and other geographic barriers as innovations in the production of steel, concrete, and bridge design allowed car users to commute from further out of the city at high speeds that enabled travel times to remain consistent with previous travel (Levinson & Krizek, 2008; Shahrooz, 2011).

Due to advancements in infrastructure and transportation technologies, commuters could now travel further distances and city centers could draw on a larger labor pool (Garrison & Levinson, 2006). Consequently, the interaction between transportation and land use began to be formally studied. One example is the research by Alonso (1964), who developed land rent models that assessed the relationship between housing prices and transportation costs. Assuming an urban area with a single market location, Alonso, as well as other researchers at the time, built statistical models to determine the trade-off costs that influence individuals' home location and transportation choices. As more people began to choose to locate on less expensive suburban land and pay for higher travel costs, congestion levels increased in urban areas. In line with the research focus on traffic flows, roads were expanded to account for the new volume of automobiles. The increases in road capacity were shown, however, to be an ineffective solution to alleviating traffic. In many cases this led to more congestion that would, in turn, lead to greater increases in road capacity, resulting in a positive feedback loop (Downs, 2004).

Given the growing interest in land use and transportation research, several regions in the United States began to develop land use and transportation plans based on large travel behavior surveys in order to relieve congestion. For example, the metropolitan transportation study known as CATS (Chicago Area Transportation Study) was the first systematic region-wide study which accounted for both transportation and land use. This study led to the release of one of the first comprehensive land use and transportation plans in the early 1960s. At this time, the plan was considered extremely progressive as "[i]t pioneered in the use of computers, trip distribution, traffic assignment, and benefit-cost analysis" (Black, 1990).

Although auto-dependent societies experienced increases in mobility, many negative externalities pertaining to the environment, the social well-being of communities, and the economy were felt in cities. As a reaction, research in transportation and land use began to place a new emphasis on understanding how to lessen the detrimental impacts on the environment that had largely been caused by the consumption of fossil fuels (Belzer & Autler, 2002; Cervero, 2004; Cervero, Ferrell, & Murphy, 2002). Furthermore, increases in congestion and infrastructure costs associated with suburban auto-dependent communities were understood to have negative economic consequences (Newman & Kenworthy, 1996; Podobnik, 2002). In recent years, these environmental, social, and economic impacts associated with auto-dependent lifestyles have continued to receive much attention. Overall, it has become increasingly clear to planners that land use and transportation planning are inherently interconnected, with land use development influencing transportation planning and vice versa (Gutierrez, 2009). Researchers are therefore

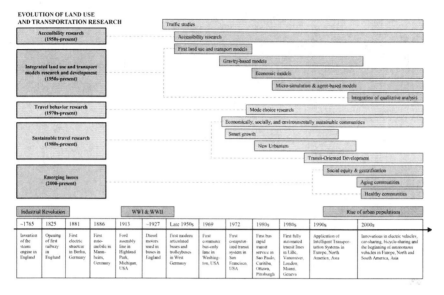

FIGURE 7.1 Evolution of land use and transportation research.

key actors in the generation of knowledge relating to complex and constantly evolving land use and transportation advancements.

This chapter illustrates how research on transportation and land use has evolved over time by briefly discussing several main research themes. The first section of this chapter discusses research related to accessibility, which is a core theme integrating land use and transport research, and this is followed by a discussion of integrated land use and transportation models. Research on travel behavior is then presented, followed by a discussion of environmentally sustainable urban forms. The chapter concludes with a discussion on emerging research trends; namely, equity, gentrification, and planning for sustainable cities. Figure 7.1 depicts the evolution of land use and transport research that is discussed. At the bottom of the figure, important dates in the history of transportation are included for reference. These dates are primarily based on Vuchic's (2007) book on urban transit technology. Furthermore, the boxes on the left side of the figure correspond to the subsections presented in this chapter.

Integrating Transportation and Land Use through Accessibility

One of the most important trends in the literature on land use and transportation is related to accessibility research. While transportation research started as an isolated field focusing on mobility, which refers to the ability to move from one place to another, most people travel because they need or want to access particular destinations. Thus, researchers recognized that transportation policies should aim at increasing access to destinations rather than solely focusing on mobility. Whereas traffic studies, which were primarily focused on mobility, depended solely on the transportation system itself, the concept of accessibility, understood as the ease of reaching various destinations (Preston & Rajé, 2007), was developed to be contingent also on the location of urban opportunities. Accessibility research hence addresses the complex interaction between the location of economic and residential activities and the transportation network in a city (Guiliano, 2004). It also helps to understand the impacts of such interactions on location patterns, travel behavior, and most importantly, quality of life.

The concept of accessibility was introduced by Hansen in 1959. In his widely cited paper "How accessibility shapes land use," Hansen proposed a method for determining accessibility patterns in a region. He defined accessibility as "the *potential* of opportunities for interaction" (1959, p. 73), which he measured based on the travel time to various opportunities from a specific location (employment, shopping opportunities, and residential activity [population density]). In this gravity-based model, each opportunity was weighted based on the travel time associated with reaching the opportunity. The further an opportunity was located from an origin, the less it contributed to accessibility, meaning that closer opportunities were deemed to be more desirable. Using this model, Hansen was interested in predicting the development of residential land use in a region.

Inspired by Hansen's early work on accessibility, researchers continued to focus on the relationship between land use development and accessibility (Ball & Kirwan, 1977; Nelson, 1973), looking at the trade-offs between accessibility and housing prices, and the location choices of households as a function of accessibility. These studies provided researchers with a better understanding of land use development patterns as a function of proximity to opportunities, in terms of time or distance.

Another branch of accessibility research emerged in the 1970s, evaluating the impacts on individuals of access to urban opportunities. At this time, accessibility was framed as the benefit resulting from a transportation and land use system (Ben-Akiva & Lerman, 1979). The influence of accessibility on the quality of life of individuals was highlighted, specifically with respect to transportation costs and employment opportunities (Wachs & Kumagai, 1973). In line with this new perspective, Wachs & Kumagai made the case for including accessibility in the evaluation of transportation and regional plans. More specifically, they studied the "distributional effects of policies" using accessibility indicators, which they defined as "the physical accessibility of population groups to a variety of activities and opportunities" (1973, pp. 437–438).

These accessibility indicators were presented to complement mobility indicators, which dominated transportation planning throughout most of the 20th century. As noted in the introduction, the first transportation and land use plans were based on travel behavior surveys with the aim of alleviating congestion. In this context, several researchers argued that accessibility measures, typically based on the number of opportunities that could be reached from a specific location using a specific mode, more accurately emphasized the needs of individuals (Koenig, 1980; Wachs &

Kumagai, 1973), whereas mobility measures merely addressed travel time minimization and fluidity of car traffic (Banister, 2008). Transportation planning today continues to be dominated by mobility indicators, although many researchers are actively attempting to demonstrate the relevance of accessibility-based approaches (Banister, 2008; Levine, Grengs, Shen, & Shen, 2012).

Up until the year 2000, the concept of accessibility had been researched and discussed but was not often translated into practical performance measures (Handy & Niemeier, 1997). These discussions were mainly conceptual and theoretical given the lack of advanced computational methods. However, due to increases in computational power and development of advanced software, a plethora of measures and empirical studies were developed at the end of the 20th century and applied to research concerning mode choice, (un)employment, land values, and social equity (Armstrong & Rodriguez, 2006; Blumenberg & Ong, 2001; Currie, 2010; Du & Mulley, 2006; El-Geneidy & Levinson, 2006; Geurs & van Wee, 2004; Grengs, 2010; Martens, Golub, & Robinson, 2012; Paez, Scott, & Morency, 2012; Sanchez, Shen, & Peng, 2004). In addition some recent research focused on evaluating the benefits from different scenarios in transportation plans (El-Geneidy, Cerdá, Fischler, & Luka, 2011; Golub & Martens, 2014; Manaugh & El-Geneidy, 2012). More recent developments have focused on methodological aspects; for instance, integrating fluctuations of accessibility throughout the day (Anderson, Owen, & Levinson, 2012; Boisjoly & El-Geneidy, 2016).

Although accessibility has been the focus of much research, both conceptually and empirically, its application to planning is still limited. While regional and transportation plans are increasingly including accessibility goals and indicators, the focus still lies largely on mobility aspects. Research has thus emerged on the implementation of accessibility in planning (Halden, 2011; Proffitt, Bartholomew, Ewing, & Miller, 2015), and further research in the formal and practical application of accessibility is needed.

Integrated Land Use and Transportation Models

One way that researchers have formalized the study of the relationship between land use and transportation is by developing mathematical and statistical methods analyzing the complex relation between changes in land use, economic activity, and transportation options. The first land use and transportation models appeared in the 1950s (Batty, 2008), and by the 1960s many operational models were developed to better understand the relationship between land use and transportation. The most advanced of these early models was Lowry's (1964) *Model of Metropolis*, which was developed for the Pittsburgh region and used various simulation techniques including complex econometric analysis as well as gravity modeling. Lowry's model represented a breakthrough in the development of methods used to analyze and simulate the spatial interaction between residential and service locations, which marks an important beginning to modeling the interactions between land use and transportation. Lowry's model was further developed by Garin

(1966) to improve how the interaction between land use and transportation was modeled (Iacono, Levinson, & El-Geneidy, 2008). During the 1970s, researchers continued to develop spatial interaction models to predict how policy changes in land use and transportation would influence one another.

The first fully complete software package integrating land use and transportation was developed in the early 1980s by Putman. Putman's Integrated Transportation and Land Use Package (ITLUP) included two land use sub-models, one representing household characteristics and the other accounting for employment details. With respect to transportation, this model accounted for travel time and was the first to account for congestion at different times of the day (Putman, 2013). Other spatial interaction models were also developed (Iacono et al., 2008; Mackett, 1983), but most of these models soon lost their popularity for four main reasons:

> most were static equilibrium models incapable of capturing the dynamics of urban systems; none of the models actually represented land markets with explicit prices; zones were highly aggregate and lacked spatial detail, and the models were inadequately supported by theory.
>
> (Iacono et al., 2008, p. 5)

By the mid-1980s, random utility theory and economic methods became increasingly popular as researchers searched for ways to better capture individuals' choices (for example, travel behavior and location preferences) in their modeling methods. The new land use and transportation models were based on theories that had previously been used for regional economic models and land market models (Iacono et al., 2008). For example, TRANUS was developed to simulate the interactions between land use, transportation, activities, and the real estate market using discrete choice logit models (De la Barra, 1989). This research was further developed in the 1990s when dynamic models were able to integrate multiple sub-models that included information on topics such as housing markets, employment, vacant lands, households, and travel behavior (Anas & Arnott, 1994; Iacono et al., 2008; Martinez, 1996).

In the late 1990s and early 2000s, Waddell developed UrbanSim to assist urban planners in making decisions about land use, transportation, and environmental planning (Brail & Klosterman, 2001; Waddell, 2000; Waddell, Outwater, Bhat, & Blain, 2002). UrbanSim symbolized an advancement in land use modeling as it was based on spatially disaggregated analysis and could be associated with complex transportation models (Waddell et al., 2002). Extensions were developed to incorporate a traditional four-step transportation model, to predict trips based on activities (Waddell et al., 2002), and to include environmental analyses (Waddell & Borning, 2004). Furthermore, UrbanSim was designed to be integrated with Geographic Information Systems (Iacono et al., 2008). UrbanSim progressed for more than two decades and eventually incorporated agent-based modeling techniques. Agent-based modeling systems, which are also based on disaggregate analyses, are considered to be more useful than aggregate modeling systems because they more accurately account for complexities related to modeling human socio-economic activities. UrbanSim continues to be used today in many regions around the world due to the open-source nature of the project, the absence of initial costs, and the various successes made by developers in implementing it.

Another agent-based model that was developed in the early 2000s is Salvini and Miller's ILUTE (2005), which uses a variety of modeling approaches to accurately simulate land use, location choice, car ownership, and travel patterns, otherwise referred to as activities. This model, which currently is being applied to the Greater Toronto Area, also accounts for temporal elements. Miller also worked with Roorda (2003) to develop the Travel/Activity Scheduler for Household Agents (TASHA) model. Similarly to other activity-based travel demand models, this model uses a micro-simulation system (Acheampong & Silva, 2015). This is helpful for modeling the complexities of how transportation and land use are interconnected at the individual level, and this has also been applied in Toronto, Canada. Additionally, environmental aspects were later incorporated into the TASHA model (Hatzopoulou, 2009). Currently, researchers are continuing to develop similar models in different metropolitan regions (Katoshevski, Glickman, Ishaq, & Shiftan, 2015; Waddell, Wang, Charlton, & Olsen, 2010).

Even though these agent-based models represent a major advancement in the simulation of land use and transportation interactions and are commonly used today in practice, they remain computationally complex, require large amounts of data, and must be developed as context-specific models. Given these constraints, integrated models are not easily transferrable, although it is often believed that they are. Today, many researchers are continuing to develop and improve land use and transportation models as they are important for testing planning theories and potential policies – especially with regard to accessibility. Wegener's (2004) comparative review of integrated land use and transportation models provides a detailed assessment of available models according to their predicted ability to impact policy. One new area of focus is the use of qualitative tools to examine, and better model, the relationships between transportation and land use. For example, Pfaffenbichler's Metropolitan Activity Relocation Simulator (MARS), developed in Vienna, Austria, integrated qualitative measures into an otherwise quantitative model (Pfaffenbichler, 2003, 2011). Other authors have suggested that a paradigm shift in land use and transportation modeling is needed to account for land use and transportation variations within existing urban areas, changes in the behavior of different populations (van Wee, 2015), and the effects of climate change (Wegener, 2011).

The development of integrated land use and transportation models has progressed along a similar timeline as accessibility research as these two topics are closely related. Accessibility is dependent on transportation and land use systems and, in turn, affects both land use development and individuals' travel patterns. Accordingly, many of these models incorporated and benefited from advancements in accessibility and travel behavior research. The ongoing development of integrated models has significant impacts on the ground, with many agencies adopting them to help in the decision-making process. Further research will contribute to developing finer models that account for a greater diversity of qualitative and quantitative measures as well as spatial and individual variations.

Understanding and Influencing Travel Behavior

Research on travel behavior emerged at the same time as research on accessibility and integrated land use and transportation models. In the context of widespread automobile use, suburbanization, and traffic congestion, planners and researchers became interested in understanding and predicting travel flows in order to better plan the transportation and land use system to meet demand. This was done through the expansion of the road network and the development of new residential areas. The aim was to understand when and where people traveled, focusing on private motorization. This traditional planning approach was based on predicting the demand and then providing infrastructure to meet that demand. This led to the development of the four-step model implemented in the 1950s in Detroit and Chicago (Weiner, 1999a), designed to predict travel demand and account for trip generation, trip distribution, mode choice, and route choice (McNally, 2007).

Mode choice later became predominant in travel behavior studies. While transportation models were generally used to predict travel patterns at the regional level and to understand how policies would influence land use and transportation, research on mode choice focused on investigating travel patterns from an individual's perspective (Hurst, 1969). More specifically, it concentrated on predicting whether investing in public transit would be an effective policy as an alternative to expanding highways and whether it would contribute to reducing automobile ownership and use (Button, Pearman, & Fowkes, 1982; McFadden, 1973). As a result, a considerable amount of research started to focus on assessing individuals' transit usage and automobile ownership (Banister, 1978; Kain & Beesley, 1965; McFadden, 1973). The goal of this research was to understand automobile ownership in relation to transit infrastructure (Button et al., 1982; Kain & Beesley, 1965) in an effort to identify policies that could help reduce automobile ownership and, thus, traffic congestion. With respect to transit use, McFadden (1973) developed a discrete choice model and predicted the probability of using public transit based on trip and individual characteristics, such as travel time by different modes, income, and ethnicity. Using this model, McFadden and his colleagues predicted travel demand and financial feasibility for the Bay Area Rapid Transit (BART) system in the San Francisco region (McFadden, 1973). McFadden's predictions about the BART turned out to be accurate. Official forecasts predicted 15% of commuting trips would be made on the BART, whereas McFadden's prediction was 6.3%; the actual mode share turned out to be 6.2% (McFadden, 2001). Although McFadden's model accurately predicted ridership, the transport planners working at BART never used his modeling techniques to develop policies (Button, Doh, Hardy, Yuan, & Zhou, 2010). Interestingly, McFadden later won a Nobel Prize for his work on discrete choice analysis.

Following McFadden's research, multiple modal split models have been developed to capture the diversity of factors influencing mode choice. Namely, land use characteristics such as employment and residential density have been included in later models (Kain & Fauth, 1978; Train, 1980). Furthermore, a concurrent growing interest for accessibility research influenced other researchers to investigate the impact of accessibility on travel behavior; namely, trip rate and mode choice (Ben-Akiva & Lerman, 1974; Koenig, 1980). Today, similar mode choice models continue to be developed and used, specifically with respect to accessibility (Legrain, Buliung, & El-Geneidy, 2015; Levinson, 1998; Owen & Levinson, 2015).

In addition to quantitative modal split models, travel behavior research has been characterized by a will to understand psychological factors influencing mode choice. Researchers became interested in understanding how individuals' habits, perceptions, and motivations affected where, when, and by which mode people traveled (Hensher, 1975). While the quantitative studies looked at personal characteristics such as gender and age, this new branch of mainly qualitative research went beyond these characteristics to understand how psychological factors like personal perceptions and values affect mode choice.

The travel behavior research described here contributed to a greater awareness of the influence of the urban form and the transportation network on travel behavior of individuals. Together with the growing environmental concerns related to automobile use, this led to a greater focus on the built environment and its relation to transportation infrastructure and travel behavior.

Promoting Sustainable Travel through Urban Form

As researchers began to identify elements of the built environment that impacted on travel behavior, developing urban forms promoting the use of sustainable modes became one of the most popular and most practiced strategies aiming to counter the negative effects of auto-dependent lifestyles (Cervero, 2004; Chatman, 2013; Samuelson, 2009). Following the oil and energy crisis experienced by industrial countries during the 1970s, many cities around the world have actively focused on developing communities where walking, cycling, and public transit are viable alternatives to private motorized vehicles. Research in this area has accordingly focused on understanding how to best integrate land use and transportation infrastructure with the goal of decreasing auto-dependent lifestyles while developing urban environments that yield social, economic, and environmental benefits.

Planners and researchers first focused on inner-area revitalization as a way to redirect a portion of urban growth closer to the city center, combined with controlled and limited outward urban development. Researchers emphasized that inner-area revitalization should be composed of attractive communities with integrated living and working environments, supporting non-motorized modes of transportation and inter-modalism (Burchell, Listokin, & Galley, 2000; Duany, Speck, & Lydon, 2010; Podobnik, 2002). This strategy, now referred to as Smart

Growth, was first discussed in the 1970s, and it continues to be discussed today although not often applied in practice (Downs, 2005).

Following the emergence of the Smart Growth principles, increasing attention was given to the integration of land use and transportation at the neighborhood level. This led to the New Urbanism movement, which was informally developed in the United States in the early 1980s to promote the development of sustainable neighborhoods and formally documented through the publication of the *Charter of the New Urbanism* in 1999 (Congress for the New Urbanism, 1999; Duany, 2013; Talen, 2013). New Urbanism is similar in principle to Smart Growth, but more codified in its prescriptions for design standards. Overall, it aims to generate compact, pedestrian-friendly, and livable communities by including vibrant public spaces, amenities located at the center of the development, and a transit station or stop (Burchell et al., 2000; Leccese & McCormick, 2000).

As with Smart Growth and New Urbanism, transit-oriented development (TOD) has received much attention among both planners and land use and transportation researchers since the early 1990s, especially throughout North America (Dunphy, Cervero, Dock, McAvery, Porter, & Swenson, 2004). The application of TOD theory seeks to increase land use densities and develop mixed-use communities near rail stations in order to encourage public transit use and dissuade auto-dependent lifestyles, the goal being to generate more sustainable communities. Similarly to other strategies aimed at developing sustainable communities, TODs focus largely on the built environment. Researchers, therefore, further explored the interconnections between public transit infrastructures and the built environment in this context. Cervero and Kockelman (1997) identified three elements that are essential components in the integration of land use and transit for reducing auto use: density, diversity, and design, also called the "3Ds." In general, researchers and practitioners agree that these three elements are essential components for developing vibrant built environments necessary for the success of TODs (Cervero & Kockelman, 1997; van Lierop, Maat, & El-Geneidy, 2016). Recently, these three components have been expanded upon to include destination accessibility, distance to transit, and demand management, which includes parking supply and cost (Ewing & Cervero, 2010; Translink, 2010). Ewing and Cervero (2010) continued research in this area and found a seventh "D," demographics, highlighting its influence as a confounding factor with respect to travel behavior while recognizing that it is not a component of the built environment. However, Cervero and Kockelman's original 3Ds comprising the built environment are still predominant in the literature, and research in this area often focuses on understanding whether the densification and discouragement of automobile use associated with both existing and new TODs successfully yield significant environmental, social, and economic benefits for cities (Dunphy et al., 2004; Hofstad, 2012; Renne & Wells, 2004). Knowing that the spatial structure of homes, jobs, and facilities creates the context within which people travel, several studies have found that planned sustainable communities influence the use of active and sustainable modes (Langlois, van Lierop, Wasfi, & El-Geneidy,

2015). Accordingly, Ewingand Cervero emphasized that "[t]he potential to moderate travel demand by changing the built environment is the most heavily researched subject in urban planning" (2010, p. 267).

However, not all researchers agree on the extent to which the built environment influences mode choice and travel behavior. Several researchers have found that individuals who have an inclination to commute by public transportation or active modes tend to locate themselves in walkable neighborhoods with sufficient access to transit, which is referred to as self-selection (Chatman, 2006, 2009; Handy, Cao, & Mokhtarian, 2006; Manaugh & El-Geneidy, 2014). Yet, regardless of the current academic debates, in practice, urban planning theories that accept the influence of the built environment on travel behavior and seek to decrease automobile use and mitigate the impacts associated with automobile dependency, continue to receive much attention (Burchell et al., 2000; Cervero & Kockelman, 1997; Hofstad, 2012; Renne & Wells, 2004).

Overall, the abundant research on the influence of the built environment has helped planners develop local policies supporting the development of sustainable communities. In turn, the implementation of such policies by practitioners has provided researchers with a variety of empirical case studies to deepen their understanding of the impact of the built environment on travel behavior.

Emerging Issues in Transport and Land Use Research

In parallel with inner-city revitalization projects such as Smart Growth, there has been a dramatic return to the city movement. These urban locations became more desirable, particularly for more affluent, educated professionals, and as a result triggered the onset of gentrification. The term "gentrification" was originally coined by sociologist Ruth Glass (1964) and later researched by Neil Smith (1982), who found that land in proximity to transportation systems was more desirable, which in turn led to higher land values. The widespread effect of gentrification has attracted considerable research to uncover its processes as well as the effects of gentrification on less affluent populations. While some studies have found a positive change associated with the process of gentrification – namely, as a result of neighborhood revitalization (Freeman, 2005) – the majority of literature describes the adverse effects of gentrification (Grube-Cavers & Patterson, 2015; Walks & Maaranen, 2008). The growth of income polarization within newly gentrified neighborhoods is seen as the main negative impact of gentrification (Walks & Maaranen, 2008). Furthermore, the process of gentrification poses a range of problems for planners as it displaces low-income households, who often must settle for accommodation in regions with poorer transit accessibility, farther distances from work, and having fewer public services (Walks & Maaranen, 2008). Consequently, gentrification research is largely tied to concerns for social equity. In the context of transportation planning, inequities often result from the distribution of transportation supply. This can be due to inequitable planning, population displacements, or limited location choices, resulting in the transportation system offering benefits to different populations (Jones & Lucas, 2012).

In parallel with research on public transit accessibility and land values, similar trends have been found for active transport modes. A positive relationship has been observed between housing prices and neighborhoods with higher walkability (Pivo & Fisher, 2011) and availability of bicycle share stations (El-Geneidy, van Lierop, & Wasfi, 2016). The desirability of neighborhoods that facilitate the use of active modes of transportation may reflect higher levels of social and community engagement found in more walkable, mixed-use neighborhoods when compared to automobile-oriented suburban neighborhoods (Leyden, 2003). In addition, the potential benefits to inidividuals' health through increased physical activity (Shephard, 2008) and the affordability and convenience offered by active travel have been found to be desirable. However, while progressive transportation planners have promoted investments in active transport infrastructure, recent evidence of an inequitable distribution of cycling infrastructure investment has been observed (Flanagan, Lachapelle, & El-Geneidy, 2016), and concerns about infrastructure improvements as a reflection of gentrification efforts have been expressed (Lubitow & Miller, 2013). The inclusion of equity principles in transportation planning as well as the acknowledgement of inequalities in the transportation system is now seen as crucial to ensuring that all individuals can access desired opportunities. Research in this field contributes to defining equity in the context of transportation (Martens et al., 2012; Pereira, Schwanen, & Banister, 2016), and researchers today are continuing to develop tools to measure inequalities in the distribution of transportation supply (Delbosc & Currie, 2011; Manaugh & El-Geneidy, 2011).

As the world's urban population continues to rise, transit agencies and governments are also faced with the challenge of meeting the increased demand for intra-urban transportation, primarily by increasing the share of individuals who choose sustainable modes of transportation. Traditionally, cost, time, and distance were believed to be the most significant factors driving the selection of an individual's transportation mode (Button, 2010). However, while trip characteristics remain important determinants of travel behavior, research has shown that travel behavior is a function of both internal and external factors unique to the individual, including personal motivation, values, and socio-demographics (Boarnet & Sarmiento, 1998; Van Acker, Van Wee, & Witlox, 2010). Furthermore, attitudes towards travel are important considerations within travel behavior modeling. For example, Ory and Mokhtarian (2005) observed that individuals with a positive attitude toward travel in general may be less likely to reduce their travel through behavioral changes such as living in a mixed-use neighborhood.

Additionally, an individual's mode choice has several implications on health, and new areas of research related to how the built environment affects health and overall well-being have emerged. For example, Ettema, Gärling, Olsson, and Friman (2010) found that daily travel can be a stressful event affecting subjective well-being. Similarly, other researchers have suggested that commuting stress is related to adverse effects on individual's health, such as exhaustion, depression, and feelings of poor health (Gee & Takeuchi, 2004; Hansson, Mattisson, Björk, Östergren, & Jakobsson, 2011). Moreover, the negative effects of stress while commuting are likely felt most by drivers, whereas active transport modes are less stressful (Legrain, Eluru, & El-Geneidy, 2015) and increase levels of physical activity. Given that research has demonstrated the multiple health benefits associated with active modes, walking was given high priority on the public health agenda after the 1996 United States Surgeon General's report on physical activity (United States Department of Health & Human Services, 1996). This led to widespread research on environmental influences of physical activity and best practices and policies for urban design (see review by Heath, Brownson, Kruger, Miles, Powell, Ramsey, & Task Force on Community Preventative Services, 2006). More recently, the Surgeon General reiterated the need to address public health through walkable communities in his 2015 Call to Action (United States Surgeon General, 2015). The growing evidence of the impact of land use and transportation patterns on our health and our social well-being spurs considerable interest in this field for the future.

Finally, land use and transportation planners and researchers today are presented with the challenge of how to adapt systems based on the needs and desires of an aging population. By 2030 at least 25% of the population of major urban areas in the developed world will be 60 years and older (United Nations, 2013). This demographic shift presents far-reaching implications for society. Cities produce advantages for older people, such as higher accessibility to essential services as well as leisure and social activities, and developing age-friendly cities remains an important planning goal (Phillipson, 2011) and research agenda. Trends of increasing auto-dependency among contemporary and future generations of seniors (Newbold, Scott, Spinney, Kanaroglou, & Páez, 2005; Rosenbloom, 2001) present researchers with the challenge of how to develop age-friendly cities with viable transportation options. Access to different modes of transportation has been identified as a key factor affecting the mobility of seniors and, consequently, their quality of life (Banister & Bowling, 2004).

Another population of interest to researchers is the Millennials, who have embraced the sharing economy, generating interest in research on car-sharing as well as emerging transport technologies such as electric vehicles and autonomous vehicles. Accordingly, research in these areas has started to emerge in recent years. Yet, due to the new nature of this topic, the impacts on land use have been limited and are up until now solely theoretical. However, major land use changes resulting from the influence of emerging transportation technologies are expected to occur in the near future.

Chapter Wrap Up

This chapter has demonstrated that land use and transportation planning are strongly interconnected. Moreover, land use and transportation research is now a mature subfield of both transportation and urban planning research, and research in this area was consolidated through the establishment of the World Society for Transport and Land Use Research (WSTLUR) in 2008 to support the dissemination of the growing body of literature on land use and transportation. The *Journal of Transport and Land Use* (JTLU) is now the official journal of WSTLUR. Also WSTLUR organizes a World Symposium on Transport and Land Use Research every three years, and selected articles form this symposium are published in JTLU.

Overall, this chapter has brought attention to the major themes that have emerged in land use and transportation research over the past century. While well-established research areas such as those related to accessibility, land use and transportation modeling, mode choice, and the development of sustainable communities continue to be studied, today's research tends to emphasize the less tangible aspects of land use and transportation, such as social equity, individuals' perceptions and experiences of transportation, and attractiveness of the built environment for different populations. Considerable progress has been made towards a greater understanding of these factors. Nevertheless, as new technologies continue to emerge in cities, a new era of transportation and land use research is beginning to emerge. For example, there are many opportunities for land use and transport interaction with regard to Intelligent Transportation Systems and other Smart City technologies both in the near and distant future. These technologies will inevitably bring significant changes to land use and transportation systems and thereby add new dimensions to all subfields of land use and transportation research. Major challenges therefore remain in bridging the gap between research and planning practice, and these must be fully considered by researchers in order to develop sustainable cities that meet the needs of all individuals.

Acknowledgments

The authors would like to thank Prof. David Levinson for providing feedback on an earlier version of the manuscript. Also thanks to Prof. Thomas Sanchez for his feedback and help in putting this chapter together.

References

Acheampong, R., & Silva, E. (2015). Land use–transport interaction modeling: A review of the literature and future research directions. *Journal of Transport and Land Use* 8 (3): 11–38.

Alonso, W. (1964). *Location and land use. Toward a general theory of land rent.* Cambridge, MA: Harvard University Press.

Aman, F. (1911). Vienna: The tramway system and sections of boulevards: Illustrated. *Town Planning Review* 1 (4): 294–298.

Anas, A., & Arnott, R. (1994). The Chicago prototype housing market model with tenure choice and its policy applications. *Journal of Housing Research* 5 (1): 23–90.

Anderson, P., Owen, A., & Levinson, D. (2013). The time between: Continuously-defined accessibility functions for schedule-based transportation systems. *92nd Annual Meeting of the Transportation Research Board*, Washington, DC, January 13–17.

Armstrong, R., & Rodriguez, D. (2006). An evaluation of the accessibility benefits of commuter rail in eastern Massachusetts using spatial hedonic price functions. *Transportation* 33 (1): 21–43.

Ball, M., & Kirwan, R. (1977). Accessibility and supply constraints in the urban housing market. *Urban Studies* 14 (1): 11–32.

Banister, D. (1978). The influence of habit formation on modal choice: A heuristic model. *Transportation* 7 (1): 5–33.

Banister, D. (2008). The sustainable mobility paradigm. *Transport Policy* 15 (2), 73–80.

Banister, D., & Bowling, A. (2004). Quality of life for the elderly: The transport dimension. *Transport Policy* 11 (2): 105–115.

Barrett, P. (1983). *The automobile and urban transit: The formation of public policy in Chicago, 1900–1930*. Philadelphia: Temple University Press.

Batty, M. (2008). Fifty years of urban modeling: Macro-statics to micro-dynamics. In S. Albeverino, D. Andrey, P. Giordano, & A. Vacheri (eds.), *The dynamics of complex urban systems* (pp. 1–20). Heidelberg/New York: Physica-Verlag.

Belzer, D., & Autler, G. (2002). *Transit–oriented development: Moving from rhetoric to reality*. A discussion paper prepared for the The Brookings Institution Center on Urban and Metropolitan Policy and The Great American Station Foundation. Washington, DC. Brookings Institution.

Ben-Akiva, M., & Lerman, S. (1974). Some estimation results of a simultaneous model of auto ownership and mode choice to work. *Transportation* 3 (4): 357–376.

Ben-Akiva, M., & Lerman, S. (1979). Disaggregate travel and mobility choice models and measures of accessibility. In D. A. Hensher & P. R. Stopher (eds.), *Behavioural travel modelling* (pp. 654–679). Andover, UK: Croom Helm.

Black, A. (1990). The Chicago area transportation study: A case study of rational planning. *Journal of Planning Education and Research* 10 (1): 27–37.

Blumenberg, E., & Ong, P. (2001). Cars, buses, and jobs-welfare participants and employment access in Los Angeles. In National Research Council, *Sustainability and environmental concerns in transportation 2001: Planning and administration; energy and environment* (pp. 22–31). Washington, DC: National Academy Press.

Boarnet, M., & Sarmiento, S. (1998). Can land-use policy really affect travel behaviour? A study of the link between non-work travel and land-use characteristics. *Urban Studies* 35 (7): 1155–1169.

Boisjoly, G., & El-Geneidy, A. (2016). Daily fluctuations in transit and job availability: A comparative assessment of time-sensitive accessibility measures. *Journal of Transport Geography* 52: 73–81.

Brail, R., & Klosterman, R. (2001). *Planning support systems: Integrating geographic information systems, models, and visualization tools*. Redlands, CA: ESRI, Inc.

Burchell, R., Listokin, D., & Galley, C. (2000). Smart Growth: More than a ghost of urban policy past, less than a bold new horizon. *Housing Policy Debate* 11 (4): 821–879.

Button, K. (2010). *Transport economics*: Cheltenham, UK: Edward Elgar Publishing.

Button, K., Pearman, A., & Fowkes, A. (1982). *Car ownership modelling and forecasting*. Aldershot, UK: Gower.

Button, K., Doh, S., Hardy, M., Yuan, J., & Zhou, X. (2010). The accuracy of transit system ridership forecasts and capital cost estimates. *International Journal of Transport Economics* 37 (2): 155–168.

Cervero, R. (2004). The built environment and travel: Evidence from the United States. *European Journal of Transport and Infrastructure Research* 2 (3): 119–137.

Cervero, R., & Kockelman, K. (1997). Travel demand and the 3Ds: Density, diversity, and design. *Transportation Research Part D: Transport and Environment* 2 (3): 199–219.

Cervero, R., Ferrell, C., & Murphy, S. (2002). *Transit–oriented development and joint development in the United States: A literature review*. Transit Cooperative Research Program research results digest, Number 52. Washington, DC: Transportation Research Board.

Chatman, D. (2006). *Transit–oriented development and household travel: A study of California cities*. Los Angeles: Institute of Transportation Studies, School of Public Affairs, University of California, Los Angeles.

Chatman, D. (2009). Residential choice, the built environment, and nonwork travel: Evidence using new data and methods. *Environment and Planning A* 41 (5): 1072–1089.

Chatman, D. (2013). Does TOD need the T? On the importance of factors other than rail access. *Journal of the American Planning Association* 79 (1): 17–31.

Congress for the New Urbanism. (1999). *Charter of The New Urbanism*. New York: McGraw-Hill Professional.

Currie, G. (2010). Quantifying spatial gaps in public transport supply based on social needs. *Journal of Transport Geography* 18 (1): 31–41.

Davis, K. (1955). The origin and growth of urbanization in the world. *American Journal of Sociology* 60 (5): 429–437.

De la Barra, T. (1989). *Integrated land use and transport modelling: Decision chains and hierarchies*. Cambridge, UK: Cambridge University Press.

Delbosc, A., & Currie, G. (2011). Using Lorenz curves to assess public transport equity. *Journal of Transport Geography* 19 (6): 1252–1259.

Downs, A. (2004). *Still stuck in traffic: Coping with peak–hour traffic congestion*. Washington, DC: The Brookings Institution.

Downs, A. (2005). Smart growth: Why we discuss it more than we do it. *Journal of the American Planning Association* 71 (4): 367–378.

Du, H., & Mulley, C. (2006). Relationship between transport accessibility and land value: Local model approach with geographically weighted regression. *Transportation Research Record* 1977: 197–205.

Duany, A. (2013). 20 years of New Urbanism. In E. Talen (ed.), *Charter of the New Urbanism*, Second edition (pp. 9–13). New York: McGraw-Hill Education.

Duany, A., Speck, J., & Lydon, M. (2010). *The smart growth manual*. New York: McGraw-Hill.

Dunphy, R., Cervero, R., Dock, F., McAvery, M., Porter, D., & Swenson, C. (2004). *Developing around transit: Strategies and solutions that work*. Washington, DC: Urban Land Institute.

El-Geneidy, A., & Levinson, D. (2006). *Access to destinations: Development of accessibility measures*. St. Paul, MN: Minnesota Department of Transportation, Research Services Section.

El-Geneidy, A., Cerdá, A., Fischler, R., & Luka, N. (2011). Evaluating the impacts of transportation plans using accessibility measures. *Canadian Journal of Urban Research* 20 (1): 81–104.

El-Geneidy, A., van Lierop, D., & Wasfi, R. (2016). Do people value bicycle sharing? A multilevel longitudinal analysis capturing the impact of bicycle sharing on residential sales in Montreal, Canada. *Transport Policy* 51: 174–181.

Ettema, D., Gärling, T., Olsson, L., & Friman, M. (2010). Out-of-home activities, daily travel, and subjective well-being. *Transportation Research Part A: Policy and Practice* 44 (9): 723–732.

Ewing, R., & Cervero, R. (2010). Travel and the built environment. *Journal of the American Planning Association* 76 (3): 1–30.

Flanagan, E., Lachapelle, U., & El-Geneidy, A. (2016). Riding tandem: Does cycling infrastructure investment mirror gentrification and privilege in Portland, Oregon, and Chicago, Illinois? *Transportation Research Board 95th Annual Meeting*, Washington, DC, January 10–14.

Foster, M. (1981). *From streetcar to superhighway* (pp. 151–176). Philadelphia: Temple University Press.

Freeman, L. (2005). Displacement or succession? Residential mobility in gentrifying neighborhoods. *Urban Affairs Review* 40 (4): 463–491.

Garin, R. (1966). A matrix formulation of the Lowry model for intrametropolitan activity allocation. *Journal of the American Institute of Planners* 32 (6): 361–364.

Garrison, W., & Levinson, D. (2006). *The transportation experience: Policy, planning, and deployment*. New York: Oxford University Press.

Gee, G., & Takeuchi, D. (2004). Traffic stress, vehicular burden and well-being: A multilevel analysis. *Social Science & Medicine* 59 (2): 405–414.

Geurs, K., & van Wee, B. (2004). Accessibility evaluation of land-use and transport strategies: Review and research directions. *Journal of Transport Geography* 12 (2): 127–140.

Glass, R. (1964). *London: Aspects of change* (Vol. 3). London: MacGibbon & Kee.

Golub, A., & Martens, K. (2014). Using principles of justice to assess the modal equity of regional transportation plans. *Journal of Transport Geography* 41: 10–20.

Grengs, J. (2010). Job accessibility and the modal mismatch in Detroit. *Journal of Transport Geography* 18 (1): 42–54.

Grube-Cavers, A., & Patterson, Z. (2015). Urban rapid rail transit and gentrification in Canadian urban centres: A survival analysis approach. *Urban Studies* 52 (1): 178–194.

Guiliano, G. (2004). Land use impacts of transportation investments: Highway and transit. In S. Hanson, & G. Guiliano (eds.), *The geography of urban transportation*, Third edition. (pp. 237–273). New York: The Guilford Press.

Gutierrez, J. (2009). Transport and accessibility. In R. Kitchin & N. Thrift (eds.), *International Encyclopedia of Human Geography* (pp. 410–417). Oxford: Elsevier.

Halden, D. (2011). The use and abuse of accessibility measures in UK passenger transport planning. *Research in Transportation Business & Management* 2: 12–19.

Handy, S., & Niemeier, D. (1997). Measuring accessibility: An exploration of issues and alternatives. *Environment and Planning A* 29 (7): 1175–1194.

Handy, S., Cao, X., & Mokhtarian, P. (2006). Self-selection in the relationship between the built environment and walking: Empirical evidence from Northern California. *Journal of the American Planning Association* 72 (1): 55–74.

Hansen, W. (1959). How accessibility shapes land use. *Journal of the American Institute of Planners* 25 (2): 73–76.

Hansson, E., Mattisson, K., Björk, J., Östergren, P., & Jakobsson, K. (2011). Relationship between commuting and health outcomes in a cross-sectional population survey in southern Sweden. *BMC Public Health* 11: 834. https://doi.org/10.1186/1471-2458-11-834

Hatzopoulou, M. (2009). *An integrated multi–model approach for predicting the impact of household travel on urban air quality and simulating population exposure*. University of Toronto.

Heath, G., Brownson, R., Kruger, J., Miles, R., Powell, K., Ramsey, L., & Task Force on Community Preventative Services (2006). The effectiveness of urban design and land use and transport policies and practices to increase physical activity: A systematic review. *Journal of Physical Activity & Health* 3 (Suppl 1): S55–S76.

Hensher, D. (1975). Perception and commuter modal choice: An hypothesis. *Urban Studies* 12 (1): 101–104.

Hofstad, H. (2012). Compact city development: High ideals and emerging practices. *European Journal of Spatial Development* Article 49. www.nordregio.se/Global/EJSD/Refereed articles/refereed49.pdf

Hurst, M. E. (1969). The structure of movement and household travel behaviour. *Urban Studies* 6 (1): 70–82.

Iacono, M., Levinson, D., & El-Geneidy, A. (2008). Models of transportation and land use change: A guide to the territory. *Journal of Planning Literature*. Published online February 13. https://doi.org/10.1177/0885412207314010.

Jones, P., & Lucas, K. (2012). The social consequences of transport decision-making: Clarifying concepts, synthesising knowledge and assessing implications. *Journal of Transport Geography* 21: 4–16.

Kain, J., & Beesley, M. (1965). Forecasting car ownership and use. *Urban Studies* 2 (2): 163–185.

Kain, J., & Fauth, G. (1978). The impact of urban development on auto ownership and transit use. *Real Estate Economics* 6 (3): 305–326.

Katoshevski, R., Glickman, I., Ishaq, R., & Shiftan, Y. (2015). Integrating activity-based travel-demand models with land-use and other long-term lifestyle decisions. *Journal of Transport and Land Use* 8 (3): 71–93.

Koenig, J. (1980). Indicators of urban accessibility: Theory and application. *Transportation* 9 (2): 145–172.

Langlois, M., van Lierop, D., Wasfi, R., & El-Geneidy, A. (2015). Chasing sustainability: Do new Transit-Oriented Development residents adopt more sustainable modes of transportation? *Transportation Research Record: Journal of the Transportation Research Board* 2531: 83–92.

Leccese, M., & McCormick, K. (2000). *Charter of the new urbanism*. New York: McGraw-Hill Professional.

Legrain, A., Buliung, R., & El-Geneidy, A. (2015). Who, what, when and where: Revisiting the influences of transit mode share. *Transportation Research Record* 2537: 42–51.

Legrain, A., Eluru, N., & El-Geneidy, A. (2015). Am stressed, must travel: The relationship between mode choice and commuting stress. *Transportation Research Part F: Traffic Psychology and Behaviour* 34: 141–151.

Levine, J., Grengs, J., Shen, Q., & Shen, Q. (2012). Does accessibility require density or speed? A comparison of fast versus close in getting where you want to go in US metropolitan regions. *Journal of the American Planning Association* 78 (2): 157–172.

Levinson, D. (1998). Accessibility and the journey to work. *Journal of Transport Geography* 6 (1): 11–21.

Levinson, D. (2007). Density and dispersion: The co-development of land use and rail in London. *Journal of Economic Geography* 8 (1) 55–77.

Levinson, D., & Krizek, K. (2008). *Planning for place and plexus: Metropolitan land use and transport*. New York: Routledge.

Leyden, K. (2003). Social capital and the built environment: The importance of walkable neighborhoods. *American Journal of Public Health* 93 (9): 1546–1551.

Lowry, I. (1964). *A model of metropolis*. Santa Monica, CA: The RAND Corporation.

Lubitow, A., & Miller, T. (2013). Contesting sustainability: Bikes, race, and politics in Portlandia. *Environmental Justice* 6 (4): 121–126.

Mackett, R. (1983). *Leeds Integrated Land–Use Transport Model (LILT)*. Crowthorne, UK: Transport and Road Research Laboratory.

Manaugh, K., & El-Geneidy, A. (2012). Who benefits from new transportation infrastructure? Using accessibility measures to evaluate social equity in transit provision. In K. Geurs, K. Krizek & A. Reggiani (eds.), *Accessibility analysis and transport planning: Challenges for Europe and North America* (pp. 211–227). Cheltenham: Edward Elgar.

Manaugh, K., & El-Geneidy, A. (2014). *Disentangling self-selection and transit availability influences in mode choice decision making*. Paper presented at the *World Symposium on Land use and Transport* (WSTLUR), Delf in the Netherlands, June 24–27.

Martens, K., Golub, A., & Robinson, G. (2012). A justice-theoretic approach to the distribution of transportation benefits: Implications for transportation planning practice in the United States. *Transportation Research Part A: Policy and Practice* 46 (4): 684–695.

Martinez, F. (1996). MUSSA: Land use model for Santiago city. *Transportation Research Record* 1552: 126–134.

McClintock, M. (1926). *Report and recommendations of the Metropolitan Street Traffic Survey.* Chicago: Chicago Association of Commerce.

McFadden, D. (1973). *Travel demand forecasting study. Bart Impact Studies Final Report Series Part III.* Berkeley, CA: Institute of Urban and Regional Development, University of California.

McFadden, D. (2001). Economic choices. *The American Economic Review* 91 (3): 351–378.

McNally, M. (2007). The four-step model. In D. A. Hensher & K. J. Button (eds.), *Handbook of transport modelling* (Handbooks in transport, Vol. 1) (pp. 35–53). Amsterdam: Pergamon.

Miller, E., & Roorda, M. (2003). Prototype model of household activity-travel scheduling. *Transportation Research Record* 1831: 114–121.

Neff, J., & Dickens, M. (2013). *2013 public transportation fact book.* Washington, DC: American Public Transportation Association.

Nelson, R. (1973). Accessibility and rent: Applying Beckers "time price" concept to the theory of residential location. *Urban Studies* 10 (1): 83–86.

Newbold, K., Scott, D., Spinney, J., Kanaroglou, P., & Páez, A. (2005). Travel behavior within Canada's older population: A cohort analysis. *Journal of Transport Geography* 13 (4): 340–351.

Newman, P., & Kenworthy, J. (1996). The land use–transport connection: An overview. *Land Use Policy* 13 (1): 1–22.

Ory, D., & Mokhtarian, P. (2005). When is getting there half the fun? Modeling the liking for travel. *Transportation Research Part A: Policy and Practice* 39 (2): 97–123.

Owen, A., & Levinson, D. M. (2015). Modeling the commute mode share of transit using continuous accessibility to jobs. *Transportation Research Part A: Policy and Practice*, 74, 110–122.

Paez, A., Scott, D., & Morency, C. (2012). Measuring accessibility: Positive and normative implementations of various accessibility indicators. *Journal of Transport Geography* 25: 141–153.

Pereira, R., Schwanen, T., & Banister, D. (2016). Distributive justice and equity in transportation. *Transport Reviews* 37 (2): 170–191.

Pfaffenbichler, P. (2003). *The strategic, dynamic and integrated urban land use and transport model MARS (Metropolitan Activity Relocation Simulator).* Unpublished PhD Thesis, Technische Universitaet Wien.

Pfaffenbichler, P. (2011). Modelling with systems dynamics as a method to bridge the gap between politics, planning and science? Lessons learnt from the development of the land use and transport model MARS. *Transport Reviews* 31 (2): 267–289.

Phillipson, C. (2011). Developing age-friendly communities: New approaches to growing old in urban environments. In R. A. Settersten & J. L. Angel (eds.), *Handbook of Sociology of Aging* (pp. 279–293). New York: Springer.

Pivo, G., & Fisher, J. (2011). The walkability premium in commercial real estate investments. *Real Estate Economics* 39 (2): 185–219.

Podobnik, B. (2002). The social and environmental achievements of new urbanism: Evidence from Orenco Station. Paper presented at the *Annual Meeting of the American Sociological Association* San Francisco, California.

Preston, J., & Rajé, F. (2007). Accessibility, mobility and transport-related social exclusion. *Journal of Transport Geography* 15 (3): 151–160.

Proffitt, D., Bartholomew, K., Ewing, R., & Miller, H. (2015). Accessibility planning in American metropolitan areas: Are we there yet? Paper presented at the *Transportation Research Board 94th Annual Meeting*, Washington, DC.

Putman, S. (2013). *Integrated urban models: Policy analysis of transportation and land use.* (Routledge Library Editions: The City). Abingdon, UK: Routledge.

Raff, D. (1991). Making cars and making money in the interwar automobile industry: Economies of scale and scope and the manufacturing behind the marketing. *Business History Review* 65 (4): 721–753.

Renne, J., & Wells, J. (2004). Emerging European-style planning in the USA: Transit-oriented development. *World Transport Policy & Practice* 10 (2): 12–24.

Rosenbloom, S. (2001). Sustainability and automobility among the elderly: An international assessment. *Transportation* 28 (4): 375–408.

Salvini, P., & Miller, E. (2005). ILUTE: An operational prototype of a comprehensive microsimulation model of urban systems. *Networks and Spatial Economics* 5 (2): 217–234.

Samuelson, M. (2009). Reducing cars and increasing development: How the creation of a viable transit oriented development corridor in Arlington, Virginia has sparked growth. *Cities of the 21st Century* 1 (1): Article 4. http://digitalcommons.macalester.edu/cities/vol1/iss1/4

Sanchez, T., Shen, Q., & Peng, Z. (2004). Transit mobility, jobs access and low-income labour participation in US metropolitan areas. *Urban Studies* 41 (7): 1313–1331.

Shahrooz, B. (2011). *Design of concrete structures using high–strength steel reinforcement* (Report 679). Washington, DC: National Academies Press.

Shephard, R. (2008). Is active commuting the answer to population health? *Sports Medicine* 38 (9): 751–758.

Smith, N. (1982). Gentrification and uneven development. *Economic Geography* 58 (2): 139–155.

Special Roads Act 1949, Chapter 32. www.legislation.gov.uk/ukpga/1949/32/enacted

Talen, E. (2013). *Charter of the new urbanism*: New York: McGraw-Hill Prof Med/Tech.

Train, K. (1980). A structured logit model of auto ownership and mode choice. *The Review of Economic Studies* 47 (2): 357–370.

Translink. (2010). *Transit–oriented communities: A literature review on the relationship between the built environment and transit ridership.* Vancouver: Translink.

United Nations. (2013). *World Population Ageing 2013.* New York: United Nations.

United States Department of Health & Human Services. (1996). *Physical activity and health: A report of the Surgeon General.* Atlanta, GA: Centres for Disease Control and Prevention.

United States Surgeon General. (2015). Step it up! The Surgeon General's call to action to promote walking and walkable communities. Retrieved from www.surgeongeneral.gov/library/calls/walking-and-walkable-communities/

Van Acker, V., Van Wee, B., & Witlox, F. (2010). When transport geography meets social psychology: Toward a conceptual model of travel behaviour. *Transport Reviews* 30 (2): 219–240.

van Lierop, D., Maat, K., & El-Geneidy, A. (2016). Talking TOD: Learning about transit-oriented development in the United States, Canada, and the Netherlands. *Journal of Urbanism: International Research on Placemaking and Urban Sustainability* 10 (1): 49–62.

van Wee, B. (2015). Viewpoint: Toward a new generation of land use transport interaction models. *Journal of Transport and Land Use* 8 (3): 1–10.

Vuchic, V. (2007). *Urban Transit: Systems and Technology.* Hoboken, NJ: John Wiley and Sons, Inc.

Wachs, M. (1993). Learning from Los Angeles: Transport, urban form, and air quality. *Transportation* 20 (4): 329–354.

Wachs, M., & Kumagai, T. (1973). Physical accessibility as a social indicator. *Socio–Economic Planning Sciences* 7 (5): 437–456.

Waddell, P. (2000). A behavioral simulation model for metropolitan policy analysis and planning: Residential location and housing market components of UrbanSim. *Environment and Planning B: Planning and Design* 27 (2): 247–263.

Waddell, P., & Borning, A. (2004). A case study in digital government: Developing and applying UrbanSim, a system for simulating urban land use, transportation, and environmental impacts. *Social Science Computer Review* 22 (1): 37–51.

Waddell, P., Outwater, M., Bhat, C., & Blain, L. (2002). Design of an integrated land use and activity-based travel model system for the Puget Sound region. *Transportation Research Record: Journal of the Transportation Research Board* 1805: 108–118.

Waddell, P., Wang, L., Charlton, B., & Olsen, A. (2010). Microsimulating parcel-level land use and activity-based travel: Development of a prototype application in San Francisco. *Journal of Transport and Land Use* 3 (2): 65–84.

Walks, A., & Maaranen, R. (2008). Gentrification, social mix, and social polarization: Testing the linkages in large Canadian cities. *Urban Geography* 29 (4): 293–326.

Weber, A., & Pick, G. (1909). *Über den Standort der Industrien: Reine Theorie des Standorts*. Tübingen: JCB Mohr.

Wegener, M. (2004). Overview of land-use transport models. In D. Hensher, K. Button, K. Haynes, & P. Stopher (eds.), *Handbook of transport geography and spatial systems* (Handbooks in Transport, Vol. 5) (pp. 127–146). Oxford: Elsevier.

Wegener, M. (2011). From macro to micro: How much micro is too much? *Transport Reviews* 31 (2): 161–177.

Weiner, E. (1999a). *Urban transportation planning in the United States: An historical overview*. Westport, CT: Greenwood Publishing Group.

Weiner, E. (1999b). *Urban transportation planning in the United States: History, policy, and practice*. New York: Springer.

8

MONITORING SUSTAINABILITY CULTURE

An Overview of a Multi-Year Program of Evaluation Research at the University of Michigan

Robert W. Marans and John Callewaert

Introduction

In their comprehensive book *Basic Methods of Policy Analysis and Planning*, Patton and Sawicki (1986) devote several pages to the final stages of the policy analysis process – *monitoring and evaluating policy outcomes*. They argue that these stages are essential to the analysis process for several reasons. First, programs designed to implement policies and plans consist of ongoing activities, and there may be doubts about whether these activities are addressing the most important aspects of the problem originally identified. Second, better and more recent data may suggest that changes in program implementation are warranted. Finally, there may be concerns about whether a program designed to implement a policy is being carried out in the most effective manner.

As part of their discussion, Patton and Sawicki review a policy analysis–policy evaluation continuum culminating in ex-post evaluations or assessments designed to determine the extent to which policy objectives and their measurable outcomes have been or are being achieved (1986, 304–306). They emphasize that ex-post evaluations should be used to determine whether a policy and the programs designed to implement the policy should be continued, modified, or terminated. That is, ex-post evaluations may involve periodic monitoring of an ongoing program designed to create change. Periodic monitoring during the implementation phase of land use planning has also been suggested (Loh, 2018, this volume).

Over the past 30 years, the literature covering evaluation and its methods as they relate to urban planning have expanded greatly (Chelimsky & Shadish, 1997; Hatry, 2007; Wholey, Hatry, & Newcomer, 1994). In part, evaluations are associated with social impact assessment of planned interventions, such as new roads and other infrastructure projects (Barrow, 2001; Nijkamp & Blaas, 2010). Similar evaluations or post-occupancy evaluations have been used to assess the effectiveness of governmental buildings and to provide feedback to policy makers as well as architects (U.S. General Services Administration, 2011; Zimring & Rashid, 2014). Finally, ex-post evaluations have been used in evaluating governmental programs of interest to planners (Marans, Driver, & Scott, 1972; Burby & Weiss, 1976; Peroff, Davis, & Jones, 1979).

In recent years, ex-post evaluations have also been used in the corporate world to assess policies and programs aimed at making organizations more sustainable (Epstein & Buhovac, 2014; Farver, 2013). Similarly, the Association for the Advancement of Sustainability in Higher Education (AASHE) established a self-reporting tracking, assessment and rating system (STARS) to measure and evaluate sustainability performance at universities throughout the world (AASHE, 2016). The University of Michigan (U-M) is one of several universities that improved its performance since the inception of the program in 2010.[1] U-M is also employing an ex-post evaluation approach to monitoring the university's shift toward a more sustainable culture on its Ann Arbor campus.

In this chapter, an overview of sustainability activities at the University of Michigan is presented. One of those efforts is designed to promote a greater understanding of sustainability among members of the university community and, more generally, to create a stronger culture of sustainability among its students, faculty, and staff. The chapter then describes an ex-post evaluation called the Sustainability Cultural Indicators Program (SCIP), which was designed to monitor progress in moving toward this goal. SCIP involves annual web surveys to measure the extent to which levels of awareness and pro-environmental behaviors are changing over time. The survey data provide regular feedback to policy makers and operational personnel. Furthermore, they are used to evaluate specific sustainability initiatives, indicating the power of evaluative tools for decision-making. The chapter concludes with a discussion of how the evaluative approach could be replicated in other universities and organizations where plans and programs aimed at changing the culture of sustainability are being implemented.

Sustainability at the University of Michigan

For more than a decade, U-M has embarked on multiple programs aimed at enhancing sustainability on its Ann Arbor campus. A key component of this planning initiative involves renovation projects and the construction of new buildings reflecting LEED (Leadership in Energy and Environmental Design) standards. The construction of green buildings is only one of the mechanisms in place to address the university's sustainability goals, particularly with regard to reducing greenhouse gas emissions and waste prevention.[2] U-M's sustainability goals go beyond buildings however. They involve programs and activities covering transportation, environmental protection, procurement, and a movement toward more sustainable foods on campus. These goals, the result of a year-long Campus Sustainability Integrated Assessment, were formalized in 2011.

Campus Sustainability Integrated Assessment

In October 2009, former U-M President Mary Sue Coleman elevated the university's commitment to sustainability in teaching, research, operations, and engagement by creating the U-M Environmental Sustainability Executive Council.[3] One of the first actions of the Council was to endorse a Campus Sustainability Integrated Assessment (CSIA) to analyze U-M's sustainability efforts to date, benchmark against other institutions, and chart a course for the future through identifying long-term goals for sustainable operations on its Ann Arbor campus, including the Athletic Department and the Health System. The CSIA builds on a long history of sustainability commitments in campus operations, such as implementing cogeneration technology at the Central Power Plant in the 1960s, adopting the EPA Green Lights and Energy Star programs in the 1990s, and more recently, establishing LEED Silver certification as the standard for new nonclinical construction projects where the construction value exceeds $10 million. The final CSIA report outlines four high-level themes – *Climate Action*, *Waste Prevention*, *Healthy Environments*, and *Community Awareness*. Accompanying the themes are time-bound and quantifiable Guiding Principles to direct U-M's long-range strategy and 2025 Goals.[4] Table 8.1 provides an overview of U-M's 2025 Sustainability Goals.

Whereas goals for climate action, waste prevention, and creating healthy environments are prevalent at other universities, the focus at U-M on raising community awareness and dealing with the behavioral aspects of campus sustainability is viewed as important and innovative. The articulation of the fourth theme of community awareness and its goal of moving toward a campus-wide culture of sustainability reflects U-M's belief that institutes of higher education have a critical role to play in bringing about a societal shift toward a more sustainable future.[5]

Community awareness involves multiple actions to educate and engage members of the university community with the intent of creating a *culture of sustainability* on campus. A culture of sustainability has been defined as "a culture in which individuals are aware of major environmental (and social/economic) challenges, are behaving in sustainable ways, and are committed to a sustainable lifestyle for both the present and future" (Marans & Edelstein, 2010).

Mechanisms for bringing about a cultural shift within universities and colleges are varied, complex, and often not well articulated (see Leal, 2015). Under the heading of "Planet Blue," efforts at U-M involve programs to expand recycling and reduce energy use in buildings, to encourage alternative modes of travel to/from campus, to promote the use of foods from sustainable sources, and to introduce the concept of sustainability in coursework throughout the university. Many are voluntary programs, such as Planet Blue Ambassadors and Planet Blue Student Leaders, coordinated through the university's Office of Sustainability and the Graham Sustainability Institute (see Marans, Callewaert, & Shriberg, 2015).

Whereas these initiatives are seen as essential to creating a more sustainable campus culture, the Cultural Indicators Sustainability Program (SCIP) represents a critical and complementary component of the Community Awareness theme.

TABLE 8.1 CSIA themes, guiding principles, and 2025 goals

Theme	Guiding principle	2025 Goals
Climate Action	We will pursue energy efficiency and fiscally responsible energy sourcing strategies to reduce greenhouse gas emissions toward long-term carbon neutrality.	Reduce greenhouse gas emissions *(scopes 1 and 2)* by 25% below 2006 levels. Decrease carbon intensity of passenger trips on U-M transportation options by 30% below 2006 levels.
Waste Prevention	We will pursue purchasing, reuse, recycling, and composting strategies toward long-term waste eradication.	Reduce waste tonnage diverted to disposal facilities by 40% below 2006 levels.
Healthy Environments	We will pursue land and water management, built environment, and product sourcing strategies toward improving the health of ecosystems and communities.	Purchase 20% of U-M food from sustainable sources. Protect Huron River water quality by: • minimizing runoff from impervious surfaces *(outperform uncontrolled surfaces by 30%)*, and • reducing the volume of land management chemicals used on campus by 40%.
Community Awareness	We will pursue stakeholder engagement, education, and evaluation strategies toward a campus-wide ethic of sustainability.	*There is no goal recommendation for this theme. However, the report recommends investments in multiple actions to educate our community, track behavior, and report progress over time.*

That is, SCIP is the mechanism for measuring, evaluating, and tracking progress in moving toward a sustainable campus culture at the University of Michigan. SCIP is also being used to evaluate experimental or trial sustainability programs that could be tested in one or a few buildings before being implemented throughout all university buildings.

The Sustainability Cultural Indicators Program

U-M cultural change initiatives stem from the principles outlined under the theme of Community Awareness. They indicate that U-M will "pursue evaluation strategies toward a campus-wide ethic of sustainability and scientifically measure and report progress and behavior as a community" (Coleman, 2011).

The evaluation strategy, begun in 2012, involves a groundbreaking program for monitoring U-M's progress in moving toward a culture of sustainability and providing regular feedback to university policy makers and operational personnel. Progress is determined by annual web surveys of students, faculty and staff regarding sustainability awareness and behavior and tracking changes over time.

Questionnaires and Their Content

Two questionnaires – one for staff and faculty and one for students – are used. While many of the questions are similar, different time frames and sequences are used in the two versions. For example, while staff and faculty survey questions are primarily set within a time frame of the past year, students are often asked questions based on their experiences since the start of the fall semester. Also, students are asked several demographic questions at the start of the survey; for example, they are asked whether they live in campus housing so that those students who do can skip questions which do not apply to students living in campus residence halls. Staff and faculty demographic questions are asked at the end of their survey. As a primary objective of SCIP is to work closely with the goals of the CSIA, questionnaire modules were developed with questions focusing on transportation, waste prevention, the natural environment, food, and climate change as well as U-M sustainability efforts. The average completion time for the online survey is about 15 minutes.

Table 8.2 presents an overview of the question types and modules. In total, the questionnaires each contain approximately 242 questions. A limited number of modifications have been made to the questionnaires each year – adding questions, deleting questions, or clarifying questions – with the goal of maintaining the amount of time required by respondents to complete the survey.

Population and Sample

In order to ensure proportional representation from all segments of the university community and from all geographic parts of the Ann Arbor campus, the sample design aims to obtain relatively large numbers from the entire student body and from the population of staff and faculty. Specifically, a stratified sample is selected by the Registrar's Office so as to yield approximately 1,000 respondents from the freshmen class, 350 respondents from each of the sophomore, junior and senior classes, and 400 graduate student respondents.[6] In addition, a panel of undergraduate students is selected so that individual changes can be tracked in addition to cohort change from year to year. In order to maintain the panel over time, graduating seniors are replaced with the freshmen from the prior year, yielding approximately 900 panel respondents. Finally, a stratified sample is selected by the university's Office of Human Resources with a target of 750 staff and 750 faculty members.

TABLE 8.2 SCIP survey questions by module and question type

Survey module	Question type					
	Knowledge	Disposition	Behavior	Other	Demographics	Total
Transportation	9	10	21	1	0	41
Conservation	5	5	33	1	0	44
Environment	4	2	9	1	0	16
Food	7	6	19	2	0	34
Climate	1	2	0	2	0	5
Sustainability (gen)	0	20	13	3	0	36
U-M efforts	8	0	8	8	0	24
Demographics	0	0	0	0	42	42
TOTAL	34	45	103	18	42	242

Since the inception of the surveys in 2012, we have been successful in reaching or exceeding the targeted number of students, faculty and staff. Annual response rates have ranged from 44 percent (2012) to 22 percent (2013).[7] Completion of questionnaires is attributable to several factors, including the personalized pre-notification email encouraging participation from the U-M President, a series of reminder emails including a video reminder from a coach of one of the athletic teams, and an opportunity for respondents to participate in a gift card drawing.

Overview of Findings

Results from the questionnaires are shared in several ways with the U-M campus community and others. Each year an annual report is prepared, providing detailed information on the respondent population and response distributions for every question. In addition, a publicly available composite table is maintained online for sharing the responses to questions and how these are changing or staying the same over time. Where indicated, statistical significance is reported between the current year and the previous year, and the current year and the first year (2012) of data collection.

In order to summarize findings covering key concepts reflecting a culture of sustainability, 15 indicators were created that combined responses to closely related questions or items about a common idea, concept, or action.[8] Items used to create the indices are shown in Table 8.3.

As shown in Table 8.4, several conclusions can be drawn by examining the indicator scores covering the four years. First, there is considerable room for improvement with regard to pro-environmental behaviors, levels of awareness, degrees of engagement and expressed commitment to sustainability among members of the university community. Second, the travel behavior of students is more in line with the goal of greenhouse gas reduction than is travel to and from campus by staff and faculty. Not surprisingly, students are most likely to walk, bike, or bus to campus. Similarly, students are likely to know more about transportation options available to them and are more engaged than either staff or faculty in sustainability activities on campus.

Third, compared to students and staff, faculty tend to behave in a more sustainable manner with respect to conserving energy, preventing waste, purchasing food, and, more generally, engaging in pro-environmental activities outside the university. Faculty members also express a higher level of commitment to sustainability than staff or students. Fourth, students tend to be less knowledgeable than staff or faculty about protecting the natural environment, preventing waste, and sustainable foods. But they know more about sustainable transportation options than staff and faculty and are equally knowledgeable about the university's sustainability initiatives. Nonetheless, the staff is more aware than other groups of the full range of sustainability activities on campus.

Finally, a review of the indicator scores over the four-year period shows that awareness or knowledge about sustainability increased among members of the

TABLE 8.3 Items used for creating sustainability indicators

Name of index	Name of items	No. of items
Primary		
Climate Action		
Conservation Behavior	turn off lights, use computer power-saver, turn off computer, use motion sensor	4
Travel Behavior	most often mode of travel to campus since fall semester	1
Waste Prevention		
Waste Prevention Behavior	print double-sided, recycle paper, etc., use reusable cups, etc., use property disposition	4
Healthy Environments		
Sustainable Food Purchases	buy sustainable food, organic, locally grown	3
Protecting the Natural Environment	use fertilizer, use herbicides, water lawn	3
Community Awareness		
Sustainable Travel & Transportation	Ann Arbor Area Transportation Authority, U-M buses, biking, Zipcar rental	4
Waste Prevention	recycle glass, plastic, paper, electrical waste, property disposition	5
Natural Environment Protection	dispose of hazardous waste, recognize invasive species, residential property, protect Huron River	4
Sustainable Foods	locally grown, organic, fair trade, humanely treated, hormone-free, grassfed, sustainable fish	7
U-M Sustainability Initiatives	save energy, encourage bus or bike, promote ride-sharing, recycling, sustainable food, reduce greenhouse gas, maintain grounds, protect Huron River	8
Secondary		
Sustainability Engagement at U-M	participate in sustainability organization, Earthfest, take a sustainability course (not for staff/faculty)	3
Sustainability Engagement generally	give money, vote, volunteer, serve as officer	4
Sustainability Commitment	how committed to sustainability	1
Sustainability Disposition	willingness to pay for expanded waste prevention, alternative transportation, and greenhouse gas reduction efforts at U-M	3
Rating U-M Sustainability Initiatives	save energy, encourage bus or bike, promote ride-sharing, recycling, sustainable food, reduce greenhouse gas, maintain grounds, protect Huron River	8

TABLE 8.4 Index scores for students, staff and faculty

Indices	Students				Staff				Faculty			
	2012	2013	2014	2015	2012	2013	2014	2015	2012	2013	2014	2015
Primary indicators												
Climate action												
Conservation behavior (4)★	6.1	6.1	6.1	6.1	6.6	6.6	6.5	6.5	6.9	6.9	7.0	7.0
Travel behavior (1)	7.6	7.5	7.4	7.6	1.6	1.6	1.7	1.5	2.2	2.0	1.8 ⇒	2.3
Waste prevention												
Waste prevention behavior (4)	6.6	6.6	6.7 ⬆	6.9 ⬆	7.0	7.0	7.0	7.1 ⬆	7.3	7.3	7.4 ⬆	7.6 ⬆
Healthy environments												
Sustainable food purchases (3)	5.5	5.3	5.6	5.5	5.7	5.8	5.8 ⬆	5.9 ⬆	6.3	6.2	6.3	6.4
Natural environment behavior	8.6	8.9 ⬆	8.8	8.8	6.5	6.4	6.6	6.7	6.1	6.1	6.4	6.6
Community awareness												
Sustainable travel awareness (4)	4.4	4.3	4.2 ⇒	4.1 ⇒	3.0	3.0	3.2	3.1	3.4	3.3	3.4	3.5
Waste prevention awareness (5)	4.0	4.2 ⬆	4.2 ⬆	4.1	5.0	5.1	5.0	4.9	5.1	5.4 ⬆	5.5 ⬅	5.3

Natural environment awareness (4)	3.1	3.3 ⬅	3.4 ⬅	3.4 ⬅	4.1	4.3 ⬅	4.3 ⬅	4.2	4.3	4.6 ⬅	4.6 ⬅	4.5
Sustainable food awareness (7)	4.3	4.5 ⬅	4.8 ⬅	4.7 ⬅	4.7	5.1 ⬅	5.0 ⬅	5.2 ⬅	5.6	5.7	5.7	6.0 ⬅
U–M sustainability initiatives (8)	5.1	5.1	5.0	5.1	5.4	5.6	5.3	5.3	4.9	5.1	5.1	5.1
Secondary indicators												
U-M sustainability engagement	1.3	1.4	1.6 ⬅	1.4	0.9	0.7	0.7	0.5 ➡	0.7	0.7	0.7	0.6 ➡
Sustainability engagement generally	1.9	1.8	2.0 ⬅	2.0	1.9	1.9	1.8	1.8	3.0	2.9	3.0	2.7 ➡
Sustainability commitment (1)	6.3	6.3	6.3	6.5	6.3	6.4	6.4	6.4	7.0	7.2 ⬅	7.1	7.2
Sustainability disposition (3)	3.5	3.3	3.4	3.4	2.9	2.6 ➡	2.6 ➡	2.5 ➡	5.3	4.8 ⬅	4.9 ➡	4.8 ➡
Rating UM sustainability initiatives (8)	6.6	6.4	6.5	6.7	6.7	6.8	6.6	6.7	6.4	6.5	6.4	6.5

★ Numbers in parentheses are the number of items used to create the index. For U-M sustainability engagement, 3 items and 2 items are used for students and faculty/staff, respectively. Significant changes reflect the differences between each year's mean score and the 2012 mean scores.

➡ significant change (p<.001)
⬅ significant change (p<.01)
⬅ significant change (p<.05)

university community. In some instances, indicator scores for 2015 are significantly higher than 2012 scores. In the case of sustainable foods, there is a significant and positive change between the 2015 scores and the earlier scores, reflecting a growing understanding of sustainable foods over the four years.

The relatively large numbers of student, faculty and staff respondents each year enable the calculation of index scores for each of Ann Arbor's campuses, regions, and subregions. The regions have been developed in collaboration with U-M's energy management team (see Figure 8.1). Differences in indicator scores by campus,

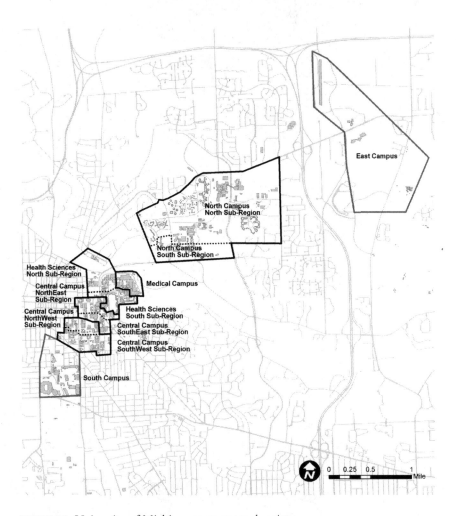

FIGURE 8.1 University of Michigan campuses and regions.

region and subregion help the energy management personnel and other operational units identify where their outreach activities have been successful and where they need to be enhanced. It is also possible to examine relationships between hard measures covering energy use (BTU/square feet) for buildings within a region or subregion and behavioral responses of the occupants in those regions.

Finally, the different geographic areas present opportunities to conduct experiments or trial programs in some places and not in others in order to test the effects, if any, of new initiatives. That is, experiments or trials can take place in clusters of buildings as well as in individual buildings.

Using SCIP to Test New Initiatives

SCIP data are also to be used in evaluation of the impacts of proposed new sustainability initiatives that are set up as experiments or trials. That is, SCIP data collected before and after a particular intervention in a selected region or building could reveal if and by how much change has occurred in selected behaviors and levels of awareness of new sustainability initiatives, such as those dealing with energy conservation, waste reduction, or environmental protection.[9]

As noted earlier, U-M has started numerous sustainability programs during the past decade. The programs have been designed to conserve energy, reduce waste, and change behaviors of students, faculty, and staff. In some cases, the programs have proved successful and continue to flourish. In other instances, they have been discontinued.[10]

In 2015, several new initiatives were recommended as part of a series of sustainability reports to the university's new President.[11] While some of the recommended initiatives will be relatively inexpensive and easy to implement, others will require substantial planning and financial resources. For cases where initiatives are relative easy and inexpensive to implement, annual SCIP data could be used to demonstrate to decision-makers whether the initiative accomplished what it was intended to do. If it did not, the initiative could be discontinued with relatively little cost to the university. However, for recommended new initiatives requiring substantial resources in terms of time and money, it would seem prudent to set up trials or experiments in one part of campus or in one or two buildings, evaluate their impact, and based on the evaluations, determine whether they should be extended to other parts of the campus, modified, or discontinued. SCIP data could be instrumental in making that assessment. One current initiative deals with composting.

In recent years, food composting has become an increasingly important vehicle for waste reduction at U-M. For undergraduate students, it has been actively promoted in the recently remodeled dining facilities within the residence halls. SCIP questions about composting were first asked in the 2014 surveys.[12] At that time, only a third of the undergraduate student body was aware of the university's efforts to promote composting. Few staff and even fewer faculty members knew about what the university was doing with regards to composting.[13] In the 2015 SCIP report, the percentage of undergraduate students who knew about this increased to 39 percent with more than half of the freshmen saying they were "very aware" or "somewhat aware" of the university's efforts to promote composting. Most of these freshmen lived in the residence halls.

According to the report to the President covering waste reduction, "composting, the managed decomposition of organic material into a nutrient-rich soil amendment, is an integral component to reaching the University of Michigan's waste reduction goal."[14] Currently, only a small amount of the university's compostable waste is diverted from landfills. Much of that waste is food scraps coming from dining facilities in residence halls. In efforts to expand composting beyond the dining halls into other parts of the students' living-learning environment, it was decided to launch a pilot or trial program in one of the university's residence halls. The pilot project was conceived within the office of the university's Vice President for Student Life (SL) in collaboration with the Graham Sustainability Institute. It would take place in Bursley Hall, one of the university's largest co-ed residence halls. Bursley was built in 1967 and accommodates approximately 1,270 students, most of whom are freshmen.

Composting Experiment

The pilot program was planned and implemented by a team of Planet Blue Student Leaders under the guidance of key staff from SL and the Graham Institute. The program, launched at the beginning of the winter semester – January 2016 – enlisted participants who were Bursley residents. The participants would regularly collect their individual food scraps or other compostable material and deposit them in a composting container located in the waste closet nearest their room.[15] The residence hall custodians would collect the compost material daily and deposit it to the building's Waste Center (along with recyclables and other trash) where it is weighed weekly prior to its being picked up by a private industrial composting company. In order to encourage participation, a competition was established between volunteers living in the east wing of Bursley and those living in the west wing. At the end of the first month of the experiment, nearly 100 students had volunteered to participate and approximately 150 pounds of composting material had been collected.

Whereas the experiment appeared to be successful as a result of the composting material collected during the three-month implementation period, the results of a short survey conducted at the end of the semester were inconclusive and raised questions.[16] Consequently, the decision was made to extend the experiment for an additional academic year (2016–2017) and use SCIP data collected in fall 2017 to evaluate the program's impact.

Evaluation Plan

The first model, labeled "Residence Hall Change" in Figure 8.2, considers the impact of the experiment on residence halls, whereas the second model, "Individual Student Change," examines the impact of the experiment on individual students.

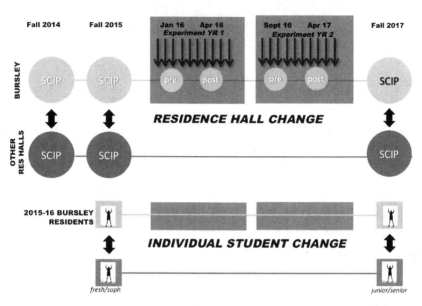

FIGURE 8.2 Bursley composting evaluation.

In the Residence Hall Change model, the plan shows that prior to the experiment, SCIP data covering survey participants in Bursley Hall are compared to survey participants in other university residence halls. Specific data to be compared cover students' general understanding of composting, their composting behavior, and their awareness of U-M's efforts to promote composting. It is hypothesized that there would be no significant differences between students in Bursley and those living in all other undergraduate residence halls in both the 2014 and 2015 surveys.

During the initial three-month intervention period (January–April 2016), short surveys were administered at two points in time to all Bursley residents. The first (pre) survey, administered a few weeks after the pilot composting program was launched, indicated whether or not residents had volunteered to compost and, for those who had, the difficulties they were having in doing so. Students who had not participated in the composting experiment were asked why they had not done so. Both participants and non-participants were asked the SCIP questions covering their overall understanding of composting, their composting behavior, and their awareness of U-M's composting efforts. As noted, a similar short (post) survey was administered to Bursley students prior to their leaving the residence hall at the end of the semester in late April. As the experiment continues during the 2016–2017 academic year, pre and post surveys are administered to the new Bursley students.

The Residence Hall Change model shows that SCIP data collected in fall 2017 will compare Bursley Hall residents with residents living in other undergraduate residence halls. The expectation is that as a result of the experiment over a year and a half, Bursley residents would be most likely to (a) know more about composting, (b) engage in composting, and (c) be more aware of what U-M was doing to promote composting on campus.[17]

In the Individual Student Change model, shown in the lower half of Figure 8.2, the emphasis is in tracking both 2015–2016 and 2016–2017 Bursley residents through the fall of 2017. Some of these students will have been participants in the composting experiment, while many others will not have participated.

It is hypothesized that because of the experiment, those who lived in Bursley during the 2015–2016 and the 2016–2017 academic years would be more aware of composting at U-M and more likely to engage in composting than students who had not been exposed to the Bursley composting program and the composting experience.[18]

Using the findings from the SCIP surveys and the short interim surveys conducted during the year and a half of the experimental period, university officials will be in a position to determine whether the composting program should be expanded as it is to other residence halls, extended but modified, or discontinued.

Applying the University of Michigan Approach in Other Settings

Since the inception of the sustainability culture change program at the University of Michigan, we have learned that other universities are making efforts to address aspects of sustainability culture. Initiatives abound to promote pro-environmental behaviors, to increase environmental literacy through coursework, and more generally to create more sustainable campuses. For the most part, these efforts target students although some are designed to reach the entire university community. Such planning initiatives should be lauded and expanded to other universities as well as to other organizations employing large numbers of people. There are technological mechanisms to deal with issues of climate change and resource depletion, but society's capabilities and will to address these challenges remain questionable. Universities and the corporate world can play a leading role in fostering a societal shift toward a more sustainable culture. And by virtue of their comprehensive outlook and understanding of public engagement, planning educators can be instrumental in guiding that shift.

While such efforts are necessary, there is also a belief that evaluation programs such as SCIP are important in determining the most effective means of bringing about cultural change. As noted, there are universities that are attempting to raise the sustainability consciousness and pro-environmental behaviors among students and staff. Many, including campus planners, have expressed interest in replicating the SCIP model in assessing progress toward those goals. If such efforts were to take place, opportunities for comparative evaluation research would enable policy makers, planners, and operational personnel to better understand what initiatives work best under different circumstances in bringing about necessary cultural changes.

Overview

This chapter has posited that systematic approaches to conducting ex-post evaluations of environment-related programs are a critical component to the planning and plan implementation processes. That is, evaluations and evaluation research are important in providing feedback on the degree to which a planned initiative is successful in achieving the goals it was intended to achieve. That feedback informs decision-makers whether the policies and the programs designed to implement policies should be continued, modified, or discontinued. An example of evaluation and monitoring of a set of programs aimed at changing the culture of sustainability on the University of Michigan campus was presented. The approach involved annual surveys of students, faculty, and staff in order to determine the extent to which levels of awareness and pro-environmental behaviors change after program implementation. Finally, the use of the annual data collection as part of the evaluation of a specific sustainability initiative was presented, indicating the power of evaluative tools in decision-making.

Notes

1 U-M's initial STARS rating of Silver was increased to a Gold rating in AASHE's 2015 report: https://stars.aashe.org/institutions/university-of-michigan-mi/report/2015-06-30/
2 Green buildings and efforts to evaluate their effectiveness represent one movement in dealing with environmental sustainability (see Mallory-Hill & Westlund, 2012). Such buildings are becoming the norm on university campuses in the United States and elsewhere as well as in the private sector.
3 The Council is comprised of the university President, the Provost and Executive Vice President for Student Affairs, the Vice Presidents for Research, Student Affairs, Development, and Global Communications & Strategic Initiatives, the Executive Vice President for Medical Affairs, and the Executive Vice President and Chief Financial Officer.
4 More information on the CSIA process, outcomes, and evaluation can be found at: http://graham.umich.edu/knowledge/ia/campus. Information on progress towards the 2025 Climate Action, Waste Prevention, and Healthy Environments goals can be found at: www.ocs.umich.edu/goals.html.
5 The need for a societal shift to a culture of sustainability is discussed more fully in Callewaert and Marans (2017) and in Marans, Callewaert & Shriberg (2015).
6 During the first year of the survey, the sample design targeted 1,000 students from each class: first-year students, sophomores, juniors and seniors. This was done in part to ensure that in the second year, there would be a sizeable number of juniors and seniors who could participate in the panel.
7 The low response rate in 2013 was attributed to U-M's transition to Gmail during the period of data collection and the fact that many emails with links to questionnaires ended up in spam folders. New email distribution plans were implemented in 2014 and 2015 and response rates improved.
8 See Callewaert and Marans (2017) for a detailed discussion of the indices and the process of creating them.
9 For experimental or quasi-experimental designs, a control group of people and or places is required where no intervention takes place. Comparing outcomes between the control and experimental groups would determine if the intervention targeting the

experimental group is having an impact. For a discussion of control groups and the planning of experiments, see Campbell and Stanley (1966) and Patton & Sawicki (1986, 313–316).

10 One initiative that proved ineffective and was eliminated was a campaign involving energy-saving signage throughout the university. The signs were designed to encourage students, faculty and staff to save energy by reminding them to: "Use Your Power Wisely." A pilot study in five university buildings revealed that few occupants recognized the signs when they were presented to them in a questionnaire; and for those who did recognize the signs, a limited number had read them (Marans & Edelstein, 2010). Had the signs been first tested in pilot buildings rather that printing and posting them in the university's 450 buildings, there could have been a saving of several thousand dollars.

11 Three committee reports were prepared for U-M's new president in 2015. The University of Michigan reports covered landfill waste reduction, greenhouse gas reduction, and sustainability culture. The latter with its recommendations can be found at: http://sustainability.umich.edu/media/files/Sustainability-Culture-Committee-Report-2015.pdf.

12 Composting was not viewed as an important component of the university's waste reduction program by the advisory team guiding the design of the initial SCIP questionnaires. Subsequent discussions with university personnel dealing with waste and food services resulted in the addition of four questions about composting.

13 See Appendix Table C15 of the SCIP report covering 2014 findings (Marans and Callewaert, 2015).

14 The University of Michigan report covering waste reduction can be found at: http://sustainability.umich.edu/media/files/Landfill-Waste-Reduction-Committee-Report-2015.pdf.

15 Student volunteers were given small buckets with removable disposable liners to collect their composting material and guidelines as to what was compostable and what was not. In addition to food scraps, paper products such as napkins, paper toweling, plates, and cups are also compostable.

16 Of the more than 1,200 Bursley residents who were asked to complete the survey, only 48 students responded and just two-thirds of them said they were very aware of U-M's efforts to promote composting in their residence hall.

17 Although it was difficult to know how many of the current Bursley Hall students would return to live there during the academic year 2016–2017, none will be living there during the 2017–2018 academic year since Bursley is designated as primarily a freshmen residence hall, with some students choosing to remain there during their sophomore year. Nonetheless, it is expected that the effects of the Bursley composting program will carry over in time, showing a greater understanding among its residents of composting at U-M than what would be found in other U-M residence halls.

18 The 2015 SCIP data indicate that most university freshmen (96 percent) live in a residence hall and 17 percent of them reside in Bursley Hall. Assuming future SCIP surveys target the same number of sophomores and juniors as in the past (350 of each), there will be approximately 200 future respondents who were Bursley Hall residents during the year and a half of the experiment.

References

AASHE, 2016. *Stars 2.1 Technical Manual: Administrative Update One* www.aashe.org/files/documents/STARS/stars_2.1_technical_manual_-_administrative_update_one.pdf.

Barrow, C. J. 2001. *Social Impact Assessment: An Introduction*. New York: Oxford University Press.

Burby, R. & Weiss, S. 1976. *New Communities U.S.A.* Lexington, MA: Lexington Books.

Callewaert, J. & Marans, R. W. 2017. Measuring Progress over Time: The Sustainability Cultural Indicators Program at the University of Michigan. In: Leal W. L., Skanavis, C., do Paço, A., Rogers, J., Kuznetsova, O., & Castro, P. (Eds.) *Handbook of Theory and Practice of Sustainable Development in Higher Education*. Volume 2. Berlin: Springer, 173–187.

Campbell, D. T. & Stanley, J. C. 1966. *Experimental and Quasi–Experimental Designs for Research*. Chicago: Rand-McNally.

Chelimsky, E. & Shadish, W. R. 1997. *Evaluation for the 21st Century: A Handbook*. Thousand Oaks, CA: Sage Publications.

Coleman, M. S. 2011. U-M Sustainability Commitment. http://sustainability.umich.edu/commitment.

Epstein, Marc J. & Buhovac, A. R. 2014. *Making Sustainability Work: Best Practices in Managing and Measuring Corporate Social, Environmental, and Economic Impacts*, 2nd Edition. San Francisco: Berrett-Koehler Publishers.

Farver, S. 2013 *Mainstreaming Corporate Sustainability: Using Proven Tools to Promote Business Success*. Cotati, CA: GreenFix.

Hatry, H. 2007 *Performance Measurement: Getting Results*. Washington, DC: Urban Institute Press.

Leal, W. L. 2015. *Transformative Approaches to Sustainable Development at Universities: Working Across Disciplines*. Cham, Switzerland: Springer.

Loh, C. G. 2018. Learning from Practice, Learning for Practice in Local Land Use Planning Research. In Sanchez, T. W. (Ed.) *Planning Research and* Knowledge. Abingdon, U.K.: Routledge, 24–34.

Mallory-Hill, S. & Westlund, A. 2012. Evaluating the Impact of Green Building on Worker Productivity and Health: A Literature Review. In Mallory-Hill, S., Preiser, W., & Watson, C. (Eds.) *Enhancing Building Performance*. Oxford, U.K.: Wiley-Blackwell, 167–178.

Marans, R. W. and Edelstein, J. Y. 2010. Human Dimensions of Energy Conservation and Sustainability: A case Study of the University of Michigan's Energy Conservation Program. *International Journal of Sustainability in Higher Education*, Vol. 11, No. 1, 6–18.

Marans, R. W. & Callewaert, J. 2015. *Monitoring the Culture of Sustainability at the University of Michigan: Fall 2014*. Ann Arbor, MI: Graham Sustainability Institute.

Marans, R. W., Driver, B. L., & Scott, J. C. 1972. *Youth and the Environment: An Evaluation of the 1972 Youth Conservation Corps*. Ann Arbor, MI: Institute for Social Research, University of Michigan.

Marans, R. W., Callewaert, J., & Shriberg, M. 2015 In Leal, W. L (Wd.) *Transformative Approaches to Sustainable Development at Universities: Working Across Disciplines*. Cham, Switzerland: Springer, 165–180.

Nijkamp, P. & Blaas, E. W. 2010. *Impact Assessment and Evaluation in Transportation Planning*. Dordrecht: Kluwer Academic Publishers.

Patton, C. V. & Sawicki, D. S. 1986. *Basic Methods of Policy Analysis and Planning*. Englewood Cliffs, NJ; Prentice-Hall.

Peroff, K. A., Davis, C., & Jones, R. 1979. *Gautreaux Housing Demonstration: An Evaluation of its Impact on Participating Households*. Washington, DC: U.S. Department of Housing and Urban Development, Office of Policy Development and Research.

U.S. General Services Administration. 2011. *Green Building Performance: A Post Occupancy Evaluation of 22 GSA Buildings*. www.gsa.gov/graphics/pbs/Green_Building_Performance.pdf.

Wholey, J. S., Hatry, H., & Newcomer, K. E. (Eds). 1994. *Handbook of Practical Program Evaluation*. San Francisco, CA: Jossey-Bass.

Zimring, C. & Rashid, M. 2014. Facility Performance Evaluation (FPE). https://www.wbdg.org/resources/fpe.php.

PART III
Planning Research on Objects and Design

9
TOWARDS AN OBJECT-ORIENTED CASE METHODOLOGY FOR PLANNERS

Robert Beauregard and Laura Lieto

Some decades ago, Donald Schön (1982) pointed out, quite perceptively, that planning academics were not the only ones who use theory. Actively engaged in planning, practitioners carry with them a "knowing-in-practice" that synthesizes past experience and current realities, much like "theory" is meant to do. A similar comment can be made about planning research. Academics are not alone in doing it. To have plans adopted and implemented, practitioners gather and analyze information and, based on this new knowledge, decide how to proceed. And while the research of practitioners might be ad hoc, task-specific, and loosely guided by scientific standards, it is still research.

We do not see a problem here. What does concern us is the extent to which academic research is made applicable to the pressing concerns of non-academic planners.[1] The key for bridging the two rests with methodology. Even the most neophyte researcher knows that research can be done in a variety of ways. This understanding is captured in the common, though problematic, distinction between quantitative and qualitative research. From its inception, and central to its adoption by governments, academic planning has favored the quantitative end of this continuum epitomized by large-N, quantitative analyses.

Consider the landscape of academic research. A survey of the major U.S. planning journals suggests that most published research analyzes secondary data from national censuses or surveys to draw inferences from multiple cases. In a recent issue of the *Journal of Planning Education and Research*, Ewing, Reid, Hojrasouliha, Neckerman, Purciel-Hiol, and Greene (2016) applied binomial regression to data for 588 city blocks in New York City to learn how the design of streetscapes affects pedestrian activity. Shi, Chu, and Debats (2015), in the *Journal of the American Planning Association*, used a survey of 156 U.S. cities along with logistic regression to measure the impact of local leadership and municipal expenditures on the decision to engage in climate adaptation planning. Or, take the "best practice" approach of the European Union. Large surveys carried out in member-states form the basis for advising the competition for structural funds and the alignment of urban and regional policies (Vettoretto, 2009).

If academic research is to be useful to practitioners, however, it needs to attend to the complexities of both practice and implementation. Large-N, quantitative analyses inevitably underestimate differences and miss the specificities of place that need to be addressed. Case studies, despite the detail and attentiveness to decisions and actions, are also deficient. For example, Bent Flyvbjerg (1998), in an otherwise rich and insightful case analysis of an attempt to redo downtown transportation in Aalborg, Denmark, provides little in the way of guidance for planners. Despite the detail, it is not apparent what to do in this or a similar situation. This is typical. Studies that reveal the flow of projects from conception to realization and what can be done to make them successful are still too rare, despite a few valuable works on implementation (Loh, 2018, this volume). Both large-N, quantitative analyses and case studies are launched from a scholarly platform, written mainly to enlighten other academics, and are more often than not inattentive to practical planning issues.

The purpose of this chapter is to argue for a case study methodology that is more responsive to the everyday needs of planning practitioners. Undoubtedly, no single or best way of doing planning research exists. Nonetheless, whatever methodology is selected should connect to the settings in which practitioners operate and reflect on the questions that they need answered. These two concerns push us toward a case methodology (see also Duminy, Odendall, and Watson, 2016). An even stronger connection to practice can be established if greater attention is paid to the objects – housing units, wetlands, bus shelters, light standards – of planning. Although people and their various associations (e.g., city councils and business groups) are critical to planning effectiveness, they are not exclusively so. What will bring both planning practitioners and researchers more "into the world" is attention to the entanglement of social relations and material objects. This requires an object-oriented case methodology.

Arguments for a Case-Based Methodology

Practicing planners might read academic research to augment their knowledge of, say, the influence of municipal leadership on plan-making. Such research, however, seldom provides practical guidance.[2] Although the planner is more informed, what they ought to do is left unaddressed. Even when research-derived knowledge seems relevant, it still has to be related to the specific context in which the planner operates. Such translation is difficult and imposes a heavy burden on the practitioner. In large-N, quantitative analyses, the specific and the general cannot be easily reconciled (Huxley, 2011); case methodology is usually biased by its theoretical and ideological premises and rarely provides practitioners with critical feedback. "Little can be learned from single cases" (Rueschemeyer, 2003, p. 306) when they escape general accounts about how the world works. Would it not be better if more research were available that took context into account and attended to the challenges of implementation?

Although "yes" seems to be the appropriate response to this question, we should resist answering in this way until we first investigate how research might best fit into the world of practitioners. Here, Bent Flyvbjerg is helpful. In his *Making Social Science Matter* (2001, pp. 9–20), he argues that people become highly adept at what they do – become *virtuosi* – when they absorb and then transcend the principles of practice, integrate experiences into their actions, and are conscious of their place in the world. It is not enough to follow the rules of how to write a plan or advise a developer on a zoning issue. Rather, the planner is effective when she acts intuitively and embodies an understanding that enables her to make wise, not just prescribed, decisions.

Flyvbjerg further argues that action always occurs somewhere. One cannot act in the abstract. Action, context, and interpretation are inseparable and contingently related (Flyvbjerg, 2001, p. 43). When a practicing planner asks about housing affordability, he has in mind a housing market that exists at this time and in this place. The knowledge he needs must be specific to the here and now. Knowledge about other times and other cities can only be suggestive, not directly useful. The planner is faced with a problem – at this moment – that requires detailed and contextualized knowledge.

In research terms, context is what lies beyond the case (Duminy, Odendall, and Watson, 2016, p. 22). The context of an event, condition, or action is whatever is considered external to it. Moreover, it is always "fabricated and negotiated" (Latour, 1996, p. 143). For example, the response to the 2007–2008 waste crisis in Naples (Italy) can only be understood by acknowledging the national government's designation of disposal sites as having "national strategic relevance" and its declaration of a "state of exception" as regards governance (Lieto, 2009). The national government is "outside" Naples and arches over it and other Italian cities. We term this the distant context (Beauregard, 2015, pp. 89–94). Planners also exist within a proximate context. Enforcement of on-street parking in Naples is very much influenced by the width of streets. Where streets are wide and straight and their edges easily demarcated for legal parking spaces, enforcement works well. In neighborhoods where streets are narrow and configured differently, enforcement becomes an altogether different task (Lieto, 2016, pp. 31–33).

Research that pursues generalization and ostracizes context is not very helpful for practitioners. Not only is it deficient as regards specific knowledge, but it usually sets aside the contingency and sequencing inherent in actual events. No matter how much the planner knows about the city in which she works, she is always faced with a jumble of causal relationships. Multiple factors operate and appear in unpredictable combinations. Decisions and actions thus tend to be conjunctural, heterogeneous, and contingent (Ragin, 2000, pp. 21–42). To this extent, the greater the planner's mastery of actual conditions, the better she can adapt. The goal is research that "accords[s] with the pragmatic way that action is defined by the actors in a concrete social situation" (Flyvbjerg, 2001, p. 42).

Lurking behind Flyvbjerg's argument is the issue of implementation. Planners not only propose what to do, they also have responsibility for what is done in response to their advice (Beauregard, 2015, pp. 36–56). Knowing what factors transform a slum, improve transportation access for the elderly, or reduce greenhouse gas emissions is insufficient. Planners also have an obligation to assure that these factors are recognized by those with the authority and power to implement them; that is, those who are responsible and accountable. They cannot remain detached. Implementation, moreover, entails very specific decisions and actions related to who has to do what, when, and with what resources, capacities, and understandings. This requires attention to detail and to the flow of argumentation and events (Throgmorton, 2000). Any researcher focusing on implementation needs to convey how neighborhood flooding relates to climate change and how such flooding can be prevented through actions in this place and at this time. What zoning rules need to be changed or adopted? What language has to be used to make the rules legally defensible and enforceable? What consequences will likely ensue? Who will oppose these rule changes? Who supports them? How does the planner mobilize supporters to act and opponents to acquiesce?

All of this points to case studies – and the power of examples – as the most appropriate type of research for connecting to practice (Duminy, Odendall, and Watson, 2016; Gerring, 2004; Flyvbjerg, 2006; Verschuren, 2003). First, case studies are most appropriate when the researcher wants to understand a specific instance of some condition or event. That is, when she wants to focus in detail on a single case or small number of cases. Second, a case study is almost always concerned with the way things happen; that is, with the processes by which the world is performed. This directs the researcher not just to time (a key aspect of context) but also to implementation; that is, how events are moved along by decisions and actions. Third, particular attention is often paid to the actors who are involved in making these decisions and taking these actions, thus providing planners with a sense of who must decide and act and with whom they must collaborate. Fourth, a case takes place somewhere; it is situated rather than decontextualized. Fifth, a good case researcher acknowledges the complexity and contingency of any condition or event. Case study researchers are humbled by the lack of predictability and the value of specificities; their work is not meant to be formally generalized across settings, although it can still be part of the general process of knowledge accumulation (Flyvbjerg, 2006). Lastly, and as compared to their large-N, quantitative counterparts, case studies are less subservient to the scientific imperative of hypothesis-testing. This makes them more open to learning from evidence rather than being intent on testing evidence against theory. For these reasons, case study methodology seems more appropriate for the kinds of research directly useful to practitioners. Case studies put researchers in the world of planners.

Yet, we are also critical of case studies. For the most part, research of this type is still wedded to the notion that the world is primarily a product of human action. We disagree. If planners are to be effective, they need to place themselves amid both humans and nonhumans. They need to acknowledge the material world.

Objects Matter

The perspective on which our object-oriented case methodology is based views the world as profoundly material, constituted in assemblages or networks, and performed by a heterogeneous array of actors (Latour, 2005; Lieto and Beauregard, 2013). Because nonhuman things (electrical transformers, ferry boats, underground streams, and pigeons) are active and consequential, and collaborate with planners, we propose a case methodology that acknowledges these entanglements and dependencies.

Central to our argument is the assertion that the constituent form of reality is the assemblage, not the individual or the household (McFarlane and Anderson, 2011). People do not act alone, but rather in networks, comprised of other humans, their human associations, and nonhuman objects, and with cities and regions comprised of multiple assemblages.[3] Action is thus a matter of collaboration such that planners join forces with highway off-ramps, annual reports, and seasonal flooding (Lieto and Beauregard, 2016).

Consider a simple example. For "big data" to be used to manage a local government, administrative mechanisms must be in place to collect valid and reliable information, computational machines (along with the electricity to operate them) must be made available, computer software has to be properly written, and technicians need to be provided with rooms, desks, and chairs. Without these nonhuman things, planners would not be able to deploy "big data," develop climate change plans, or administer zoning regulations (Beauregard, 2012). What matters is "relationalities of composition" (McFarlane, 2011, p. 206) in which people and things are brought together around shared objectives. These assemblages are what enable concerted and coordinated action. The implication is that "[p]lanners are not so much intervening [in the world] as they are drawn into associations" (Rydin, 2014, p. 591) that enable them to influence matters that concern them.

In the material world, what matters in terms of action – and thus planning – is heterogeneity; that is, the diversity of different actors who must come together for purposive change to be made to happen. An actor is any "thing" which shifts the behavior of others, thereby causing a response. Within assemblages, action is distributed across humans and nonhumans. In brief, the sociality of the world is inseparable from its materiality (Law and Mol, 1995). More specifically, humans delegate actions (and responsibility) to things, as when transportation planners synchronize the traffic lights along a major boulevard in order to regulate vehicle flow or environmental planners pass regulations that prohibit new construction in an ecologically sensitive area. In these instances, the intent of planning is carried out by electronic devices and laws respectively.

Humans and material objects, then, are fused together, and it is impossible to accurately describe any collective action – whether it is a protest movement, a terrorist attack, or a planning commission meeting – in their absence (Molotch, 2013; Vilches and Tate, 2016, pp. 64–65). There is no "in-here" of planners and "out-there" of rivers, office towers, sidewalks, insects, and weather patterns.

Planners are "in" the world in a way that denies any delusion that, as experts, they stand above or beyond the messiness (the politics, the erratic bird migrations, the unpredictable infrastructure failures) of what lies outside their offices. Rather, they must recognize that they do not command the world "out-there," but are intricately entangled in and dependent on it. Objects matter both as relational and material entities. An object is not just a physical artifact – inert and manipulable – but has agency as an effect of "stable arrays of networks of relations" (Law, 2002, p. 91).[4] Just as planners in numerous countries have acted on a democratic impulse to open planning to the city's residents, they also must act on a material impulse to acknowledge the influence of nonhuman things.

Our sense of place follows from this understanding of how the world is constituted. We view place not as preceding action, but rather as emerging during the formation of assemblages (Murdoch, 1998). Place is assembled as actors come together; it is transient and occurs as a consequence of encounters and interactions (Tsing, 2005, p. xi). A once-buried stream in Seoul, Korea, becomes a place for strolling, contemplation, and play after the government removes the soil that covered it, adds landscaping, builds walkways, creates access points, and publicizes its accomplishment nationally and internationally. It will remain "this place" as long as humans and objects remain together in this assemblage. Even more obvious is the city itself – created as a place by plans, regulations, road networks, buildings, land forms, and shade trees. Objects have a central role to play, and a planning without objects is a delusion (Duineveld, Van Ascher, and Beuen, 2013).

Object-Oriented Case Methodology

What remains of our argument is to sketch how such a methodology might be put into effect. To simplify matters, we isolate three aspects that distinguish an object-oriented case methodology from a typical case study. They are (1) the concern with objects and their entanglements, (2) the focus on distributed action and the importance of process tracing, and (3) the search for possibilities and thus counterfactuals.

First, the methodology explicitly recognizes the importance of objects to what actors are able to do.[5] Action is almost always a collaboration between humans and nonhumans, and it makes no sense to reduce these entanglements only to their human components. Researchers thus need a methodology that returns objects to their proper place in the workings of the world. The proposed case study methodology thus attends to the objects that populate the assemblages that enable humans to carry out their projects. Objects (e.g., a development site, an air quality monitor) must be given a central role in the research, with one or more objects always present when discussing how an event or controversy unfolds.

Consider as illustration Bruno Latour's *Aramis or the Love of Technology* (1996). In it, he tells the story of an attempt in the 1980s in Paris to develop an automated, personal rapid transit system known as Aramis. After years of study and research and the development of an operable prototype, the project faltered and was never implemented. In exploring the reasons for this, Latour gives objects a central role. For him, the story is not simply about humans and their actions. Issues of funding, ministerial politics, bureaucratic routines, consultant relationships, interagency jealousies, and political will all play a role, but that role only makes sense in relation to the many objects that had to come together to enable Aramis to function system-wide and at full capacity. The list of objects is extensive: optical sensors, passenger modules, variable-reluctance motors, technical reports, scale models, test sites, stations, track switches, patents, and telescoping bumpers to name just a few. Aramis's fate was inseparable from the objects essential for its full functioning. As much as humans, they dictated the flow of events.

In presenting the case, Latour avoids calling out miscreants or pointing to when mistakes had been made. It is not for him to attribute a failure in implementation to someone or some thing; that is, to draw an evaluative conclusion. What is important is recognizing the primacy of objects in the flow of events: "Aramis is dead, but there was no murder. There is no perpetrator, no guilty party" (Latour, 1996, p. 290). Nonetheless, Latour is not opposed to explanation. What he wants is a "deep re-description of what is a social explanation" (Latour, 2000, p. 107). Yet, he cannot resist commenting on what went wrong. In a hypothetical dialogue with the project's supporters, he tells them, "You believed in the autonomy of technology" (Latour, 1996, p. 292) and failed to appreciate the socio-materiality of the world.

In an object-oriented case study, objects are always "there" in interactions and collaborations, and they deserve the same attention that a researcher gives to humans. Data must be collected on objects and analyzed to the same degree as for engineers, regional transportation agencies, and politicians. In order to understand Aramis's fate, we need to know as much about the software controlling the coupling and uncoupling of passenger modules as we do about passengers who fail to queue properly. This is not just true as regards cases that address technology or science. Because no human activity (whether it be writing a climate change plan or speaking at a public meeting) can occur in the absence of nonhuman things, all cases must attend to the efficacy of objects.

Second, our proposed methodology focuses on distributed action. Unlike a typical case, an object-oriented case methodology assumes that both humans and nonhumans act. In fact, they share in action – action is distributed. This has two implications. One is that action is always understood as emanating from collaborations and entanglements. The other is that action is always cast in terms of processes rather than as isolated acts. Consequently, action has to be studied as sequences; that is, a flow of actions, responses, and responses to those actions. The researcher traces the processes at work by following multiple and circuitous paths as they branch off and run parallel to each other. What is important for "telling" the case and also for drawing forth implications for planning is how things happen. This means learning about the sequences of events that define the assemblage (Collier, 2011; Waldner, 2015) and treating action as always entangled.[6]

As an example, we offer a case by Anique Hommels (2005, pp. 41–79) concerning the renovation of a large, mixed-use, commercial project (Hoog Catharijne) built in the 1970s in Utrecht, The Netherlands. Her story begins with the first redevelopment plan for the railway station district in 1962 and ends with a new master plan (one of many) approved in 2007 by the city council. The case revolves around the difficulties of changing physical structures that since the 1960s conditioned actors and decision-making. In telling the story, Hommels traces an unfolding series of actions as the project moves forward, stalls, is rejuvenated, and restarts. From its opening in 1973 to 1982 when it was purchased by a large pension fund, Hoog Catharijne functioned perfectly well. But, in the early 1980s, its high modernist design and years of use contributed to a sense that the complex needed to be upgraded and its layout reconfigured. Consequently, the city government developed a number of plans, each cast aside for various reasons until it finally settled, nearly three decades later, on an approach acceptable to the major actors.

To account for distributed action, Hommels takes us through sequences of launched and discarded initiatives, formed and dissolved partnerships, the rise of resident committees, an array of alternative proposals, and an extended debate regarding how to think about this concrete, megastructure that loomed over the city's downtown. Central to the redevelopment was whether to retain the original "raised level model" (which informed the initial design of pedestrian pathways and enclosed shops above street level) or to institute a "ground-floor model" that would open the project to the surrounding streets and canals and enable a more fine-grained and human-scale experience. For years, the debate was unresolved. Hoog Catharijne's bulky materiality was seemingly too obdurate to be adaptable to changing needs and actors. Only when the mayor hired the former director of development for Rotterdam was the impasse broken. The plan he produced in 1997 embraced the ground-floor model and, more importantly, satisfied the concerns of the major actors, thereby allowing the project to proceed. Throughout, Hommels heeded the chronology of planning decisions and actions by depicting the pathways along which Hoog Catharijne's obdurate materials were addressed.

This emphasis on sequence reflects how life happens and epitomizes an actor-network approach to research that embodies actions and their consequences. Moreover, it bridges the research and the practical concerns of planners who have to act and react in sequences of decisions, actions, reflection, and response. This is the essence of implementation. Consequently, the object-oriented case methodologist thinks in terms of processes and attempts to trace those processes. These sequences are not meant, however, to be causal paths, but rather possible paths. And in tracing them, the researcher makes explicit the collaborative nature of all action.

Third, the methodology that we are proposing is meant to enable planners to understand the choices that might exist and which might be available to them. The objective is not to formulate a single and exhaustive explanation of a planning event. Rather, planning research should concern itself with "always-emergent conditions" and aim to identify the array of possibilities at play (Hirschman, 1970;

Marcus and Saka, 2006, p. 101; McFarlane and Andersson, 2011).[7] Knowing this, those reading the research can then think through the options while developing an appreciation for the complexity and fluidity of the world. This absolves the researcher of the responsibility to simplify the situation for his or her readers; that is, to impose meaning and coherence. If we consider actions to be contingent and practical outcomes of assemblage formation, we must acknowledge that a "slight change could easily have led to a different outcome" (Levy, 2008, p. 630). The intent, then, is to articulate how different choices, different actions, and different responses might have occurred, thus revealing the indeterminate nature of all action. This means attending to counterfactuals (Levy, 2008; Megill, 2007, pp. 151–156). The researcher has to suggest what might have happened if an action had not succeeded or even been attempted. The point, though, is not to write counterfactual cases, but rather to entertain the possibility of doing so.

Although few case studies are written from a counterfactual point of view (but see Campbell, Tait, and Watkins, 2014), many cases suggest that things could have happened differently. Take as an example Shula Goulden's (2016) study of the adoption of "green building" standards in Israel. Her interest is in how such environmental assessment practices bring green buildings into existence. Nevertheless, the case reveals key points in the process where a different path might have been taken.

Consider two such instances. One occurred after an assessment procedure had been developed in 2005 by the Standards Institution of Israel (SII). Only a few builders took notice and coordination among key ministries such as Environment, Energy, and Interior was weak. As a result, the procedures were generally ignored. In response, the Israeli Green Building Council was formed in 2007. In order to proceed, it had to decide whether to adopt and revise the SII standards, devise new ones, or look to international standards. Here was a potential turning point. That the Council opted for the first was not preordained. The revised standards were more precise than the original, gained broader support, and enabled the convergence of green buildings with the issue of climate change. In retrospect, the decision seems wise, but political support might not have been forthcoming and it was not known in advance that climate change would be another ally.

A second critical juncture in 2010 had to do with climate change. Then, the national government adopted a plan to reduce greenhouse gas (GHG) emissions in response to pressure from local governments, global initiatives occurring outside the country, and the report of an international consulting firm. The intersection of these factors enabled a link to be made between GHG emissions and buildings and led to many city governments making environmental assessment procedures a required part of their planning regulations. If local pressure had not been forthcoming, if global initiatives had been overlooked due to more pressing domestic matters, or if the national government had not hired the consulting firm, what happened would not have happened. The adoption of green building assessments was far from inevitable.

What Goulden uncovers in her case suggests that things could have occurred differently. Coalitions might not have formed when they did, or the consultant's report might have been ignored. Consequently, the standards might have been less precise, optional rather than required by planning law, or bypassed by builders and developers. Counterfactuals make the relational nature of objects and people more evident: the green building is not a stable, univocally identified thing, but the outcome of a contingent array of relations among actors, things, and norms. A planning-oriented case methodology, then, should focus on the contingency of events and the potential for actions to go astray. To pursue explanations that imply that what happened could only have happened in this way is to undermine planning itself. It constricts possibilities and hobbles planners in their quest for purposive change and a better world (Beauregard and Lieto, 2016). In a world where life follows a script, little room exists for planners to propose and appropriate actions to follow.

Conclusion

Much more could be said about an object-oriented case methodology. What you have read is schematic and suggestive. Our goal has been to compare and contrast this approach to that of typical planning methodologies and point out that what we propose might be more useful for practicing planners. And despite our focus on context and implementation and on individual planning events, we believe that an object-oriented case methodology can also contribute to a more general understanding of planning. The methodology is meant mainly to benefit practitioners, but contributes as well to the work of scholars providing that they reject the "common [misunderstanding] about case study research" that it cannot yield generalizations (Flyvbjerg, 2006, p. 219). A focus on the specific does not necessarily limit collective learning within a broader community of inquiry. While knowledge about practice produced by an object-oriented case might not be suitable for formal generalization, it can be of broader value for two reasons.

First, by acknowledging the heterogeneity of contexts, conditions, and actors, an object-oriented case methodology offers an antidote against overextended generalizations, especially when it falsifies general theories as in the philosopher Karl Popper's famous example of the black swan.[8] Generality is not only about what happens or exists across a multitude of instances; it also involves empirical feedback on our theoretical frames, something cases are uniquely positioned to do.

Second, and most importantly, the focus on materiality and context brings to the fore how general forces of change (e.g., globalization, climate change, international migration) come to life in a specific setting where the entanglement of humans and objects creates a zone of friction (Tsing, 2005). Here, the general becomes what is engaged, incarnated, and substantial and thereby leads planners to implementation. This reverses our understanding of generalization from its usual meaning. It is now about enhancing local knowledge as the necessary counterpart to a wider discourse, one that cannot be fully understood without specific cultural assumptions that define planning's existence in diverse settings. Objects contribute by giving substance to planning aspirations as they move and change across different localities and cultures.

In sum, an object-oriented case methodology can be an effective way to mediate between academic research and professional practice. Such an approach attends to what planners need to do their job while contributing to scholarly work. It will not do so, however, without greater awareness of the importance of objects to planning.

Notes

1. The gap between theory and practice is a growing concern in the international planning community. Kunzmann and Koll-Schretzenmayr argue that "there are fewer and fewer bridges between academia and professional practice" (2015, p. 16). Their concern reflects the chasm between Anglophone scholars and those with different European languages and traditions.
2. Alexander (2010) makes a similar comment about the influence of planning theory on practice; to wit: occurring more through enlightenment than translation into action.
3. While we applaud urban morphologists for their focus on the materiality of the city, we do not consider the city's "form" as a candidate for an object-oriented case study; form is a quality of multiple, contiguous objects, not itself an object. On urban form, see Benevolo (1971), Scheer (2018, this volume), and Whitehand (1992).
4. Inseparable from materiality, objects are finite and obdurate (Hutchby, 2001). On this point, we distinguish between an object and a thing. Both are relational and material, but recalling the Latin word *res*, a thing brings additional implications derived from its original meaning as a gathering. A thing is more abstract while an object is more finite, obdurate, and politically entangled.
5. On the kinds of objects we have in mind for planning research, see Lieto (Forthcoming).
6. Although we support process tracing here, we are less favorably inclined to its fixation on linear causality. Another approach might be to deploy narrative techniques (Hart, 2011).
7. This also means that the researcher should refrain "from judging the way in which the actors analyze the society which surrounds them" (Callon, 1986, p. 198). Beauregard (2015, pp. 113–132) describes these possibilities as truths and contrasts them to realities; i.e., what actually happens in any given situation.
8. At issue is the general assumption that "all swans are white." For Popper, just one black swan, observed as a single case, falsifies this statement and triggers further theory-building. See Flyvbjerg (2006).

References

Alexander, Ernest R. 2010. "Introduction: Does Planning Theory Affect Practice, and if so, How?" *Planning Theory* 9, 2: 99–107.

Beauregard, Robert. 2012. "Planning with Things," *Journal of Planning Education and Research* 32, 2: 182–190.

Beauregard, Robert. 2015. *Planning Matter: Acting with Things*. Chicago, IL: University of Chicago Press.

Beauregard, Robert and Laura Lieto. 2016. "Does Actor Network Theory Help Planners to Think About Change?" In Yvonne Rydin and Laura Tate, eds., *Actor Networks of Planning: Exploring the Influence of Actor Network Theory*. London: Routledge, pp. 159–174.

Benevolo, Leonardo. 1971 (Orig. 1963). *The Origins of Modern Town Planning*. Cambridge, MA: MIT Press.

Callon, Michel. 1986. "Some Elements of a Sociology of Translation: Domestication of the Scallops and the Fishermen of St. Brieuc Bay." In John Law, ed., *Power, Action and Belief: A Sociology of Knowledge?* London: Routledge, pp. 196–223.

Campbell, Heather, Malcolm Tait, and Craig Watkins. 2014. "Is There Space for *Better* Planning in a Neoliberal World?" *Journal of Planning Education and Research* 34, 1: 45–59.

Collier, David. 2011. "Understanding Process Tracing," *PS, Political Science and Politics* 44, 4: 823–630.

Duineveld, Martijn, Kristof Van Ascher, and Raoul Beuen. 2013. "Making Things Irreversible: Object Stabilization in Urban Planning and Design," *GeoForum* 46: 16–24.

Duminy, James, Nancy Odendall, and Vanessa Watson. 2016. "Case Study Research in Africa: Methodological Dimensions." In J. Duminy, J. Andreasen, F. Lerise, V. Watson, and N. Odendall (eds.), *Planning and the Case Study Method in Africa*. London: Palgrave Macmillan, pp. 21–47.

Ewing, Reid, Amir Hojrasouliha, Kathryn M. Neckerman, Marnie Purciel-Hiol, and William Greene. 2016. "Streetscape Features Related to Pedestrian Activity," *Journal of Planning Education and Research* 36, 1: 5–15.

Flyvbjerg, Bent. 1998. *Rationality & Power: Democracy in Practice*. Chicago, IL: University of Chicago Press.

Flyvbjerg, Bent. 2001. *Making Social Science Matter*. Cambridge: Cambridge University Press.

Flyvbjerg, Bent. 2006. "Five Misunderstandings about Case Study Research," *Qualitative Inquiry* 12, 2: 219–245.

Gerring, John. 2004. "What is a Case Study and What is it Good For?" *American Political Science Review* 98, 2: 341–354.

Goulden, Shula. 2016. "Constructing 'Green Building': Heterogeneous Networks and the Translation of Sustainability into Planning." In Yvonne Rydin and Laura Tate, eds., *Actor Networks of Planning: Exploring the Influence of Actor Network Theory*. London: Routledge, pp. 27–43.

Hart, Jack. 2011. *Storycraft: The Complete Guide to Writing Narrative Nonfiction*. Chicago, IL: University of Chicago Press.

Hirschman, Albert O. 1970. "Paradigms as a Hindrance to Understanding," *World Politics* 22, 3: 329–343.

Hommels, Anique. 2005. *Unbuilding Cities: Obduracy in Urban Sociotechnical Change*. Cambridge, MA: The MIT Press.

Hutchby, I. 2001. "Technologies, Texts, and Affordances," *Sociology* 35, 2: 441–456.

Huxley, Margo. 2011. "The Specific and the General: The Designation of Planning Problems," *Crios* 2, July–December: 21–30.

Kunzmann, K.R. and M. Koll-Schretzenmayr. 2015. "The State of the Art of Planning in Europe," *disP: The Planning Review* 200, 1: 16–17.

Latour, Bruno. 1996. *Aramis or the Love of Technology*. Cambridge, MA: Harvard University Press.

Latour, Bruno. 2000. "When Things Strike Back: A Possible Contribution of 'Science Studies' to the Social Sciences," *British Journal of Sociology* 51, 1: 107–123.

Latour, Bruno. 2005. *Reassembling the Social: An Introduction to Actor–Network Theory*. Oxford: Oxford University Press.

Law, John. 2002. "Objects and Spaces," *Theory, Culture and Society* 19, 5/6: 91–105.

Law, John and Annemarie Mol. 1995. "Notes on Materiality and Sociability," *The Sociological Review* 43, 2: 274–294.

Levy, Jack S. 2008. "Counterfactuals and Case Studies," In Janet M. Box-Steffenmeier, Henry E. Brady, and David Collier, eds., *The Oxford Handbook of Political Methodology*. Oxford: Oxford University Press, pp. 627–644.

Lieto, Laura. 2009. "Knowledge, Power and Ethics in Extraordinary Times: Learning from the Naples Waste Crisis." In F. LoPiccolo and H. Thomas, eds., *Ethics and Planning Research*. Fornham, U.K.: Ashgate, pp. 191–205.

Lieto, Laura. 2016. "Things, Rules, and Politics: Blurring the Boundaries Between Formality and Informality." In L. Lieto and R. Beauregard (eds.), *Planning for a Material World*. Abingdon, U.K.: Routledge, pp. 26–41.

Lieto, Laura. Forthcoming. "What Counts as an Object for Urban Theory?" *City*.

Lieto, Laura and Robert Beauregard. 2013. "Planning for a Material World," *Crios* 2, July–December: 11–20.

Lieto, Laura and Robert Beauregard (eds.). 2016. *Planning for a Material World*. London: Routledge.

Loh, C. G. (2018) Learning from Practice, Learning for Practice in Local Land Use Planning Research. In T.W. Sanchez (ed.), *Planning Research and Knowledge*. Abingdon, U.K.: Routledge, pp. 24–34.

McFarlane, Colin. 2011. "Assemblage and Critical Urban Praxis: Part One," *City* 15, 2: 204–224.

McFarlane, Colin and Ben Anderson. 2011. "Thinking with Assemblage," *Area* 43, 2: 162–164.

Marcus, George E. and Erken Saka. 2006. "Assemblage," *Theory, Culture & Society* 23, 2–3: 101–109.

Megill, Allan. 2007. *Historical Knowledge, Historical Error*. Chicago, IL: University of Chicago Press.

Molotch, Harvey. 2013. "Objects and the City." In Gary Bridge and Sophie Watson (eds.), *The New Blackwell Companion to the City*. Chichester, U.K.: Wiley-Blackwell, pp. 66–78.

Murdoch, Jonathan. 1998. "The Spaces of Actor-Network Theory," *Geoforum* 29, 4: 357–374.

Ragin, Charles C. 2000. *Fuzzy–Set Social Science*. Chicago, IL: University of Chicago Press.

Rueschemeyer, D. 2003. "Can One or a Few Cases Yield Theoretical Gains?" In J. Mahoney and D. Rueschemeyer, (eds.), *Comparative Historical Analysis in the Social Sciences*. Cambridge: Cambridge University Press, pp. 305–366.

Rydin, Yvonne. 2014. "The Challenges of the 'Material Turn' for Planning Studies," *Planning Theory and Practice* 15, 4: 590–595.

Scheer, B. C. 2018. Urban Morphology as a Research Method. In T.W. Sanchez (ed.), *Planning Research and Knowledge*. Abingdon, U.K.: Routledge, pp. 167–181.

Schön, Donald. 1982. "Some of What a Planner Knows: A Case Study of Knowing in Practice," *Journal of the American Planning Association* 48, 3: 351–364.

Shi, Linda, Eric Chu, and Jessica Debats. 2015. "Explaining Progress in Climate Adaptation Planning Across 156 U.S. Municipalities," *Journal of the American Planning Association* 81, 3: 191–202.

Throgmorton, James. 2000. "On the Virtues of Skillful Meandering," *Journal of the American Planning Association* 66, 4: 367–379.

Tsing, Anna. 2005. *Friction: An Ethnography of Global Connections*. Princeton, NJ: Princeton University Press.

Verschuren, Piet J.M. 2003. "Case Study as a Research Strategy: Some Ambiguities and Opportunities," *International Journal of Social Research Methodology* 6, 2: 121–139.

Vettoretto, L. 2009. "A Preliminary Critique of the Best and Good Practices Approach in European Spatial Planning and Policymaking," *European Planning Studies* 17, 7: 1067–1085.

Vilches, Sylvia and Laura Tate. 2016. "Grants as Significant Objects in Community Engagement Networks." In Yvonne Rydin and Laura Tate (eds.), *Actor Networks of Planning: Exploring the Influence of Actor Network Theory*. London: Routledge, pp. 62–78.
Waldner, David. 2015. "Process Tracing and Qualitative Causal Inference," *Security Studies* 24, 2: 239–250.
Whitehand, J.W.R. 1992. *The Making of the Urban Landscape*. Oxford: Oxford University Press.

10
URBAN MORPHOLOGY AS A RESEARCH METHOD

Brenda Case Scheer

Introduction

Urban morphology is the study of the form of settlements over time. For some, use of the term "urban morphology" is fluid and can refer to generic ideas such as "central place theory" or "transects" (Duany and Talen, 2002). However, there are far more specific research-based methodologies that rely on measurement, analysis, and comparison of actual places. Urban morphology is often used as a term that ties the form of a place to some other attribute of the place; for example, its economy, historical events, land use, pedestrian counts, urban design, human comfort, and social hierarchies. In this chapter, urban morphology is the study of form in the sense of the physical elements exclusively, rather than the myriad relationships these elements have to other attributes or qualities (e.g. livability). This limitation in definition allows study of form per se as a separate and distinct knowledge area. At the same time, it is obvious that form is correlated with these attributes, and most studies in urban morphology are geared toward evaluating how form supports broader ideas of place or serves as a background to urban design (Gauthier and Gilliland, 2006).

The planning academy, if not the profession as a whole, is dominated by researchers who consider the social, governance, and economic aspects of the city to be determinant, an argument made by Beauregard and Lieto in this volume. At the same time, physical planning and urban design has been taken over by architects, landscape architects, and others, whose prescriptive and creative mindset is viewed with distrust or even ignored by more data-oriented researchers. As Ponzini (2018) points out in this volume, the most commonly used collections of readings in urban planning do not include topics about the physical character of the city.

Urban morphology, while making an important contribution to urban design and planning practice, is a field of study where data and methodology are at least as reliable as other social science contributions to planning. It commonly operates through case studies that use similar methodologies worldwide so that knowledge about particular places can be compared and theories can be developed based on observed patterns.

The first distinction of urban morphology as a discipline is the idea that knowledge is gained through *comparison* of the physical form of actual places, as opposed to the creation of theoretical economic and social models. The most common methods of comparison are to compare two places that exist at roughly the same time (synchronic) or to compare the same place at different times (diachronic) (see Figure 10.1).

Another way in which urban morphology is distinguished from other kinds of urban analyses relates to the starting point of acquiring formal data about specific places (Kropf, 2009). "Form" or formal is defined here to denote the semipermanent and definitively located physical elements of a place, including, for example, the tracks of the streetcar, but not the vehicles. Also not included in the term "form" are the ridership counts, the schedule, the destinations, the ownership of the streetcar track, or measurements of human comfort, although these may have important correlations or explain the form.

The researcher starts by gathering contemporary and historical maps, physical surveys, field measurements, photographs, and documentary records. The data used in urban morphology are substantially measurable or mathematically derived from measurements or coordinates of built form and, thus, for the most part objective. Formal data have scale, are associated with a particular date and a particular study area, and can be located geographically. There are large amounts of data for any area under study, and depending on the scale of inquiry, they might include density of built form, size or segment length of features, street widths, and location of footpaths and lot boundaries. For buildings, the data frequently include descriptions of materials, plans, and dates of construction. For some studies, data include topography, elevation, slope, and location of waterways. The data collected in morphology research is limited to the needs of the inquiry at hand. Tools such as GIS and Google Earth have greatly increased the reach of morphologists.

As we accumulate data about a place, we normally sort that information into categories. The categorization of these morphological elements is based on the need to easily distinguish one kind of element from another. The common urban form elements that morphologists use are buildings, streets, and plots, but a more specific categorization is *built form, the boundaries of paths and plots*, and *land* (Scheer, 2016). *Built form* has substantial reality and is man-made. The *boundary matrix*, which is defined as the combination of plots and the linear paths of public rights of way, describes lines and spaces that are measurable and traceable over time, even though they have no physical substance. Finally, *land* is the natural landscape terrain upon which the built form rests. These elements coexist in space and may have literal co-presence – a boundary may be marked by built form (e.g. a wall) or a natural feature (e.g. a stream).

Urban Morphology as a Research Method 169

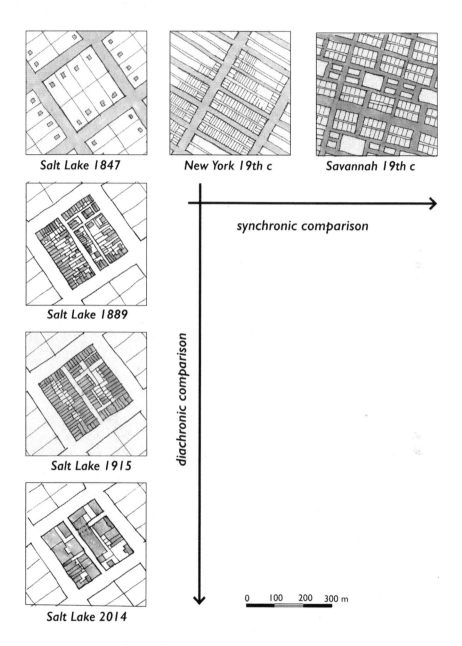

FIGURE 10.1 Morphological data is usually comparative, either diachronic or synchronic (drawn by Brenda Scheer).

170 B. Case Scheer

Figure 10.2 shows the kinds of data that are commonly collected to represent urban form, isolated from other conditions of the urban environment (that is, not land use or other nonphysical data). The following general principles about these elements are known:

1 They are universal and always present in a settled place, but their specific configuration is unique for each place. Patterns can be compared across time and space as long as reliable sources are available.

Built Form

Objects
Paving, lawn, cultivated vegetation, signs, canopies, fountains, art, signals, poles, planters, curbs

Buildings
Occupied buildings, topologically whole. Accessory buildings: shed, kiosk, garage

Infrastructure
Large scale, not occupied: bridge, stadium, canal, clock tower, city gate, city wall, triumphal arch, monuments

Boundary Matrix

Plots
Bounded, parcel or lot, signifying control

Paths
Continuous, the bounded space of the right of way of street, rail, canal

Land

Land
Watershed, natural vegetation, slope and aspect, rivers, harbors, topography.

FIGURE 10.2 Categories of morphological data (drawn by Brenda Scheer).

2   They are measurable in physical dimensions, or in relation to dates, or mathematically calculated from measurable data (e.g. paving width, density of lots).
3   They exist objectively. There may be uncertainty about the reliability of any kind of data, but our assumption is that the information gathered represents forms that exist or once existed.
4   They are coexistent in space.

Built form is further broken down in Figure 10.2 where different kinds of built form are classified. Three general categories are recognized – *objects*, which are non-occupied constructions; *buildings*; and *infrastructure*. Built forms are independent pieces, although they are always composed of subparts. A building, for example, is independent of its plot in the sense that it can be demolished without affecting the plot boundaries.

Data Analysis

After identifying, measuring, and mapping these data points, researchers identify and interpret patterns that can be seen not only in the place under study, but also occurring in multiple places. Comparison points are critical for data analysis. For example, comparison of a single place at intervals of many years can show the patterns of how that place evolved and can be useful in understanding why that place evolved the way it did. Figure 10.3 is an overlay of the tip of Manhattan in 1660 and 1996, showing just land and the path of streets. It is remarkable, and perhaps unexpected, how many streets are relatively unchanged over 300 years, while no buildings from the 17th century survive. Over time, the land has been added to substantially by fill. And the wall that appears in 1660 (one of the very few in US territory) has now become "Wall Street."

Urban morphologists are especially interested in patterns that arise in radically different places and widely spaced eras, as these patterns can tell us something of the culture of the society that created them. Figure 10.4 is compilation of a very few of these common patterns, demonstrated with real examples. Note that these patterns are visible at different resolutions of scale, with building types (a kind of pattern) being the smallest and entire regions the largest.

There are multiple principles that can be observed by comparing formal configurations. An important category of morphology is to compare buildings in a single place and time to establish the elements of a *building type*. A building type is an abstraction, a pattern, where we observe formal similarities between one building and another (say, rowhouses in Brooklyn) even though the buildings may have different architectural expression (Scheer, 2010). Note that the buildings in Figure 10.5 share many common formal characteristics, but are very different in color, materials, style, and expressiveness.

Another kind of pattern that is observed is the "plan unit" (Conzen, 1960) or "urban tissue" (Caniggia and Maffei, 2001). These are patterns that involve a group

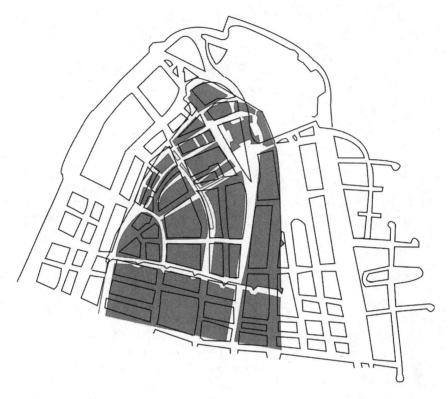

FIGURE 10.3 An overlay of two maps of lower Manhattan – one from 1660 and one from 1995. Broadway, Canal Street, and Wall Street (with wall) remain in the same location. Note the expansion of land over time (drawn by Brenda Scheer).

of buildings, blocks, and streets that are formally similar. Usually this means they were built at the same time. Plan units can be identified in existing cities by mapping and analysis of patterns.

Observing Change

The physical city is in constant flux, with buildings being torn down and replaced quite commonly. The place data that are compared over time or space allow morphologists to theorize the mechanisms of the various *changes* that are observed. Just as important are the observation and explanations of what *endures* in a city's form. Interestingly, morphologists have found that city forms change or endure in very similar patterns, regardless of culture or even era. For example, we know that the three elements (built form, the boundary matrix, and the land) change at different frequencies, as has been noted in most theories of urban morphology. (Panerai et al., 2004; Moudon, 1986; Caniggia and Maffei, 2001; Scheer, 2001).

Urban Morphology as a Research Method **173**

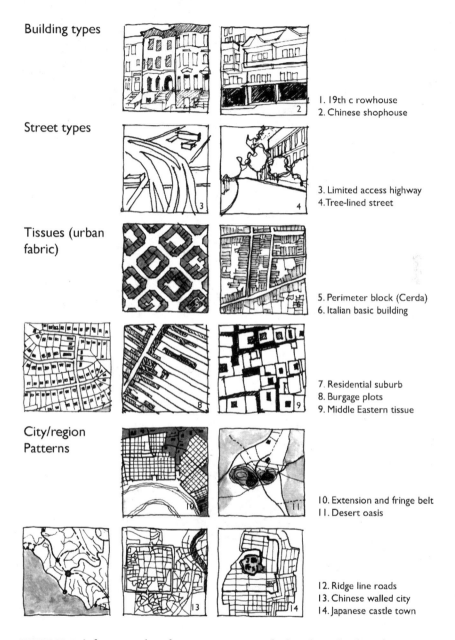

FIGURE 10.4 A few examples of common patterns of urban form that have been identified and documented in multiple settings by urban morphologists (drawn by Brenda Scheer).

FIGURE 10.5 Brownstone rowhouses in Bedford-Stuyvesant, New York City, are a clear example of a type. Note the variation in details, while the building types have similarities in scale, proportion, overall organization, and features such as the tall stoop (photo by NewYork10R. licensed under CC 3.0).

One key finding concerns the relative endurance rate of buildings vs. streets: buildings can be very long-lived, but they do not typically last as long as the boundary of paths and plots that contain them. As we just saw, the current street pattern of lower Manhattan has endured from the 17th century, but there are no buildings that survive from that time period. Similar endurances have been documented all over the world.

While a boundary matrix can endure as buildings change, when it does change, it will usually affect all the built form that touches it. For example, when a street is widened, even if buildings are retained, the objects that constitute the path's physical presence are almost all destroyed and replaced: paving, landscape, signs, etc. If a lot is combined, an existing building may remain, it may be added on to, the new plot may be subject to repletion (the addition of more buildings), or the entire plot may be redeveloped with a new, somewhat larger building.

Disruption of the boundary matrix is not like these stepwise evolutions, however, which are carried out by individual actors in a slow, evolving dance. Disruption involves a radical restructuring of boundaries caused by deliberate action of a powerful agent or a catastrophe. Just as evolutionary changes reflect subtly shifting conditions in the environment, disruption signals a radical change in those same conditions: a new regime has taken control, or a powerful agency has started a slum clearance program, or a new superhighway must be built through a neighborhood. With a disruption to the boundary matrix, most of the built form is also destroyed. The most dramatic changes, which also cause plan disruption, are those that change the landform itself: cataclysmic events like earthquakes, landslides, and floods, or a man-made land-altering event like leveling a hill to fill in the sea (e.g. Boston, Seattle, New York). Interestingly, some catastrophes (the fire of London, the bombing of Hiroshima) do not result in boundary changes – new buildings are built within the boundary matrix of the destroyed city – signaling the important endurance of this form.

North American Morphology – Common Research Themes

One of the key characteristics of the North American urban form is its response to relatively rapid change. North America is like a laboratory devoted to finding specimens that quickly reproduce. Auto-oriented building types can change so rapidly that they seem accelerated lessons in the evolution of types (Scheer, 2010). The structure of medium-sized cities and towns, which for centuries in Europe and other established urban places has changed relatively slowly, in North America has exploded in size and land coverage, even without attendant huge population gain. Change is a precondition of urban form in North America.

North American morphologists are quick to acknowledge the flexibility and persistence of the ubiquitous 18th- and 19th-century grid, which provides a framework for orderly but very rapid growth. Pioneer settlements west of the Appalachians used the grid almost exclusively to rapidly lay out streets and lots and to sell property. For example, the Oklahoma land run in 1893 created three or four small towns that were surveyed and settled in less than a month. Pierce Lewis (1990) notes the grid as a flexible framework used nearly universally after the popularity and success of the 1682 Penn plan for Philadelphia.

The theme of rapid morphological change in North America began most prominently with Anne Vernez Moudon's (1986) classic and groundbreaking study of the Alamo neighborhood in San Francisco. The title of the book – *Built for Change* – encapsulates the idea of flexibility. She notes that the streets and plots (cadaster) support not only change, but also several flexible building typologies. Looking at Savannah, GA, Anderson (1993) analyzes the extraordinary, varied, and flexible city structure that allowed a sophisticated build out and subsequent redevelopment. Scheer and Ferdelman (2001) document a 100-year period of change in the grid and built form in Cincinnati's Over-the-Rhine neighborhood. They lament the loss of flexibility as they document the partial destruction of the neighborhood's tissue and the tendency to combine plots to make larger buildings. More recently, the famous grid of Manhattan has been celebrated in detail with the 200th birthday of its foundation, especially noted for its persistence, its formal clarity, and its intense flexibility for adaptation to modern forms (Ballon, 2012).

This emphasis on the flexibility of traditional forms and their tendency to absorb change while maintaining order has also resulted in an interest in preserving and infilling the extant traditional forms (building types and the boundary matrix of plots and paths).

Suburban sprawl is another theme. A significant amount of urban morphological study in the US has been devoted to the study of the great and disruptive suburban extensions of the city, which accelerated with the streetcar and the car, starting in the late 1920s. Southworth and Owens (1993) document the change in form of suburban neighborhoods from modest, gridded extensions to the sprawling "loops and lollipops" of cul-de-sacs and curved streets. Moudon also identifies changing suburban neighborhood patterns, along with Hess, while also supporting the concept that certain categories of change could be observed in highly differentiated places (Moudon, 1998; Moudon and Hess, 2000). Scheer (2001) reports similar transformations in Hudson, Ohio, while reporting on the persistence of the 1790 gridded land survey cadaster in the overall city.

In addition to residential transformation, suburban formal commercial transformation has also been studied. One study of diachronic change in development along commercial highways as the city expands outward from its foundation grid and grid extensions led to the contribution of the concepts of "static, elastic, and campus tissues" to the morphology lexicon of patterns (Scheer, 2001, 2010, 2015). The form of "edge cities" (size, rapid expansion land area, changing building and roadway types) has been compared to that of traditional central cities (Scheer and Petkov, 1998). Gilliland and Gauthier (2006, p. 58) document the rising interest in Canada of morphological research that informs questions of affordable housing, urban sprawl, and transportation systems.

Urban Morphology in Practice

One of the primary concerns of American urban designers and planners is dissatisfaction with the contemporary form and build out of American cities. North American suburban form can be traced to the worldwide change in architecture (modernism). Modernism's disconnection from the traditional city also enabled the isolated typologies of the North American suburban form (e.g. big box stores and gas stations) while it glorified the speed and independence engendered by the automobile.

Beginning in 1990, the dispersed and disconnected suburban form was identified by reformers as a clear crisis. These sprawling forms discouraged a sense of community, neglected pedestrians, increased land coverage, required long commutes, implemented a dominating car infrastructure, and were (for urbanists) boring, unsustainable, and unlivable (Duany, 2000; Calthorpe, 1993; Talen, 1999). Over the last two decades, the complaints about suburban form multiplied (encourages obesity, contributes to air pollution, etc.) while, at the same time, suburban typologies – shopping strips and single-family neighborhoods – rapidly built out not only in North America, but also all over the world.

Practitioners, responding to this dissatisfaction with dispersed forms, have tended to reify the traditional form of the early American gridded downtown, at all scales. As Conzen (2004) points out, however, these existing gridded formations are very small compared to the conurbations that surround cities of any size in North America. Practitioners, such as New Urbanists, therefore find it advantageous to copy and invent "historical" forms, including aesthetic tropes that imitate the look of 19th-century building types, as well as mimicking the grain of the gridded block and street.

Andres Duany, the leader of the New Urbanism reformers, promotes generic solutions consisting of holistically planned, "livable" settlement areas (called *transects*), which provide blueprints and guidelines for "good" city form at all scales currently present in the North American landscape (Duany and Talen, 2002; Brower, 1996).

Urban morphology offers a more substantial background to design than a generic approach, insisting on understanding and documenting what is before proposing essentially foreign solutions. Overlaying a generic urban design idea on a place that has been created and lived in for a period of years ignores the essential evolutionary nature of the physical city. New urbanist projects are often modeled on historically accreted cities and neighborhoods, which achieve their diversity and integration through a slowly evolving set of cultural circumstances. The forms that arise from these practices can be subject to critique by morphologists, who note their lack of flexibility, or their lack of natural evolutionary character, and their generic solutions, which do not derive from the study of the historical form in a particular place (Scheer, 2010, p. 106). Neuman (2005, p. 22) writes,

> The new urbanist's town is a static product of a developer's marketing campaign rather than an evolving process of human development.... Compact settlements with an emphasis on density, pedestrians, and public transportation only address a few of the ills attending modern metropolises.

Planning Practice

Urban planners and urban designers have much to learn from applying morphological methods to a study area. Even in places where there has been no non-agricultural development, it is often the case that the pre-development boundaries of fields and farm roads are retained and become the deep structure of the city over time (Scheer, 2001; Bosselmann, 2008; Bonine, 1979). Ignoring the persistence of formal boundaries can be problematic for the planner because these boundaries signify so much for their owners. So, even planning for a new city addition may need to acknowledge the preexisting boundaries and patterns that have evolved in the place over time.

However, morphological analysis is most informative within the context of an existing settled place. Rather than the disruptive program of wiping out large areas to introduce an entirely new city form (as observed in large Asian cities), the nature of many urban design and physical planning projects in the US is generally small.

This scale of urban planning operates where *existing* cities, places, cultures, and landscapes are deliberately engaged – where the solutions to specific problems arise or emerge from the physical conditions and socioeconomic systems. This urbanism, emerging from the existing place, is as much *discovered* as it is *designed*, through systematic analysis of history, networks, and patterns. It implies a continuous urban pattern rather than a disruptive one, or it is disruptive deliberately to supply an emergent pattern. It enhances a framework, or it organizes a framework. It looks to the past and to the future – predicting and accommodating the next evolution as well as the present one. For this kind of planning, morphological analysis is a key starting point.

Urban designers and architects are increasingly looking to the following strategies, all of which rely on the methods of urban morphology to provide the historical perspective, primary data, and analysis. These strategies favor using the existing physical pattern of place to provide clues about the next development.

- *Repair.* This idea looks to repair or restore a pattern or fabric that has been disrupted or lost, especially a network of streets or open space corridors. Designers try to knit back together streets and large areas that were disrupted in the 20th century. One example of this is the redevelopment of the land previously occupied by large shopping center islands to restore street patterns and create connections to nearby neighborhoods (Dunham-Jones and Williamson, 2009). Another example of a repair strategy is proposals to rework disruptive highways that have left a path of destruction in the city. (See, for example, I-80 in Syracuse, NY.) Another notable example is Peter Bosselmann's work in Oakland, CA (2008, pp. 193–221), which draws on variations of the historic grid pattern there to knit together a city partly destroyed by freeways.
- *Appropriation of historic types and patterns.* Especially in resource-challenged times, adapting patterns for contemporary use in such a way as to preserve the general scale and grain is an effective way to preserve character but also acknowledge modern sensibility, materials, modes of transportation, and so on. This can include infill or new development that is continuous or contiguous with older patterns. Europeans seem to do this best: see, for example, the Borneo-Sporenburg houses in Amsterdam, a reinterpretation of the canal house type (West 8 Urban Design and Landscape, 1993–1996). In Savannah, GA, a waterfront redevelopment deliberately invokes the older, much beloved pattern of old Savannah in its new town plan (Conn, 2010). This strategy is used to tie old and new together in order to brand new development with the aura of nearby older places. Just as importantly, this strategy invokes climatic and environmental appropriateness by looking to low-energy, passive strategies of the past.
- *Reveal.* A more complex strategy is one that discovers or uncovers previously uncelebrated or even unknown patterns and historical artifacts in the existing place and then uses that discovery to create new public spaces or development

programs, which themselves organize newer development. A famous example of this is the Highline in New York City, which took an eyesore and made it into a development magnet and popular open space (see Highline, 2012). More recently, Canalscape, the project to bring to life the long-neglected canals in Phoenix, AZ, has provided a framework for denser activities (Ellin, 2010).

- *Rupture.* This strategy is used to deliberately break a pattern that is unhealthy, ill-adapted to changing climate conditions, and unfriendly to quality of life. Increasingly, this strategy will be used to adapt suburban fabrics that have evolved in energy-profligate times. So-called "road diets" that narrow large arterials are an example of this strategy (Rosales, 2006). This is one of the most difficult areas of urban design and one where the persistence of the existing and evolved place (e.g. a highway strip, a settled subdivision) is often ignored.
- *Regulation.* The fragmentation and weakness of development control in the US has led planners to focus on an urban design strategy of regulation rather than physical plans. Urban design in practice suffers because of the reluctance of cities to plan – streets, subdivisions, and open spaces are haphazardly proposed or tendered by land developers with commercial motivations rather than civic ones. As planners move to take firmer control over development as a way of making places more livable, they increasingly look to morphological analysis to provide validity and reduce the arbitrariness of codes and other regulations. In infill situations, the city will sometimes write codes or introduce zoning that are morphologically based. This is by far the most extensive use of morphological or typological research in North America.

Conclusions

In this paper, we have explored the nature of urban morphology as a quantifiable interpretation of the physical form of the city with its own theories to explain change in multiple urban situations. Pure morphological research adds to and enlightens other kinds of research, such as economic or demographic analysis, about a place. It also enlightens our understanding of how places are created and how they change by comparing multiple examples.

Applications of morphology in practice depend on connecting observations about form and formal change to the history, culture, and life of the city. In practice, urban planners can use the data and analysis of urban morphology to build a stronger case for continuity in cities, rather than the disruptive planning changes that have marred much 20th-century transportation and renewal planning. The strategies outlined above rely on urban morphology in some form to understand how the city has changed in the past and how it may change in the future even without a formal plan. Just as importantly, morphological analysis provides a basis for design that is unique and place-centered. It can protect valuable vernacular resources (e.g. buildings, alleys, street patterns) by recognizing their active contribution to the physical character of the place even when they are not extraordinary in terms of the usual artifacts of preservation.

By measuring and analyzing the urban fabric over time, the designer gains a realization of the subtleties and especially the particularities of a place that otherwise can be easily overlooked and misinterpreted. Whenever these historic changes over time are misunderstood, the designer misses an important analytical key that would ground the new project in the community and provide honest historic continuity.

References

Anderson, S. (1993) Savannah and the issue of precedent: city plan as resource, in Bennett, R., ed., *Settlements in the Americas*, Newark, NJ: University of Delaware Press, 110–144.

Ballon, H. (2012) *The greatest grid: the master plan of Manhattan, 1811–2011*, New York: Columbia University Press.

Beauregard, R. and Lieto, L. (2018) Towards an object-oriented case methodology for planners, in Sanchez, T. W., ed., *Planning research and knowledge*, Abingdon, UK: Routledge, 153–166.

Bonine, M. E. (1979) The morphogenesis of Iranian cities, *Annals of the Association of American Geographers*, 69(2), 208–224.

Bosselmann, P. (2008) *Urban transformation: understanding city design and form*, Washington, DC: Island Press.

Brower, S. N. (1996) *Good neighborhoods: a study of in–town & suburban residential environments*, Westport, CT: Praeger.

Calthorpe, P. (1993) *The next American metropolis: ecology, communities, and the American dream*, New York: Princeton Architectural Press.

Caniggia, G. and Maffei, G. L. (2001) *Architectural composition and building typology: interpreting basic building*, Firenze: Alinea.

Conn, L. (2010) Growing the Oglethorpe plan in downtown Savannah, *Savannah Now*, February 28.

Conzen, M. R. G. (1960) Alnwick, Northumberland: A study in town-plan analysis, *Transactions and Papers (Institute of British Geographers)*, No. 27, iii–122.

Conzen, M. R. G. (2004) *Thinking about urban form: papers on urban morphology, 1932–1998*, Oxford; New York: Peter Lang.

Duany, A. (2000) *Suburban nation: the rise of sprawl and the decline of the American Dream*, New York: North Point Press.

Duany, A. and Talen, E. (2002) Transect planning, *Journal of the American Planning Association*, 68(3), 245–266.

Dunham-Jones, E. and Williamson, J. (2009) *Retrofitting suburbia: urban design solutions for redesigning suburbs*, Hoboken, NJ: John Wiley & Sons, Inc.

Ellin, N. (2010) Canalscape: practising integral urbanism in metropolitan Phoenix, *Journal of Urban Design*, 15(4), 599–610.

Gauthier, P. and Gilliland, J. (2006) Mapping urban morphology: A classification scheme for interpreting contributions to the study of urban form, *Urban Morphology*, 10(1), 41–50.

Gilliland, J. and Gauthier, P. (2006) The study of urban form in Canada, *Urban Morphology*, 10(1), 51–66.

Highline (2012) *Visit the Highline* [online], available at: www.thehighline.org/visit [accessed 29 August, 2016].

Kropf, K. (2009) Aspects of urban form, *Urban Morphology*, 13(2), 105–120.

Lewis, P. (1990) Americanizing English landscape habits, in Conzen, M. P., ed., *The making of the American landscape*, Boston: Unwin Hyman, 91–114.

Moudon, A. V. (1986) *Built for change: neighborhood architecture in San Francisco*, Cambridge, MA: MIT Press.

Moudon, A. V. (1998) The changing morphology of suburban neighborhoods, in Petruccioli, A., ed., *Typological process and design theory*, Cambridge, MA: Aga Khan Program for Islamic Architecture, Harvard University and Massachusetts Institute of Technology, 141–157.

Moudon, A. V. and Hess, P. M. (2000) Suburban clusters, *Journal of the American Planning Association*, 66(3), 243–264.

Neuman, M. (2005). The compact city fallacy, *Journal of Planning Education and Research*, 25(1), 11–26.

Panerai, P., Castex, J., Depaule, J. C. and Samuels, I. (2004) *Urban forms: death and life of the urban block*, Oxford, UK; Boston: Architectural Press.

Ponzini, D. (2018) The unwarranted boundaries between urban planning and design in theory, practice and research, in Sanchez, T. W., ed., *Planning research and knowledge*, Abingdon, UK: Routledge, 182–195.

Rosales, J. (2006) *The road diet handbook: setting trends for livable streets*, 2nd Edition, New York: Parsons Brinckerhoff/William Barclay Parsons Fellowship Monograph.

Scheer, B. C. (2001) The anatomy of sprawl, *Places: the Journal of Environmental Design*, 14(2), 28–37.

Scheer, B. C. (2010) *The evolution of urban form: typology for planners and architects*, Chicago: American Planning Association.

Scheer, B. C. (2015) Strip development and how to read it, in Talen, E., ed., *Retrofitting sprawl*, New York: Routledge, 31–55.

Scheer, B. C. (2016) The epistemology of urban morphology, *Urban Morphology*, 20(1), 5–17.

Scheer, B. C. and Petkov, M. (1998) Edge city morphology: a comparison of commercial centers, *Journal of the American Planning Association*, 64(3), 298–310.

Scheer, B. C. and Ferdelman, D. (2001) Inner-city destruction and revival: the case of Over-the-Rhine, Cincinnati, *Urban Morphology*, 5(1), 15–27.

Southworth, M. and Owens, P. M. (1993) The evolving metropolis: studies of community, neighborhood, and street form at the urban edge, *Journal of the American Planning Association*, 59(3), 271–287.

Talen, E. (1999) Sense of community and neighbourhood form: an assessment of the social doctrine of new urbanism, *Urban Studies*, 36(8), 1361–1379.

West 8 Urban Design and Landscape (1993–1996) *Borneo–Sporenburg, Amsterdam* [online], available at: www.west8.nl/projects/borneo_sporeburg [accessed 30 November, 2016].

11

THE UNWARRANTED BOUNDARIES BETWEEN URBAN PLANNING AND DESIGN IN THEORY, PRACTICE AND RESEARCH[1]

Davide Ponzini

In the last decades, important Anglo-Saxon and American planning approaches have considered the planning process as their main focus of theorization, research and practice. Even if in the past the design of the built environment had been a central element in planners' education in multiple planning traditions, the theoretical discussion and the actual practice of design has only recently been taken into consideration to a greater extent inasmuch as it was perceived as a prerogative of other disciplines, such as architecture and urban design. Other European traditions such as the Italian and Spanish ones, as well as less conventional Anglo-Saxon and American approaches, developed a significant area of practice and study at the crossroads between urban planning and urban design, though having a limited impact on the international planning debate and receiving little attention in terms of research and theorization. Drawing on current planning and urban design literature and using the evidence of the well-known case of regeneration of Poblenou in Barcelona, this chapter highlights the relevance of the design dimension of planning with reference to theory, practice and applied research.

The first section concisely presents four perspectives on urban design that will be useful in subsequent sections. In the second section, the longstanding issue of the planning process/design divide is discussed, highlighting the relevance of the design dimension of planning and the need for a more complex interpretation of it. In the third section, selected examples regarding European and American traditions of education, research and practice that have been developed at the crossroads between urban design and planning provide an insight into the advancements that derived from a less compartmentalized understanding of planning, which is finally exemplified through the case of regeneration of Poblenou in Barcelona.

The aim of this paper is to reconsider the unwarranted boundary drawn between design-oriented and process-oriented planning approaches so as to show the challenges for planning theory and practice that may derive from trespassing such disciplinary boundaries. A number of arguments can be derived from literature and available experiments in practice without necessarily aiming to create a new grand theory or approach, or expecting to finally "fill the gap between planning and design" (also because one may consider the countless attempts at doing so in the last 60 years). At the same time, the advantages of trespassing will be clear, and they suggest that a significant area of study and experimentation has been neglected in the international planning theory debate and that facing given planning issues (such as form-related planning tools, nesting large-scale projects into spatial visions, generating local knowledge through urban design, and others) in a more integrated way could generate relevant benefits for educational programs as well (Palermo and Ponzini, 2015a, 2015b).

Four Views of Urban Design

In general terms urban design refers to a broad set of functions in planning systems that involve coordinated and intentional actions to give shape, form and meaning to (parts of) cities and various human infrastructures and settlements. It can be more or less codified and integrated with other strategic, regulative and informative functions in the institutional framework according to the national and regional context (among others, see the theoretical framework proposed by Luigi Mazza, 2003, 2004). It certainly has a relevant position and visibility in the public realm. It has a strong "transformative" connotation since it tends to concretely explore scenarios and to locate development and land uses in space, eventually according to strategic orientations and broader regulation. In this sense it is not simply related to a given scale (typically intended as the intermediate scale between the architectural and the regional) nor to a policy sector (typically related to public space and landscaping). As a planning function, in most Western countries it is simply understood as the outlining of forms and types in land-use planning or infrastructural networks.

While being more or less codified in different planning systems, urban design gained a clear position as a field of practice, that can be occupied by architects, by city planners, or by other professions, such as engineers, and does not have clear and definitive boundaries. This second acceptation (i.e. design as a field of practice) is very important for understanding the development of the cultural features of urban design and their evolution through time, especially due to the fact that several attempts at institutionalizing this field as a self-contained discipline have been occurring. Banerjee and Loukaitou-Sideris (2011) argued that the openness of this field to multiple intellectual influences has enriched it. On the other hand one might see the risks of having a somehow undefined realm and few evaluations of the (sometimes incompatible) contents and positions that are proposed under the same name. Moreover, this ambiguity hinders the relationship not only to planning but also to architecture and other disciplines that contributed to its origin and growth (Madanipour, 1996)

Third, it is clear that we perceive and understand urban design mostly as a set of products of professional, institutional and social practices (e.g. master plans, settlement schemes, sectorial plans, large-scale development projects) following diverse cultural orientations (Madanipour, 1996). Clearly, this field has a strong technical legitimization according to more or less detailed conceptions and models of the "good city form" or "better place" (Dovey, 1999; Carmona, Heath, Oc, and Tiesdell, 2003; Lang, 2005; Gehl, 2010); though the design profession is neither autonomous nor clearly defined in its nonexclusive role in designing such products. Its interdependence with other decision-makers and actors involved in shaping cities makes urban design more closely connected in this process than, say, architects dealing with less "public" matters. Knox and Ozolins (2000) discussed the definition of the urban built environment as the end product of intense interactions and decisions among landowners, investors, developers, politicians, bureaucrats and other actors.

The fourth view of urban design as a source of relevant planning knowledge depends on the approach and perspective one has in planning. The empirical-analytical (or positivist) and interactive paradigms of planning do not consider urban design projects as relevant means for generating new understanding of place and contributing to broader visions for urban development (Palermo and Ponzini, 2015a). These two paradigmatic views generally consider urban design as the final and most technical product of the planning process. On the contrary, design can be seen as a way of producing meanings that can be politically effective and change the planning process itself (among others, Hubbard, 1996, suggested that the attention to design may generate arguments disconfirming "structural" views of urbanism and become an opportunity for practice) and of eventually generating new knowledge that is relevant for transforming the built environment.

However, it is safe to say that relevant urban design activities can be an interactive practice, with inherent technical-political features given the often-needed mediation between strategic perspectives, contextual limitations and multiple urban stakeholders (Palermo and Ponzini, 2010). According to a project-oriented view of planning, urban design can be seen as a complex process of understanding and intentionally shaping the urban form in operational fields that typically include multiple actors besides urban designers.

The activities that practitioners undertake to better know and transform the urban environment have been studied for some time now (Schön, 1983). The role of urban development projects and planning in developing critical knowledge of one context has been explored for several decades (Gregotti, 1966) without a significant impact on mainstream planning theory. Despite recent attention to research by design, methodological discussions in this direction are limited in the urban planning debate (Palermo and Ponzini, 2012).

One must notice, for example, that readers in the planning disciplines rarely consider design as a central question or a relevant topic (e.g. Faludi, 1973; Hillier and Healey, 2008). *Readings in Planning Theory* (Campbell and Fainstein, 1996) and *Readings in Urban Theory* (Fainstein and Campbell, 2002) both correctly recognized the divide between planning theory and theories about the city and its transformation, but they did not make the effort to combine them in a synthetic view where the design of the urban environment has a relevant position. More than 25 years have passed since Beauregard (1990) posed this central question. Only recently have urban design debates included in-depth views of the planning process and its relationship to urban development. Among others, Tiesdell and Adams (2011) highlighted the relevance of urban design in crafting and implementing different planning tools, but this did not generate further debate.

Institutionalizing Urban Design Knowledge

As mentioned, the historical roots of the urban design discipline and knowledge are varied, and their relationship to planning may radically differ according to the planning culture in question. In general, despite the attempts at institutionalizing the design fields, urban design cannot be properly conceived of as a self-contained discipline (Madanipour, 1996; Banerjee and Loukaitou-Sideris, 2011). In this complex field of practice, Cuthbert (2010) viewed design as the conscious and purposive social production of space, both in its material and symbolic dimensions. The overlap between planning and design is evident, and the reference to architectural traditions and techniques is a feature of particular interpretations of urban design (Lang, 2005), which perhaps are not dominant in the Anglo-Saxon world.

Even if in the past the design of the built environment had been one element in planners' education, the theoretical discussion and the actual practice of design has more often been considered as if it were a prerogative of other disciplines, such as architecture and urban design; in any case, the presence and theorization of urban design in the planning discipline has been perceived as inadequate (see, among others, Punter, 1996). Other European traditions and less conventional Anglo-Saxon approaches developed a significant area of practice and study at the crossroads between urban planning and urban design, though having a limited impact on the international planning debate, which has been dominated by more process-oriented and social science based approaches to planning.

There were several attempts at making urban design a separate disciplinary field, most clearly in the United States, giving birth to specialized educational and research activities. This can be seen as the institutionalization of both cultural and professional trends that dominated the international scene. Eric Mumford (2009) explained the genesis of modern urban design practice and discipline and showed how the typical views proposed in academic debates tend to oversimplify quite a rich set of efforts. According to Cuthbert (2010), the recognition (and curbing) of the urban design discipline was originated in the 1950s by the Spanish architect Jose Lluís Sert, who was at that time Dean of Harvard Graduate School of Design. This academic experience was very important for the institutionalization of this activity, but probably served to crystallize the definition of the discipline according to what was the praxis in urban development in a specific moment and a specific geographical context and according to the specific scale that was relevant for those scholars, mainly dealing with the intermediate objects between architectural design and large-scale planning and focusing on public space. This particular take on urban design became the object of critique.

More generally, since the 1960s several prominent American schools of planning – despite being originally rooted in architectural schools and having teaching programs that to some extent combined design and planning disciplines together – developed a sort of aversion to an architectural approach and to the physical planner as they were part of the problems in urban and regional development. The targets were master planning and top-down approaches and other mainstream expressions of modernist architecture and planning. Among the criticisms of design disciplines of that time were the arguments that architectural design tended to be apolitical, that it did not have a strong scientific basis as other social sciences did, and that urban designers never realized the unrealistic expectations of environmental determinism (Sanyal, 2008).

Bish Sanyal (2008) highlighted one interesting point regarding how the divide between urban design practice and planning theory or policy disciplines evolved in prominent American planning schools and why this divide constituted a great and unresolved challenge, potentially becoming more and more determinant. In the United States this was perceived as a departure from spatial design competences and tasks toward merely procedural ones. The inclination toward consensus building rather than imposing spatially defined solutions was contested as weakening the status of planners (and architects). Rodwin and Sanyal (2000) argued that if planning knowledge departs too much from spatiality, it cannot justify its peculiar feature as specialized knowledge. Of course this does not imply a technocratic approach to form, even less a process-blind perspective.

More recently, Anselin, Nasar, and Talen (2011) examined the relationship between planning and design in American universities by assessing the performances of programs located in different departments. Their starting position stresses a recurring concern for disciplinary divides in both directions, implying a loss of focus and competence in designing the physical environment in more process-oriented planning schools and, at the same time, a loss of sociopolitical and economic understanding in architecture-and-urban-design-oriented schools. This is a longstanding issue and is far from going unnoticed (Anselin, Nasar, and Talen cited a 1952 editorial in the *Journal of the American Planning Association*).

The positions praising a more complex and reciprocal understanding in general have evidently failed if one considers the mainstream: planners often tend to have a partial view of urban design practice, mainly focusing on its products; urban design methods are seen more and more as technical devices that constitute the finalization of or even an item separated from the planning process. At the same time architects and designers have been aware of the importance of the process dimension of their work, though often resorting to more or less vague "holistic" approaches without making explicit arguments about the need for process-related knowledge well beyond managerial skills.

Recent trends such as place-making have lately had a success that can be considered a symptom of limited understanding of the complex form-process interconnection in planning theory and research (Palermo and Ponzini, 2015b). Potential sources of knowledge reside in the planning traditions that have deeper roots in architecture and design disciplines and in experiments that occurred at the crossroads between planning and design, putting process and form in tension.

Interesting Experiments at the Crossroads between Planning and Design

The separation of process-oriented planning cultures from project-oriented approaches depends on the schools and traditions that are considered relevant. In the Anglo-Saxon and American mainstream, the nexus between planning and design is understudied. In this paragraph I will try to argue that by trespassing the disciplinary boundaries, one can address theoretical questions on issues such as: the production and accumulation of usable and project-oriented knowledge in complex urban decision-making processes; the nesting of strategic and structural visions into urban morphological design and urban development projects; the use of urban design for forecasting the impacts of planning codes and other urban policy tools on the built environment.

The idea is widespread in Europe that Mediterranean countries have maintained a peculiar and still influential tradition in architectural design and physical planning and a concentration on prescriptive measures (CEC, 1997; ESPON, 2007). These planning traditions permitted interesting experiments; while they have been taken into limited consideration (for an extensive discussion, see Palermo and Ponzini, 2010), the experiments are briefly recalled here through selected examples in the Italian and Spanish context.

In Italy, the essential function of urban planning, viewed in terms of design of the physical transformation of the city, did not impede experimentation related to politically aware and interactive approaches to urban design. In practice, attempts were made to critically involve the local community and other stakeholders with concrete reference to the contents of plans and projects well before collaborative approaches emerged internationally (De Carlo, 1964, 2013).[2]

The recent works of Bernardo Secchi and Paola Viganò have had international impact; for example, the Gran Paris consultation and the long-term strategic plans produced for Antwerp and Brussels (Devron, 2009; Secchi and Viganò, 2009; Viganò, 2010; Secchi, 2010). A multifaceted role for planners can be seen in different circumstances. Besides the process-management tasks and the interaction with local stakeholders and citizens more broadly, the physical forms and their impact over social and economic development were reconnected to a broader vision for one city or metropolitan region, sometimes keeping environmental, morpho-typological, mobility and social equality issues center stage. However, the relationship with actual development projects appeared to be crucial for driving urban change. In the case of Spoor Nord Park in Antwerp, the experiments crossing process-related and design skills induced significant improvements both at the neighborhood and regional scale (Palermo and Ponzini, 2015b).

Recently, Bonfantini (2002) studied a set of master plans, urban development and redevelopment projects in Italy and highlighted different ways of integrating design and regulation. He explained the difference between illustrative design and form-based regulation. The former showed a detailed physical view of possible infrastructural and morpho-typological arrangements in existing and developing urban contexts (setting in this way final conditions and allowing further decisions and interactions regarding future urban design choices); and the latter consisted of binding rules that explicitly define a given set of urban and architectural features in their forms, building forms, access from the street, etc.

In other European schools of planning, significant research was developed for discussing the relevance of design in the definition and implementation of strategic projects in contemporary cities (Oosterlynk, van den Broeck, Albrechts, Moulaert, and Verhetsel, 2011). In this sense the discussion of complex institutional and social settings for design showed potential innovations in its conceptions. Strategic projects were intended as punctual or systemic (e.g. infrastructural), physical and functional transformation projects that induce greater change in one city or region, addressing multiple goals and involving multiple actors in a planning process with a long-term perspective. In this sense the relevance of designing as a strategic planning activity was acknowledged. In particular, on the basis of his design experiments, Jef Van den Broeck (2011) maintained that large-scale strategic visions integrating urban development projects are of crucial importance for spatial development because they mobilize multiple actors and can change the trajectory of individual planning processes.

Despite these experiments being of great interest both in theoretical and practical terms, we must note that their effects and legacy are limited; they did not substantially influence mainstream planning or design research, education and practice in Europe.

In Spain one can find long-term traditions and experiments with change of the physical environment as the prime goal for planners, but also recognizing the intrinsically political work that is required in doing so. For example, the *urbanismo estartegico* approach in the 1980s in Barcelona promoted the revitalization of the city through a large-scale vision that was implemented thanks to 140 strategically situated projects called "Urban Acupuncture" (Acebillo, 2006, p. 55) that solved local functional problems and represented the initial phase of renewal. The legacy of this approach has been significant, although there are very different positions regarding the existence and relevance of the so-called "Barcelona model" (Degen and García, 2012). For example, in the case that will be analyzed below, in order to gain further political consensus, the celebration of urban change was kept straightforward (Ajuntament de Barcelona, 2011; Pareja-Eastaway and Piqué, 2011). More generally, simplistic views of a "model" are useful for urban designers to strengthen their cultural position and eventually export their practice to other cities within their own countries or abroad. But oversimplification of the relationship between planning and design is, in practice, a problem for managing cities (González, 2011) and accumulating relevant knowledge.

If one jumps to the present day, most substantial programs of transformation in the city of Barcelona still use urban design as a means of exploring the potential modification of parts of the city, defining their morphology, typology and some of its development parameters in order to attract public and private investment. In the case of the master plan for Sagrera, the area surrounding the future high-speed train station in the northeastern quadrant, this approach to design is quite perceivable. In more detail, the large-scale process of transformation of the Poblenou neighborhood in Barcelona provides clear evidence about how interconnected the design and decision-making dimensions have been and shows the advantages both the public administration and the private stakeholders could derive from this approach.

I will briefly summarize the well-known experience of Poblenou in order to highlight how the design and planning processes related to one another, contrasting with the urban scholarly debates that have been presented through the different, often separated, perspectives of architects, urban designers and planners, geographers and policy analysts (for a more extended description and analysis of the place-making process, see Palermo and Ponzini, 2015b).

The Case of the Regeneration of Poblenou in Barcelona

Since the 1990s the strategy for development in Barcelona has assumed the high-tech and knowledge economy to be a necessary ingredient. The 2000 plan for Poblenou (literally meaning "new town") confirmed that this part of the city was a focal point given the expectation of completing the waterfront redevelopment and of improving the infrastructure system on the east side of Barcelona. The structure of the neighborhood derived from the early 19th-century light-industrial and mixed-use settlement, which was more varied than the standard morphological and functional patterns of Cerdà's grid. In this medium-density environment, small workshops and warehouses were often operated by family-owned enterprises which suffered from deindustrialization trends (Casellas and Pallares-Barbera, 2009). Converting light-industrial fabric for the new economy implied transforming a lower-middle-class and declining neighborhood into an attractive mixed-use pole for high-tech and creative industries (Clos, 2004).

In 2000 the Municipality created the public agency 22@Barcelona to support the planning and implementation of the vision for change. The design, creation and management of infrastructure and public space were perceived publicly as a way to grant the quality and international visibility that other parts of Barcelona had in the 1990s (e.g. Vila Olímpica). These aspects were targeted with systematic investments from the Municipality and with the expectation of driving private investors towards high urban design standards.

Urban design was heavily influenced by the new land-use regulation and the building code in terms of basic dimensions: higher density; functional mix and diversity in terms of public-private spaces; complexity and flexibility. In particular for each project and urban block, the negotiation between public and private parties could cover some aspects, to be approved by a Commission for architectural and urban quality (e.g. height limits), but not others (e.g. fixed indexes and parameters such as gross floor space [GFS], heritage preservation, presence of housing functions).

The broad and to some extent vague definition of the economic activities to be located in the district allowed for a fast start for the redevelopment. The proposal included the transformation of over one million square meters of productive space, over 4,000 residential units to be maintained in the area, and green areas and new public facilities related to the new projects (Clos, 2004). In general the revitalization prioritized functions related to technological enterprises and their complementary activities such as hotels, office space, retail, cultural facilities and housing (Casellas and Pallares-Barbera, 2009).

The urban design features were taken into particular consideration according to the long tradition of the public administration in Barcelona. Regeneration of the light-industrial fabric was in fact intended to confirm and strengthen the pace of the grid and to make significant height and formal variations in given exceptions (such as Glories and the new buildings and complexes along the Diagonal). The use of international architects and innovative building techniques and aesthetics was concentrated in the most symbolic interventions, such as the Agbar Tower by Jean Nouvel (for a detailed insight, see Ponzini and Arosio, forthcoming). The tower is visible from several parts of the city and along the avenues (Gran Via del las Cortes Catalanas, Avenida Diagonal, Avenida Meridiana) since it is in the main roundabout of the eastern side of Barcelona, and this quickly became a landmark.

The creation of a private company for the design and management of infrastructures and public space (the 22@bcn) was assumed to be more efficient for regeneration; but at the same time, one might see this as a potential problem in terms of including a broader set of the population (or their representatives and even elected politicians) in the decision-making process. The population was initially involved through fixed participation procedures related to each project, sometimes including public presentations and hearings in order to have feedback on the projects.

The regeneration project started in a quite successful way by converting a significant section of the city, in particular the fringe between the grid and pre-existing industrial settlements along the Diagonal. According to the agency's data, 60% of the land was already regenerated in 2008. The area was intended to become a home for the "new economy", attracting new investment and allowing new companies to be created and integrated with the significant public investments that were to be made. Some opposition emerged once the first signals of gentrification started to appear in the most revitalized blocks (Puddu and Zuddas, 2013). The pace of development became slower with the stagnation of the real estate market after the start of the 2009 financial crisis. In general terms, the redesign of the preexisting blocks was more difficult than the design of the brownfields.

The plan for the area included illustrative design of six areas with the aim of guiding stakeholders and showing good and feasible solutions in given blocks and the neighborhood's most important axes for the transformation. The initial proposal was designed to be a means of interacting with other actors and the broader population, collecting in this manner further knowledge about the possibilities for change and their meaning for different segments of local society. The six projects were the Audiovisual Campus, Central Park, Llacuna Axis, Llul Pujades East, Llul Pujades West, and Perù-Péere IV; these were to be completed in cooperation with different urban designers and the local universities in order that a critical mass of knowledge could be achieved. The Audiovisual Campus concentrated a set of activities and institutions from this sector. The project of re-establishing the grid and street hierarchy was kept while the building typology was modified through time in several blocks in order to accommodate emerging public uses and due to issues of feasibility (Ajuntament de Barcelona, 2011). The case of Central Park shows further depth of interaction derived from illustrative design and its relevance in terms of collecting local knowledge about the urban environment and managing the development process. The strong protest against the renewal of the Can Ricart factory was to do with the preservation of this mid-19th-century industrial compound and the drawing up of a detailed preservation plan with about 140 elements giving the Poblenou urban landscape a particular sense of place.

The 22@bcn agency was discontinued in 2012 after the program had achieved significant regeneration results, and the management was returned to the usual procedure of the Municipality. This example is known internationally, and in general it is portrayed as either a process of regeneration driven by the new economy or, by contrast, an explicit attempt at appreciation of the real estate stock to induce gentrification in this part of Barcelona. More rarely is attention given to urban design tools and the process of designing and managing the change of the urban form (Palermo and Ponzini, 2015b).

Conclusions: The Unwarranted Boundaries between Urban Planning and Design

The debates and views considered in this chapter have shown that the gap between process-oriented and design-oriented approaches to urban planning and transformation depends on long-term processes of institutionalization of planning disciplines as they evolved in different contexts with different planning cultures and traditions. For cultural and professional reasons, in the Anglo-Saxon and American world, urban designers attempted to create their own academic and professional field without necessarily ignoring wholesale the shared background with architects and planners. However, what is most visible in these attempts is that they consist of simple approaches, models or even urban design products (think, for example, about the transit-oriented design diagrams and the New Urbanism; Grant, 2006). These simplifications are of course common for other aspects of planning (I mentioned the Barcelona model), but a limited understanding of planning traditions that have deep design roots along with an underestimation of the experiment at the crossroads of different disciplines has limited the accumulation of knowledge regarding urban problems and solutions that are well beyond technicalities separate from the planning process (the case of Poblenou is one among many, but nonetheless it generates relevant knowledge – see Beauregard and Lieto, 2018, this volume).

Abstract questions regarding the positioning of urban design in planning (Gunder, 2011) would provide partial points of view that could be biased by the planning culture and tradition we are embedded in. More generally it is unlikely that, internationally, the so-called "gap between planning and design" will ever be filled for good (Wyatt, 2004) given the interests in promoting new programs and the good reasons for producing new practical experiments in urban design, place-making, etc. and deriving new knowledge from them. Nor will the individual progress made by such experiments and programs suffice to fill this gap if planners do not have a higher appreciation of diverse traditions and if they do not find better ways of accumulating knowledge regarding complex urban decision-making and design processes, beyond simplified models.

The scope of this chapter is quite modest. By considering design not only as a product (e.g. plan, scheme or project) but as a complex process of shaping and giving sense to urban places, I suggest that the production and accumulation of usable and project-oriented knowledge may derive from observing examples from diverse planning cultures. I am aware that the appreciation of such knowledge depends on one's paradigmatic view on planning (Palermo and Ponzini, 2015a), but the practical advantages of crosscutting planning and design are substantial and could be appreciated by a more general audience (see Brenda Case Scheer, 2018, this volume). As exemplified in Barcelona, looking at design as a way to explore and critically understand the potential physical, functional and symbolic transformation of places shows that planning codes and other urban policy tools can make use of illustrative design techniques for forecasting and public discussion of the impacts of given projects (Ben-Joseph, 2005; Carmona, 2011) as was the case for the six special projects in Barcelona. At a larger scale, a better understanding and theorization of urban design can contribute to the nesting of strategic and structural visions into actual urban development projects fitting the morphological change (Oosterlynck et al., 2011) as in Poblenou.

Contingent institutional, political, social and cultural conditions will always play a determining role in planning and in the possibilities of producing planning knowledge. Nonetheless, scholars have the responsibility to recognize some basic issues and position themselves: the explorative use of design activities for interactive land-use planning show that they are, in fact, particular kinds of social inquiry (Lindblom, 1990; Lindblom and Cohen, 1979; Palermo and Ponzini, 2015a).

The recognition of such small innovation is important but likely will not overcome, once and for all, the frontiers in theory, practice and applied research. Further debate and deeper insight into the advantages of trespassing the boundaries that planning and design disciplines defined in their different institutionalization processes can induce important advancements in theory and in practice.

Notes

1 This work is based on a long-term research project, which was published in different places: Ponzini 2013; Palermo and Ponzini 2010, 2012, 2015a, 2015b. A previous and different version of this chapter was presented in 2013 at the Joint Congress of the Association of European Schools of Planning and the American Collegiate Schools of Planning in Dublin.
2 For a brief review in the English language, see the portrait of Giancarlo de Carlo in *Architectural Review*, January 30, 2014: https://www.architectural-review.com/archive/reputations/giancarlo-de-carlo-1919-2005/8658151.article.

References

Acebillo, J. A. (2006). Barcelona: Toward a New Urban Planning Approach. *Spatium*, *2006*(13/14): 55–59.
Ajuntament de Barcelona (2011). *22@ Barcelona: 10 Years of Urban Renewal*. Barcelona: Mimeo.
Anselin, L., Nasar, J. L., and Talen, E. (2011). Where Do Planners Belong? Assessing the Relationship between Planning and Design in American Universities. *Journal of Planning Education and Research*, *31*(2): 196–207.
Banerjee, T., and Loukaitou-Sideris, A. (Eds.). (2011). *Companion to Urban Design*. London: Routledge.
Beauregard, R. A. (1990). Bringing the City back in. *Journal of the American Planning Association*, *56*(2): 210–215.
Beauregard, R., and Lieto, L. (2018). Towards an Object-Oriented Case Methodology for Planners, in Sanchez, T. W. (Ed.), *Planning Research and Knowledge*. Abingdon, UK: Routledge, pp. 153–166.
Ben-Joseph, E. (2005). *The Code of the City: Standards and the Hidden Language of Place Making*. Cambridge MA: MIT Press.
Bonfantini, B. (2002). *Progetto Urbanistico e Città Esistente: Gli Strumenti Discreti della Regolazione*. Milan: Libreria Clup.
Campbell, S., and Fainstein, S. (Eds.). (1996) *Readings in Planning Theory*. Cambridge, MA: Blackwell.
Carmona, M. (2011). Design Coding: Mediating the Tyrannies of Practice, in Tiesdell, S., and Adams, D. (Eds.), *Urban Design in the Real Estate Development Process*. Hoboken, NJ: Wiley, pp. 54–73.
Carmona, M., Heath, T., Oc, T., and Tiesdell, S. (2003). *Public Places Urban Spaces: The Dimensions of Urban Design*. Amsterdam: Architectural Press.
Casellas, A., and Pallares-Barbera, M. (2009). The Barcelona Experience: Public-Sector Intervention in Embodying the New Economy in Inner Urban Areas. *Urban Studies*, *46*(5/6): 1137–1155.
Clos, O. (2004). The Transformation of Poblenou: The New 22@ District, in Marshall, T. (Ed.), *Transforming Barcelona*. London and New York: Routledge, pp. 91–201.
Commission of the European Communities (CEC). (1997). *The EU Compendium of Spatial Planning Systems and Policies*. Regional Development Studies No. 28. Luxembourg: European Commission.
Cuthbert, A. (2010). Whose Urban Design? *Journal of Urban Design*, *15*(3): 443–448.

De Carlo, G. (1964). *Questioni di Architettura e di Urbanistica*. Urbino: Argalia.
De Carlo, G. (2013). *L'Architettura della Partecipazione*, edited by Sara Marini. Macerata: Quodlibet.
Degen, M., and García, M. (2012). The Transformation of the "Barcelona Model": An Analysis of Culture, Urban Regeneration and Governance. *International Journal of Urban and Regional Research*, 36(5): 1022–1038.
Devron, J. F. (Ed.). (2009). *Le Grand Pari(s). Consultation Internationale sur l'Avenir de la Métropole Parisienne*. Paris: Le Moniteur.
Dovey, K. (1999). *Framing Places: Mediating Power in Built Form*. London: Routledge.
Editors, Journal of the American Planning Association. (1952). Editorial: Design in Planning. *Journal of the American Planning Association*, 18: 152.
ESPON. (2007). *Governance of Territorial and Urban Policies from EU to Local Level*. Luxembourg: European Spatial Planning Observation Network.
Fainstein, S. S., and Campbell, S. (Eds.). (2002). *Readings in Urban Theory*. Cambridge MA: Blackwell.
Faludi, A. (1973). *A Reader in Planning Theory*. Oxford: Pergamon Press.
Gehl, J. (2010). *Cities for People*. Washington DC: Island Press.
González, S. (2011). Bilbao and Barcelona "in Motion." How Urban Regeneration "Models" Travel and Mutate in the Global Flows of Policy Tourism. *Urban Studies*, 48(7): 1397–1418.
Grant, J. (2006). *Planning the Good Community: New Urbanism in Theory and Practice*. London: Routledge.
Gregotti, V. (1966). *Il Territorio dell'Architettura*. Milan: Feltrinelli.
Gunder, M. (2011). Commentary: Is Urban Design Still Urban Planning? An Exploration and Response. *Journal of Planning Education and Research*, 31(2): 184–195.
Hillier, J., and Healey, P. (Eds.). (2008). *Critical Essays in Planning Theory*. Aldershot, UK: Ashgate.
Hubbard, P. (1996). Urban Design and City Regeneration: Social Representations of Entrepreneurial Landscapes. *Urban Studies*, 33(8): 1441–1461.
Knox, P., and Ozolins, P. (2000). *Design Professionals and the Built Environment: An Introduction*. Chichester, UK: Wiley.
Lang, J. T. (2005). *Urban Design: A Typology of Procedures and Products*. London: Routledge.
Lindblom, C. E. (1990). *Inquiry and Change: The Troubled Attempt to Understand and Shape Society*. New Haven, CT: Yale University Press.
Lindblom, C. E., Cohen, D. K. (1979). *Usable Knowledge: Social Science and Social Problem Solving*. New Haven, CT: Yale University Press.
Madanipour, A. (1996). *Design of Urban Space: An Inquiry into a Socio–Spatial Process*. Chichester, UK: Wiley.
Mazza, L. (2003). Appunti sul Disegno di un Sistema di Pianificazione. *CRU – Critica della razionalità urbanistica*, 14(1): 51–66.
Mazza, L. (2004). *Piano, Progetti, Strategie*. Milan: Franco Angeli.
Mumford, E. P. (2009). *Defining Urban Design: CIAM Architects and the Formation of a Discipline, 1937–69*. New Haven, CT: Yale University Press.
Oosterlynck, S., van den Broeck, J., Albrechts, L., Moulaert, F., and Verhetsel, A. (Eds.). (2011). *Strategic Spatial Projects: Catalysts for Change*. London: Routledge.
Palermo, P. C., and Ponzini, D. (2010). *Spatial Planning and Urban Development: Critical Perspective*. Dordrecht: Springer.
Palermo, P. C., Ponzini, D. (2012). At the Crossroads between Urban Planning and Urban Design: Critical Lessons from Three Italian Case Studies. *Planning Theory and Practice*, 13(3): 445–460.

Palermo, P. C., and Ponzini, D. (2015a). Inquiry and Design for Spatial Planning. Three Paradigms for Planning Research in Late Modern and Contemporary Cities, in Silva, E., Healey, P., Harris, N., and Van den Broek, P. (Eds.), *The Routledge Handbook of Planning Research Methods*. London: Routledge – Royal Town Planning Institute, pp. 121–131.

Palermo, P. C., and Ponzini, D. (2015b). *Place–Making and Urban Development: New Challenges for Planning and Design*. London: Routledge.

Pareja-Eastaway, M., and Piqué, J. M. (2011). Urban Regeneration and the Creative Knowledge Economy: The Case of 22@ in Barcelona. *Journal of Urban Regeneration and Renewal*, 4(4): 319–327.

Ponzini, D. (2013). Despite the Absence of the Public Sphere: How Common Goods Can Contribute to the Design of Public Spaces, in Serreli, S. (Ed.), *City Project and Public Spaces*. Dordrecht and New York: Springer, pp. 97–110.

Ponzini, D., and Arosio, P. M. (Forthcoming). Urban Effects of the Transnational Circulation of Branded Buildings: Comparing Two Skyscrapers and Their Context in Barcelona and Doha. *Urban Design International*, 22(1): 28–46.

Puddu, S., and Zuddas, F. (2013). Cities and Science Parks: The Urban Experience of 22@ Barcelona. *Territorio*, 63: 145–152.

Punter, J. (1996). Urban Design Theory in Planning Practice: The British Perspective. *Built Environment*, 22(4): 263–277.

Rodwin, L., and Sanyal, B. (2000). *The Profession of City Planning: Changes, Images and Challenges, 1950–2000*. New Brunswick, NJ: Center for Urban Policy Research.

Sanyal, B. (2008). Critical about Criticality. *Critical Planning, UCLA Journal of Urban Planning*, 15(Summer): 142–160.

Scheer, B. C. (2018). Urban Morphology as a Research Method, in Sanchez, T. W. (Ed.), *Planning Research and Knowledge*. Abingdon, UK: Routledge, pp. 167–181.

Schön, D. (1983). *The Reflective Practitioner: How Professionals Think in Action*. New York: Basic Books.

Secchi, B. (2010). A New Urban Question. *Territorio*, 53: 8–18.

Secchi, B. and Viganò, P. (Eds.). (2009). *Antwerp, Territory of a New Modernity*. Amsterdam: SUN.

Tiesdell, S., and Adams, D. (2011). *Urban Design in the Real Estate Development Process*. Chichester: Wiley.

Van den Broek, J. (2011). Spatial Design as a Strategy for Qualitative Social-Spatial Transformation, in Oosterlynck, S., van den Broeck, J., Albrechts, L., Moulaert, F., and Verhetsel, A. (Eds.), *Strategic Spatial Projects: Catalysts for Change*. London: Routledge, pp. 87–96.

Viganò, P. (2010). *I Territori dell'Urbanistica: Il Progetto come Produttore di Conoscenza*. Rome: Officina.

Wyatt, R. (2004). The Great Divide: Differences in style between Architects and Urban Planners. *Journal of Architectural and Planning Research*, 21(1): 38–54.

PART IV
Planning Methods, Science, and Technology

12
USE OF *PLANNING* MAGAZINE TO BRIDGE THE GAP BETWEEN RESEARCHERS AND PRACTITIONERS

Kathryn R. Terzano and Reid Ewing

"Research You Can Use" has appeared as a column in *Planning* magazine since November of 2006. Directed at planning practitioners, interested members of the public who read *Planning* magazine, and increasingly other academics who conduct the research that informs practice, the column has sought to distill the takeaway messages from select academic research studies that have the potential to be useful in planning practice.

Planning is published by the American Planning Association (APA), which is the professional association for planning practitioners in the U.S., and it is undoubtedly the best-known publication among professional planners, who receive the monthly magazine as part of their membership in the APA. Since the column's inception, more than 50 have been published, attempting to bridge the gap between planning academia and planning practice. These columns discuss nearly 100 publications (and, occasionally, work that is in press); most are academic journal articles, but several are key books in the planning field and at least two are reports prepared by planning practitioners—although the majority of the columns focus on informing the readership about the work of planning researchers, on occasion exemplary work by practitioners is presented.[1]

At the time the column was first proposed, in the summer of 2006, the column's author, Reid Ewing, wrote the following to David Sawicki, then editor of the *Journal of the American Planning Association*, and Sylvia Lewis, then head of publications at the American Planning Association:

> You asked for a prospectus of the "Planning Research You Can Use" feature or column proposed for *Planning* magazine. The feature would be a way of encouraging academics to conduct research of use to practitioners, and rewarding those who do with more exposure than they would otherwise receive. It would draw the world of research closer to the world of practice

and vice versa. It might be a monthly feature, or possibly, less regular. It would run 1,000 words max, probably less. It would report on the most practical research I can find at some stage of review or publication.

It has largely adhered to these guidelines, though it has become increasingly eclectic as the author has sought to appeal to a broader audience and increase the relevance of the column.

Methodological Approach

A recurring theme throughout the columns is the critique of methodology in the studies in question. Three columns examine the relative merits of quantitative methods compared to qualitative methods. "When Qualitative Research Trumps Quantitative—Cultural Economy and Smart Growth" (October 2007) features two academic journal articles that use qualitative methods to provide unique insights where quantitative work would have been found lacking. "When Quantitative Research Trumps Qualitative—What Makes Transfer of Development Rights Work?" (January 2009) takes a very different approach in critiquing a qualitative study that would have made a stronger contribution to the literature if the authors had also employed quantitative methods; the column further discusses how a quantitative or mixed-methods study could have been carried out. "Mixing Methods for Clearer Results" (February 2013) more directly addresses three different ways that quantitative and qualitative data can be combined for a mixed-method design: merging the data, connecting the data, and embedding the data. An additional column, "Observation as a Research Method (and the Importance of Public Seating)" from (February 2014) highlights observational methods of research and focuses on a dissertation-turned-book that used observation in the same vein as William H. Whyte, Allan Jacobs, and others with the addition of a quantitative analysis of the observations. Finally, "Finding Happiness in Public-Private Partnerships: The Case for Case Studies" (January 2007) advocates for the qualitative research method of employing case studies for in-depth analysis. The examples in the January 2007 column come from Lynn Sagalyn's article on public-private partnerships in the Winter 2007 issue of the *Journal of the American Planning Association*.

Other columns review (or, depending on the reader, introduce) quantitative methods. Most of these columns use existing studies as examples to illustrate or critique a given method, but several columns delve into the method directly. Regression, in its various iterations, is discussed in several columns. "Not Your Grandparents' Regression Analysis" (April 2014) provides an introduction to how regression analysis functions and what its common pitfalls are, ending on a cautionary note about the need to consult experts for the advanced analyses required by today's standards. "Different Models of Metropolitan Economic Performance" (June 2008) discusses the relative merits of structural equation modeling over multiple regression analysis through the example of an academic study that used multiple regression analysis when structural equation modeling would have been a better approach. "Compact Development and Good Outcomes—Environmental Determinism, Self-Selection, or Some of Both?" (July 2009) reopens the discussion of ordinary least squares regression, negative binomial regression, and structural equation modeling within the context of a larger discussion of the effects of self-selection on study outcomes. Similarly, "A 'Natural Experiment'—Closing Broadway" (April 2010) makes an argument for structural equation modeling as being preferable to simple linear regression. "Using Safe Streets as a Research Priority" (May 2009) introduces the reader to Poisson regression and negative binomial regression as possible options when the dependent variable is a count variable with many zero values.

One other quantitative method, propensity score matching, was discussed in the January 2015 column entitled "Assessing BIDs Using Propensity Score Matching." This column praises the use of propensity score matching specifically because it led to a different conclusion than less sophisticated methods may have reached. The importance of choosing the right method, such as propensity score matching, is discussed since the wrong method could lead to the wrong conclusion.

Meta-analysis as a research method is discussed in two columns. The earlier column, "Regional Scenario Plans and Meta-Analysis," from March 2007, defines meta-analysis and goes on to highlight Keith Bartholomew's meta-analysis of 80 regional scenario plans, based on his (then) forthcoming article in *Transportation*, "Land use-Transportation Scenario Planning: Promise and Reality." Meta-analysis was, and still is, rare in planning; as of the March 2009 column, "Meta-Analysis of Plan Quality—More than a Literature Review," only ten meta-analyses had appeared in the planning literature. This latter column provides a more detailed description of meta-analysis than the earlier column, and it encourages scholars to think beyond traditional literature reviews to instead use meta-analysis to summarize and examine the existing literature.

Still other columns examine the theoretical underpinnings for research studies in planning. The first column that topically addressed theory was "Make Way for a New Theory," published in February 2011. This column summarizes the argument that planning does not have its own theoretical basis but, rather, borrows theory from cognate fields. An exception to the rule of borrowing from other fields has historically been rational planning theory, which is discussed in the column. The column continues with an explanation of the theory of collaborative rationality, another theory with its origins in planning, which had been introduced in the Winter 2011 issue of the *Journal of the American Planning Association*. Other theories are discussed in different columns. In "Toward a Grounded Theory of Sustainable Zoning" (May 2015), sociology-based grounded theory is introduced. Grounded theory has been applied in the study of concepts in diverse fields, and this column reviews John Landis' article "Growth Management Revisited: A Reassessment of its Efficacy, Price Effects, and Impacts on Metropolitan Growth Patterns" to describe how grounded theory can be applied to zoning. Another column that same year, "A Physicist Tries to Solve the City" (December 2015) points out flaws in urban scaling theory, a theory developed by physicists that has proved problematic in its actual application to urban phenomena.

Finally, two columns discuss translational research—or that research which provides a ready translation of basic research findings into practice. The first half of the October 2010 column, "Translational Research: The Next New Thing," is devoted to explaining translational research. The next column, "Translational Research in Action" (December 2010) summarizes six planning tools that exemplify translational research.

Journal Reputation and Peer Review

In addition to columns that have primarily discussed the methods or research design of studies, several columns can be grouped together in terms of how they center on journals and peer review. The first-ever column, "Does Growth Management Work? Program Evaluation at its Best" (November 2006) named the *Journal of the American Planning Association (JAPA)* specifically as a source for academic research articles and went on to discuss an article from the most recent issue at the time. The February 2010 column, "A Bonanza of Journal Articles," defines impact factors and relates their importance. *JAPA* is praised in this column for the increase in the journal's impact factor, and four articles from *JAPA* are discussed.

"Peer Review Clarifies Lots of Things, Including the Relationship of Sprawl and Air Pollution" (July 2010) describes the process and benefits of academic peer review. "Reviewing the Reviews" (October 2013) explains the process of peer review in more detail, citing the criteria used for the *Journal of Planning Literature (JPL)*. Perhaps the column that has garnered the most attention, "Brouhaha over *JAPA* Article: Is Flawed Peer Review to Blame?" (October 2012), discusses an article that sparked controversy because of the possibility that inadequate peer review allowed the article, which is argued to be subpar, to be published in a well-regarded journal. *JAPA* is once again discussed as the topic of the July 2013 column, entitled "Come Home to *JAPA*." This column is a straightforward defense of the journal, which was coming out of a tumultuous period of long delays in manuscript review, and an encouragement for planning researchers to submit manuscripts to the journal.

Throughout the history of the column, many journals are given prominent attention in individual columns and others are, at least, referred to in passing. Aside from *JAPA* and *JPL*—the two journals from which articles are most frequently cited—other journals mentioned include *Journal of Planning Education and Research*, *Housing Policy Debate*, *Economic Development Quarterly*, *Journal of Urban Design*, *Landscape and Urban Planning*, *Transportation Research*, and *Journal of Transport and Health*. The August–September 2014 column, "Hot Journal, Hotter Cities," discussed the journal *Landscape and Urban Planning* in comparison to *JAPA*, *JPL*, and *Journal of Planning Education and Research*. The December 2013 column, "Costs of Sprawl Revisited," predicts a trend toward more open access journals, such as *Sustainability*, within the urban planning field.

Smart Growth, Sprawl, and the D Variables

Given the longstanding research interests of the column's author, Reid Ewing, many of the articles that have stood out as notable for inclusion are those related to smart growth, sprawl, and the so-called D variables (density, diversity, design, destination accessibility, distance to transit, and demographics).[2] The very first column, "Does Growth Management Work? Program Evaluation at its Best" (November 2006), introduces the then forthcoming *JAPA* article by John Landis, entitled "Growth Management Revisited: A Reassessment of its Efficacy, Price Effects, and Impacts on Metropolitan Growth Patterns," in which three growth management techniques are found to be successful in their aims and two growth management techniques are found to be ineffective.

Two columns later, the March 2007 column entitled "Regional Scenario Plans and Meta-Analysis" examines meta-analysis of scenario planning projects, which typically compare development patterns that range the spectrum from being compact to exemplifying sprawl. The particular article being summarized in this column, as mentioned above, is Keith Bartholomew's "Land use-Transportation Scenario Planning: Promise and Reality." Bartholomew's findings are contradicted in an article by Marcial Echenique et al.—"Growing Cities Sustainably: Does Urban Form Really Matter?" published in *JAPA*'s Spring 2012 issue. The column in October 2012, "Brouhaha over *JAPA* Article: Is Flawed Peer Review to Blame?" picks apart Echenique et al.'s article and its claims that there is no "clearly superior" type of development among different development types (compact development, sprawl, edge expansion, and new towns) and that compact development has only a minimal impact on sustainability.

The article at the center of the July 2010 column, "Peer Review Clarifies Lots of Things, Including the Relationship of Sprawl and Air Pollution," takes a close look at the relationship between compact metropolitan regions and ozone concentrations. The article's authors, Lisa Schweitzer and Jiangpin Zhou, find that compact metropolitan areas have lower ozone concentrations than less compact metropolitan areas, but that ozone exposures are greater in these same compact areas. This topic is revisited in "Is Anyone Listening as Climate Change Speeds Up?" (December 2011), which draws a connection among a regional planning act in California aimed at climate mitigation (SB 375, Sustainable Communities and Climate Protection Act of 2008), metropolitan planning organizations (MPOs) encouraging more compact development in response, and the predicted levels of carbon dioxide reduction resulting from more compact development. Sprawl is further discussed in the column entitled "Costs of Sprawl Revisited" (December 2013). This column reviews three articles: one that examined the loss of agricultural land as a result of sprawl; a second that looked at transportation-related costs of sprawl in the U.S.; and a third that found impacts of sprawl on air, energy, land, and water. The relationship between regional planning and air quality is also discussed in the April 2013 column, "Coordinating Land Use and Transportation in Sacramento".

An additional column, "Mapping Mobility" (June 2014), first reviews a study of upward mobility conducted by a team from Harvard and University of California-Berkeley, which found that intergenerational mobility varies across geographic areas of the U.S. The column goes on to report on a University of Utah study that linked sprawl to upward mobility and found that another cost of sprawl is upward mobility: children born into families of lower economic status were less likely to achieve upward mobility if they lived in sprawling areas as compared to compact areas.

The December 2007 column, "The Demand for Smart Growth: What Survey Research Tells Us," is one of the columns in which smart growth is more directly addressed. This discusses the 2004 National Survey on Communities, which was carried out for the nonprofit organization Smart Growth America. The column makes the case for a latent demand for the kind of compact, walkable neighborhoods that are the antithesis of sprawl and are encouraged through smart growth policies. The February 2010 column, "A Bonanza of Journal Articles," briefly discusses an article by Paul Lewis and Mark Baldassare entitled "The Complexity of Public Attitudes Toward Compact Development: Survey Evidence from Five States." The article reports on the finding that at the time of their study at least half of Americans would consider living in a compact, mixed-use neighborhood, reinforcing the idea from the December 2007 column that a latent demand exists for development of this kind. Smart growth is briefly mentioned again in the December 2010 column, "Translational Research in Action," since one of the tools created by Uri Avin, FAICP, of the PlaceMaking group at Parsons Brinckerhoff was a Smart Growth Audit, although details of this tool are not given in the column.

In December 2009, the column entitled "Top Academics vs. Top Thinkers" in part critiques a report from the National Academy of Sciences on the relationship between driving and the built environment, specifically on different scenarios of energy use that in turn are based on differing degrees of intensity of residential development. The column further critiques the report's use of residential development only, rather than including commercial development as well. The April 2011 column, "Traffic Generated by MXD: New Prediction Methods Ahead," returns to the subject of traffic and its relationship to smart growth, or at least one significant feature of smart growth: mixed-use development (MXD). The column explains how, within the MXD area, mixed-use developments create favorable conditions for walking, biking, and taking transit, thus reducing the number of external car trips. The column then introduces research by a team (Michael Greenwald, Ming Zhang, Robert Cervero, Jerry Walters, Mark Feldman, Larry Frank, and John Thomas) whose article was slated for publication in the *Journal of Urban Planning and Development*. In their then forthcoming article, the researchers report on their study of 239 MXDs and their findings that the internationalization of trips in these areas related to the MXD's land area, employment, balance of jobs and population, and intersection density. The researchers then validated their results by comparing their model's predictions with actual traffic counts from 22 MXDs.

The connection between the built environment and travel is described in relation to urban design in the July 2011 column, "Urban Design vs. Urban Planning: A Distinction With a Difference". This discusses the three original D variables (density, diversity, and design) as well as the additional D variables that have been added since Robert Cervero and Kara Kockelman's 1997 article. The column approaches the field of planning from a rational planning perspective, arguing that the object of planning is utility, and then explains how researchers studying the built environment and travel may operationalize design as it relates to street network characteristics, rather than design as it concerns art and aesthetics. The D variables are discussed again in the February 2016 column, "Contribution of Urban Design Qualities to Pedestrian Activity," which notes the existence of over 200 studies on the association between the built environment and travel that assess one or more of the D variables. The D variable of design is once again the subject, and this time the column delves into ways of measuring aspects of urban design. The column begins with a discussion of a 2009 *Journal of Urban Design* article by Reid Ewing and Susan Handy, "Measuring the Unmeasurable: Urban Design Qualities Related to Walkability," which operationalized imageability, enclosure, human scale, transparency, and complexity to create a link to walkability. The column also reports on a later study that found transparency (measured by proportion of first-floor façade with windows, the proportion of active uses at street levels, and the proportion of continuous building frontage) was the most significant design variable in terms of its influence on walkability. Finally, the column summarizes the findings of a third study, again from the *Journal of Urban Design*—"Do Better Urban Design Qualities Lead to More Walking in Salt Lake City, Utah?" by Ameli et al.—which also examined urban design and walkability, finding both transparency and imageability to be highly significantly related to walkability.

Other Aspects of Transportation

"Using Safe Streets as a Research Priority" (May 2009) notes that while there was already a significant body of work on the relationship between the built environment and household travel, far less research had been published on the relationship between the built environment and traffic safety. The column highlights the work of Eric Dumbaugh, specifically his *JAPA* article from Summer 2009, co-authored with Robert Rae, entitled "Safe Urban Form: Revisiting the Relationship between Community Design and Traffic Safety." Dumbaugh and Rae advocate for traditional street design features such as pedestrian-oriented retail uses and interconnected streets. The March 2015 column, "Golden Age of Street Design," makes the connection between poor street design and factors such as overly conservative geometric standards, road widening as a solution to congestion, lack of investment in street trees and special materials, among others. The column optimistically predicts the dawning of a golden age of street design based on the rise of the complete streets movement, which advocates for streets that accommodate pedestrians, bicyclists, and transit riders in addition to automobile users. Part of the rise of the complete streets movement is seen through the increased number of complete streets design manuals being adopted by various jurisdictions. Lastly, the column notes that we are already seeing streets being redesigned through road diets, the installation of curb-separated protected bike lanes, and centerline medians designed for pedestrian comfort.

A 2012 *JAPA* article entitled "Does Accessibility Require Density or Speed? A Comparison of Fast Versus Close in Getting Where You Want to Go in U.S. Metropolitan Regions" (by Jonathan Levine, Joe Grengs, Qingyun Shen, and Qing Shen) is described in the July 2012 column, "Accessibility vs. Mobility: The Right Methodology." In the column, the article's argument (that accessibility is more important than mobility) and the authors' methods (structural equation modeling) are both praised.

In April 2016, the column, entitled "*JAPA*, A Year in Review," highlights three transportation-related articles that were published in *JAPA* in 2015. The first article mentioned (Noreen McDonald's "Are Millennials Really the 'Go-Nowhere' Generation?") presents evidence that younger generations travel fewer miles than previous generations at comparable ages. The second article ("How Differences in Roadways Affect School Travel Safety" by Chia-Yuan Yu) describes school travel-related crash data in Austin, Texas. The third article ("Parking Infrastructure: A Constraint on or Opportunity for Urban Redevelopment? A Study of Los Angeles County Parking Supply and Growth" by Mikhail Chester et al.) estimates how parking affects travel and urban form.

Aside from the connecting of active transportation with compact development in a number of columns, active transportation is at the forefront of several additional columns, beginning with the May 2007 column entitled "The Perils of Causal Inference: Bicycling in Davis, California." The main point of this column was to critique a study in which the author made a causal inference that, while probably correct, was not sufficiently supported within the parameters of the study itself. However, the column also describes the qualities of a city—in this case, Davis, California—that are helpful for facilitating a high bike mode share. "A 'Natural Experiment'—Closing Broadway" (April 2010) presents findings that pedestrian malls may be feasible under special circumstances. Bicycling to school and Safe Routes to School programs are briefly mentioned in the October 2011 column, "Another Bonanza," and more expansively in the November 2014 column, "Correlation Does Not Imply Causation (When It Comes to Childhood Obesity)". The latter column highlights four *Journal of Planning Education and Research* (*JPER*) articles about healthy schools. Finally, the August–September 2016 column, "Active Living: A Planning Subfield Comes of Age," describes the origin and immense growth of active living as a planning subfield, including the relationship of active living to public health.

Urban Design

As previously mentioned, several columns focus on urban design issues. The columns already discussed were mentioned because of their link to walkability:

"Urban Design vs. Urban Planning: A Distinction With a Difference" (July 2011) and "Contribution of Urban Design Qualities to Pedestrian Activity" (February 2016). Other columns touch on the issue of urban design in different ways. For example, the July 2007 column, "Security of Public Spaces: New Measures Are Reliable, But Are They Valid?" presented a then forthcoming *JAPA* article—"Toward a Methodology for Measuring Security in Publicly Accessible Spaces" by Jeremy Nemeth and Stephan Schmidt—that, in part, linked the physical design of public spaces to issues of security and natural surveillance.

The February 2014 column entitled "Observation as a Research Method (and the Importance of Public Seating)" describes how observational methods are often appropriate for urban design research, particularly when it comes to what makes an active and successful street, plaza, or park, using examples of well-known observers such as Jane Jacobs, Donald Appleyard, and William H. Whyte. The column continues by describing the work of Vikas Mehta, whose 2013 book *The Street: A Quintessential Social Public Space* combined observational work with quantitative analysis. Among Mehta's findings was that social activity is positively correlated with commercial seating.

Land-use and Development Regulations

The February 2008 column, "Land Readjustment—Learning from International Research," promotes the technique of land readjustment, where property owners in a given area allow a third party to replat (and, sometimes, rezone) the property in a way that enhances its value and makes for more efficient use of the land overall. The column notes how land readjustment has its origins in Germany but is well used in planning throughout the developed world, with the exception of the U.S. and the U.K.

The August–September 2008 column, "Graduated Density Zoning—The Danger of Generalizing from a Sample of One," introduces graduated density zoning and critiques it as a potential method for creating higher-density development through promoting site assembly. The column discusses two Maryland counties that used site assembly-density bonuses, and recommends exercising caution in adopting graduated density zoning by itself.

Taking a nongovernmental approach, Rebecca Retzlaff's *JPER* article, "The Use of LEED in Planning and Development Regulation," is described in the September–October 2009 column, "What Planners Need to Know About Evaluating LEED," along with a second article from *JAPA*, "Sustainable by Design? Insights from U.S. LEED-ND Pilot Projects" by Ajay Garde, which was much more critical of LEED.

Climate Change and the Natural Environment

In addition to the above-mentioned column on climate change ("Is Anyone Listening as Climate Change Speeds Up?"; December 2011), the November 2008 column, "First Look at Climate Action Planers—So Much More to Be Done," also addresses this important issue. In fact, the latter column even states that "climate change will be the *defining issue* for urban planners in the 21st century." This prediction was based on, among other things, Stephen Wheeler's *JAPA* article from Autumn of 2008 ("State and Municipal Climate Change Plans: The First Generation") and the then recent passage of California's SB 375, mentioned earlier in this chapter. Climate action plans are again discussed in "Mixing Methods for Clearer Results" (February 2013), which describes two studies by Adam Millard-Ball, who finds little evidence for a causal relationship between climate action planning and emission-reduction measures. Finally, urban heat islands and ecological planning are discussed in the August–September 2014 column "Hot Journal, Hotter Cities".

Diversity of Topics

Other topics are given coverage in at least one column. Public-private partnerships are discussed in two columns, years apart—"Finding Happiness in Public-Private Partnerships: The Case for Case Studies" (January 2007) and "A Bonanza of Journal Articles" (February 2010). The public health tool of Health Impact Assessments (HIAs) is introduced to planners in the October 2010 column, "Translational Research: The Next New Thing". The relationship between tax credits and the production of low-income housing units is briefly discussed in the October 2011 column, "Another Bonanza". The April 2012 column entitled "Great Topic (Urban Agriculture) and Good Start (to Academic Career)" introduces urban agriculture as a research topic that was newly trending in urban planning at the time of writing. Livability and, specifically, AARP's Livability Index are discussed in the July 2015 column, "Measuring Livability". The October 2015 column, "Edgy Planning Issues," provides summaries of articles on three very different yet "edgy" topics: property rights challenges to regional planning, the relationship between travel behavior and social connections in neighborhoods with a large share of gay and lesbian residents, and land-use issues related to medical marijuana dispensaries.

Looking Ahead

As noted in the introduction, the column has become increasingly eclectic. The three most recent columns have identified and profiled the five most highly cited academic planners, most of whom planning practitioners have probably never heard of but should know about (Luc Anselin, Michael Storper, James W. Varni, AnnaLee Saxenian, and Robert Cervero); described the birth of a new planning subfield and a new journal (active living by design and the *Journal of Transport and Health*); and described the use of research by an APA expert planning panel to challenge a massive freeway widening project in Denver (the I-70 East Reconstruction project, which would be wider than a football field is long and which would severely impact minority neighborhoods).

The column will undoubtedly continue to pick out the most important and groundbreaking new research to share with the readers of *Planning* magazine. As new research directions arise, new topics are written about, and new methods are developed, the column will highlight the research that planners should know about. Co-authors, like the lead author of this chapter, will be enlisted by the second author to make the column even more useful.

Notes

1 All past columns are available for free online at: http://cmpweb.arch.utah.edu/research_projects/research-you-can-use.
2 Cervero, R. and Kockelman, K. (1997) Travel demand and the 3Ds: Density, diversity, and design. Transportation Research D, 2(3), 199–219.

13
PLANNING OUR FUTURE CITIES

The Role Computer Technologies Can Play

Robert Goodspeed, Peter Pelzer, and Christopher Pettit

Introduction

One of the most notable changes to cityscapes worldwide in the past 20 years has been the steady expansion of information and communications technologies (ICTs). Today, urban residents navigate cities with smartphones, track their own activities with digital devices, access public transportation systems with smart cards, and interact with governments through web portals. In urban planning, there is a growing interest in how ICTs may result in new knowledge about cities and be used to improve urban quality of life. Some researchers have begun to probe the burgeoning data sets these new ICTs produce in search of previously hidden patterns (e.g. Townsend, 2015; Bettencourt and West, 2010). For others, ICTs open the possibility of creating new ways to tackle longstanding urban problems; for example, smart city strategies utilizing new technologies to improve urban management (Batty et al., 2012; Goodspeed, 2014; Neirotti et al., 2014). Planning scholars are beginning to tap the new data sources to shed light on classic urban social science questions (e.g. Thakuriah et al., 2014). Finally, new technologies have fueled work by practitioners and scholars to tailor ICTs to support planning tasks with visualization, modeling, and analysis. This category of ICTs has been dubbed planning support systems (PSS) (Harris and Batty, 1993; Klosterman, 1997; Klosterman and Pettit, 2005; Geertman and Stillwell, 2004, 2009; Geertman et al., 2013, 2015).

In our view, although ICTs have become ubiquitous in urban management and planning scholarship has begun to use the new data sources, existing technologies continue to be poorly suited to addressing the long-term and strategic issues facing cities (Couclelis, 2005; Klosterman, 2013). Writing over a decade ago, Couclelis urged planners to "dare to build the right kinds of models for planning"

(2005, p. 1359), observing that computer models (which often form the heart of PSS) "only pretend to be about the future" since surprises and unexpected changes play such an important role in the evolution of urban regions. Nonetheless, we agree with her conclusion that computer models are valuable despite their limitations, since they can be used to test policy strategies, back-cast from desirable futures, and construct validated and visual future scenarios. This is consistent with Batty's argument elsewhere in this volume that urban models may be useful even if their assumptions cannot be fully tested and that using multiple models can be one way to investigate their uncertainty (Batty, 2018, this volume). Moreover, the planning process often features freewheeling discussions, where such models can ensure proposals are grounded in a thorough and integral analysis that systematically considers multiple dimensions of a planning issue. Although such analysis tends to be equated with using different sorts of *quantitative* information, the results of computer models can be combined with experiential knowledge and qualitative information through techniques such as storytelling (Batty, 2018, this volume; Couclelis, 2005).

Despite their long period of scholarly development, PSS lack widespread real-world applications and are often not perceived as usable by professionals (Brömmelstroet, 2010; Goodspeed, 2013; Vonk et al., 2005). Previous work on PSS have been slowed by technical challenges, which in our view are rapidly being overcome by three important general trends. First, development of PSS has been hampered by a lack of needed data, but the proliferation of novel data sources and growing maturity of public sector data providers has greatly reduced this problem. Second, use of PSS has been limited by the technical challenge of running complex computer programs, an obstacle overcome by new web-based technologies which allow sophisticated analyses to be run on websites accessible from web-connected devices like smartphones, tablets, laptops and desktop computers. Third, computing hardware useful in supporting collaborative planning activities, such as large touch-sensitive screens, continues to improve in performance and decline in price. However, technological development is not inevitable, and taking advantage of these trends will require a concerted research and development effort by professionals and scholars to create PSS that are useful for planning practice.

The purpose of this chapter is to describe the future planning research needed to realize the potential of creating new PSS that apply emerging ICTs. Whereas cities have begun to buy into smart city concepts centered on sensors, control rooms, and expensive IT systems (e.g. Goodspeed, 2014), we believe they also need new PSS which foster the collaborative engagement with strategic planning issues. The following sections draw on our research and professional activities in Australia, the Netherlands, and the United States to illustrate both trends in ICTs and associated planning research. The chapter is organized as follows: first, we discuss why we believe PSS are potentially valuable to planning and what types of research on them are needed; second, we elaborate on trends in ICT relevant to planning and provide examples of how each development is being applied in innovative research and practice in PSS. These areas feature *design science research* to build and test PSS as well as *social science research* to investigate how PSS can result in desirable and beneficial improvements to planning processes and outcomes.

New ICT and the Future of Planning

The trends in ICTs described above have the *potential* to improve PSS. However, PSS often require significant investments of time and money, so their development should be conducted when there is a documented link to positive influence on planning processes and outcomes. We think there are two primary ways PSS could have such a positive influence on planning for better urban futures.

First, PSS can provide an antidote to the dominance of rather naïve exclusively deliberative approaches in planning, which are based on the premise that a good participatory process alone will also lead to a good and informed outcome. As Klosterman (2013, p. 166) puts it:

> Community-based planning and forecasting using simple analytical models and tools can be extremely helpful in augmenting the partial, poorly defined, and often faulty tacit knowledge stored in individuals' mental models with explicitly defined public knowledge, helping reduce the influence of expedient viewpoints and resist overly wishful or pessimistic thinking.

The important emphasis on incorporating participants' tacit and experiential knowledge must be matched with an effort to engage in "knowledge claim testing" through the application of the explicit and systematized knowledge contained in PSS (Pelzer et al., 2015a). One example of this is the public participation GIS (PPGIS) project described in Thompson (2018, this volume), where a community-university collaboration in New Orleans produced a detailed GIS database after Hurricane Katrina which demonstrated that at the time, more residents had returned to the Ninth Ward and more properties were structurally sound than authorities had previously thought.

Second, many applications of ICTs in planning are very much focusing on management and efficiency rather than exploring city futures. For instance, a close scrutiny of the recent edited volumes on PSS by lead editors Geertman and Stillwell reveals that several case studies are about short-term decisions rather than long-term options; urban *management* rather than *strategic planning* (e.g. Bond and Kanaan, 2015; Rasouli and Timmermans, 2013; Zomer et al., 2015). However, these volumes also reveal the richness of PSS that deal with strategic and long-term issues and have proved their value in practice, such as LEAM, What if?, and CommunityViz (Deal and Pallathucheril, 2009; Pelzer et al., 2014; Pettit et al., 2013). Next to providing an antidote to naïve and unfounded discussion as outlined above, these PSS also help frame discussions towards the long-term future, rather than the more usual focus on short-term decisions (cf. Klosterman, 2013; Pallathucheril and Deal, 2012).

We see the need for several distinct forms of planning research related to the creation and improvement of innovative PSS, including creating technologies and studying their use in planning. These fall into the general research categories proposed by March and Smith (1995) for research on information systems. On the one hand, there is a need for what they term *natural science*, which involves discovery and justification, to develop theories of how the world works. For PSS, this primarily involves the basic science about cities that provides the knowledge contained within PSS. In this volume, Batty describes this type of knowledge, after Faludi, as theories *in* planning. However, we would add another category. As the number and type of PSS have proliferated, we believe there is a role for *social science* research focused on the planning process that investigates the relationship between use of PSS and desirable outcomes such as stakeholder learning, collaboration, and plan quality. In our view, theories of planning should be not only normative, as described by Faludi and Batty, but also scientific.

In addition to such natural science, another way scientific investigation can be applied in planning is in the development of PSS. March and Smith (1995) call this type of research *design science*; this form of research does not aim to produce the general theoretical knowledge of natural science, but instead results in the ingredients of new technologies: constructs, models, methods, and instantiations (prototypes). Design science involves not only invention but also rigorous testing to demonstrate that technical innovations solve particular problems. March and Smith propose that design research activities include *build, evaluate, theorize, justify*, and subsequent scholarship has suggested additional guidelines for design research (Hevner et al., 2004).

Too often, technical scholarship on PSS has presented descriptions of models which were unavailable to outsiders and lacked evidence of their effectiveness. Design research would encourage researchers to publish about each element of their PSS, make available their technology as open-source software, and subject their technology to empirical testing. However, we acknowledge that such practices require tool designers to have expertise in open-source programming and empirical testing methodologies. Yet there are existing communities of practice, such as OpenCitySmart, which are endeavoring to promote open-source planning tool development.[1] Planning tool developers could also conduct empirical testing of the usability of their tools with frameworks such as those proposed by Barton et al. (2015) and Russo et al. (2015). In addition, we believe planning should emulate more technical fields such as engineering to recognize technology creation and testing as a scholarly activity which both requires and can result in generalizable knowledge. To summarize, in addition to ongoing research that investigates cities themselves as empirical phenomenon, urban planning requires further research spanning technical and social domains which (1) conducts research on how computer technologies can be effectively used within planning settings, and (2) applies a scientific approach to the design and testing of new ICTs for planning.

ICT Trends and Emerging Applications

This section briefly describes three noteworthy recent developments in ICT relevant to planning: open data, web-based geoprocessing, and touch-sensitive screens. We provide examples of how each are leading to innovative research and practice in planning, inspiring new research avenues for planning scholars. Each section concludes with several research questions we think are ripe for investigation by planning researchers.

Visualizing New Data Sources

Open data policies and practices make raw data available to planners. Notable examples of open data include the London datastore, Europe's INSPIRE program, the US Open Data program, and data portals at the local, state, and national government levels in Australia (Huijboom and Van den Broek, 2011). In the United States, the US City Open Data Census has catalogued 364 fully open data sets (Open Data Census Project, 2016). Drivers of these developments have been the perceived political, economic, and operational benefits of open data to government (Janssen et al., 2012). In addition to these official efforts, PPGIS and citizen science projects such as the one described by Thompson (2018, this volume) are also producing novel open data sets. Readily accessible data is valuable for understanding current urban conditions, as well as serving as a crucial input to many PSS, so this trend is potentially beneficial for communities and planners alike. However, this data deluge has resulted in an urgent need for PSS to visualize and analyze the data in an accessible and timely way—the first area where future research is needed.

The advent of big urban data, which is increasingly becoming available to citizens and researchers at no cost, provides the opportunity to develop data analytics and visualization techniques that can provide evidenced-based planning support. One such example is the CityViz online platform, which includes map-based indicators of city housing and city movement across Sydney derived from new data sources.[2] Housing indicators include the growth of million-dollar properties (see Figure 13.1), the increase of strata (condominium) properties, and a housing affordability index, all of which are generated using the land sales sourced openly from New South Wales Land and Property Information (a Division of the Department of Finance, Services and Innovation). These maps can better help professionals and researchers understand the spatial characteristics of urban housing markets. Another map features city movement indicators derived from data collected via bicyclists using the Bicycle Network RiderLog app, which provide detailed information about how riders are traversing the City of Sydney (Pettit et al., 2016b). A series of interactive map layers illustrate the various dimensions of bicycling, including the strikingly different patterns of male and female riders as shown in Figure 13.2.

Such visual analytical platforms as CityViz provide data depicting our cities in new and engaging ways and are accessible to communities, planners and decision-makers alike. We believe such visual analytical platforms which include elements of map interactivity and digital storytelling offer exciting possibilities for

Planning Our Future Cities **215**

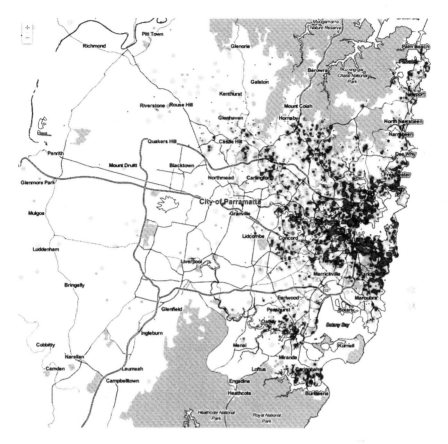

FIGURE 13.1 CityViz Housing Indicator—the change in million-dollar property sales in Sydney between 2009 and 2015 (produced by Laurence Troy).[3]

how ICTs can be harnessed to support city shaping endeavors. However, we realize that data maps alone are insufficient for planning. They serve to illuminate problems, but do not necessarily allow communities to consider the impact of alternative policies. Such future-oriented analysis is often the objective of PSS, described in the next section. Finally, the maps may prove illegible or confusing to their intended audience, and the third section describes social science research that addresses the question of how to best integrate ICTs within the planning process.

Design Science Research Questions:

- What new techniques of data summary, analysis, and representation are needed to extract intelligence from novel sources of urban big data?
- How can new visualization techniques be utilized to promote participation; for instance, by communicating experiential or tacit knowledge and/or allowing for a two-way flow of information?

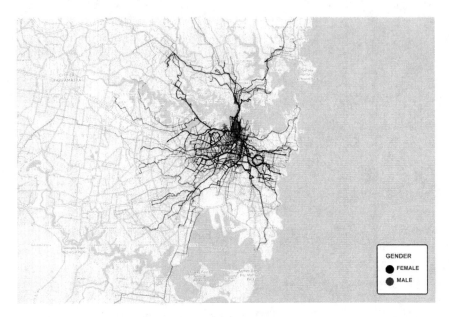

FIGURE 13.2 CityViz City movement indicator—spatial distribution of female versus male cyclists in Sydney based on RiderLog data collected from 2010 to 2014 (Pettit et al., 2016b).[4]

- How can visualizations be used to effectively convey complex information to stakeholders with different disciplinary backgrounds?

Social Science Research Questions:

- What is the added value of new digital visualization techniques compared to analogue means (paper, pen)?
- What is the most appropriate visualization technique to use for a particular audience (planner versus policy-maker versus citizen)?
- What is the rationale for depicting some aspects and not others (i.e. the rationale for what is *not* in the visualization)?

Expanding Access with Online Geocomputation

Alongside changes in data access have come a revolution in mapping technologies, a trend suggested by the rise of striking web maps like those shown in Figures 13.1 and 13.2. At the heart of many planning support system applications are geographic information systems (GISs) which allow for the storage, manipulation, and visualization of spatial information. To avoid the need to reinvent the growing base of GIS software, many planning support system applications were designed to rely on existing GIS software for these functionalities, often utilizing ESRI's

ArcGIS Desktop software. However, this choice in software architecture has had profound implications for the flexibility and usability of PSS since it requires integrating into a highly complex desktop application which is frequently updated. One well-known example is CommunityViz, which, since it operates as an ArcGIS extension, must be upgraded for each new version of ArcGIS (Walker and Daniels, 2011). However, the rapid development of web-based GIS technology has meant that PSS can now leave the desktop and be run via a web browser from almost any computer that interacts with GIS software running on a server over the internet. The growing collection of GIS server software includes the open-source options GeoServer, Mapnik, and MapServer as well as the commercial option ESRI ArcGIS Server (Rubalcava, 2015).[5]

Several innovative projects are using web-based GIS as building blocks for fully online PSS, realizing the vision of a digital planning infrastructure proposed by writers like Klosterman (1997). In one notable example, we have seen the creation in Australia of the AURIN online workbench, which provides machine-to-machine access to over 2,000 data sets, comprises more than 100 spatial-statistical tools, and includes a suite of visualization interfaces (Sinnott et al., 2014; Pettit et al., 2015a). This online workbench is made available to researchers and analysts from across academia and government. It has been accessed by over 1,000 users. Interestingly the workbench is not available to the community and the commercial sector due to some of the underlying data agreements stipulating that the data is for research and government purposes only. It is also important to note there are challenges in using such online urban analytics infrastructures to undertake complex spatial-statistical analysis without the support of other software packages (Pettit et al., 2016a). AURIN also includes an instantiation of the What if? planning support system developed by Klosterman (1999). PSS are now being applied in real-world decision-making in Australia, and the new source code has been released for others to build on (Pettit et al., 2013, 2015b).

Another example of a planning support system embedded within a web-based information system is the UrbanFootprint software created by California consulting firm Calthorpe Associates (2012). This software is being used to power the Southern California Association of Government's Scenario Planning Model, an ambitious project which will facilitate the sharing of spatial information as well as the construction and analysis of land-use scenarios at the local and Los Angeles region scales.[6] This project builds on other pioneering online planning tools in California, including I-PLACE^{3}S, an innovative tool created by the Sacramento Area Council of Governments for regional spatial planning (McKeever, 2011), and MarineMap, a web-based marine spatial planning tool used to designate protected areas off the state's coast (Cravens, 2015).

Community-based and participatory mapping projects in planning are also taking advantage of web-based technologies. Thompson's (2018, this volume) case study of a participatory GIS data collection project in New Orleans describes how the resulting data was shared on the online mapping website WhoData.org. In another example, technology developed by the organization Ushahidi for mapping spatial information during crises has been applied in collecting spatial knowledge within a planning process (Brandusescu et al., 2015).

We fully expect similar technologies will be developed and adopted in a growing number of cities and regions. However, we have observed that these tools raise difficult questions about who should be provided access to the tools, how their analysis can be aligned with community concerns, and how to tell if such models are resulting in more intelligent plans. The last section discusses how practitioners are beginning to tackle these questions through collaborative workshops, and researchers have begun to systematically document evidence of planning support system usefulness.

Design Science Research Questions:

- How can online platforms be designed in such a way that they not only function as databases but actually support the strategic and future-oriented endeavor of planning?
- What interfaces are required to support the involvement and needs of diverse stakeholders?
- How can online platforms be designed in such a way that nonexperts can also fruitfully use them?

Social Science Research Questions:

- How can the ownership of data in online platforms be organized to support access for all involved in the planning process, including not only academia and government but also community and private sectors?
- How can online technology be best used to align local and regional planning activities?
- What kind of planning tasks are best supported by online platforms, and how can this be improved?

Facilitating Stakeholder Collaboration and Learning

However exciting, PSS which provide insightful data visualizations and the ability to analyze proposals are irrelevant if they are not used by real-world planners to draw up plans and weigh alternative options in decision-making. These activities are typically conducted in collaborative settings, something which has been noticed by planning support system researchers and developers. Increasingly PSS are now available that combine software and hardware in such a way that interaction among stakeholders is facilitated, and this often takes advantage of the declining costs of computing hardware. A case in point are MapTables, which are large, touch-sensitive computer screens, usually depicting a map of the plan area and allowing some kind of interaction with software (e.g. impact analysis) (Vonk and Ligtenberg, 2010). While this idea is certainly not new—Hopkins et al. discussed the idea of a "sketch-planning workbench" in 2004—these instruments have become much more affordable and commonly used in practice in recent years. A recent study found that a range of governmental bodies in the Netherlands use MapTables in their daily practice, in particular because practitioners believe it leads to better communication and better collaboration. As one practitioner noted about a MapTable: "the added value is that you engage in a dialogue. That one can anticipate . . . things that are being said. . . . You either react on what is being said or react to the things you see" (in Pelzer et al., 2014, p. 22). In several instances, these MapTables are used in combination software such as CommunityViz, which can be used to create tailored, project-specific analysis interfaces (Walker and Daniels, 2011). However these improvements in hardware have raised process questions: How and when should such devices be used? How can PSS be best integrated into the planning process to integrate analysis, deliberation, and design activities? These questions are the focus of the final research area for social science research on use of PSS.

These developments in data, computational architectures, and hardware and software to support collaboration, make PSS now much easier to use in day-to-day planning practice. It is debatable, however, if this has also led to better engagement when planning for city futures. Improved availability of data, the advent of planning support system infrastructures, user-friendly hardware, and compelling visualization possibilities might overcome many of the usability issues raised in earlier studies (cf. Vonk, 2006; te Brömmelstroet, 2010). However, both scholars and practitioners should be very careful not to make the mistake of means-end conflation.

Improved usability of PSS is never an aim in itself, but is a way to achieve a positive influence on planning practice. Based on earlier work in group model building and group support systems, this 'added value' of PSS can be subdivided into three levels: individual, group, and outcome (Pelzer et al., 2014). The *individual* level is usually conceived as the extent to which the PSS improves the learning process among participants; for instance, in terms of single or double-loop learning (Goodspeed, 2013) or interdisciplinary learning (Pelzer et al., 2015a). Workshops which provide users with rapid feedback on their ideas and do not overwhelm novices with complex interfaces seem to produce the greatest reported learning (Goodspeed, 2016). The *group* level includes improved collaboration and consensus because of the usage of PSS and often requires specific types of facilitation (Pelzer et al., 2015b). The above-mentioned MapTable is typically applied in planning support system configurations to achieve this kind of positive influence. The *outcome* level, finally, refers to the extent to which a plan is more rational, informed, and logical because of the influence of a planning support system (Hopkins, 2001; Klosterman, 1997). The outcome level has hardly been studied empirically. In a set of Dutch studies with students, no strong effect (a higher rating of the plan quality by an external rater) of applying a planning support system was found, an issue which is the subject of more detailed ongoing research (e.g. te Brömmelstroet, 2014). Conceptually, it would also be very relevant to look beyond the words, logics, and maps of a plan and to the physical changes in the world 'out there' to see what the effect has been of applying a planning support system on buildings, roads, and people. Distilling this effect empirically is a daunting, if not impossible, task however.

FIGURE 13.3 Dutch stakeholders working with a CommunityViz application on a MapTable during a session on December 12, 2012, about improving the sustainability of municipalities in the region of Utrecht (Peter Pelzer).

Design Research Questions:

- What are the characteristics of workshops which achieve desirable outcomes, such as learning, encouraging consensus, changing stakeholder perceptions, and producing high-quality plans?
- How can PSS be designed to improve their empirically validated performance in real-world planning tasks?

Social Science Research Questions:

- How do different types of hardware (tablets, tables, etc.) influence the dynamics of technology-supported workshops?
- How can the typical process of divergence-convergence be understood in technology-supported planning workshops?
- How do technology-supported planning workshops connect to the wider planning process of power and interests?

Conclusion

In order to ensure cities draw up plans which draw upon relevant new information and robust analysis, one of the most significant developments for the future of planning research will be ongoing advances in ICTs and the urgent need to adapt them to planning. To do so, we foresee a continued need by planning scholars to engage in two fundamentally different, but related, forms of research: *design research* which aims to produce useful planning support system technologies through rigorous methods and *natural science* research about how such technologies can best be used in planning. Both of these research activities complement ongoing efforts to develop deep theoretical understanding of urban systems, which are necessary but not sufficient for intelligent planning.

To illustrate these ideas, we have described three examples where advances in ICTs are inspiring innovative forms of research and practice. While these are among the most significant, there may very well be other technologies arising that are of interest to planning, such as the rapidly developing augmented and virtual reality. Similarly, shifting planning priorities and problems mean it seems inevitable that planning will continue "making and breaking" its tools, including PSS (Mandelbaum, 1996). Indeed, the specific examples cited above were stimulated by recent planning priorities: the CityViz examples are to investigate high housing costs and encourage sustainable transportation; and the Southern California Association of Government's (SCAG's) Scenario Planning Model is intended for use in planning for reduced automobile miles traveled—and thus decreased greenhouse gas emissions—under the state's climate change legislation (Rose, 2011).

Finally, we think there are ample research opportunities associated with many of the topics mentioned here. For each of the three topics, we have identified research questions from both a design science and a social science perspective that can be studied in the future. While doing so, we urge researchers and developers not be blinded by an excessive focus on new technologies. All too often in our empirical research we have experienced that the technology rather than the planning process gets center stage in the discussion. With an ever-continuing development of technology, this will likely remain an important issue. In order to prevent this, we urge both planning researchers and more technically inclined scholars (e.g. GIS scholars) to remain reflexive at all times about the research they are undertaking. For instance, this involves continuous awareness about preventing means-end conflations, recognizing that usable technology is never an aim in itself and that planning is about creating better urban futures as supported through collaboration and consensus building processes. Technology can potentially support this, but is never a silver bullet; moreover, it can also have negative effects (e.g. Pelzer et al., 2015b).

Planning technologies face many challenges. They are embedded within diverse urban and professional contexts, must respond to evolving substantive concerns, and must be useful to the heterogeneous professionals and stakeholders who actually conduct planning activities. While these challenges explain the slow and halting development of technologies, they are not insurmountable, and technologies remain a crucial means of making available rich empirical information and support for the intelligent consideration of long-term decisions in planning. For that reason, we think the future is bright for planning research which tackles the multifaceted challenge of improving planning through the development and application of PSS.

Notes

1. See https://wiki.osgeo.org/wiki/Opencitysmart
2. See https://cityfutures.be.unsw.edu.au/cityviz/
3. Online version available at: https://cityfutures.be.unsw.edu.au/cityviz/million-dollar-sales/https://cityfutures.be.unsw.edu.au/cityviz/million-dollar-sales/
4. Online version available at: https://cityfutures.be.unsw.edu.au/cityviz/cycling-sydney/ https://cityfutures.be.unsw.edu.au/cityviz/cycling-sydney/
5. For a list of GIS software, see https://en.wikipedia.org/wiki/List_of_geographic_information_systems_software
6. See http://sp.scag.ca.gov

References

Barton, J., X. Goldie, and C. J. Pettit. 2015. Introducing a usability framework to support urban information discovery and analytics. *Journal of Spatial Sciences* 60(2): 311–327.

Batty, Michael. 2018. Science in planning: Theory, methods and models. In T. W. Sanchez (ed.), *Planning Research and Knowledge*. Abingdon, UK: Routledge, pp. 241–254.

Batty, Michael, K. W. Axhausen, F. Giannotti, A. Pozdnoukhov, A. Bazzani, M. Wachowicz, G. Ouzounis, and Y. Portugali. 2012. Smart cities of the future. *The European Physical Journal Special Topics* 214(1): 481–518.

Bettencourt, Luis, and Geoffrey West. 2010. A unified theory of urban living. *Nature* 467(7318): 912–913.

Bond, Russell, and Ammar Kanaan. 2015. MassDOT Real Time Traffic Management (RTTM) system. In S. Geertman, J. Ferriera, R. Goodspeed, and J. Stillwell (eds.), *Planning Support Systems and Smart Cities*. Cham, Switzerland: Springer, pp. 471–488.

Brandusescu, Ana, Renée E. Sieber, and Sylvie Jochems. 2015. Confronting the hype: The use of crisis mapping for community development. *Convergence: The International Journal of Research into New Media Technologies* 22(6): 616–632.

Brömmelstroet, M., 2010. *Making Planning Support Systems Matter: Improving the Use of Planning Support Systems for Integrated Land Use And Transport Strategy–Making*. PhD thesis, University of Amsterdam.

Calthorpe Associates. 2012. *Urban Footprint Technical Summary Model Version 1.0.* Unpublished Report.

Calthorpe Associates. 2014. SCAG Scenario Planning Model local review and project overview. Presentation *at SCAG SPM Working Group about SPM Local Review and Project Overview*, 7 May 2014. Accessed 15 July 2016. http://sp.scag.ca.gov/Pages/Documents.aspx.

Couclelis, H. 2005. Where has the future gone? Rethinking the role of integrated land-use models in spatial planning. *Environment and Planning A* 37(8): 1353–1371.

Cravens, Amanda E. 2015. Negotiation and decision making with collaborative software: How MarineMap 'changed the game' in California's Marine Life Protected Act Initiative. *Environmental Management* 57(2): 474–497.

Deal, Brian, and Varkki Pallathucheril. 2009. A use-driven approach to large-scale urban modelling and planning support. In S. Geertman and J. Stillwell (eds.), *Planning Support Systems Best Practice and New Methods*. Dordrecht: Springer, pp. 29–51.

Goodspeed, Robert. 2013. A survey of US metropolitan spatial planning infrastructures: Institutions, models, and tools. *The 13th International Conference on Computers in Urban Planning and Urban Management*, Utrecht, Netherlands, 2–5 July.

Goodspeed, Robert. 2014. Smart cities: Moving beyond urban cybernetics to tackle wicked problems. *Cambridge Journal of Regions, Economy and Society* 8(1): 79–92.

Goodspeed, Robert. 2016. Digital knowledge technologies in planning practice: From black boxes to media for collaborative inquiry. *Planning Theory & Practice* 17(4): 577–600.

Geertman, S., and J. Stillwell. 2004. Planning support systems: An inventory of current practice. *Computers, Environment and Urban Systems* 28(4): 291–310.

Geertman, S., and J. C. H. Stillwell. 2009. *Planning Support Systems Best Practice and New Methods*. Dordrecht: Springer.

Geertman, S., F. Toppen, and J. Stillwell (Eds.). 2013. *Planning Support Systems for Sustainable Urban Development*. Heidelberg: Springer.

Geertman, S., J. J. Ferreira, R. Goodspeed, and J. Stillwell. 2015. *Planning Support Systems and Smart Cities*. Cham, Switzerland: Springer.

Harris, Britton, and M. Batty. 1993. Locational models, geographic information and planning support systems. *Journal of Planning Education and Research* 12(3): 184–198.

Hevner, A. R., S. T. March, J. Park, and S. Ram. 2004. Design science in information systems research. *MIS Quarterly* 28(1): 75–105.

Hopkins, Lewis D. 2001. *Urban Development: The Logic of Making Plans*. Washington, DC: Island Press.

Hopkins, Lewis D., Rajiv Ramanathan, and Varkki George Pallathucheril. 2004. Interface for a sketch-planning workbench. *Computers, Environment and Urban Systems* 28(6): 653–666.

Huijboom, Noor, and Tijs Van den Broek. 2011. Open data: An international comparison of strategies. *European journal of ePractice* 12(1): 4–16.

Janssen, Marijn, Yannis Charalabidis, and Anneke Zuiderwijk. 2012. Benefits, adoption barriers and myths of open data and open government. *Information Systems Management* 29(4): 258–268.

Klosterman, Richard E. 1997. Planning Support Systems: A new perspective on computer-aided planning. *Journal of Planning Education and Research* 17(1): 45–54.

Klosterman, Richard E. 1999. The what if? collaborative planning support system. *Environment Planning B: Planning and Design* 26(3): 393–408.

Klosterman, Richard E. 2013. Lessons learned about planning: Forecasting, participation, and technology. *Journal of the American Planning Association* 79(2): 161–169.

Klosterman, R. E., and C. J. Pettit. 2005. An update on planning support systems. *Environment and Planning B: Planning and Design* 32(4): 477–484.

Mandelbaum, S. J. 1996. Making and breaking planning tools. *Computers, Environment and Urban Systems* 20(2): 71–84.

March, S. T., and G. F. Smith. 1995. Design and natural-science research on information technology. *Decision Support Systems* 15(4): 251–266.

McKeever, Mike. 2011. Visioning Sacramento. In C. K. Montgomery (ed.), *Regional Planning for a Sustainable America*. New Brunswick, NJ: Rutgers University Press, pp. 333–345.

Neirotti, Paolo, Alberto De Marco, Anna Corinna Cagliano, Giulio Mangano, and Francesco Scorrano. 2014. Current trends in Smart City initiatives: Some stylised facts. *Cities* 38: 25–36.

Open Data Census Project. 2016. US City Open Data Census. Accessed 6 July 2017. http://us-city.census.okfn.org/.

Pallathucheril, Varkki, and Brian Deal. 2012. Communicative action and the challenge of discounting. Paper presented at the *53rd Annual Conference of the Association of Collegiate Schools of Planning*, Cincinnati, Ohio, November 1–4.

Pelzer, Peter, S. Geertman, R. van der Heijden, and E. Rouwette. 2014. The added value of planning support systems: A practitioner's perspective. *Computers, Environment and Urban Systems* 48: 16–27.

Pelzer, Peter, Stan Geertman, and Rob van der Heijden. 2015a. Knowledge in communicative planning practice: A different perspective for planning support systems. *Environment and Planning B: Planning and Design* 42(4): 638–651.

Pelzer, Peter, Robert Goodspeed, and Marco te Brömmelstroet. 2015b. Facilitating PSS workshops: A conceptual framework and findings from interviews with facilitators. In S. Geertman, J. Ferriera, R. Goodspeed, and J. Stillwell (eds.), *Planning Support Systems and Smart Cities*. Cham, Switzerland: Springer, pp. 355–369.

Pettit, C. J., R. E. Klosterman, M. Nino-Ruiz, I. Widjaja, M. Tomko, and R. Sinnott. 2013. The online What if? planning support system. In S. Geertman, F. Toppen, and J. Stillwell (eds.), *Planning Support Systems for Sustainable Urban Development*. Berlin: Springer, pp. 349–362.

Pettit, C. J., J. Barton, X. Goldie, R. Sinnott, R. Stimson, and T. Kvan. 2015a. The Australian Urban Intelligence Network supporting smart cities. In S. Geertman, J. Ferreira, R. Goodspeed, and J. Stillwell (eds), *Planning Support Systems and Smart Cities*. Cham, Switzerland: Springer, pp. 243–259.

Pettit, C. J., R. E. Klosterman, P. Delaney, A. L. Whitehead, H. Kujala, A. Bromage, and M. Nino-Ruiz. 2015b. The online What if? planning support system: A land suitability application in Western Australia. *Applied Spatial Analysis and Policy* 8(2): 93–112.

Pettit, C. J., R. Tanton, and J. Hunter. 2016a. An online platform for conducting spatial-statistical analyses of national census data. *Computers, Environment and Urban Systems* 63: 68–79.

Pettit, C. J., S. N. Lieske, and S. Z. Leao. 2016b. Big Bicycle Data Processing: From Personal Data to Urban Applications. *ISPRS XXIII Congress*, Prague, Czech Republic, July 12–19.

Rasouli, Soora, and Harry Timmermans. 2013. What-ifs, if-whats and maybes: Sketch of ubiquitous collaborative decision support technology. In S. Geertman, F. Toppen, and J. Stillwell (eds.), *Planning Support Systems for Sustainable Urban Development*. Berlin: Springer, pp. 19–29.

Rose, E. 2011. *Leveraging a new law: Reducing greenhouse gas emissions under Senate Bill 375*. Berkeley, CA: Center for Resource-Efficient Communities, University of California, Berkeley.

Rubalcava, Rene. 2015. *ArcGIS Web Development*. Stamford, CT: Manning.

Russo, P., F. M. Costabile, R. Lanzilotti, and C. J. Pettit. 2015. Usability of planning support systems: An evaluation framework. In S. Geertman, J. Ferreira, R. Goodspeed, and J. Stillwell (eds.), *Planning Support Systems and Smart Cities*. Cham: Switzerland: Springer, pp. 337–353.

Sinnott, R.O., C. Bayliss, A. Bromage, G. Galang, G. Grazioli, P. Greenwood, G. Macauley, D. Mannix, L. Morandini, M. Nino-Ruiz, C. J. Pettit, M. Tomko, M. Sarwar, R. Stimson, W. Voorsluys, and I. Widjaj. 2014. The Australia urban research gateway. *Concurrency and Computation: Practice and Experience* 27(2): 358–375.

te Brömmelstroet, M. 2010. Equip the warrior instead of manning the equipment: Land use and transport planning support in the Netherlands. *Journal of Transport and Land Use* 3(1): 25–41.

te Brömmelstroet, M. 2014. *Do planning support systems improve planning or not: A measurement framework and randomized experiment*. Centre for Urban Studies Working Paper Series

No. 12. Amsterdam: Centre for Urban Studies. Available via: http://urbanstudies. uva.nl/working-papers/working-papers/working-papers/content/folder/working-paper-series-no.12.html

Thakuriah, Piyushimita, Nebiyou Tilahun, and Moira Zellner. 2014. *Proceedings of the Workshop on Big Data and Urban Informatics*. Accessed 30 January 2015. http://urbanbigdata.uic.edu/proceedings/.

Thompson, M. M. 2018. Citizen science as a research approach. In T. W. Sanchez (ed.), *Planning Research and Knowledge*. Abingdon, UK: Routledge, pp. 226–240.

Townsend, Anthony. 2015. Cities of data: Examining the new urban science. *Public Culture* 27(2 76): 201–212.

Vonk, G. 2006. *Improving Planning Support: The Use of Planning Support Systems for Spatial Planning*. PhD thesis, Utrecht University.

Vonk, Guido, and Arend Ligtenberg. 2010. Socio-technical PSS development to improve functionality and usability: Sketch planning using a Maptable. *Landscape and Urban Planning* 94(3–4): 166–174.

Vonk, Guido, Stan Geertman, and P. P. Schot. 2005. Bottlenecks blocking widespread usage of planning support systems. *Environment and Planning A* 37(5): 909–924.

Walker, Doug, and Thomas L. Daniels. 2011. *The Planners Guide to Communityviz: The Essential Tool for a New Generation of Planning*. Chicago: Planners Press, American Planning Association.

Zomer, L. B., W. Daamen, S. Meijer, and S. P. Hoogendoorn. 2015. Managing crowds: The possibilities and limitations of crowd information during urban mass events. In S. Geertman, J. Ferreira, R. Goodspeed, and J. Stillwell (eds.), *Planning Support Systems and Smart Cities*. Cham, Switzerland: Springer, pp. 77–97.

14
CITIZEN SCIENCE AS A RESEARCH APPROACH

Michelle M. Thompson

Introduction

Citizens who reside in neighborhoods deemed 'marginal' or 'distressed' have become accustomed to being part of the great social experiment that the academic community considers progressive. The City of New Orleans has endured the international microscope of planners who specialize in all facets of hazard mitigation and post-disaster management. Although post-Katrina aid focused on the immediate catastrophe in 2005, systemic issues persist in reflection of a shrinking, weak market city. Due to the collapse of social, economic, and environmental systems in New Orleans, the planning community was challenged to identify and implement creative solutions to address failures. Traditional models of hazard response, post-disaster planning, and community engagement were considered insufficient due to the magnitude of this unprecedented event. In order to make short- and long-term recovery decisions, all of these models rely on primary or secondary data, which was not readily available. This paper reflects to how community data information systems (CDIS) advance the post-disaster response using advocacy and neighborhood planning. This approach reflects the application of 'citizen science' in planning practice, based upon a traditional model of citizen participation.

In the recent past, planning 'experts' have developed or deployed disaster response plans based on theoretical models. The *neighborhood planning model* suggests that using a top-down or bottom-up strategy is not as effective as one that is "middle through" (Sieber, 2006). Applied models that consider critical system failures (such as the New Orleans disaster) can only present 'what if' scenarios that rarely reflect the extent of emotional, financial, environmental, and health and safety issues faced by the affected population. As a result, 'success' cannot be measured according to the rate of implementation since many of the short-term recovery responses have long-term effects that are difficult to disentangle. The focus must be on community-centered planning instead of administrative or municipal planning as the means to encourage recovery, revitalization, and reinvestment. One of the consistent themes that runs through theoretical or applied planning is the use of data that has been transformed into information. Public and private business decisions are based on fundamental data that, in Post-Katrina New Orleans, was not readily available, was not verifiable, and in most cases was not accurate. Therefore discussion will focus on the data and how this was developed in the "Lessons from the ACORN Housing/University Collaborative" (Reardon et al., 2009) and the implementation of a New Orleans-based public participation geographic information system (PPGIS) that reflects a more modern and responsive geospatial community planning which may also be considered an applied citizen science model.

This paper will evaluate the lessons learned and expands the discussion presented in the top-down planning exercise as part of the post-Katrina Unified New Orleans Planning (UNOP) process. The process of completing a 'successful' community intervention was frequently challenging but, in the end, the completion of the plan was a significant accomplishment. Examining this participation geographic information systems (PGIS) project through the lens of citizen science suggests that this is typical in such applied research. It was further argued that the "nation's willingness to rebuild New Orleans and its poorest neighborhoods [w]as a litmus test of society's commitment to racial justice and equality" (Reardon et al., 2008, p. 66). This chapter will evaluate the applied citizen science model which focused on PGIS as a data collection and citizen engagement model.

Planning Practice and Applied Citizen Science in Pre- and Post-Katrina New Orleans

The major actors in the pre-Katrina planning community were the New Orleans Regional Planning Commission, the University of New Orleans College of Urban and Public Affairs (CUPA), and those in practice. While there is general agreement that the City planning department was understaffed and under-resourced, their counterparts in CUPA provided planning services beyond typical academic planning research. The typical model of 'university-community partnerships' considers the role of the university followed by the duration of engagement, which can be short-term 'projects' or long-term 'programs.' "As a primary community outreach arm of the university, CUPA had developed name recognition with many neighborhood groups, nonprofits, and city agencies" (Evans and Lewis, 2009, p. 52). However, shortly after the storm, the University of New Orleans administration decided to dissolve CUPA and reintroduce it as the Department of Planning and Urban Studies, thus reducing influence over the planning process at the university level and diminishing its identification as an influencer in the community at large.

Unfortunately, there were assumptions that local and regional planning agencies as well as universities (e.g. Tulane School of Architecture and Dillard University Program in Urban Studies) were not fully able to manage the recovery planning process. The diminished resources further exacerbated the ability of local resources to engage with each of the proposed plans (Nelson et al., 2007). Further, there was a lack of process whereby post-planning information could be warehoused, systems of engagement adequately documented, and the one-time private, public, and philanthropic resources extended beyond the short-term recovery plans. In an effort to mitigate the unintended negative impacts of using outside planning 'experts' to evaluate and recommend planning options for post-Katrina New Orleans, a community-focused and citizen-led model was born.

This type of model is now known as citizen science, which is defined as "the involvement of non-professional scientists in data collection and, to some extent, its analysis" (Haklay, 2013, pp. 105–106). This particular model assures that the focus of the project is determined by the community, with the support of planning professionals (academic and/or in practice), in order to organize, develop, analyze, report, and implement a neighborhood plan. The challenge in a post-disaster scenario remains the lack of preexisting data streams and systems necessary to create a benchmark that community data can be compared against. In order to establish a framework for estimating the existence, level, and extent of post-Katrina blight, the university partnership developed a data collection methodology that was refined and adopted by residents and volunteers in the field before and during data collection.

Before the ACORN Housing/University Collaboration

In the fall of 2006, a team of Cornell University student volunteers raised funds to gut houses in the Lower Ninth Ward/Holy Cross during their winter break. Students also led a community charrette in the Ninth Ward that impressed the leaders of the Association of Community Organizations for Reform Now (ACORN Housing/University Collaborative, 2007). It has been suggested that ACORN provided adequate representation for the 'voiceless, invisible residents' of the Lower Ninth Ward who had been marginalized due to spatial segregation based upon physical, racial, and economic barriers (Reardon et al., 2009). Since the Lower Ninth Ward/Holy Cross neighborhood was completely decimated after the storm, many existing and newly formed neighborhood groups were used as proxies for the displaced residents.

In response to the City of New Orleans action plan call, ACORN Housing Corporation and the University Partnership submitted a successful proposal to become the neighborhood planner for the UNOP process (Reardon et al., 2008). ACORN leadership agreed to advance the application as a UNOP Planner. In the fall of 2006, the Cornell University departments of Planning and Urban Studies and Landscape Architecture and the College of Architecture, Art and Planning committed to developing courses that would form the basis of planning teams to support the ACORN Housing/University 'Partnership.' Due to a legal evaluation of the term by Cornell University, the team was renamed the ACORN Housing/University Collaboration (Thompson, 2015). In August 2006, ACORN Housing Corporation, Cornell University, Columbia University, and the University of Illinois at Urbana-Champaign agreed to align resources and formally work together

(Reardon et al., 2008). The planning consultant, Concordia, in response to the UNOP Preliminary Scope of Services, designed the work plan requirements. However, the AHUC team was concerned by its singular focus on restoring infrastructure systems and public facilities to their pre-Katrina status. ACORN activists questioned the accuracy of many of the initial damage and risk assessment reports that had prompted policy analysts to propose various forms of planned neighborhood shrinkage (City of New Orleans, 2007).

At the end of the summer of 2006, Dr. Kenneth Reardon, then Chair of the Department of City and Regional Planning at Cornell University, asked the author to serve as co-instructor of the Neighborhood Planning Workshop with Dr. Richard Kiely. With Reardon focusing on overall project management and 'planning in the face of power' and Kiely working on adapting the community participation model and developing and delivering a qualitative survey, the author was tasked with developing a data management collection strategy. Dr. Rebekah Green outlined the plan for measuring the level of damage, calculating this with a property condition survey and summarizing the total assessments.

While the AHUC team recognized limitations to community engagement in the planning process, the AHUC was not prohibited from creating a separate 'reporting' site or providing ACORN with media that would aid residents, other nonprofits, and adjacent neighborhoods with the planning process goals and timeline. While advocacy planning calls for identifying and including a wide range of stakeholders, absent from the AHUC were the local universities, particularly the University of New Orleans Department of Planning and Urban Studies (formerly known as the College of Urban and Public Affairs).

In order to meet the minimum neighborhood plan development requirements, the AHUC expanded the project scope to include primary data analysis among the tasks. The tasks were reinterpreted as course syllabi and reassigned to the different university teams. At Cornell University, classes responded to the reporting requirements and were led by the planning and landscape architecture faculty. The immediate challenge to creating the necessary database and geospatial data infrastructure was the lack of a parcel layer and direct access to resources collected by GCR, who served as the data management arm for UNOP. As the Spatial Data Project Coordinator, this author developed an alternative plan for identifying the street grid, parcel centroids and neighborhood boundaries without a verified coordinate system. Lack of cooperation from the City of New Orleans Geographic Information Systems department initially limited the base mapping efforts, but this was resolved prior to final mapping and data analysis due to the heroic efforts of the student data management teams.

In order to collect data on property conditions, survey methodology, training, and team management had to be organized remotely from Ithaca, NY. With a team of 80 consisting of undergraduates, graduates, faculty and volunteers, there was an orientation addressing the data collection process, the community, and potential in-field security issues. The lack of local leadership and knowledge of on-the-ground survey conditions (e.g. lack of street signage) and other local knowledge was not initially considered in this phase of research development. In preparation for the mixed-methods data collection, the University Collaborative held a training workshop where all of the data collection tools were identified and materials for data gathering were distributed. The customized quantitative data collection tools were refined based upon prior project-based fieldwork in non-disaster community projects.

The travel team orientation also included in-class discussion on the cultural history of New Orleans. As a result of these sessions, it was found that there was an unspoken discomfort among students about the upcoming travel plans. With an agreement of anonymity, the author was informed of the concerns of the students, who were primarily white, middle class and from the northeast, having had limited exposure to historic urban decay. The author reached out to Cornell Mental Health Services to provide a round table to discuss issues related to fear of the unknown and concerns about race relations and safety. As a result of this effort, there was reflection by students each evening after doing fieldwork and upon return from New Orleans.

The contract between ACORN Housing and the University Collaboration was discussed and the scope defined, based upon the UNOP deliverables. However, the contract between ACORN Housing, Concordia, and the City of New Orleans was never executed. A turning point in the project came when the AHUC was 'realigned' (Reardon et al., 2009) or 'fired' as a UNOP Planning Team. ACORN had been provided property sites to develop affordable housing as well as community development block grant (CDBG) funding that was potentially related to this. This 'conflict of interest' was the reason given for the contract loss with both ACORN and the City of New Orleans. What was unknown to the Cornell administration was that funds provided by the College of Architecture, Art and Planning to support this project were not going to be reimbursed. The cost of the faculty, course materials, and the non-reimbursable airline tickets and hotel rooms for 80 persons had been an added incentive to travel to New Orleans. The plan moved forward because there was a belief that the

> analysis reveals that structural and flood damage is not the only, or perhaps even the primary, impediment to recovery. Instead, it is the limited resources of residents, the widespread assumptions of non-viability and the slow pace of infrastructure recovery in these neighbourhoods have played a significant role in retarding repair and re-occupancy—especially in the Lower Ninth Ward.
>
> (Green et al., 2007 p. 312)

The Collaborative brought approximately 80 students and faculty to New Orleans during October 25–29, 2006, to carry out the following field-based research activities:

- inspecting 3,500 residential properties to determine their structural integrity;
- surveying Ninth Ward sidewalks, streets, and curbs to evaluate their current condition;

- evaluating the maintenance levels of 29 local playgrounds, parks, parkways, and residual open spaces;
- documenting business sites along the Ninth Ward's four busiest commercial corridors;
- interviewing 230 individuals from households in which members had returned to the Ninth Ward; and
- facilitating focus groups involving members of a dozen civic groups active within the Ninth Ward.

The AHUC convened in New Orleans with a mandate to collect the data, with the support of residents/nonresidents, using the applied citizen science model. Due to the lack of administrative oversight from the City of New Orleans, the project held more promise with a visioning process that was community-led. The importance of the data, and its ownership, became apparent in the pre-field orientation when the former Director of ACORN International stated that the information collected would "not be made available to anyone outside of the AHUC" (ACORN Housing/University Collaborative, 2007). The value of the Lower Ninth Ward data (which included the Lower Ninth Ward and Holy Cross) could not be overestimated. Since the City of New Orleans failed to release the parcel layer (or any spatial layer) that would allow all of the UNOP data to be seamlessly integrated, this unique data set provided an important resource that was not available before the storm or for five years after.

By the end of the semester, all of the deliverables were complete, and the AHUC partnership was ready for dissolution. As an agreement between the project partners, the AHUC's report was to extend beyond the classroom and be delivered back to the citizens of New Orleans. "In mid-December, AHUC representatives traveled to New Orleans to present the preliminary draft of *The People's Plan for Overcoming the Hurricane Katrina Blues: A Comprehensive Strategy for Building a More Vibrant, Sustainable, and Equitable 9th Ward* to ACORN's leaders" (ACORN Housing/University Collaborative, 2007). Following suggested revisions and a format that addressed demographic and economic issues beyond the collected data, the plan was again presented to residents and to both the New Orleans Department and City Planning Commission. The Commission was unanimously directed by the City Council to incorporate the *People's Plan* into the soon-to-be-ratified comprehensive plan (Reardon et al., 2009).

While many University-generated reports provide important information that can be life-changing or provide a scientific breakthrough, the importance of *The People's Plan* for developing process and 'model' as a neighborhood planning tool cannot be fully measured. The process of citizen participation, garnering pre- and post-Katrina community knowledge, and adapting the geospatial data collection methods to a post-disaster environment provides a now classic example of applied citizen science. It is difficult to know whether the process of collecting the GIS and qualitative data, and the findings and reporting were significant or if the contribution had long-lasting effects. Since August 2005, the findings of the report have provided a look at Ninth Ward property conditions that would not be provided by any public or private entity until 2011 (WhoData, 2012).

The major Plan findings included the following:

1   Eight out of ten of the residential structures surveyed were structurally sound.
2   The vast majority of the flood-affected homes appeared to be strong candidates for cost-effective rehabilitation.
3   The percentage of families that had returned to the Ninth Ward was, in fact, much higher than previously reported.
4   A significant portion of the 'returnee' families had removed debris from their properties and prepared them for rehabilitation.
5   Most families had undertaken the above-mentioned activities without the benefit of insurance or federally supported Road Home funds.
6   Those interviewed reported being in regular contact with others who were committed to returning to the Ninth Ward provided that: neighborhood schools could be reopened, access to primary health care was available, living wage employment was accessible, and a higher level of public safety could be guaranteed.

After the Report: Master Plans with the Community in Mind

The ability to track the status of the properties is less inhibited since the City of New Orleans parcel layer was released to the public in the spring of 2010 when the City of New Orleans GIS Department received new administrative oversight. In 2010, the City of New Orleans approved a comprehensive master plan that has the force of law (Eggler, 2010). The City Planning Commission formally urged adoption of the *People's Plan* after the City Council passed a unanimous resolution directing the Department of City Planning to incorporate the People's Plan into the master plan. The Lower Ninth Ward/Holy Cross continues to be the 'face of Katrina' and remains an icon. Among the specific ideas that were identified as key to the successful rejuvenation of the Lower Ninth Ward were public resources such as schools, infrastructure reinvestment, housing rehabilitation, and a sustainable and healthy foods grocery market. In 2016 the community still struggles to obtain significant public facility improvements and still lacks a tier 1 grocery store, though it has increased access to non-Hollywood (Make It Right[1]) affordable rental and homebuyer houses.

WhoData.org: Putting Planning into Practice

In New Orleans, there have been a number of approaches that have served to address the gap between planning theory and practice (Praxis). Neighborhood planning principles suggest the importance of the 'four Ds': *deprofessionalization, decentralization, demystification* and *democratization* (Jones, 1990, p. 11). Key to these approaches have been that neighborhood knowledge, local leadership, and nonprofit innovation has led the way to recovery and reinvestment in the City of New Orleans. Community leaders have introduced approaches to solving problems that the City administration, politicians, and planners alone could not solve.

In an effort to evaluate what plans were ready to advance from UNOP, including the People's Plan, US Senator Mary Landrieu proposed a 4-series forum in 2011 and 2012 to evaluate the state of infrastructure, housing, education, and employment as part of the Raise Up the Lower Ninth Ward initiative. The goals of these forums were not to create a new planning process but to evaluate how to move the ideas to reality (Thompson et al., 2004). These forums were by invitation and included local, state and federal municipal managers, private companies, nonprofits, universities, residents and philanthropists who were focused solely on the recovery of the Lower Ninth Ward. Although each entity had access to a plethora of data, none could accurately depict the state of the community in real terms.

As a result, WhoData.org completed a 100% on-the-ground property condition survey and commercial business inventory with the help of Rebuilding Together, the Regional Planning Commission, lowernine.org, residents, University of New Orleans students and local/international volunteers. As a result of this summer-long effort, this new model of applied citizen science produced a comprehensive quality-of-life needs-assessment open-source map of property conditions after Hurricane Katrina. The result of the survey resides on a web-enabled internet mapping system, www.whodata.org, which can be accessed 'anytime, anywhere' for free. The WhoData project extended this work to include other data sets that remain critical to reinvestment and rebuilding strategies on a unique resource known as the 'Gumbo' map. Figure 14.1 includes the location of Louisiana Land Trust properties (e.g. Road Home), City-designated blight, and the New Orleans Redevelopment 'Lot Next Door' properties.

This theoretical model of community-municipal-university partnership is an example of the efforts of applied citizen science using participation geographic information systems science (CS/PGIS). The theoretical framework of PPGIS considers a wide range of collaboration models. In all cases, the goal is to promote community engagement which would lead to autonomy through capacity building. In December 2011, the City of New Orleans announced the success of a pilot 'Lot Clearing' program that involved 12 former prisoners and unemployed Lower Ninth Ward residents mowing 775 parcels (London, 2011). In order to prioritize the lots and locate those in the greatest need, the City of New Orleans requested a copy of the WhoData.org map and the data files of the Lower Ninth Ward map in order to develop their work plan. The WhoData project directly increased the capacity of the City and aided in reducing potential costs of their staff undertaking a survey of over 9,000 parcels.

Based upon these experiences, this author puts forth a new model of citizen participation (Thompson, 2015) that puts decisions, data, and technology in the hands of those most affected by change – the residents. This model includes

234 M.M. Thompson

FIGURE 14.1 Property condition survey, Lower Ninth Ward, 2011 and 2012.

'top-down,' 'bottom-up' and 'middle-out' data analysis approaches (Carerra and Ferreira, 2007). The nature of this approach to 'design science' is to "design research [that] would encourage researchers to publish about each element of their PSS [planning support systems], make available their technology as open-source software, and subject their technology to empirical testing" (Goodspeed et al., 2018, this volume, p. 213).

What follows in the next section is a model that considers this new era of 'participatory and planning advocacy' using technology through applied citizen science.

Evaluating the Citizen Science Model: The Thompson Technology Tree

The integration of technology has improved the type, frequency and legitimacy of community engagement in the neighborhood planning process. The level of engagement depends on how well the technology barriers are overcome and the ability and/or willingness of the citizen to manage responsibilities that were formerly relegated to the municipality. The Thompson Technology Tree (TTT) model (Figure 14.2) explores engagement not in a linear way but iteratively; in practice, it has many feedback loops that allow reflection and new strategy development. In this case, the process of identifying how and when citizens can support the management of their public resources is not solely at the discretion of the municipality.

Citizen		Municipality or University
^	Technology-based decision support	>
^	IMS Monitoring and Data Maintenance	>
+	Program Implementation	+
+	Evaluation/Reporting	+
>	Data Collection	^
>	Training/Education	^
>	Phase Project Plans	^
+	Partnership	+
+	Values/Goals Definition	+
+	Communication	+
>	Identification	^

FIGURE 14.2 The Thompson Technology Tree (Thompson, 2015).

Note: > = reliance; ^ = primary driver/coordinator; + = equal participation.

Like the Meta Domain model, the TTT model suggests that citizen engagement varies within the different phases of project development. Depending upon what, or how, technology is brought into the planning process, community is more or less reliant on the university or municipality. The management process allows for equal participation, reassessment of roles and modifications of the power relationships through a feedback system. Understanding and interpretation of PPGIS roles, their influence on the planning process, the impact on the outcomes and how 'success' is measured have changed over time.

Outlined below is a summary of how these changes are manifest throughout the project development implementation process and what remains at project end:

- *Partnership.* There are times when the initial stages of a technology project must be 'driven' by the university or municipal partner but in constant consultation with the Community-Based Organization.
- *Data.* The issue of who owns the data and how it can be used, distributed and maintained will be a negotiated issue throughout the project process.
- *Independence/reliance.* It should be the goal for the citizen planner, and related organization, to become independent from the university-municipal partners in order to manage their own GIS.
- *Training/education.* In order for PPGIS to expand beyond a concept and towards a 'science,' there must be a way to document the knowledge transfer and brand the policies, practice and methods in measureable, quantifiable and verifiable terms.

While many forms of technology focus on complex and data-heavy models, simple and nontechnical methods should also be considered. PPGIS has helped to create a wider array of choices for the community. There isn't a standard formula for engagement; nor is there a template that will fit all circumstances. The premise, however, is that the model should have a community focus, be neighborhood-centric, and be supported with technology and tools provided by the academic community or a data intermediary using municipal data and resources. The following section explores some of the limitations to PPGIS and its impact on community engagement.

Best *Applied* Practices for CS/PGIS

The success of project implementation with this community-municipal-university collaboration was based upon the following factors:

1 All projects should include a scope of services, a data-sharing agreement and contracts for services signed by appropriate administrative entities.
2 University participants must consider the sweat equity and indirect costs that cannot be recaptured if or when external funds are not obtained.

3   Students should create specific descriptions of their roles and outline the skill sets (both soft and hard) that were obtained as part of the course or independent study when working on community-university projects.
4   Construct a map of social networks of informal and formal planning organizations who will become resources for post-disaster planning activities.
5   Create a virtual data repository using the Federal Geographic Data Center (FGDC) standards for collecting, storing, and evaluating data resources; this includes a data dictionary and metadata that use FGDC standards to maintain data reliability and accuracy.
6   When inviting residents to meetings, outline the overall process from concept to implementation, provide a variety of means to continue engagement after the meeting, include multilingual and multimedia devices to provide special accommodation and post all meeting notes on an interactive website.
7   Create a community website that allows residents to be up to date and/or prepared for the next community meeting. Eliminate project reporting that serves only the interest of the university and has no practical application for the client.
8   Planning is a dirty word; use alternative phrases and focus on implementation, outlining theoretical processes.
9   Prepare nonresident teams with relevant training in sensitivity, cultural awareness, and community history prior to community engagement.
10 Make sure that data is collected and can be distributed in a format that can be integrated with municipal data should it follow the FGDC conventions.
11 Only promise what you can provide.
12 Leave the community-based organization with adequate information so that the project can easily be replicated or extended.
13 Do no harm.

Empowerment is commonly defined in terms of efforts that PPGIS experts make to increase participation and involvement of less powerful groups in public policy decisions (Kyem, 2002). When participation is conducted as a therapy, manipulation, or education, the process creates opportunities for co-opting less powerful groups. The participatory process in PPGIS applications therefore takes on different forms, many of which entail conditions and abuses that also can make it difficult for organizations to achieve their goals. Consequently, the methods employed to ensure public participation in PPGIS projects can themselves become obstacles to effective empowerment.

Conclusion

A number of well-intentioned, and some opportunistic, planners focused on dropping into New Orleans to test new planning theories, apply classic ones and/or create alternatives for how to respond to one of the worst natural disasters on US soil. The key to success in sustainable neighborhood planning has been planning with the community in mind. Over 25 years ago residents who founded the Dudley Street Neighborhood Initiative (DSNI)[2] declared and proved that the most successful efforts in neighborhood revitalization comes when the vision and plans are made through a collaborative process with local government. One of the key components in making this approach work is access to and ability to freely share data on which business decisions can be made.

During the fall of 2006, a team of conscientious academic planners joined with ACORN housing to take on the role of UNOP team for the Ninth Ward. The goal was noble but this was taken on without understanding the political ramifications of undertaking this role as 'carpetbagger planners' who did not understand the local issues, history, and extent of recovery planning needed. The assumption that legacy residents could not adequately identify, communicate and prioritize the recovery needs led to an immediate polarization within neighborhoods and between planning teams.

Whether a man-made or natural disaster, neighborhood planning education and practice must start to put 'community back into community development.' In doing so, the process will receive the type of grounding and buy-in that does not come readily when, as Ché Madyun put it, 'planning never happens with the people who are going to have to live with the day to day result' (Holding Ground Productions, 1996, p. 6).

The 'best applied practices' mentioned here are based on an observation of successful community-university partnerships, such as DSNI, and modern collaboration using technology such as public participation geographic information systems (PPGIS) with the WhoData.org project. The commitment to go beyond a semester-long project, a popular article, or a catastrophe-driven book will continue to impact how planning, as a profession, is perceived.

The goal of neighborhood planning after a disaster is to quickly improve conditions in order for the community to be as good, or better, than before. While the local planning community may not be in a position to take on this task, a combination of talents and resources from the community-municipality-university will achieve what each entity individually could not. The future of planning is dependent on a major shift in ideology, but this is necessary in order for communities to re-embrace the importance of planning, recognizing that it is not just a process but also a solution. On February 8, 2017, the EF tornado – the "strongest recorded in the city since recordkeeping began in 1950" (Nobles, 2017) hit New Orleans East. Beyond social media, expanded public-private spatial data partnerships have already changed the way in which information has been shared from and to the public. This is another situation where we'll be able to test the "theories in planning and of planning" (Batty, 2018, this volume, p. 250) in a post-disaster planning operation in motion.

UNOP and the Cornell team used a traditional approach to *participatory action planning* that did not meet the needs of the residents. The residents were locked into a process that met the idea of engaging community but the outcomes of which were not required to be implemented (as was found out afterwards when many of the community plans were not adopted). Residents were faced with more immediate needs (housing, health care, safety, and schools) and continued to be frustrated by the number of meetings that resulted in an action list and another meeting instead of concrete solutions. It is now apparent that the "planned exercise quickly broke down as many of the race and class divisions and resentments reflective of past inequities emerged" (Reardon et al., 2009).

The planning process did not reflect how 'crisis planning' is very different when outside community planners are not fully aware of the cultural differences, which have less to do with race and class than they do with being from the North or South. It is future planning academics who have experienced how the triumphs and tragedies of uninformed, short-sighted planning processes can adversely impact the hope and promise of new beginnings. Citizen science holds hope, and a way forward, to drive the community engagement process from the middle in an objective, systematic, and holistic manner. Applied GIS now has a home and can go beyond PGIS into the realm. Science, Technology, Engineering & Math (STEM) does not just begin with Science, but should also take into consideration the value of community knowledge in applied citizen science for planning.

Notes

1 See http://makeitright.org/where-we-work/new-orleans/.
2 See www.dsni.org.

References

ACORN Housing/University Collaborative. 2007. *The People's Plan for Overcoming the Hurricane Katrina Blues: A Comprehensive Strategy for building a More Vibrant, Sustainable, and Equitable 9th Ward*. Ithaca: NY: Cornell University, Department of City and Regional Planning. Accessed 20 October 2016: https://works.bepress.com/michelle_m_thompson/51/.

Batty, M. 2018. Science in Planning: Theory, Methods and Models. In T. W. Sanchez, Ed., *Planning Knowledge and Research*. Abingdon, UK: Routledge, pp. 241–254.

Carrera, F. and Ferreira, J. 2007. The Future of Spatial Data Infrastructures: Capacity-Building for the Emergence of Municipal SDIs. *International Journal of Spatial Data Infrastructures Research* 2, 49–68.

City of New Orleans. 2007. *Unified New Orleans Plan (UNOP): Citywide Strategic Recovery and Rebuilding Plan*. Accessed 12 February 2017: http://resilience.abag.ca.gov/wp-content/documents/resilience/New%20Orleans-FINAL-PLAN-April-2007.pdf.

Eggler, B. 2010. New Orleans Master Plan Approved by City Council, *The Times–Picayune*, August 12. Accessed 3 August 2013: www.nola.com/politics/index.ssf/2010/08/new_orleans_master_plan_approv.html.

Evans, P. and Lewis, S. 2009. A Reciprocity of Tears: Community Engagement after a Disaster. In A. Koritz and G. J. Sanchez, Eds., *Civic Engagement in the Wake of Katina*. Ann Arbor, MI: University of Michigan Press, pp. 44–58. Accessed 20 August 2016: https://www.press.umich.edu/923684/civic_engagement_in_the_wake_of_katrina.

Goodspeed, R., Pelzer, P. and Pettit, C. 2018. Planning our Future Cities: The Role Computer Technologies can Play. In T. W. Sanchez, Ed., *Planning Knowledge and Research*. Abingdon, UK: Routledge, pp. 210–225.

Green, R., Bates, L. and Smyth, A. 2007. Impediments to Recovery in New Orleans' Upper and Lower Ninth Ward: One Year after Hurricane Katrina. *Disasters* 31(4): 311–335.

Haklay, M., 2013, Citizen Science and Volunteered Geographic Information: Overview and Typology of Participation. In Sui, D. Z., Elwood, S. and Goodchild, M. F. Eds., *Crowdsourcing Geographic Knowledge: Volunteered Geographic Information (VGI) in Theory and Practice*. Berlin: Springer, pp. 105–122.

Holding Ground Productions. 1996. Holding Ground: Final Script. Accessed 12 February 2017: https://www.newday.com/sites/default/files/transcripts/Holding%20Ground,%20 transcript,%2058%20min.pdf.

Jones, B. 1990. *Neighborhood Planning: A Guide for Citizens and Planners*. Chicago: Planners Press.

Kyem, P. A. K. 2002. Examining the Community Empowerment Process in Public Participation GIS Applications. *Proceedings, First International PPGIS Conference* held by URISA, Rutgers University, New Brunswick, 20–22 July.

London, C. 2011. BlightStat 29, December 15, 2011. *Charlie's Neighborhood News, New Orleans*. Accessed 3 September 2017: https://katrinafilm.wordpress.com/tag/oliver-wise/page/2/

Nelson, M., Ehrenfeucht, R. and Laska, S. 2007. Planning, Plans and People: Professional Expertise, Local Knowledge, and Governmental Action in Post-Hurricane Katrina New Orleans. *Cityscape: A Journal of Policy Development and Research* 9(3), 23–52.

Nobles, W. P. 2017. New Orleans East Tornado was an EF-3 – The Strongest Recorded in the City, *The Times–Picayune*, February 8. Accessed 12 February 2017: www.nola.com/weather/index.ssf/2017/02/new_orleans_east_ef3_tornado.html.

Reardon, K., Ionescu-Heroiu. M. and Rumbach, A. J. 2008. Equity Planning in Post-Hurricane Katrina New Orleans: Lessons from the Ninth Ward. *Cityscape. Design and Disaster: Higher Education Responds to Hurricane Katrina* 10(3), 57–76. Accessed 20 October 2016: www.huduser.org/portal/publications/cityscapevol10num3.pdf.

Reardon, K. M., Green, R., Bates, L. K. and Kiely, R. C. 2009. Commentary: Overcoming the Challenges of Post-disaster Planning in New Orleans: Lessons from the ACORN Housing/University Collaborative. *Journal of Planning Education and Research* 28(3), 391–400.

Sieber, R. 2006. Public Participation Geographic Information Systems: A Literature Review and Framework. *Annals of the Association of American Geographers* 96(3), 491–507.

Thompson, M. 2015. Public Participation GIS and Neighborhood Recovery: Using Community Mapping for Economic Development. *International Journal of Data Mining, Modeling and Management* 7(1), 24–38 (original publication 2010; updated online 2015). Accessed 20 October 2016: works.bepress.com/michelle_m_thompson/62/download/.

Thompson, M. 2016. Upside-Down GIS: The Future of Citizen Science and Community Participation. *The Cartographic Journal*, 53(4), 326–334.

Thompson, M. M., Acosta, D., Anderson, A. A., Arceneaux, B. N., et al.. "WhoData.org 2012 Newsletter" WhoData.org 2012 Project Newsletter Vol. 1, Iss. 1 (2013). Available at: http://works.bepress.com/michelle_m_thompson/13/

Thompson, M., Aman, L., Chen, J., Karwowska, A., Lee, K.-S., Luger, J. and Neafsey, E. J. 2004. *Building Bridges Between Community Based Organizations and Technology: Exploring Tools for Community Participation and Economic Development for the Dudley Street Neighborhood Initiative*. Thompson RE Consultants. Accessed 20 October 2016: https://works.bepress.com/michelle_m_thompson/48/.

15
SCIENCE IN PLANNING
Theory, Methods and Models

Michael Batty[1]

Preamble

In his book *Planning Theory*, Andreas Faludi (1973) emphasises the point that there are theories *in* planning as well as theories *of* planning. His book was all about the latter, but he was very conscious that those studying and practising planning used theories within the activity of planning, specifically theories about their system, sector or domain of interest – the city and the region – which were very different from the theories that guided planning as an activity. Although this separation between cities and their planning has been long-lasting, there is an argument in the social sciences suggesting that to produce a relevant view of cities and planning, the separation between them is something that should be resisted. As planners, so the argument goes, we need to consider ourselves as part of the city system, and only in doing so are we able to produce an integrated and workable perspective on how to practice. Indeed both Alexander (2018) and Burton (2018) in their chapters in this book take a very different view of theory from that espoused here. They articulate theory as it relates to the activity and practice of planning, implicitly subsuming the city system as the domain that the activity applies to without inquiring into the science that might be used to progress our understanding of cities per se. Our treatment of the science of cities here however does not embrace the planning activity as such for we tend to divide the world into the objects that we study and ways in which we must change these objects – that is, into cities and their planning – and it is particularly difficult to avoid this schism. So we will begin by accepting that this is the case and sketch ways in which conventional theory in both domains is elaborated.

This difference between cities and planning has a profound impact on the science that we develop to enable us to plan better. The science needed to integrate them both is highly variegated; some is structured in classic terms according to the way positivist physical science has developed since the 17th-century Enlightenment in the West, some is based on powerful philosophies of political science and economy, but much is developed in more ad hoc and pragmatic terms in a practical context as Burton (2018, this volume) describes. This is reflected in both urban theory where planning is implicit and in contexts such as that presented by Alexander (2018, this volume) where he argues that planning theories have evolved through three perspectives: the radical-communicative model coming from rational action, the post-structuralist approach, and then the institutionalist focus – all viewpoints that are highly planning- rather than city-centric and which are somewhat different from the emphasis in this chapter. Here we will explore how the traditional science of cities has developed in planning, beginning with the classical scientific method and then illustrating how the power of theory has weakened as a much more pluralistic view of cities has emerged.

We will first focus on how theory is developed and then gradually show how models have come to supplant theory, how theory as a terminology has fallen out of fashion, and how a much more pragmatic approach to developing planning knowledge is now developing. We will also focus on the various tools and techniques that have been developed to aid and inform the planning task, showing how these depend in part on high theory but are developed and adapted in practice to deal with more immediate and practical concerns. Any essay on science in planning could cover an enormous range of theory and practice, but we will bound our domain by focussing on more classical scientific methods. These are of course being rapidly changed as the content of our concern – the city itself – also changes dramatically as the world automates, and as cities become ever more complex. In this, we will also sketch how our view of cities as systems in which we intervene through planning and management is gradually giving way to a much wider-ranging philosophy of complexity, which is now one of the emerging paradigms of the social sciences.

Building Theory: The Scientific Method

The basic idea that most of us have grown up with is the notion that through science, we are able to make firm predictions about the future. To do this, we need to understand the ways in which our systems of interest work; and in the last 250 years, we have articulated this focus through the concept of mechanism. In general, we develop theories which are simplifications or abstractions of the salient points that concern the way the system functions, and from these abstractions, we can make predictions. We usually do this using mathematics as the basis for such generalizations. If the generalisation – in essence the theory – works over and over again in predicting the system under many different conditions, we gain confidence in the theory; and eventually this confidence may be so strong that it acquires the status of a law. The best examples are those of classical mechanics whereby we have developed laws of motion that tell us how objects move when forces are applied to them under all kinds of conditions that we are able to generate in terms of our immediate experience.

The theories that are generated are often very different from the systems that they are applied to, but they are nevertheless sufficiently close to enable them to be good predictors of some aspects of the system of interest. The way we generate these theories, and of course any laws we are able to derive from them, is called the *scientific method*. This consists of two interrelated processes which we call *induction* and *deduction*. The most basic way of deriving theory usually begins with a succession of observations that seem to imply some degree of regularity in the system of interest (Batty, 1980). To fix ideas, let us consider observations about how population is distributed in cities. Several commentators looking at big cities over the last 100 years have observed that the density of city population declines with increasing distance from the city centre. By the mid 20th century, enough observations had been accumulated for the idea to be considered seriously that one could fit well-defined regular functions of density versus distance to such phenomena. In 1951, Colin Clark became one of the first to do so, illustrating that if one was able to fit such a function to a city, then one could make predictions about future population densities. This is not a strong theory per se, but it has sufficient force to be a promising way of thinking about how populations are distributed in cities and provides a rationale for further explanation. It is hardly a law, but it is illustrative of what happens as observations mount up and as theorists begin to infer generalizations of the kind first developed by Clark (1951). This, in essence, is the process of induction.

If we then assume that this theory has the status of a law, we might use it to generate predictions that all present and future cities would have population density profiles that decline with increasing distance from their city centers. This process of generating a prediction is in fact deduction. You could argue that if you started with a theory and had no observations, you could then deduce predictions from it over and over again under different conditions, and if the predictions matched reality, then this would be akin to the inductive process of gaining confidence in the theory. In fact, no one ever starts with a blank slate – we always have preconceptions about how the world works and we have observations – facts that we can agree on – and thus we have rudimentary hypotheses. We improve these by a circular process of scientific reasoning, which involves a loop between induction and deduction where we infer or induce theory and then deduce predictions following the logic of the loop, making our theories stronger and stronger and hopefully generating insights that eventually reveal laws. In fact, in our world, anything approaching a law is rather rare; even in the harder sciences, we now consider that laws are never as firm or as strong as previous generations of scholars and practitioners considered them to be. To illustrate the scientific method, the block diagram in Figure 15.1 demonstrates the significant features of this process.

Before theories are assumed to be laws, they are often referred to as hypotheses, and as such, the scientific method is a process of testing hypotheses – by confronting them with data to see if they can be confirmed. In fact, simple hypotheses constitute the subject matter of statistics for most observations contain noise and error which means that exact confirmation of a hypothesis against data is rare; data

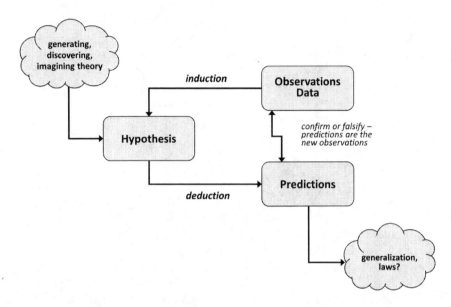

FIGURE 15.1 The classical scientific method.

tends to confirm or reject a hypothesis, but within certain statistical limits, and this is usually a matter for interpretation and judgement.

No True Theory: The Role of Falsification

Until the 18th century, most philosophers and scientists assumed that theories about the world could be true or false, but once the scientific method became institutionalised, doubts about the truth of any generalisation gained ground. In the late 19th century, the edifice that had been erected in modern physics from Newton onwards, widely regarded as the ultimate truth, no longer appeared as solid as had been assumed. Nagging doubts from inconsistent facts eventually led to an enormous paradigm shift in which these inconsistencies were found to be key to the limits of classical science (Kuhn, 1962). These limits did not mean that the science of Newton was 'wrong' but that it was limited in scope and could not deal with the very large – vast distances – or the very small – subatomic interactions. Relativity and quantum theory stepped into the breach, and an entirely new paradigm (or set of paradigms) was developed to deal with these respective scales.

In essence, what happened alongside these paradigm shifts was the gradual realization that where human systems are involved, the future is largely unknowable. If we are in charge of our own destinies, then we are in a position to invent the future; and thus the notion of predicting the future – accurately and precisely – is inevitably flawed. In terms of the scientific method, no amount of new facts which confirm a hypothesis can lead to the truth for there is always the possibility that a new fact will emerge that refutes the theory or hypothesis under consideration. Thus induction is fatally flawed. Continuous induction cannot lead to truth for there is always the possibility that a contradictory fact will emerge. This notion is encapsulated by the idea of the black swan (Taleb, 2007). 'All swans are white' was the empirical law until the discovery of Australia, where there are black swans. Bertram Russell's concept of the inductivist turkey is even more graphic. The turkey woke each morning, day after day, and at 9 am was fed. Being a good inductivist, the turkey assumed that this would always be the case – until the day before Christmas when it woke to have its throat cut (Chalmers, 1999). The turkey did not consider, could not consider, the wider context.

In short, what this means is that all one can ever do is falsify a hypothesis. One cannot confirm it. But the wider question relates to why this is so, and in the case of our swans and turkeys, it is because the system of interest onto which the hypothesis or theory is anchored is bounded. If we had known of Australia before its discovery (which to some extent is a contradiction in terms), then we would already have observed back swans. Had the turkey been able to stand back and look at what happened to successive generations of its kind, it would have realised that the good life always ends. In short, by broadening the frame of reference, the context changes, and what was considered impossible becomes possible and vice versa. This realization has to an extent always been part of science, but it was Karl Popper (1959) who first articulated it formally by arguing in his book *The Logic of Scientific Discovery* that all that science could do was falsify a hypothesis, not confirm it. He popularized the notion that good science should seek conjectures that could be refuted, with progress in science being measured by the extent to which a hypothesis resisted falsification but set against a background where any hypothesis could always be wrong.

Popper's demonstrations of the idea that science can only falsify, not confirm, are nicely illustrated by his reference to the closed solar system. In this system, we can apply the complete laws of Newtonian mechanics as we do so routinely in launching satellites and unmanned probes to the planets. In short, we can use Newton's equations to compute with complete certainty the trajectories of rockets within this system, but once we scale to the universe, all this breaks down and we are forced to consider relativities. An even more profound example relates to our science of economics and the increasing doubt we have in the scientific policy instruments that were established in the early years of the 20th century. The conventional wisdom of the modern economy is that monetary policy such as the control of interest rates is able to change patterns of demand and supply. If the economy is growing too slowly, then lowering interest rates will increase the demand for loans – for investment because it is cheap to borrow – whereas when the economy is growing out of control, raising interest rates will suppress demand. For many years this kind of policy was the *modus operandi* of the central banks and their governments. But these policy measures no longer work, and one of the reasons (amongst many) is that new factors have entered the way the economy functions: it has become more complicated, producers and consumers second-guess one another in much more complex ways than hitherto, information technologies now intervene, and globalization makes our individual and even collective behaviour more convoluted than ever before. Network effects beyond our understanding are increasingly rife. Moreover, historically, once interest rates fall below a certain threshold, it has always been assumed that people would no longer save but spend and that the economy would reverse any decline. In fact, it would appear that these forces no longer work to reinforce one another and that the economic system no longer behaves as the theories assume. This is similar to broadening the context by broadening the system of interest but with the notion that it is now impossible to know how broad the context is.

There are several features in developing scientific theory that need to be noted. First, no theory produces perfect predictions as there are always limits to the way we measure and observe. A theory may appear to be very promising when confronted with observations, but there may be some uncertainty over the observations. There may be a tendency to discount uncertain or ambiguous observations, but this does not increase the veracity of theory – quite the opposite. Sometimes the theory is altered to omit the suspect observations by adding auxiliary hypotheses that reduce its power, but if this is continually done, eventually the theory will lose any power that it has. Another key feature relates to observations themselves. For any science, there needs to be agreement about what the observations constitute. There may be substantial disagreement about what the relevant observations are, and if this is the case, then there can be no scientific theory. Any theory that is proposed cannot be falsified if there is no agreement about what the relevant facts are. Indeed in science, facts like theory are slowly built up and established. There are countless cases where theory has ultimately been abandoned because what were once seemingly incontrovertible facts are no longer agreed upon. Indeed facts represent the strongest of all observations, but there are much weaker forms of these that are used to test theory, sometimes called 'factoids' or 'factlets'. These tend to be observations which are not confirmed in any way and often appear as fictional but plausible information. Indeed recently the notions of 'alternative' facts and 'fake' facts have been introduced.[2] However, some facts are much clearer in their meaning for when a theory cannot be tested, a synthetic but plausible situation can be generated as a sort of average of many situations. This produces 'stylised' facts. Wikipedia says: "A stylized fact is often a broad generalisation that summarizes some complicated statistical calculations, which although essentially true may have inaccuracies in the detail".[3] What is clear from this is that science, like much of life, is an ambiguous and ill-defined activity, especially when it comes to the social domain. In short, science and its facts are socially constructed, never neutral.

Theories and Models

If you trace the history of the term 'model', you will find that its growth in usage dates from the mid 20th century, about the time when digital computers first appeared (Batty, 2007). In scientific method, we can define a model as a means of transforming a theory into a structure that is testable against observations. A model is clearly an abstraction or simplification, as is a theory; but it is more starkly so for a model only contains that which is relevant to the prediction in hand, whereas a theory may contain substantial information of a qualitative kind that is not immediately relevant to operationalising the prediction. In our world of cities and planning, models developed hand in hand with theory, and it is worth describing the way urban economic and geographic theory has been used to develop models that not only test theory but also enable one to make predictions which inform planning.

In the 1950s and 1960s, three theoretical perspectives were drawn together to provide a rudimentary basis for forecasting the future form and function of cities. First, theories of transportation flows and interactions were developed in analogy to models of force in social physics, picking up on a long tradition of building analogies between gravitation and potential with social dynamics. Second, notions about how populations were distributed in cities with respect to their social group and density relative to their work were articulated by urban geographers in such a way that these ideas led to good qualitative explanations of how the Western city in particular was structured as a series of concentric rings of different activity and land use around the central business district (CBD). Third, theories of spatial structure and location were developed from notions about how individuals traded off distance for space where economic utility theory was invoked to construct models of the urban economy, which could explain why densities decline with distance from key economic centers. This led to the development of a new urban economics that provided a basis for thinking of cities as markets where what ultimately came to be established in terms of densities and prices (rents) was seen as a process of market clearing. Added to this, industrial location theory, economic base theory and input-output analysis all complemented what quickly became a series of ideas around which predictive models of the urban system could be fashioned.

These theories became the rationale for the first wave of urban and transportation models developed in the 1960s. These models essentially took basic ideas about how aggregate populations in different areas of the city interacted with respect to retailing, housing, and work and introduced a series of algebraic functions that enabled predictions to be made about the location and density of these activities. But in the first instance, these predictions needed to be confirmed against actual observations, so the first stage of the model-building process was to engage in testing the model theory against an observed situation. These processes involved verification and validation of the model against data – in short, testing how good the theory was with respect to observations, which lies at the heart of the scientific method shown in Figure 15.1. In Figure 15.2, we elaborate on this for the model-building process, introducing the concept of calibration, which represents a kind of fine-tuning of the model, a tuning that establishes how well the model fits the particular situation. No model or theory, however good, can be applied 'cold', so to speak, to the real world. There are always parameters that pertain to the real situation that have to be calibrated, and thus the first stages of model building are to find these as well as to validate how well the model reproduces what we observe, be it in the past or the present or both.

Figure 15.2 elaborates this sequence, building on the scientific method in Figure 15.1, but extending this to the use of such theories and models to make predictions in situations which we have not yet encountered. Strictly speaking, if we want to really test a theory, we build a model and calibrate and validate it on one set of observations, generating its parameters, and then take it to another situation and see how well it works there. So, for example, in our many models of the London metropolis, we first use observations from, say, the 2011 Census, then we apply the same model to 2001, then we apply it to another city at a different date, and so on, building our confidence in its ability to make good predictions as we go along. What we rarely do is divide the data set into two and develop the model on one part of this, using the fitted model to predict the other part. This, of course, is what happens in remote sensing where one has considerable volumes of satellite image data; you can define a training sample on one part of the data, use this for interpretation, and then transfer these interpretations to the whole data set to see how good they are.

In fact the situation of developing these kinds of theory for use in planning is even more different from the received wisdom than one might imagine. Rarely, if ever, do we build a model on a real city and then transfer its results to some other city or the same city at another time. This is largely because getting a model to work on even one city is a huge feat. It is also compounded by the fact that data is often only available for the cross-section or time interval for which the model is to be built, and in terms of any scientific quest, very often the model builders

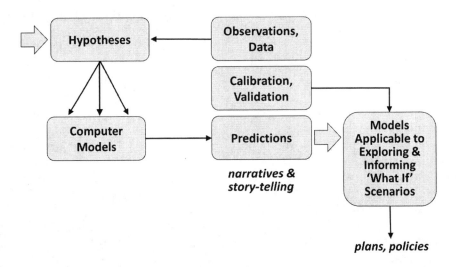

FIGURE 15.2 Models in scientific method.

do not have the luxury of being able to apply their model elsewhere because of organizational and resource constraints.

The sort of theories and models we have in mind here are considerably more intricate and involved than a simple testing of gravitational theory or economic base analysis. Large-scale models for cities have many details and idiosyncrasies that make their construction expensive and lengthy. Compared to their beginnings half a century ago, the computational problem has almost disappeared, but the models are ever bigger in scale and detail, and many additional features involving visualisation are now essential in their interpretation and usage. In short, new elements to these models are always being added, and there are now classes of urban model that are highly detailed, operating at the level of individuals or agents over multiple time periods. Their construction is often plagued by missing data despite advances in open data and the emergence of big data during the last decade.

In general, our quest in science is to simplify and develop the essence of any explanation, taking away details which are irrelevant to the task in hand. In this sense, science tends to value parsimony in developing theory, which as Einstein once said, should be "as simple as possible but not too simple". However, parsimony is often not consistent with the need to incorporate features that are plausible but untestable, and thus many theories and their models contain assumptions that appear correct but cannot be tested because data is not available. In social situations where we are modelling human behaviour, the processes of decision-making are often simply not observable, or if they are, we find it difficult to observe the factors that are important to making such decisions. New classes of model have emerged in cities during the last 20 years involving very rich descriptions of how individuals behave, which contain multiple assumptions that cannot be tested and will never be because of limits on observation and data. In terms of classical science, these kinds of model do not meet the standards of testability and validity that we assume, nor do they meet the criteria of parsimony; but they are nevertheless useful. This implies that we must take a different view of science than the one that most of us have been conditioned to believe in and that science is a good deal more uncertain and unclear than we always hoped.

This new view of science as being useful rather than truthful is entirely consistent with our view of how we might use theory and models in helping us to plan. Half a century ago, the prevailing attitude was that we should be able to build models that could at least predict the short-term future. In fact as daily events now show, this is a pious hope. As we learn more about the world and as it gets ever more complex as we invent new technologies and evolve new behaviours, we can never be certain our theory is equivalent to the task of predicting even the shortest-term events. Why we ever thought we could is something of a mystery for now that we have absorbed the chilling message of Popper (1959), all we can hope for is falsifiability. In any case, it is now widely agreed – and in some senses this is an inevitable consequence of our view of cities as social systems – that theories and models are not primarily for prediction but for structuring and focussing debate. This is widely acknowledged in economic forecasting where, quite routinely, a basket or ensemble of model predictions is assembled from many different groups who build their own econometric models. These predictions are then pooled and some average agreed upon. This reflects the diversity of views and the uncertainty of theory, and it is slowly but surely becoming the *modus operandi* of using any theory or model in thinking about the future of cities.

In Figure 15.2, we go one step further and show that from any one theory, a plurality of models needs to be considered that can be tested against the same sets of observations. The notion that we might build more than one model in a policy context is something that emerged very quickly when it was found that the uncertainties of modelling were such that to get some perspective on policy, different models were required. The idea of counter-modelling emerged in which alternative models were developed to enable us not only to construct the future but also to deconstruct it (Greenberger, Crenson and Crissey, 1976). To some extent, many of these notions are now included in the way we are developing decision and planning support systems. Here, a variety of models, techniques and tools are being implemented to support what is an eclectic process of to-ing and fro-ing between future alternative plans in such a way that one is able to converge on a plan or policy that reflects a balanced view of many different theoretical perspectives (Brail, 2008).

Theories of Planning and Theories in Planning

The study of cities crosses the boundary between the social and physical sciences, but it is widely accepted that unlike the physical sciences, we cannot develop and test our theories on the subject matter of the city itself, largely for ethical reasons. In various unguarded moments, commentators talk of our experiments with 'new towns', 'social housing', 'pedestrianisation', and so on, but rarely do we consider these akin to laboratory experiments that are conducted to advance physical science. In fact, when we refer to these kinds of experiment in the social sciences, we usually mean schemes that were never intended as experiments but, in hindsight, almost appear as though they were, often with disastrous consequences. A term which recently has grown in popularity in the social sciences is 'natural experiment', referring to experiments existing in the 'wild' so to speak. These are defined as situations where outcomes appear which are relatively well defined but outside the control of any particular scientist or investigator (Dunning, 2012). In this sense, they occur 'naturally' in that they meet some of the requirements for traditional experiments without being planned or controlled from the top down. Traditional experiments in science essentially set up environments (sometimes these are called media) whose conditions are very closely controlled to the point where slight variations lead to changes that confirm (in a limited sense, of course) or falsify hypotheses. Usually such experiments endow these artificial environments with the same reality as that in which the phenomena exist; and in this sense, there is an intuition that confirming instances of these hypotheses is somewhat more satisfying than in non-physical environments that dominate many social experiments.

In a world where experiments cannot be in the same medium as the phenomena being explained, it is possible to have as much control but in a virtual environment – one that is artificial in that the investigator has total control over the form of the media. The best examples of this kind of theory development are through the medium of thought experiments, which are logical deductions based on formal reasoning – mathematical, symbolic, verbal – defined as a way of demonstrating the principles associated with any hypothesis through derivations of outcomes and ancillary hypotheses. These experiments are entirely theoretical in that they are not confronted by facts of any kind and consist purely of deductive consequences. These kinds of experiment may vary much more widely than traditional experiments in that they might consist of generating counterfactuals based on all kinds of 'what if' scenarios, and in this sense, they can be close to planning situations. To an extent these types of experiments are dominated by analogies and metaphors between different types of system, and their value lies in providing a context for informed discussion and speculation.

Of course, most models in planning are now essentially developed and tested in computational – digital – environments. The original motivation for computer models was to provide an environment where non-intrusive experiments could be developed for generating robust and relevant theories that could explain human systems of various kinds. In fact during the time such models were first being developed in the social sciences, computation was also being extended to complex physical (as well as human) systems. Now computer modelling and the ability to compose, predict and test futures without actually having to construct them has become the *modus operandi* of many varieties of theory building. The computer thus constitutes a virtual environment in which the future can be explored – in which many digital futures can be computed – with a view to converging on the best option with this being the focus of the plan or policy to be developed. This was one of the basic motivations for applications of computer models to urban systems in the 1960s. Computers themselves were regarded as laboratories in which to experiment about the future without needing to let it run its course. The argument was that this strategy could produce the best possible future or at least avoid the worst. More recently, the most extreme of these contexts have emerged as virtual environments where users can experiment with the actual environment itself by immersing themselves totally within an artificial context.

Theories in the form of computable models do not exist in a vacuum. Because our ability to predict the future is highly limited and because we still need computer models to structure the debate, the debate must be accomplished with a whole series of different media which support formal modelling. Thought experiments thus pervade this usage, and so does 'storytelling', which has become popular in softening the outcomes of models and introducing qualitative information and data that cannot be formally part of the computation itself. Morgan (2012) has sketched the many ways in which economic modelling and forecasting is enriched by such storytelling, which she argues is an essential part of any formal application of modelling to policymaking. Her view that such narratives are an important test bed for model development, particularly in the domain of economics, resonates extremely well with processes that broaden the experimental context to include thought experiments and virtual environments.

We now need to return to planning theory rather than theories in planning, but before we do so, we must say something of the major styles of philosophy that dominate our world of cities. Essentially both classical and contemporary science tend to assume a weak positivist position where theory is always to be confronted with facts or facts with theory. This is in contrast to theory that is largely regarded as normative, pertaining to norms or standards that may have everything or nothing to do with the real world. In terms of theories about how cities work, these are largely positivist, but there are some which suggest that how cities evolve is highly individualistic and not susceptible to theorizing about the kinds of behaviour that make this possible. Much of the theory about the cognitive powers of individuals in manipulating processes and structures that constitute cities tends to be normative.

Theories of planning are themselves largely normative although there has been a strong imperative to attempt to ground them in the social and political context of everyday behaviours. Such theories, however, tend to be prescriptive rather than predictive in that they instruct how planners should proceed by solving problems and generating solutions to them. In computational modelling terms, such theories deal with optimisation. For example, blueprint planning, where an end state is articulated as an ideal, is an example of such normative thinking, while incrementalism is somewhat less idealistic but equally hard to ground in any factual basis of how planners and the planned might engage in rational planning. Theories of planning as advocated by Faludi (1973), which were first formally posed half a century ago, are much more diverse than theories about cities, but these tend to pertain to a much wider style of theorizing more akin to philosophy. We will not explore these any further here but simply note that elsewhere in this book, the chapters by Alexander (2018), Burton (2018) and Lieto and Beauregard (2018) approach planning theories in this more direct manner. A useful and wide-ranging compendium of the views of many well-established planning theorists whose ideas have been developed over the last half century is a good complement to the arguments introduced here (see Haselsberger, 2017).

Prospects: A Science for Planning?

There is no magic procedure for deriving the best theories and models to inform our plan-making. As we have hinted in this brief synopsis, the path to discovery is paved with obstacles and challenges pertaining to data, observation, insight, and intuition. Science is as much a voyage of inspiration as it is of painstaking, routine analysis, and to use it effectively in exploring and designing the future is a matter of assembling many different perspectives, which range from formal computational simulation to effective and enticing storytelling, from reflecting on what is feasible and possible to thinking laterally and unconventionally about the nature of the planning problem (Guhathakurta, 2003). Even though science is a generic activity, it needs to be adapted to context, and the particular idiosyncrasy that is featured here is the fact that we require at least two kinds of theory – a theory of cities and a theory of how we should best plan. Fifty years ago, it was assumed that these were one and the same. Indeed the systems approach to planning suggested that cities were like cybernetic systems which had structure, purpose and function that could be steered or managed, controlled or planned. But this model, like many, ignored the pluralistic nature of society, whose artefacts were cities which revealed the many problems of fashioning a world composed of many different viewpoints. It ignored the definitional issues about what is planning, what are its methods, and how is it and how should it be implemented in different contexts, such as those noted by Alexander (2018) and others in this book. Readers of this chapter are urged to reflect on how science as we have portrayed it here might help inform the wider task of making planning function better, which is woven through the contributions to planning knowledge and research collected here.

Notes

1. Michael Batty is Bartlett Professor of Planning at University College London, where he is Chairman of the Centre for Advanced Spatial Analysis (CASA). He has worked on computer models of cities and their visualisation since the 1970s and has published several books such as *Cities and Complexity* (MIT Press, 2005) and most recently *The New Science of Cities* (MIT Press, 2013). He is editor of the journal *Environment and Planning B*. His research group is working on simulating long-term structural change and dynamics in cities, as well as urban analytics for smart cities.
2. See: https://en.wikipedia.org/wiki/Alternative_facts
3. See: https://en.wikipedia.org/wiki/Stylized_fact

References

Alexander, E. (2017) How Theory Links Research and Practice. 70 Years' Planning Theory: A Critical Review, in T. W. Sanchez (ed.) *Planning Research and Knowledge*, pp. 7–23, Routledge, Abingdon, UK.

Batty, M. (1980) Limits to Prediction in Science and Design Science, *Design Studies*, 1 (3), 153–159.

Batty, M. (2007) Model Cities, *Town Planning Review*, 78 (2), 125–151.

Brail, R. K. (Editor) (2008) *Planning Support Systems for Cities and Regions*, Lincoln Institute of Land Policy, Cambridge, MA.

Burton, P. (2018) Striving for Impact Beyond the Academy? Planning Research in Australia, in T. W. Sanchez (ed.) *Planning Research and Knowledge*, pp. 51–65, Routledge, Abingdon, UK.

Chalmers, A. F. (1999) *What Is This Thing Called Science?* Third Edition, The Open University Press, Milton Keynes, UK.

Clark, C. (1951) Urban Population Densities, *Journal of the Royal Statistical Society, Series A (General)*, 114 (4), 490–496.

Dunning, T. (2012) *Natural Experiments in the Social Sciences: A Design-Based Approach*, Cambridge University Press, Cambridge, UK.

Faludi, A. (1973) *Planning Theory*, Pergamon Press, Oxford, UK.

Greenberger, M., Crenson, M. A. and Crissey, B. L. (1976) *Models in the Policy Process*, Russell Sage, New York.

Guhathakurta, S. (2003) Urban Modeling as Storytelling: Using Simulation Models as a Narrative, *Environment and Planning B: Planning and Design*, 29 (6), 895–911.

Haselsberger, B. (Editor) (2017) *Encounters in Planning Thought: 16 Autobiographical Essays from Key Thinkers in Spatial Planning*, Routledge, London.

Kuhn, T. S. (1962) *The Structure of Scientific Revolutions*, First Edition, University of Chicago Press, Chicago.

Lieto, L. and Beauregard, R. (2018) Towards an Object-Oriented Case Methodology for Planners, in T. W. Sanchez (ed.) *Planning Research and Knowledge*, pp. 153–166, Routledge, Abingdon, UK.

Morgan, M. A. (2012) *The World in the Model: How Economists Work and Think*, Cambridge University Press, Cambridge, UK.

Popper, K. (1959) *The Logic of Scientific Discovery*, Routledge, London.

Taleb, N. N. (2007) *The Black Swan: The Impact of the Highly Improbable*, Random House, New York.

POSTSCRIPT

Thomas W. Sanchez

Some will argue that planning research has paid insufficient attention to a broader range of themes, including those related to feminism, indigenous and postcolonial approaches to planning/planning knowledge, political ecology, and other critical perspectives. They assert that traditional and mainstream topics dominate the planning academy and profession. I agree. An objective of this volume was to step back and consider the "research about research." With reflection and evaluation being vital elements of planning process, where do they come into play with respect to scholarly practice?

INDEX

AARP's Livability Index 208
academia 163, 217–218
academic planners 53, 61, 238; research, 51, 57–58, 60, 153–154, 163
accessibility 113–115, 117–119, 124, 206; measures 114; research 113–114, 117, 119
ACSP (Association of Collegiate Schools of Planning) 70, 72
advocacy 8, 17, 226
American Planning Association (APA) 7, 70–72, 76–77, 87, 96, 153, 186, 199–202
analysis, quantitative 3, 153–154, 200, 207
analytics, urban 253
applied citizen science 227, 231, 233, 235, 239
applied ecology 96
architecture, 56, 80, 176, 182–183, 185, 187, 227–228, 230
assessment 61, 81, 117, 132–133, 143
Association of Collegiate Schools of Planning (ACSP) 70, 72, 224
auto-dependent lifestyles 112, 119–120

benefits 46, 54–55, 100, 114–115, 122, 202, 232; economic 120; environmental 99, 119
betweenness centrality 74–75, 78–82
bibliometrics 72–73
bicycling 206, 214
big data 157, 249
biking 139, 204
biodiversity 86, 88, 92, 94–97, 99–100

boundaries 2–3, 27, 168, 174, 177, 183, 185, 187, 189, 191–193, 250
buildings, green 133, 161–162
building typology 191
buses 138–139

capacity 55, 156, 159, 233; road 112
case studies 2, 16, 25–26, 36, 55, 98, 154, 156, 161, 168, 200, 208, 212, 217
CBD (central business district) 247
CDBG (community development block grant) 230
change detection 3
changes, urban 59, 187–188
citations 62, 72
cities; edge 176; emerging world 55; healthy 55–56; livable 26; right to the 12, 20
citizen science 3, 226–229, 231, 233, 235, 237, 239
City Beautiful Movement 88
city centers 111–112, 243
city council 27, 154, 160, 231–232, 239
city governments 160–161
cityscapes 210, 240
CityViz 214–216, 221
climate change 55–58, 117, 136, 156, 161–162, 207–208
Climate Protection Act 203
collaborations 58, 142, 144, 157–159, 213, 221
communities 26–27, 35, 42, 73–75, 78, 81, 135–136, 176, 180, 214–215, 217–218, 227–229, 232–233, 236, 238; academic

226, 236; active research 59; mixed-use 120; sustainable 120–121, 124, 203; walkable 123
community activism 76
community development 20, 70, 74, 238
community development block grant (CDBG) 230
community engagement 55, 122, 226, 229, 233, 235–237, 239; participation 76, 240; planning 13, 19, 226
CommunityViz 212, 217, 219
commuting 123
comparative studies 40–42, 44–45
complexity 17, 20, 30, 36, 69, 117, 154, 156, 161, 190, 204–205, 242, 253
comprehensive plan 16, 30, 91
computation 251
congestion 112, 114, 116, 205
connectivity 74, 93
consensus building 186
conservation 80, 86–87, 96–97, 137
context; artificial 251; professional 221
control groups 147–148
correlation 56, 206
counterfactuals 158, 161–162, 251
crisis 42, 47, 176, 190, 218, 239
cultural studies approach 41–42, 47
culture; auto-dependent 111; political 41; sustainable 133, 146
culture of sustainability 133–134, 136, 138, 146–148

data; accessible 214; big urban 214; open 249; parcel-level land use 30; qualitative 200, 231; secondary 153, 226
data analysis 171, 229
data collection 97, 100, 138, 147, 227–228
data mining 240
data sets 73, 75, 210, 217, 233, 248
decentralization 232
decision-making processes 45, 118, 190
demographics 16, 81, 120, 137, 203
density 73–74, 120, 125, 168, 171, 177, 203, 205, 243, 247; residential 119; urban 20
design; architectural 186–187; institutional 13, 16; practice of 182, 185; street 205; sustainable 75, 79
design research 188, 207, 213, 221, 235
design science 213, 221, 235
development; compact 203–204, 206; residential 204; transit-oriented 120
development control 13, 38–39, 179
development processes 191
digital futures 251

disaster 79, 238–240
discrete choice analysis 118
disruption 55, 174–175
domains; cultural 45; public 18–19, 56, 60, 62; social 213, 246
dynamics, institutional 13

ecological; footprint 86; integrity 95; planning 208
ecology 80, 86, 88, 94–96, 100
economic base analysis 249
economic development 37, 39, 71, 75, 78, 87, 187, 240
economic impacts 112
economy 19, 82, 86, 112, 167, 242, 245–246
ecosystems 88, 96, 135
empirical evidence 54
employment 114–116, 119, 204, 233
engagement, citizen 236
environment; physical 186, 188; urban 170, 184–185, 191; virtual 251–252
environmental design 133
environmental determinism,186, 201
environmental justice 57
environmental protection 133, 143
e-planning 8–10, 13, 20
equity 81, 113, 115, 121, 124
evaluation, ex-post 132–133, 147
evaluation research 2, 147
experiments, social 226, 250

factors; endogenous 36; external 28, 62, 122; psychological 119
faculty interests 73–74, 76
findings 20, 25, 30, 41, 61, 138, 146, 148, 204–206, 231
food, sustainable 133, 138–140, 142
forecasting 48, 100, 187, 192, 212, 247, 249, 251
form; building 188; physical 88, 168, 179, 187
framework; conceptual 8; theoretical 183, 233
function; land-rent 20; regression analysis 200

Gap; mind the 19; planning theory-practice 18–19
gender 81, 119
generations, trip 118
gentrification 113, 121, 190–191
geography, urban 16, 101
geospatial data collection methods 231
Gephi 73

GIS (geographic information systems) 30, 80, 91, 97, 116, 168, 216, 227, 229, 231, 233, 236, 238, 240
governance 13, 39, 44, 57–58, 78, 155, 167
governments; federal 53; national 155, 161
graph theory 71, 73
greenbelt 96
greenhouse gas 139, 161
greenway planning 2, 86–88, 94–102
grid 17, 175, 177, 190–191
grounded theory 25, 201
growth, urban 119
growth management 51

habitat 88, 91, 93–94, 96, 99
habitat loss 85
habitat protection 92–93
hazard 34
hazard mitigation 27, 34, 226
health 81, 91–92, 122–123, 135, 202, 208, 226
hermeneutic thinking 18
hierarchies, 9; social 167
higher education 69, 134, 240
highways 95
households 11, 114, 116, 157, 231; low-income 121
housing 16, 56–58, 71, 75, 78, 109, 155, 176, 190, 230, 233, 239, 247, 250
housing indicators 214
housing markets 15, 116, 155; urban 214
housing policy 55
housing prices 112, 114, 122
housing units 154; low-income 208

ICTs 3, 210, 212, 214–215, 221
impact analysis 218; fiscal 13
implementation 13, 28–31, 35, 39, 45–46, 97, 110, 115, 121, 154–156, 159–160, 162, 188–189, 226–227, 237
inclusion 122, 203
index 139, 141; housing affordability 214
indicators 115, 138, 214, 216
inequalities 57, 121–122, 239
infrastructure 81, 112, 118, 171, 176, 189–190, 233
infrastructure planning 18, 132
infrastructure system 189
initiatives, global 161
institutions 2, 12, 38, 42, 54, 63, 134, 191; academic 2; professional planning 96
integration 2, 72, 87, 99, 111, 120, 177, 235

interactions 43, 77, 88, 100, 112, 114–116, 158–159, 187–188, 191, 218, 247
internet 56, 217
investments 135, 205, 245

jobs 24–25, 31, 120, 163, 204; professional planning 24
journal articles 87, 96–97, 199–200, 202, 204, 208
justice; racial 227; social 57–58

knowing-in-practice 153
knowledge; accumulating 192; body of 1, 72; collective 43; contextualized 155; disciplinary 72; experiential 11, 211–212; project-oriented 187, 192; research-based 19; social construction of 8, 11
knowledge domain of planning 2, 71, 73, 77
knowledge economy 189

land 15, 53, 78, 85, 94–95, 100, 104, 121, 168, 171–172, 178, 183, 190, 203, 207
land; agricultural 31, 203; conserving 93
land forms 158
land rent 20
landscape 79, 86, 91, 96, 99, 153, 174, 178; urban 191
landscape architecture 95, 228
landscape biodiversity 92
landscape change 95
landscape ecology 91–92, 95, 108
land use 20, 29, 32, 79, 85–86, 93, 110–117, 119–121, 123–124, 130, 167, 170, 247
land use; residential 114; sustainable 94
land use and transportation 110–111, 113, 115–116, 120, 124
land use change 123
land use development 112, 114, 117
land use planning 13, 15, 27, 31, 40, 87, 94–97, 132, 183
land use plans 114; comprehensive 99
land use regulation 51
land use systems 114, 117–118
land values 115, 122
laws 79, 90, 157–158, 164, 232, 242–243
learning 25–27, 29, 31, 156, 159, 207, 218, 220; social 10
levels, congestion,112
limitations 40, 97, 99, 167, 211, 236; contextual 184; recognized 229; technological 30
linear regression 201

livable communities 120, 167, 208
local governments 52, 62, 157, 161, 238
local knowledge 162, 191, 240
local land use planning research 24, 28
local planning 26, 39, 46
location 114, 168, 172, 233, 247
location choices 114, 117
loop, positive feedback 111–112

Management; adaptive 95; post-disaster 226; water 135
mapping 69, 71–73, 75, 77, 79, 81, 91, 97, 171–172
mapping technologies 216
maps 41, 72–73, 77, 100, 172, 214–215, 218–219, 237; open-source 233
markets 12, 20, 36, 41, 78, 247; land-property 16–17; real estate 116, 190
master plans 184, 188–189, 232; comprehensive 232
measurable objectives 29
media 8, 229, 250–251; social 238
meta-analysis 101, 201, 203
metadata 62, 237
methodology 10, 16, 43, 73, 77, 101, 153–154, 158–160, 162, 167–168, 200, 207; research-based 167
methods; analytical 3; qualitative 200
metropolitan planning organizations (MPOs) 203
metropolitan regions 117, 187, 206
mobility 112–115, 123, 187, 206; intergenerational 204; upward 204; urban, 111
mode choice 115, 118–119, 121–122, 124
modeling 3, 55, 75, 80, 115, 117, 210, 240, 249-251; structural equation 200–201, 206
modeling techniques 91, 100, 118
models; activity-based travel demand 117; agent-based 117, citizen engagement 227; computer 211, 251; discrete choice 118; four-step 118; integrated land use and transportation 115, 117–118; quantitative 117; spatial interaction 116; urban 211, 249
modes 74–75, 111, 114, 118, 134, 139; active transport 122–123; sustainable 119–120
moral choices 16
morphological change 192
morphological methods, applying 169–171, 177, 179, 189
morphology, urban 3, 17, 163, 167–169, 171–173, 175, 177–179, 181

morphology research 168
MPOs (metropolitan planning organizations) 203
multiple regression analysis 200–201
municipalities 95, 189, 191, 220, 235–236

natural environments 88, 92–93, 136, 138–139, 207
natural heritage 95–97
nature 19, 25, 37, 51, 56, 59, 76, 87–88, 90–92, 100–101, 177, 179, 235, 252
negative impacts 94, 119, 123, 221
negotiation 190
neighborhood planning 20, 226, 237–238, 240
neighborhood revitalization 121, 238
neighborhoods 78, 86, 122, 155, 175, 177–178, 188–189, 191, 208, 226, 238; gentrified 121, 127; walkable 121, 204
neoliberalism 53–54, 61
network analysis 71–72, 74–75
network effects 246
networks 55, 71–75, 77, 92, 99, 157–158, 178
New Science 253
New Urbanism 14, 17, 120, 177, 191
norms 9, 36–37, 40, 42, 44, 69, 147, 162, 252

official plans 85, 93, 95
online 217
open data policies 214
open-source programming 213
open spaces 88, 93, 95, 179
organizations 20, 133, 146, 174, 236–237; metropolitan planning 203; state planning 107
outcomes; evaluating policy 132; informed 212; intended 69; measurable 132
overlay 91, 171–172

PAB (Planning Accreditation Board) 70, 72
Paradigms; emerging 242; interactive 184
parks planning 87, 92, 96, 100, 207, 231
participation 17, 82, 138, 144, 215, 227, 233, 237, 240; active, 17–18
participatory process 27, 237
paths 31, 38, 160–161, 168, 171, 174, 176, 178, 252
pattern recognition 3
patterns 1, 46, 72, 76, 93, 170–172, 176–179, 214
pedestrian activity 153, 205, 207
peer review 202–203

260 Index

performance 29, 35, 39–41, 46, 61, 133, 186, 211
perspectives; historical 44, 178; social science 221; theoretical 247, 250; philosophy 11, 100, 252
physical activity 123
physical determinism 59
plan implementation 25, 27, 29–30, 147
planners; citizen 236; community 239; professional 1, 36, 43, 199; urban 100, 116, 179, 208
planners and researchers 118–119
planning; adaptive 14, 16; advocacy 9–10, 235; applied 227; climate action 208; collaborative 12, 16, 18; communicative 13; community-based 32, 212, 226; participatory 74; physical 167, 187; rational 14, 252; science in 239, 242–243, 245, 247, 249, 251, 253; social 8, 15; strategic 10, 14, 17–19, 212; theory in 13, 15; theory of 13
planning and design, urban 183, 185, 187, 189, 191, 193
planning codes 187, 192
planning consultants 27, 229
planning decisions 17, 160
planning disciplines 92, 96, 100, 184–186, 191
planning domains 10, 72, 75–76
planning educators 69, 146
planning faculty 2, 70–71, 73, 75, 77
planning field 27, 47, 199
planning knowledge 1, 186, 253
planning outcomes 28, 31
planning paradigms 11, 16
planning policies 61
planning practices; contemporary 36, 61; contextuated 10, 15; diverse 7–10, 13; enacted 15, 19; globalized 36; hybrid 36, 42; knowledge-centered 9, 13, 20; modes of 69
planning practitioners 38, 51–52, 54, 60, 100, 154, 199, 208
planning problems 2, 69, 253
planning process 25–27, 29, 41, 69, 182, 184–186, 188–189, 192, 211–213, 215, 218–221, 227, 229, 236, 239; comprehensive 26
planning profession 2, 47, 55, 58, 71, 77, 93, 96
planning-related research 7–8, 15–17
planning research 1–3, 7, 16–19, 24–25, 52–55, 59, 61–63, 74, 76, 153–154, 160, 163, 211, 213, 221–222; contemporary 57

planning researchers 32, 52, 57, 59, 199, 202, 214, 221
planning research methods 1
planning scholars 1, 13, 25, 27, 31, 70, 72, 86, 210, 214, 221
planning scholarship 1–2, 25, 210; academic 1, 59
planning students 19, 25, 61, 88
planning studies 8, 30
planning theorists 7–8, 19–20, 54, 252
planning thought 1, 10–11, 72
planning tools 97, 99–100, 185, 202
planning traditions 40, 187, 192
plan outcomes 28
plan quality 28, 201, 213, 219
plan quality research 29
plans; municipal 93; regional 46, 114
policies; regional 35, 154; urban 39
policy analysis 10, 44, 132
policy development 60, 240
policymaking 60–61, 251
policy processes 61
politics 8, 11, 78, 158
population density 111, 114, 243
positivism 18, 20, 41, 54, 184, 252
power 9, 12, 42, 46–47, 69, 73, 133, 147, 156, 217, 220, 242, 246
PPGIS (public participation geographic information systems) 212, 214, 227, 233, 236, 238, 240
Practice; communicative 11–12, 16, 18–19; epistemic 9, 19; knowledge-centered 9–10, 15, 18–19; learning for 25, 27, 29, 31; planning theory and planning 18, 53, 58; professional 46, 163; social 184
Practitioners; research of 56, 153; skills 24
predictions 208, 242–243, 247–250
problems; complex 70; computational 249; economic 88; wicked 69
processes; communicative 26; complex 184, 192; model-building 247
processes of change 30, 36–37
process tracing 158
professionals 69, 96–97, 211
professional training, 1
programs; educational 183; pilot 144; slum clearance 175
progressive agenda, 11
projects; large-scale 95, 183; open space conservation 98; participatory mapping 217; strategic 188
properties 79, 175, 207, 212, 214, 232
publications, practitioner-oriented 32
public facilities 229

public involvement 27
public meeting 159
public participation GIS 212, 240
public policy 55, 75, 78, 237
public-private partnerships 200, 208
public spaces 120, 183, 186, 189–190, 207
public transit systems 111

Quality; environmental 87; urban 190, 210
quantitative methods 200–201
question types 136–137

rail stations 111, 120
rational choice 8, 19
rebuilding 233
recovery 227, 230, 233, 238, 240
recreation 87, 96
recycling 134–135, 139
redevelopment 17, 52, 81, 160, 175, 178, 190; waterfront 178, 189
redevelopment projects 188
regeneration 190–191
regional cooperation 46
regional development 186
regional planning 7, 35, 39, 203, 208, 229, 239
regional spatial planning 217
reinvestment 227, 233
relationship, causal 155, 208
reliability 57, 171
renewal 61, 188, 191
research; applied 52, 58, 182, 192, 227; case study 162; comparative 35, 38, 47; funded 60; innovative 211, 214; morphological 176, 179; practice-oriented 1–2, 31–32; pragmatic 24–25; published 61–62, 100, 153; qualitative 25, 31, 119, 153; social science 212–213, 215, 219; translational 202, 208
research design 3, 202
researchers; advocacy 62; data-oriented 167; urban 59; researchers and practitioners 120; research on travel behavior 113, 118; research topics 31, 72, 76–77, 208
response; behavioral 143; hazard 226; post-disaster 226
revitalization 188, 190, 227; inner-area 119; local urban 20
revolution 216
risk 29, 31, 41, 183
roads 85, 112, 205, 219

safety 230, 239
sample 57, 70–72, 136, 207; stratified 136
sample design 147
scales 2, 9, 53, 59, 73, 108, 168, 171, 174, 177–178, 186, 192, 217, 245, 249; urban 3, 93
scenario-building 26
scenarios 115, 183, 204, 211
scholarship 1–2, 25, 73, 213; academic 72; disengaged 53; engaged 60, 62; public 32; technical 213
science; basic 213; classical 244, 249; computer 72; environmental 16, 20, 96; natural 18, 87, 101, 213; physical 241, 250; political 12, 242
scientific method 3, 18, 242–244, 247–248
self-selection 121, 201
seniors 53, 123, 147
settlement, mixed-use 189
settlements 167, 183; industrial 190
simulation 115–117, 252
smart cities 55–56, 124, 253
smart growth 120–121, 200, 203–204
smartphones 210–211
social capital 61
social problems 60
social sciences 18, 60, 185–186, 241–242, 250–251
sociology 12, 16
software, open-source 213, 235
space 16–17, 20, 24, 79–80, 168, 170–172, 183, 185, 247
spatial 7, 9, 13, 19, 43, 80, 118
spatial information 216–217
spatial planners, 16–18
spatial planning 8, 14–17, 19, 36, 38–40, 46; strategic 18, 20, 36
spatial structure 120, 247
specializations, professional 71
sprawl 86, 100, 176, 202–204
stakeholders 26–27, 29, 187, 216, 218, 221, 229
standards 31, 133, 162, 200, 237, 249, 252
state, welfare 38, 40
state planning 10, 39
strategies; data management collection 229; rebuilding 233; smart city 210
structure, social 43
students 3, 15, 52, 61, 70, 96, 133, 136, 138, 140–148, 219, 228, 230, 237
subdivisions 179
subregions 142–143
suburban 112, 176
suburbanization 91, 118
suburbs 55, 86, 111–112

survey 25, 57–58, 63, 100, 136, 138, 143, 145, 147–48, 153, 233
sustainability 57–58, 76, 80, 96, 133–134, 136–139, 147, 149, 202–203, 220; environmental 80, 147
sustainability engagement 139, 141
sustainability initiatives 133, 139, 141, 147
sustainable development 98
sustainable transportation 221
systems; economic 246; existing protective 91; human 244, 251; natural 88; political 69; socioeconomic 178
systems approach 253

tacit knowledge 215
teaching 53, 71, 75–77, 96, 134
techniques, innovative building 190
technological change 36
technology 3, 29, 80, 97, 110–111, 124, 158–159, 213, 217–218, 221, 233, 235–236, 238–240
theoretical models 20, 226, 233
theories; deriving 243; developing 249
theories and models 19–20, 246, 248–249
theories of practice 42–43
theorists 25, 53, 243
theory and practice 25, 51, 57–58, 163, 242
tools; analytical 75; neighborhood planning 231; qualitative 117; urban policy 187, 192
towns 8, 17, 86, 175, 189, 203, 250
traditions; scholarly 52; social reform 10, 12
traffic 112, 115, 204
transects 167, 177
transit accessibility 121
transit use 118
transparency, 205
transportation; 20th-century 179; modes of 123, 178; public 73, 121, 177; urban 111
transportation access 156
transportation and land use 112–113, 117
transportation costs 112, 114
transportation network, 114, 119
transportation plans 112, 115
transportation systems 114, 121–122, 124, 176

travel; active 122; daily 122; household 205
travel behavior 113–114, 116, 118–122, 138–140, 208
travel behavior research 117, 119
travel patterns 117–118

undergraduates 136, 143, 145, 229
university community 133–134, 136, 138, 142, 146
university-community partnerships 227
urban design 17, 39, 71, 86, 88, 96, 99, 167, 177, 179, 182–187, 189, 192, 202, 205–207
urban development 45, 52, 92, 119, 184–185, 188
urban economics 15–16
urban form 55–56, 119, 163, 170, 173, 175, 184, 191, 203, 206
urbanism 79, 126, 178, 184
urbanization 82, 85, 92–93, 110
urban policy issues 52
urban problems 210
urban research 54, 59
urban systems 116, 221, 247, 251

validity 19, 179, 249
values; normative 15; subjective 17
variables 35, 61, 201, 203, 205
vehicles, autonomous 123
visibility 45, 183
vision 17, 29, 188–189, 217, 238
visioning process 231
visualization 210, 216, 249, 253
volunteers 139, 144, 228–229

walkability 122, 205–206
waste 133–136, 138–140, 143–144, 147–148
water 80, 92, 203
waterways 112, 168
web-based geoprocessing 214
web-based technologies 211, 217
websites 70, 211
workbench, sketch-planning 218

zones, buffer 92, 99
zoning 97, 99, 179, 201
zoning regulations 157